COMMUNITIES, NETWORKS AND ETHNIC POLITICS

Communities, Networks and Ethnic Politics

KEN HAHLO

Ashgate

Aldershot • Brookfield USA • Singapore • Sydney

© Ken Hahlo 1998

Published by
Ashgate Publishing Ltd
Gower House
Croft Road
Aldershot
Hants GU11 3HR
England

Ashgate Publishing Company
Old Post Road
Brookfield
Vermont 05036
USA

British Library Cataloguing in Publication Data
Hahlo, Ken
    Communities, networks and ethnic politics. - (Research in ethnic relations series)
    1. South Asians - Great Britain 2. Great Britain - Ethnic relations - Political aspects
    I. Title
    305.8'914 '041

Library of Congress Catalog Card Number: 98-73405

ISBN 1 85628 949 4

Printed in Great Britain by The Ipswich Book Company, Suffolk

Contents

Abbreviations

Assistant Community Relations Officer	ACRO
Bolton Council for Community Relations	BCCR
Bolton Evening News	BEN
Bolton Racial Equality Council	BREC
Commission for Racial Equality	CRE
Community Relations Council	CRC
Community Relations Officer	CRO
Islamic Culture Centre	ICC
Minorities Joint Consultative Committee	MJCC
Racial Equality Council	REC
Vishwa Hindu Parishad	VHP

Acknowledgements

This book is based on research carried out between 1973-76 and I would like to acknowledge my thanks to the late Clyde Mitchell for his support and Peter Braham. Many people have contributed directly and indirectly to this book. I would like to thank Tom Tootell and Raymond Halliwell, who as CROs for Bolton Council for Community Relations and the latter as Director of Bolton Race Equality Council, always offered support and encouragement over many years. Ron Mather, John Urry, Roger Penn, and Muhammad Anwar have very kindly read drafts of the book and commented on it. Although I have incorporated most of their comments, the responsibility for what is written is mine.

The research for this book was originally supported by the SSRC (now ESRC) and Bolton Metropolitan Borough Council. I would like to acknowledge my thanks to the ESRC for this grant. This research would not have been possible without the support and help of the Gujarati Hindu and Muslim communities, the Vishwa Hindu Parishad, and the late Yusuf Suleman. I would like to thank Sandra Whittleston, Margaret Gilmour, Ingrid Bevan and Tony Heywood for their help in preparing the book for publication.

The tables, diagrams and maps are drawn from my Ph.D thesis, and most have been modified.

Introduction

There are few studies of South Asian ethnic politics in Britain and most of these were done in the 1960s. With the mistaken view that CRCs were buffer organisations (Katznelson, 1973), interest in ethnic politics waned with changes in the role of CRCs. Also with the emergence of ethnic social and religious organisations at the end of the 1960s (Ballards, 1977), attention shifted to other forms of political participation, in particular voting. A number of significant community studies confirmed the importance of these developments (Robinson, 1986; Shaw, 1988; Werbner, 1989; Eade, 1989). These studies either stressed assimilation or integration (Robinson, 1986), or pointed to the robustness of ethnic communities and their cultures (Werbner, 1989), or to a combination of these approaches in the context of a community framework (Eade, 1989). The relationships between ethnic communities and political participation were explained in terms of their political commitment to voting in elections (Anwar, 1980, 1994) and to support of political parties (Solomos and Back, 1994; Lawrence, 1974). The importance of ethnic politics was set aside as being another form of political participation along with withdrawal from political participation and opposition to racism (Layton-Henry, 1984). However, as Ben-Tovim *et al* (1986) demonstrated in their analysis of ethnic politics in Liverpool, the importance of ethnic politics and CRCs was central to the political representation of ethnic communities in a political situation in which white political parties held sway. This book will add to existing community studies, but more importantly will focus attention on ethnic politics.

The studies of ethnic politics in the 1960s and early 1970s concentrated on issues of ethnic and racial discrimination and the reactions of ethnic communities to them (John, 1969; Scott, 1972/73; Beetham, 1970). Strikes at Grunwick and Imperial typewriters brought into focus other situations in which organised ethnic opposition had a political element. Saggar (1990) in his review of ethnic political participation pays little attention to ethnic politics and concentrates principally upon participation in formal politics. Ethnic politics was interpreted as a form of local political activity. It became seen as a form of political activity that had to be discouraged. Anwar (1994; 1986; 1980) has demonstrated over many years that

Asians' commitment to participation in elections as voters has not brought them success in terms of seats locally or nationally. Layton-Henry (1984) identified some other forms of political participation in addition to voting. He makes the point that buffer organisations did give ethnic minority communities an additional degree of political participation. This raised the issue of ethnic minorities benefiting from additional forms of political participation compared to white communities (Solomos, 1989). Although Solomos did raise the issue of some form of political organisation which could represent ethnic communities, possibly regionally, this idea seemed to be unrealistic.

My argument is that ethnic politics should be regarded not as a form of local politics that only emerges when a local community chooses to oppose some rule that conflicts with their ethnic culture. Ethnic politics, as the term is used here, is seen as a form of political participation, in addition to voting, which enables ethnic communities to influence local political decisions. As such it needs some arena and this, I shall argue, was provided by local Community Relations Councils (CRCs, now called Racial Equality Councils, RECs). In Britain democracy is based upon political parties and their competition in elections. Other forms of organised political participation are generally regarded as lying outside politics or are accepted as a form of fringe activity, such as lobbying and interest group pressure. Ethnic politics, which depends upon non-political forms of organisation, developed alongside the emergence of ethnic social organisations and communities. Because these organisations have no political standing, politicians see them at best as non-political 'voluntary' organisations and at worst as pressure groups. Thus their assumption of a political role was regarded as unacceptable in a political democracy which is based on political parties. Though membership of political parties is open to all people irrespective of their ethnic origins, control of the allocation of seats in local and national politics lies in the domain of predominantly white members. Black sections, once seen as a possible way of increasing ethnic participation, came to nothing (Hall, 1985). Through the 1970s CRCs provided ethnic communities and their men in influential positions (so-called leaders) with opportunities to participate in local politics (Ben- Tovim et al, 1986).

CRCs, far from being buffer organisations, actively assisted ethnic communities to increase their political participation. Katznelson (1973) did not consider the activities of local CRCs. Hill and Issacharoff's (1971) analysis of CRCs provides an instructive study of their political strengths and weaknesses. Later reviews of CRCs, their functions, roles and relationship to the Commission for Racial Equality (CRE) viewed their political support for grassroots support as both a sign of commitment and a potential danger. This support brought them closer to those whose interests they served, but it increased their vulnerability to ethnic take-overs and focused their work on immigration and nationality. Such work became seen as unproductive, costly, migration was detached from its close association with racialised control of immigrants and became seen as not in keeping with a changing world in which accountability came first. Once the role and functions of CRCs were changed, they lost their grassroots supporters and their immigration and nationality casework. With these changes in the late 1980s and early 1990s disappeared their support for ethnic politics. Now ethnic communities are dependent upon voting as their main form of political participation and on political parties for opportunities for selection for seats.

A number of issues impinge upon any explanation for the existence of ethnic politics, which are not brought out clearly in the literature. These include firstly, recognition of the demise of Fordism and the rise of post-Fordism. Secondly, they include recognition of the role of the state in maintaining institutionalised racism, that is, an awareness of implicit state policy that supports racism.

The literature tends to give the impression that migration is closely associated with capitalism and the demand for cheap and powerless labour (Miles, 1982; Miles and Phizaklea, 1984; Bohning, 1982). In the earliest period of migration this association is well established. However, by the 1970s this form of capitalism (Fordist) was in decline and gradually being replaced by a new form of post-Fordist capitalism. The argument offered her claims that this form of capitalism also implicitly supported institutionalised racism (Jessop et al, 1988; Brown, 1992). Post-Fordism was marked by both the rise of Thatcherism and the decline of the manufacturing sector and the rise of the service sector. Once the demand for replacement and/or supplementary labour and its relationship dominated the relationships between migration and racism, with the decline of the manufacturing industry the demand for labour decreased. The Keynesian form of capitalism was in decline and was being replaced by a post-Fordist economy based upon a Schumpeterian form of capitalism. Ethnic politics should be seen against a background of emerging consumerism, the rise of the flexible firm and globalisation. This study of ethnic politics is located in a theoretical framework that draws upon debates about the decline of the Keynesian Welfare State and the rise of the Schumpeterian Workfare State (Jessop, 1994; 1993; 1992 a and b; 1989); the relationship between post-Fordism and the state (Lash and Urry, 1994); the control of space (Urry, 1990a) and the relationship between authority, consumerism and freedom (Bauman; 1995; 1988).

My thesis is that the shift from exploited and exploitable to consumer entails a move from a state of constraint (racism and racialised) to more a greater state of freedom (a consumer with power). This shift involves more precisely a move from an ethnic population to the emergence of ethnic communities with ethnic identities. These ethnic communities and organisations found an outlet through ethnic politics in the 1970s. This window of opportunity arose as a consequence of a declining economic and political system that by the late 1970s was replaced by an emergent post-Fordist society and state associated with the rise of Thatcherism. All over the next twenty or so years have become increasingly subject to the power of the consumer, a role which the state now openly promotes. However, in the search for a new form of state in an internationalised and globalised world, some of the powers of the state have become displaced (Jessop, 1994; Hay, 1994). One of these powers is that the state can no longer control racialisation as a local and national governmental process, although it can address racism as a criminal act. Competition for space and for control over the exchange of capital has shifted from the producers to the consumers. In this new competitive arena, the question about how ethnic communities participate is critical to their freedom as consumers. These issues are addressed in this book.

3

The second issue concerns the role of the state. Much of the established literature concentrates upon governments and their decisions to control migration. After 1970 the demand for labour decreased, and the literature focuses on the numbers game, the reduction in numbers of migrants and on new laws enacted to reduce still further migration of black people. These debates kept attention focused on migration, nationality and racism. What this book argues is that it was the state that was racialised and that it implicitly supported racism well into the 1980s. In a post-Fordist economy the role of the state itself came under scrutiny (Jessop, 1992; 1989); Jessop suggests that the state had to face the difficulty of losing power to others, for instance the European parliament, in a rapidly globalising world. These issues are explored in Chapters One and Two.

As Solomos (1989) noted ethnic minorities have no politically recognised form of participation that allows them to voice ethnic issues. Parekh (1991) raised this same issue in the context of pluralism. Recently, Modood (1996) notes how the notion of justice might assume new importance in politics in a plural society. McLennan (1995) opens up this debate when he considers pluralism within the context of postmodernism. Using this approach I shall consider the position of ethnic communities in Bolton today (Conclusion).

Location

This is a study of ethnic politics in a Gujarati population in Bolton, a town in the North West of England. The research was done in the period between 1973 and 1976 and was based on a combination of semi-participant observation and the use of a survey. Thus it combines qualitative with quantitative research methods (Appendix I). Three important points need to be made about Bolton and the Gujaratis. Bolton shares three important characteristics with both other northwestern towns and cities as well as with other towns and cities nationally. Firstly South Asian migrants came here, as they did to many others, looking for work in a town that was heavily dependent on a labour intensive manufacturing industry. Secondly today Bolton shares with many, although not all, towns and cities to which these migrants went, a declining, if not already declined, manufacturing sector and a developing service sector. Thirdly, it shares with many towns the pressures of competing in a globalised local and national economy. Therefore, as a place, Bolton and what is written here about Gujaratis and the events that occurred could be found in any other town in Britain.

Growth of ethnic populations

The ethnic population of most northern English towns grew rapidly in the post-war years between 1950 and 1970 (Robinson, 1986; Werbner, 1989; Hahlo, 1980). This growth in the past and the continuing present has contributed to the political situation that exists today. Control over migration and the labour process within Britain contributed to the formation of ethnic communities here. The arrival of

4

South Asian peoples after 1950 in towns across north western England was a response to the needs of a declining textile industry, which some capitalists believed could be remedied or controlled through the employment of immigrant labour. This book is concerned with how a Gujarati population used ethnic politics to change from poor and powerless migrants into initiators of a new and developing consumer culture.

At least three significant processes contributed to the changing political importance and impact of South Asian populations in British towns and cities: the first is chain migration; the second is the demand for goods and services and the third is the acquisition of citizenship. As Bohning (1981) noted, chain migration is virtually unstoppable and it still continues to bring new people to join those already settled here. Today far from the population profile being mainly young men, the profile now includes older men, their wives and young children, and children of children, but it is beginning to include a significant number of elderly people who comprise both a growing number of first generation migrants and their parents.

Secondly, this population expansion from the 1960s to the present day created a complex of demand for ethnic goods and services that shifted from being focused on meeting ethnic needs (Desai, 1963; Werbner, 1989; Smith, 1989) to meeting the needs of consumers generally. In a growing number of instances ethnic enterprises are becoming more aware of national and even international markets. Initially, areas were transformed by growing ethnic competition for space for housing, ethnic business development, and temples and mosques in existing buildings or as new developments, the latter symbolising community identity, wealth and presence in areas. This development which took place during the first two decades of their settlement led to demands that both identified Asians as an economic presence and as a political force in local politics.

Thirdly, the process of settlement transformed rightless migrants into citizens. The acquisition of citizenship gave South Asians, who came to find work, the right to settle here as citizens, even though many once harboured (Anwar, 1979), and some still harbour the idea of returning to the subcontinent. Along with other ethnic social identities (Cohen, 1994), South Asians are British. More significantly, the acquisition of citizenship has generated an expanding body of demands that can be met by both ethnic and white services. Chain migration, population growth and acquisition of citizenship encouraged the formation of ethnic communities, which required their leaders to construct a complex set of social, economic and political needs. These needs could be met only through (a) some form of participation in local politics, (b) their equal access to local scarce resources, (c) their recognition as consumers of services, and (d) their membership in South Asian diaspora. To this extent, the analysis of the Gujaratis population in Bolton is no different from that of other Gujaratis populations in Britain.

This book contributes to politics and in particular to ethnic politics, but it also is a contribution to studies of South Asian populations in northern English textile towns. Furthermore, it uses material gathered in the middle 1970s in Bolton to show how ethnic/ community politics flourished, and then considers how the changing economic and industrial profile of the town has influenced the South Asian community and racism. The importance of the local is first linked to the

5

national and then to the global. The arrival of South Asians here made those in the local political arena aware of contestable or 'ungoverned' space. However, the shift from the Keynesian Welfare State (KWS) to Schumpeterian Workfare State (SWS) moved the control of the boundaries of this space away from the national state to the local and global. Therefore, this study is also concerned with the localised identification of space and social boundaries.

Chapter One establishes the theoretical framework, drawing upon post-Fordism, arguing that the change from poor and powerless migrants to recognised consumers and producers of culture involves competition for urban space. Chapter Two sets the scene by focusing on immigration, housing and employment in Bolton and will argue that these aspects of settlement need to be seen against the four dimensions of state control and regulation. The particular nature of exploitation matched the form of capitalism that was embodied within the Keynesian Welfare society of this period. Chapter Three will look at the consequences of the population expansion through the development of ethnic organisations. It will analyse the structures of these organisations arguing that some allow for hierarchical reorganisation uniting them into a single effective organisation, while others comprise a collection of organisations under a single banner. Both sets of organisations effectively mobilise South Asians into leaders and supporters, that is, organisations that can take on a range of functions - religious, social, economic and political. Chapter Four looks at the development of communities within this South Asian population. Social networks of friendship underpin communities. The characteristics of the structures of these networks may enhance or impede community mobilisation. To cope with the political issues that arose as a consequence of the expansion in the population, the leaders/ representatives of community organisations held a model view of the space between the various communities in the town. This space is explored in Chapter Five. Chapter Six considers the formal political position between the ethnic communities and the elected politicians. Chapter Seven looks at how the leaders attempted to achieve influence over the politicians by manipulating identities of space. Chapter Eight brings the analysis of the South Asian communities in Bolton up-to-date and also looks at the place and meaning of racism in a post-Fordist society.

guises is dominant' (1994:16). Post-Fordism embodies three processes: (a) as 'a labour process post-Fordism can be defined as a flexible production process based upon flexible machines or systems and an appropriately flexible workforce'; (b) 'as a stable mode of macro-economic growth would be based on the dominance of a flexible and permanently innovative pattern of accumulation'; and (c) 'as a social mode of economic regulation would involve supply-side innovation and flexibility in each of the main areas of regulation' (Jessop, 1994:19-21). The search 'by economic and political forces for a new state form to resolve the contradictions and crises of Fordist accumulation and re-stabilise the state system led to a *structural transformation* and *fundamental strategic reorientation* of the capitalist state' (Jessop, 1994:24). This search produced a new state, which Jessop refers to as a Schumpeterian Workfare State (1994:24). He defines 'hollowing out' as a consequence of two contradictory trends: firstly, a weakening of the state through a shift towards internationalisation and globalisation of production systems leading to a reduction in its autonomy. Secondly, he argues that this 'creates a need for supra-national co-ordination and the space for subnational resurgence'. The powers of the nation-state are 'limited through a complex displacement of powers upward, downward, and outward' (1994:24). Jessop's argument holds for a strictly economic analysis, but it does not take account of social, cultural and political issues with which I am concerned. I shall argue that the economic decline of the Fordist state in the 1970s, which culminated in the rise to power of Thatcherism, provided a framework for the transition from labour regulation based on demand to a post-Fordist state in which labour regulation is supply-based. This transition made apparent the ungoverned space that allowed ethnic politics to flourish in a way that was not possible either before or after this period. Regulation covers a wide range of economic control and I shall argue initially that the forms it took reflected the project of the state in attempting to extend its control to these immigrants as workers, as members of families and as members of communities. The importance of the regulation of the circulation of labour in a post-Fordist state is that it has a central role to play in the changing face of racism in British society. Within this theoretical framework the formation of ethnic communities and organisations and their competition for space for the development of ethnic organisations and the production of ethnic culture provided a fertile ground for the development of ethnic politics. One view claims that such development was supported by mainly one dedicated organisation, namely local CRCs (Ben-Tovim *et al*, 1986), another claims that such development should be seen as a form of anti-racism (Ballard *et al*, 1994).

The second part of the book forms an ethnographic case study of ethnic politics. It concentrates on the development of religious communities, the social networks that underpin them and the social perceptions of their place within the wider racialised world. These developments are related to their inability to participate meaningfully in local politics and, by implication, national politics. It will then explore how these representatives capitalised upon their temporary political roles to develop ethnic politics. The rise and fall of ethnic politics should be seen against a background of emerging post-Fordism.

The final part of the book provides a conclusion, and brings the analysis up-to-date by locating the present socio-economic characteristics of the Gujarati population in a post-Fordist framework. I argue that this ethnic population is an apt example of how ethnic communities have developed in a 'hollowed out' Schumpeterian Workfare State (Jessop, 1994) based upon the notion of flexible accumulation (Lash and Urry, 1994). The importance of locality emerges as an important force in the restructuring of ethnic communities and their social identities, because flexibility and reregulation, as opposed to deregulation, have removed the organisations and relationships that were critical to ethnic political participation by undermining the established authority of the men and the young unskilled. As the older men in ethnic communities are deskilled, their authority has shifted to women and younger people, reducing ethnic organisations to little more than welfare groups. However, the strategies employed by local government, attributed to a flawed Schumpeterian state (Hay, 1994), suggest that ethnic communities are still seen as cohesive units whose economic potential can be exploited for the benefit of the town by local 'movers and shakers' and central government. Racism that was once prevalent as a society-wide issue has now become reduced to the level of individual complaints, and social identities are little more than social badges sported by bidders for lottery monies. At the other extreme, racism has become elevated to the level of a global ideology. Globalisation offers the ethnic entrepreneur new potential for development unrestricted by local or national political decisions.

The theoretical approach

The aim of this book is to set race relations and ethnic politics within (a) the wider context of the state (Jessop, 1990; 1993; 1992 a and b; 1994; Jessop *et al*, 1988); (b) the regulation of labour migration in a post-Fordist state (Amin, 1997), (c) changes in the enskilling and deskilling of South Asians and the restructuring of ethnic communities within an analysis of circulation of capital, in particular, flexible accumulation (Lash and Urry, 1994); and (d) consumerism (Featherstone, 1996). The importance of this framework is that it:

1. sets race relations within the context of security as expressed by the state through various dimensions of social control;
2. focuses on the process of transition (Amin, 1997) of ethnic populations from immigrant to citizen;
3. integrates the process of social change within the transition from Fordism to post-Fordism which, through the shift to innovation, the flexible firm, market transactions and choice, gave importance to the local and the global by restructuring ethnic economic activities. This in turn led to changes in the contexts of ethnic social identities, racism and the racialisation of social boundaries;
4. locates within this process of transition the circulation of various forms of capital (Lash and Urry, 1994), and in particular the shift from labour power to

subject power within a context of cultural change (Hall, 1988; Hall and Jacques, 1989); and

5. symbolises a shift from the exploited immigrant to the unconstrained consumer as part of a larger body of citizens and consumers (Bauman, 1988; Urry, 1990a and b). What is absent is the shift in (ethnic) authority from legislators to interpreters (Bauman, 1995).

Within this framework I shall concentrate on three areas: firstly, state control, secondly, the ethnic political community and thirdly, the changing ethnic community. In this part I shall concentrate upon the first of these three areas. I shall begin by making four broad generalisations.

Firstly, an aspect of the Fordist state is its direct involvement in the regulation of labour; for the purposes of this argument it encompasses the initial period of labour migration from the New Commonwealth. The argument is not only that a racialised state expresses power through different dimensions, but that this power is exemplified through the state's regulation of migrant labour, and the relationship between capital and labour (Miles, 1982; Miles and Phizacklea, 1984; Castles and Miller, 1993; Castles et al, 1984; Bohning, 1981). The regulation of migrant labour impinged upon the wider aspects of the social, the economic (Jessop et al, 1988) and the political life of members of ethnic communities (Ben-Tovim et al, 1986; Solomos and Back, 1995). This control extends down to and over the ethnic family, influencing the positions of South Asian men, women and children in British society (Mama, 1992; Knowles and Mercer, 1992; Brah, 1992).

Secondly, the debate about the transition from Fordism to post-Fordism (Amin, 1994) involves change (Lash and Urry, 1994) and for ethnic minorities this has been expressed in some of the following ways. Individuals, as representatives of migration chains, have become members of distinctive ethnic communities. Their social identities have shifted from immigrant to citizen and from the presumed welfare dependent to independent consumer. The position in which the state held the migrant has moved from being seen as a threat located in an ageing colonial construct (Hall, 1981; Benyon and Solomos, 1987) to a potential cultural asset associated with cultural diversity. The control of immigration was (Bohning, 1981) and still is invested in governments and particularly the state; while once the state was concerned with the control of immigrants to fill gaps in the labour market; now it is concerned with individuals seeking rights to citizenship (Castles and Miller, 1993; Cohen, 1994).

Thirdly, the position of the immigrant has changed from being needed as a person with the potential to be quickly enskilled to replace and/or supplement labour to being no longer needed, deskilled, unwanted and, to an extent, still regarded as exploitable labour. The social implication of this shift is that an immigrant who was considered poor and powerless has become a citizen and individual consumer who has both buying power and freedom to exercise choice as consumer (Bauman, 1988). While the individual is accepted as a consumer, the ethnic community is still seen as a totality that can be targeted for improvement and development. This, I shall argue, conceals a contradiction or a racialised barrier (Small, 1994) that

11

separates the ethnic community as a target for improvement from the ethnic consumer who is encouraged to spend and invest.

Fourthly, the post-Fordist state does not just pertain to economics and industrial relations, but has an impact upon ethnic culture (Hall, 1988; Hall and Jacques, 1989); and more importantly upon the relationship between ethnic communities as consumers over producers whether they are white or ethnic (Urry, 1990a). Ethnic communities came of age when they recognised themselves as consumers and became recognised by others as consumers rather than as a body of people on whom money is spent to improve their opportunities, that is, as the object of consumers. The state, the local community and ethnic minorities share in the process of defining their gazes as consumers. This situation encouraged Gujaratis (and other South Asians) to development their social identities as consumers and a collective ethnic political identity. However, the state initially saw ethnic politics as threatening. Shifts in status from immigrant to citizen, from perceived benefit-dependent to consumer are supported by the emergence of ethnic communities. For instance South Asians have emerged as a major group of homeowners (Saunders, 1990; Smith, 1989), and as niche ethnic entrepreneurs, whose businesses range from food to clothing to computers and electronics. Warde (1994) notes there are different kinds of consumers; the freedom to purchase is a freedom that is not bound by constraints (Bauman, 1988). Three processes are central to this development. Firstly, there is the transition of ethnic members of communities to move from poor migrants to active and major consumers. Secondly, there is a conflict between the constraints of racism and their freedom to become consumers. Thirdly, there is a choice that ethnic producers can make: either they can become niche market exploiters with no major consumption other than labour, or they can become consumers of scarce resources, such as labour, landlords, and other natural resources, in order to produce goods for local and global markets. The recognition of this process of transition from migrant to consumer is a political one. This incorporates a shift in the status of the migrant from being dependent upon financial and social welfare support with little freedom from the constraints of racial discrimination (exploited and exploitable) to becoming an active consumer with the freedom (Bauman, 1988) and power (Urry, 1990b) to exploit new markets with new sources of authority (Bauman, 1995). It is these shifts that I shall explore through an analysis of ethnic politics in the 1970s.

The impact of these changes has led to an expansion in the capacity of ethnic consumers to benefit from markets transactions, innovation and flexibility by expanding the range of ethnic goods and services. It has also transformed the impact of both the ethnic producers and consumers on wider markets as well as giving ethnic community members' power as consumers. Through these changes the transition to post-Fordism has brought about a restructuring in the ethnic community through consumerism, deskilling of the older workers and enskilling of the younger workers. This restructuring has created schisms between the older and younger generations, between men and women, between community and consumer, and between deskilled and enskilled.

What seems to have been overlooked are the changes that have arisen as a consequence of the transition to post-Fordism. Notably, the shift in the state's use of immigration legislation and control over citizenship set in motion a process leading to a restructuring of ethnic communities. They have changed from being political communities with the potential to globalise their identities to a locally oriented collection of voluntary organisations with consumer identities. Both of these changes embrace aspects of social control and elements of resistance: they are the consequences of the circulation of money-capital, commodities, and labour power (Lash and Urry, 1994). The combination of labour regulation and state security with the circulation of these elements of capital has set in motion changes in the space within and between communities, which impacts upon those living within them. It is this aspect of the change which eludes Lash and Urry (1994: Chapter 6) in their analysis of ungovernable spaces. The spaces are not ungovernable as a consequence of the circulation of capital; they are 'ungoverned'. It is not the social characteristics of the people within the space that make it ungovernable (Lash and Urry, 1994), but the creation of ungoverned spaces as a consequence of ethnic expansion linked to the increasing power of ethnic communities to participate as consumers. Neither local nor central were prepared to recognise control over these spaces. In a sense they represented the interfaces between and within ethnic and white communities open to competition for control.

While Jessop is not concerned with such space, Hay (1994) draws attention to its importance in his analysis of the role of the state and local government as 'movers and shakers'. He summarises the argument as follows. The changing contours of capitalist accumulation have increasingly privileged local development, making it a condition of national development. Many of these processes are present in the 'hollowed-out' Schumpeterian Workfare State nationally, which are linked to new forms of local governance reinforcing the subordination of welfare to workfare and legitimising accumulation. Hay raises doubts about whether the SWS is the best framework for post-Fordism, since it restricts 'supply-side intervention to innovation, structural competitiveness and sustained economic growth'. This may limit non-economic development. The adaptation of local governance to these constraints is expressed through various formal and informal structures which construct, operationalise and legitimise strategies for development. However, local developments can be undermined by the property-led development model favoured by central government and by the Schumpeterian deficit which restricts the amount of local intervention necessary to create the conditions for a 'stable mode of insertion within regional, national and supra-national economic dynamics'. He argues that the 'central state remains the most important single constraint on local and regional economic development' (1994:38-39). The contribution that this argument makes is that it draws attention to a social process of control through which local government on behalf of the state can take a post-Fordist view of the need to expand consumerism by encouraging the growth of businesses. When this is set within a Fordist approach to race, the ethnic community is reaffirmed as an economic and political entity, which, if protected from change, is set apart ideologically from other communities.

Since the post-war migration the circulation and control of black labour has been a significant processes within a declining Fordist state and a rising post-Fordist state. To summarise: racism developed in a context of economic regulation that allowed for the exploitation of migrant workers by capitalists. The regulation of these migrant workers was centred upon their freedom and otherwise to cross external boundaries as a definable group. Once the criteria of immigration controls were met, their settlement here became of concern only when their impact upon local services, such as employment, housing, education, health, and benefits, became a significant explanatory factor for the lack of access to these services. By explaining scarcity in terms of racism, the demands of the black community for equal opportunities were racialised. This focused white resentment on ethnic communities whose members became seen as source of evermore immigrants. Ethnic communities took this opportunity to challenge such political control through competition for governed spaces. The challenge for control over these spaces made apparent choices which were new and which identified weakness in the structure of authority in local government and state. The importance of control over these ungoverned spaces was that nobody had seen them as being important. Ethnic politics developed as a response of ethnic communities to control the space around them politically and to this extent to exercise their rights as consumers. As such, ethnic politics was recognised as a threat that needed to be controlled. The refusal of political parties and local authorities to participate in ethnic politics removed any opportunity for either to become embroiled in recognising the importance of this space. The change in the role of CRCs removed grassroots leaders from membership and CRCs from taking any political part in ethnic politics. To this extent state theory provides a framework for the analysis of race which can take account of ethnic politics.

The emergence of these choices for ethnic and white communities was reflected in the moral crisis, which with the crises of security in the state (Hall *et al*, 1978), accompanied the demise of mass production and formed part of the move towards a post-Fordist society divided into 'two nations'. Arguably, this shift to post-Fordism centred on the process of searching for new forms of state organisation that could resolve the 'contradictions and crises of Fordist accumulation and re-stabilise the state system' (Jessop, 1994:24). Jessop argues that the post-Fordist form of the new state to emerge from a Fordist economy is a SWS with a distinct set of objectives. These are 'to promote product, process, organisational, and market innovation in open economies in order to strengthen as far as possible the structural competitiveness of the national economy by intervening on the supply-side; and to subordinate social policy to the needs of labour market flexibility and/or the constraints of international competition' (1994:24). By reducing the importance of full employment, raising the priority of international competitiveness and placing productivist re-ordering of social policy above redistributive welfare rights, the new functions of the SWS seem to meet the new dynamic of global capitalism. Jessop argues that internationalised, flexible, and regionalised production systems have weakened the power of the national state. These changes have focused the struggle for power on the region and the local area and thus have shifted the maintenance of the ideology of racism from the state to the locality and the individual. This, in turn, led to the demise of ethnic politics, ethnic communities and ethnic identities. It transferred competition for economic and political space on to the individual and the flexible firm, which arguably has led to increasing opportunities to racialise at the level of the locality and region by reducing equal opportunities to an exercise in consumer competition. Furthermore, this has led to changes in the structuring of the ethnic community, which has subordinated its commitment to economic and political development to a commitment to welfare. In losing some of its power the state has transferred to the local the ideology of racism and the process of racialisation in a form that is more flexible, less accessible and individualised.

To unpack this argument I shall begin by concentrating upon a dominant aspect of post-Fordism, which is the regulation of labour and racist ideologies. Furthermore I shall suggest (a) that regulation of labour within the SWS permeates all aspects of the state project; (b) that regulation underpins the concept of flexible accumulation and (c) that regulation influences cultural changes within ethnic communities. Hay neatly summarises the differences between the KWS and SWS in terms of the former being characterised by 'demand-side intervention in relatively closed economies, whereas the latter is characterised by supply-side intervention in more open economies' (1994:13).

Although the emphasis is on post-Fordism, it is necessary to recognise that the post-war period is one during which a Fordist state, in some form, existed but was in decline. According to Jessop *et al* (1988) it had been in decline virtually since the turn of the century. The key characteristics that identify a Fordist state incorporate the nature of the labour process, the state sector's direct economic role and the state's wider role in the social mode of economic regulation (Jessop, 1994:16; Geddes, 1994:161). A 'typical form of Fordist state is the Keynesian Welfare State' (KWS), because firstly 'it aims economically to secure full employment in relatively closed national economies and to do so primarily through demand-side management' and secondly 'it tries to regulate collective bargaining within limits consistent with full employment levels of growth, generalise and extend norms of mass consumption to all citizens and to promote collective consumption favourable to a Fordist environment' (Jessop, 1994:17). This structure, which Bohning (1981) describes as liberal capitalist, incorporates a rigid occupational structure that in a Fordist society ensures that growth in employment and work can only be resolved by immigration. What is less clear is how the boom affected the industries that required these migrant workers. For instance, two separate forces determined the need for migrant workers in the local textile industry. The first was to modernise - initially to convert from coal to electricity, and then to automate and later computerise - in order to meet demands to clean up the environment and compete with foreign imports (Hahlo, 1996). The pressure of competition from foreign imports in textile manufacturing had begun before World War II. The second force for change came from a need on the part of some employers to contain and delay modernisation and automation while remaining competitive until the need to change became unavoidable and then either to modernise or fold. Industry met the need to change by employing replacement and supplementary labour that was cheap, powerless and rightless. In towns dependent on the textile industry a further difficulty arose, this took the form of the departure of white women workers for work in cleaner, better paying, more middle class employment. The departure of these woman workers gave South Asian women the opportunity to find work in the mills, which many did. While the women worked day shifts, their husbands worked night shifts. For Britain this solution to the post-war boom years, which provided an 'Indian summer' for the mass producing industries whose futures were already vulnerable, led to the encouragement of immigration of black people from the ex-colonies to provide a solution to a shortage in labour. It also signalled the end of Fordism.

Regulation of labour is a central element in Fordism and therefore in the KWS, but regulation is also a key process within the SWS. This suggests that different aspects of labour regulation exist and that different authorities through different channels at different levels apply them. The period from 1968 to 1990 was marked by the rise of Thatcherism as a social movement, the consolidation of Thatcherism and post-Fordism leading to radical Thatcherism (Jessop, 1993; 1992 a and b). Although the model of the SWS implies that regulation may be replaced by deregulation, Hay (1994) argues that it has been replaced by reregulation. Immigration controls today are an example of this, but it is no longer control over labour circulation. Regulation forms a key role in the state and the state expresses its authority through its efforts to control over labour. The regulation of migrant labour is distributed across four dimensions of power, all of which share a commitment to racist ideologies deriving from past and present histories. Through these dimensions of power, namely the prerogative, bureaucratic, capitalist and liberal dimensions, the state regulates a wide range of social activities that concern black people and women (Brown, 1992). The translation of this complex of power into exploitation and forms of social control has an immediate effect at the local level. Regulation at the international level, however, takes the form of immigration control, and as such reflects changing concepts of a national social identity (Cohen, 1994) and citizenship (Castles and Miller, 1993). I am concerned here with the implementation of this form of social control at the local level through the power invested by the state in local and national government, police, Department of Social Security (DSS), health services, and the onus placed on employers to act as agents of surveillance.

Others have already drawn attention to racism within a Fordist state, but they have reduced this to the implementation of immigration controls as a form of regulation (Lee, 1995; Bakshi *et al*, 1995). Regulation of labour as a consequence of ideologies of racism goes far beyond immigration controls for the purpose of exploitation at work and permeates into other areas of everyday life. The site of the wider effects of regulation of ethnic minority communities is local, not national, and in the post-war years the effectiveness of this regulation lay in its implementation locally. Furthermore, the impact of national and local governmental decision-making emerges at the local level. This is where ethnic minorities react to and experience the effects of decisions in terms of pay, pensions, employment and unemployment, promotion or otherwise, and the enforcement of legislation pertaining to immigration, visiting of family, kin and friends. It is at the local level in everyday life that ethnic minorities experience the disadvantages of the processes of regulation that form such an important role within the Keynesian Welfare and Schumpeterian Workfare states.

Reaction to regulation can take many forms: the differences between local and national reactions are relatively clear. The formation of CARD (Heineman, 1972) was a response nationally, but it also failed. The arguments about black anti-racist reactions are interpreted as an attempt to keep a national protest alive (Sivanandan, 1990), even though some ethnic minorities, such as Gujaratis, chose to see themselves as anything but black (Modood, 1988; 1992). A form of protest which was regarded as a sign of the despair felt by all ethnic minorities is urban unrest and public disorder (Benyon and Solomos, 1987; Hall *et al*, 1978). Scarman (1981) in his report argued that the local situation contributed as much to the unrest as did the national one. Another attempt to give a broader base to the response of minority communities to regulation is the argument that the recreation of ethnic cultures should be seen as a form of opposition to the hegemony of white British culture (Gilroy, 1987; 1993; Hall, 1990; Ballard, 1994; Khan, 1982). Local opposition to regulation, narrowly defined as opposition to immigration and nationality legislation, rarely takes the form of organised protest. Such protest is often channelled through local CRCs to national bodies that are involved in working with migrants, refugees and asylum seekers. The most common form of opposition to regulation in various forms at various levels is locally situated either in the place of work, local government, schools, or local CRCs. Therefore, this form of protest involves local CRCs, local political parties and ethnic organisations in some form of ethnic politics (Ben-Tovim *et al*, 1986, 1992; Eade, 1989; Werbner and Anwar, 1991). The decline of the KWS was signalled by its inability to cope with a change in the economic environment from being nationally orientated to being localised and globalised (Jessop *et al*, 1988). The state's perception of anti-social black behaviour was regarded as a national symptom of unrest (Hall *et al*, 1978). Opposition to KWS forms of regulation allowed ethnic minorities the freedom to organise their protest and to protest in a number of different ways. By the beginning of the 1970s, however, the state's tendency to panic in the face of local anti-racist protest gave way to increasing economic and political uncertainty, as the pressure to globalise the economy was matched by the failure of Fordist forms of production. Anti-racist protest in the 1970s benefited from the disintegration of Fordism; this allowed ethnic minorities to contest ungoverned space for development of cultural signs to a degree that was not possible in the previous decade (Rex and Moore, 1971:117; John, 1969; Wright, 1968; Beetham, 1970; Scott, 1972/73; Bentley 1972/73) or after this decade.

The 1970s were a watershed in the emergence of post-Fordism; these early years in the development of Thatcherism as a social movement allowed ethnic communities to exploit the ungoverned spaces between communities. These included certain forms of ethnic political participation that, with rapid population growth, gave minorities an opportunity to develop structures of leadership and social networks of support whose functions could be both social and political. During this period local CRCs were able to extend their role to form close links with ethnic communities based upon the services they provided on immigration and nationality. In addition CRCs had access to funds for ethnic development through the Commission for Racial Equality (CRE) and which they had the power to allocate. The question of political participation is important, because it imposes a form of regulation on people which dictates how they can participate in local and national political processes (Saggar, 1992). Furthermore, the development of ethnic forms of participation depends upon social formations or movements and political socialisation. Political participation, whether it is expressed through social class ideology, buffer organisations, withdrawal from participation, the formation of anti-racist black organisations or in some combination (Layton-Henry, 1984; Solomos, 1989) recognises implicitly that minority communities are located outside the established political relationship between political parties and government. Layton-Henry identifies five different forms of political participation available to ethnic minorities. The include participation through political parties and the working class, buffer organisations, a withdrawal of participation in politics, black opposition to racism and a combination of all four. These forms of participation are consequences of the racialised relationships that link ethnic minorities to the state. Excluding voting and participation in political parties, the other four forms of participation are only available to ethnic minorities. Participation through the ballot box has given minority communities generally little or no access to politically important positions locally or nationally (Anwar, 1996) and little influence of local or national decision-making processes. Setting aside the withdrawal of ethnic minorities from politics and the formation of anti-racist organisations which have not developed into major forms of participation, the chief form of participation other than the ballot box has been the development of ethnic politics through CRCs, arguably mistakenly identified as buffer institutions. The emergence of ethnic communities in the late 1960s and early 1970s and South Asians' commitment to political participation gave importance to the political position of the ethnic voter. In electoral politics since 1974 (Anwar and Kohler, 1975) the ethnic vote has been much sought after by politicians (Anwar, 1994). The importance of this vote lies not only in it being a committed vote to the Labour Party (Anwar, 1994; Lawrence, 1974), but also in it being seen by politicians as a possibly a block vote (Scott, 1972/73; Bentley 1992/73).

I shall first discuss the ethnic community and then address the political implications. The growth in the size of the ethnic population in the 1960s and 1970s contributed to the emergence of ethnic communities within the South Asian ethnic minority in Britain generally. Within this population ethnic identities were not merely shifting points of reference in changing social situations, but their origins lay in membership of actual communities based upon faction, caste, sect and religion. Immigration to Britain provided members of these communities with a new situation in which they had not only to recreate their culture (Werbner, 1989), but also had to establish new relationships between communities from different regions and countries. Ungoverned spaces between these communities were as open and unchallenged as were those between them and the other ethnic communities and the white community. They became the signs that invited contest for control over the daily life of the members of ethnic communities. Domination of these spaces is a central issue in the relationship between ethnic communities and the local authority. Therefore, control of ungoverned spaces between ethnic communities and the white community developed into a political issue. This was translated into a demand by ethnic communities for physical, social, economic, political and cultural space. Ethnic communities developed organisations with structures of leadership and support to compete for control of this space.

Underpinning these communities and their organisations are social networks which provide both a structure and a set of reference points to define social boundaries of spaces within which social identities can be associated in different social situations. Furthermore, these networks provided channels of support, communication, identity, and acted as social, economic, religious, political and cultural resources upon which ethnic communities depended for their links with communities in their places of origin and for their development here (Werbner, 1989). These networks represent the social matrix upon which much of the ethnic social expansion and economic and political action occurred.

Against this expansion of ethnic communities it is necessary to consider some of the implications of the process of regulation of immigration and the controls that formed part of developing post-Fordism in a declining KWS. The process of exploitation shaped ethnic communities into a disadvantaged section of the population in response to local and national governmental decision-making and policies, e.g. the containment within disadvantaged housing areas (Smith, 1989; Rex and Tomlinson, 1979), the placing of ethnic children in less advantaged schools, and the temporary enskilling of a workers who were soon to be deskilled (Miles, 1992). For ethnic communities this contributed to the maintenance of their vulnerability to unemployment, and the continuing experience of racism in local government, the statutory services and in the forces of law and order. By the 1970s the state no longer reacted in a panic mode to ethnic politics, but it was also not prepared to accept it. Now local government attempted to make contact with ethnic political figures and listen to ethnic demands through local CRCs and later Joint Consultative Committees (JCCs). This enabled local government to control ethnic communities where possible, meeting them where politically expedient, ignoring them where politically advantageous, but drawing upon ethnic voting power at every opportunity. Thus the main political opportunities for ethnic organisations to participate in local and national politics were local, and were by perceived by some to give a advantage to ethnic communities over others (Solomos, 1989). The development of an informal political arena within local CRCs, of which there were over a hundred in the 1970s in British towns and cities, made competition for the control over ungoverned spaces possible within and between expanding ethnic communities and the white community. In this context, representatives of ethnic organisations became regarded as leaders due to the belief held by politicians and local government officers, that they spoke for and could influence the voting intentions of their members (Scott, 1972/73; Eade, 1989 and Bentley 1972/73). Regulation as a national form of control over ethnic minorities could not control local political activities, because local politicians recognised the importance of the ethnic vote, while the forms of regulation targeted members of ethnic communities on the basis of their status as immigrants. As ethnic politics was of little concern to the government or the state for a time, the threat it posed was initially local. Central to the development of ethnic politics were local CRCs (now known as Race Equality Councils or RECs). The Government established these in towns and cities which had large or significant black populations, to facilitate the development of harmonious relations between them and the white communities. Although these councils pre-dated the Commission for Racial Equality, they survived the various changes through which the Commission went, prior to its development, and through various reorganisations implemented by the Commission between 1978 (CRE), 1988 (Gay and Young) and 1997 (CRE 1997). Other than reports on these reorganisations, the work of Hill and Issacharoff (1971) and Ben-Tovim *et al* (1986), the roles of CRCs and their relationships with ethnic communities have not been the subject of sustained research. Katznelson (1973) ignored them, concentrating upon other local and national organisations which worked with ethnic communities, such as the Community Relations Commission. Therefore, the importance of their political role has been overlooked with the exception of the two above mentioned studies and the reports on their reorganisations in 1978 and 1988, the most recent of which has still to be published. In the early 1970s these locally based organisations extended their role to facilitating ethnic politics by providing an arena in which ethnic leaders could debate local and national political issues with elected politicians to the extent of developing a significant influence. Underlying ethnic politics were demands from ethnic organisations for a political identity within a situation in which their access to space and scarce resources was restricted by racism and where racialised social boundaries favoured the white community (Small, 1994). In the process of being controlled or acceded to, ethnic political demands brought to the attention of the wider local and to some extent national political arenas the presence of ethnic communities. The rejection of Rushdie's *The Satanic Verses* by Islamic communities across Britain exemplifies the potential of one section of these ethnic communities to exploit ungoverned space and present a united political opposition outside existing politically recognised organisations.

Ethnic politics is a form of anti-racism and as such allowed ethnic communities to express their views locally in a way that would not have been acceptable nationally. The central part of this book is concerned with immigration (regulation), development of communities, social networks and ethnic politics (Chapters Two to Six). Other than signalling that this analysis is to follow, my concern here is with establishing the bases of my argument. The reaction of black workers, and South Asians in particular, to regulation led to the formation of ethnic communities and to ethnic politics. The development of these communities was not just a result of population growth, but also a response to immigration legislation (Anwar, 1979), to economic conditions in the countries of origin, and to economic conditions in British towns and cities (Smith, 1989; Rex and Tomlinson, 1979), and to employment and citizenship. As the position of black people within the economy generally needs to be recognised in the Fordist and post-Fordist state, my concern here is with Fordism and post-Fordism and therefore with regulation in its wider aspects. In the final Chapter I shall turn my attention to the relationship between ethnic communities and the post-Fordist state.

Most analyses of post-Fordist regulation concentrate upon control of economic relationships and the circulation of labour; the primary reason for bringing migrant labour to Britain was economic (Power, 1976; Miles, 1982; Castles *et al,* 1984; Miles and Phizacklea, 1984). However, the regulation of this labour appears to have moved beyond that of purely economic relationships to impinging upon social and familial relationships. It is possible to argue that regulation of black workers and their families was extended beyond the economic: it involved the control over migration generally, control over migrants and their skills, control over the women who accompanied them both as workers, as women, and as producers of children. Regulation as used here draws upon a wider range of economic and associated economic implications than is envisaged by Jessop (1990; 1992; 1993; 1994) or Hay (1994), but comes closer to the Jessop *et al* (1988) analysis of the place of post-war migration in their analysis of Thatcherism. In general it is the economic relationships associated with migration that have dominated studies of race relations, and where a different approach has been taken, the cultural aspects have emerged (Watson, 1977; Ballard *et al*, 1994; Westwood, 1984; Miles, 1982; Power, 1976). In terms of this understanding it is reasonable to speak of regulation of migrant post-war labour as being essentially economic in character. To this extent the use of regulation transfers some of the essential economic elements of Fordism to a post-Fordist state, but also extends it in terms of the economic implications of racism for black communities. This analysis will explore some of the consequences of regulation on ethnic communities at different levels and in different ways but in the local context.

Conclusion

In a Fordist state the producer and the market have power over the consumer; in a post-Fordist state the consumer has power over the producer (Urry, 1990a and b). The consumer also has freedom to gaze (Bauman, 1995; 1988). For migrants to become consumers, they need to consume. The employment of family labour and the development of a production process to meet the needs of a niche market do not involve the consumption of scarce resources. Where the ethnic community and its members compete for scarce resources as consumers they acquire similar power to other consumers.

Arguably, the displacement of state power as a consequence of its being 'hollowed out' is a central element in the process that transformed ethnic communities from those employed by consumers to increase their profits to active consumers in their own right. Producers can be separated into two categories: firstly, those who as producers are also consumers of power, land, property, buildings, water, and state benefits. Secondly, there are those who give them a role as employers of labour, both of which make them subject to the power of consumers. In a Fordist state, control over labour amounted to control over black workers. By using these controls to construct their private life in the public domain, the state not only controlled their labour, but also their women and children. The transition to post-Fordism has both given these workers and their families a degree of wealth, and with it they have become consumers. It is as consumers that they share power with other consumers over producers and markets. The contradiction is that as both exploited migrants and consumers they are targets for racism. Racism has become displaced within an ideology of choice and subcontracting. Only the consumer can initiate action against racism.

The central factors that underlie this analysis are the state's control of migration, the formation of ethnic social and religious organisations, the lack of political representation in the formal local and national political systems, the emergence of ethnic politics as a form of local political participation and the attempt by ethnic communities to locate themselves in the new world of internationalised and globalised consumerism.

Chapter Two explores the state and the dimensions of control through which it expresses its power and shapes notions of security in relation to ethnic communities. Furthermore, through an analysis of these dimensions of power, I shall argue that the post-Fordist framework imposes a need to recognise the local, the national and the global. Local data on migration will be used to establish a connection between the national and the local. Although the trend has been to treat such data at a national level, this usage of such data is intended to focus the national issues on a local context. This will set the scene for Chapters Three to Seven, which will explore the emergence and development of ethnic communities and organisations as political organisations. A description of the research methods is set out in Appendix One.

2 State, dimensions of control and migration

This Chapter explores the processes of state control in relation to the rightless, poor and powerless South Asian migrants as they became aware of their need to resist racial discrimination, to recognise state forms of control and to shift towards becoming consumers and thus to establish their cultural position. This process forms part of two general changes to the location of migrants living in a post-Fordist society. Firstly, their status shifted from that of migrant to that of citizen. Secondly, this involvement in ethnic politics increased their awareness of racism into recognition that as ethnic communities they could generate cultural signs of resistance, that is, they could become consumers and producers of their own cultural signs. Thirdly, the shift towards consumerism enabled Gujaratis and other ethnic communities to establish a link between the national and the local and the global.

The inter-relationship between state control and migrants' resistance to racism (Ballard, 1994) is the focus of this Chapter. By doing this, the scene is shifted from a national context to a local one, a shift that lies at the heart of the post-Fordist state with its localised and globalised markets. This implies treating migration as a process of control by the state and a process that symbolises ethnic resistance. In turn, this turns attention to employment and housing which located these migrants in the occupational structure and defined their position within the wider social class structure. By relating these movements to dimensions of social control by the state, the scene was set for the development of a situation in which social control was matched by resistance. To an extent, the development of ethnic communities with political and ethnic identities should be seen as a consequence of the state's attempts to maintain control. I shall discuss the socio-economic position of Gujaratis in Bolton in the early to middle 1970s and argue that the pattern of arrival of the Gujaratis enhanced their tendency to form small exclusive communities divided along social and religious lines, which were generally invisible to outsiders. As a whole, they were perceived by members of the white community to be part of one growing and visible immigrant community in the town. The characteristics of visibility and exclusiveness were expressed through skin colour and patterns of migration, employment, settlement and a complex structure of social identities. The analysis situates what was happening in Bolton in a national context. The intention is to show that Bolton, as a sunset industrial town, was and is both similar to many other northern industrial towns and different from towns in the south of England.

This Chapter is divided into two major sections. The first deals with the state and its commitment to control. The second separates state control into four dimensions of power, namely, the prerogative, bureaucratic, capitalist and liberal dimensions. By relating these dimensions of power to migration, employment and housing in Bolton, the state will be related to the local; it is the relationship between the national and the local which is assumed to be similar (Yancey *et al*, 1976).

State

The commitment of post-war South Asians in the late 1960s to remain in Britain is supported by evidence of the deferment of their intentions to return to the subcontinent (Anwar, 1979). This was in part a reaction to measures adopted by successive governments to control immigration and access to citizenship (Bohning, 1981; Layton-Henry, 1984; Solomos, 1989). Over the period from 1962 to the present, there has been an ideological and political shift in the form of the State's regulation from the politics of immigration to generalised control of immigration. The focus on immigration control was shifted from the control of black migrants from New Commonwealth countries to reduce racism (the politics of immigration) to the control of all migrants' access to citizenship. The control of migration has switched to the question of citizenship (Miller and Castles, 1993), and identity (Cohen, 1994) in relation to more rigorously enforced laws of immigration, nationality and the Asylum Act 1996. However, the effect of these changes remains a central concern not only for new immigrants, refugees and asylum seekers, but also for members of settled South Asian communities whose elderly parents increasingly wish to migrate to England to join their children. What has changed over thirty years is not only the increasing stringency of immigration controls and the extension of rules to all who seek entry into Britain, but also from the point of South Asians living here, it seems to continue to penalise them. South Asians are no longer the largest group of migrants seeking entry: the majority come from Africa and other third world non-Commonwealth countries (*Dept. of Immigration and Nationality Annual Report*, 1995). Though the emphasis has shifted away from the 'politics of immigration' to citizenship and identity, South Asian immigration to Britain has not ceased and remains a major issue for these communities.

Spatial movement enabled South Asians to change the social value of their labour from being regarded by capitalists as poor, powerless, cheap, unskilled and rightless to being better off, empowered, less cheap labour with rights. The acquisition of citizenship confirmed this shift in empowerment, and for those who came in the period from 1950s to the 1970s and beyond, it brought to them a realisation of their new status, with a growing recognition of their power and wealth. The political concern with immigration controls that was reflected in a

24

range of legal and technical devices, including deportation, X-raying, virginity testing, and dividing families, serves as evidence of the commitment of the state to control black migration (Solomos *et al*, 1982). This concern is supported now by the implementation of more refined techniques such as genetic testing, and the implementation of new policies, which attempt to undermine the rights of refugees to have access to the health services, housing and education for their children. These measures, while no longer directly linked to racism, remain associated with employment, public expenditure and citizenship. The government has extended the onus of national control of immigrants to employers and the major service providers, such as the NHS and local authorities.

State security is central to any analysis of race. The state's responses to its own changing circumstances need to be explained not just in terms of immigration control, but more importantly in terms of threat or risk posed (a) by the unintended consequences of migrants' social empowerment deriving from their movement through space from India and Africa to Britain and (b) an awareness of the 'growing opacity of the state' (Lyotard, 1988) in a globalising society. Four elements are central to this argument: the state, the notion of a social contract, the four modalities of power, and the political significance of the ethnic community. The 'core of the state apparatus comprises a distinct ensemble of institutions and organisations whose socially accepted function is to define and enforce collectively binding decisions on the members of a society in the name of their common interest or general will' (Jessop, 1990: 341). As an apparatus the state cannot be capitalist, racialised or gendered (Jessop, 1990: 353ff.), but the extent to which it is characterised depends upon 'the changing balance of forces engaged in political action both within and beyond the state' (Jessop, 1990: 353). In terms of its political actions the state can be capitalist, gendered, racialised and racist at the same time with no single characteristic dominating the state. The character of the state apparatus emerges through four modalities of power (Brown, W, 1992: 16-24.). Firstly, the prerogative dimension involves the 'actualisation of the state through its control and ownership of political power and ability to employ violence, sexuality and political purpose for its own ends'. Secondly, the bureaucratic dimension bridges state and civil society and is both 'an end and an instrument and thus operates as a power in the service of other powers while presenting itself as extrinsic and neutral'. Thirdly, the capitalist dimension separates women from men on the grounds that the former do both waged and unwaged work and the latter do waged work. Finally, the liberal dimension rests upon a 'division of the polity into ostensibly autonomous spheres of family, civil society (economy) and the state'. The balance of these modalities of power gives the black observer the impression that the state is racialised.

Racism in post-war Britain is set within a framework which stresses the needs of capitalism (Miles and Phizacklea, 1984; Miles, 1982), while overlooking, arguably, an equally important aspect of state and governmental need to control black people in the name of security. This Chapter argues that state control emerges most forcefully through the four dimensions of power, namely, the prerogative, capitalist, liberal and bureaucratic dimensions which impact directly upon three aspects of the process of migration. These forms of control are expressed through the debate about the politics of immigration (Cohen, 1994; Layton-Henry, 1992; Bohning, 1981), local and national governmental legislation and funding for housing and education (Smith, 1989; Troyna, 1992; Rex and Moore, 1971) and patterns of employment (Brown, 1984; Rex and Tomlinson, 1979). The prerogative dimension, the right of the state to use power, overshadows the other three dimensions, and in part is expressed through acts of deportation, and also control of asylum seekers and refugees (Cohen, 1994; Castles and Miller, 1993). Racism is embedded in decisions and actions that were taken by governments at local and national levels within the context of a racialised ideology typical of the period between the 1950s and 1970s (Smith, 1989). These affected the lives of migrants, who were politically and racially constructed as black, poor and powerless (Sassen, 1990). The state saw them as a threat to its security, a legacy of colonialism buried in the histories of Britain and black peoples. Consequently, actions and decisions taken by the state to control black people are socially and politically constructed, and both white Britons and migrants reacted to them.

Prerogative dimension

Analyses of immigration legislation and administration blur the distinction between state, government and civil society; by identifying the four dimensions of the state apparatus it is possible to disentangle the powers and the boundaries between the state, government and civil society. Two aspects of this dimension of power impacted on all newcomers and visitors, and many members of ethnic communities resident here in the 1970s. These were and still are firstly, the state's determination to regulate and control black immigration and settlement, and secondly, the stop and search power of the police. The state's use of these powers rested upon a distinction of who was in the Commonwealth and who was not, whose social identity is acceptable (white) and whose is not (black). From this the state constructed an ideology of security that dominates its policies towards black people to the present day. Politics of immigration describes the means by which the state developed control over black people through the implementation of legislation and administration. This dimension of the state is experienced through the use of force, sexuality, discrimination, violence and politics to achieve its own ends. Immigration and nationality acts should be seen as the most direct form of state control over members of the civil society.

Post-war British governments encouraged the immigration of labour from ex-colonies as a result of pressure particularly from capitalists and industrialists to support their declining industries (Layton-Henry, 1992; Solomos, 1989; Miles and Phizacklea, 1984; Miles, 1982) in a de-industrialising national economy that was seeking an entry into globalised markets. During these years, people and politicians explained racism in terms of increasing difficulties associated with access to scarce resources, such as council housing, reducing opportunities for employment, overcrowding in schools, deterioration of inner urban areas and issues of law and order (Hall, 1981; Hall et al, 1978). A solution to these difficulties was presented in the form of improving the control over the entry of black people into Britain. The form of control chosen by governments was through political means (Bohning, 1981), which proved to be difficult to implement because it attracted political criticism both at home and abroad, and, more importantly, because it was ineffective. As Bohning (1981) observed, a liberal-capitalist economy with a rigid structure of occupations could not cope with changes such as de-industrialisation which brought unemployment after the economic boom of the 1950s. There is a political logic which was constructed and added to by successive governments that is reflected in the commitment to control black migrant immigration, but to exercise less control over the immigration of white people from European countries including Ireland. Attention was focused on settled black minority populations, their cost to the public purse, and a belief in their willingness to resort to public disorder and violence (Hall *et al*, 1978). The logic of this political debate is now established through government efforts to define migrants who can be admitted to and who can not be admitted to citizenship (Cohen, 1994). The application of new and more refined definitions of citizenship led to the removal of those who do not match the categories (e.g. Joy Gardner), but the logic of these policies has become extended to all migrants. Solomos (1989:61-63) rightly notes that the analysis of immigration needs to be linked to particular social, political and economic changes which impose their characteristics on the industrial and economic periods. He also recognises that the debate about control of those wanting to enter and settle here was displaced on to the size of settled black communities in Britain. The complex of policies surrounding immigration control forms a set of categories that allow governments to draw even finer distinctions between visitors, migrants, refugees and asylum seekers than has hitherto been possible. A developing structure of policies exists to give these distinctions legal force, thus ensuring that most who enter the country can be categorised according to their status as refugees, asylum seekers, and immigrants. This structure of control supports the view that the state is committed to erecting racialised barriers (Small, 1994) which will make immigration control even more effective.

A recent instance of the determination of the state to erect racialised boundaries is embodied in the power of the police to stop and search. This dimension was clarified when the chief of the Metropolitan Police commented on the prevalence of young black men involved in street robbery in London and justified the power invested in the police to stop and search under Section 1 of the Police Criminal and Evidence Act 1984. Statistics suggest that most stop and search activities occur in black rather than white areas and that in proportion more black people than white people are subjected to such searches (*Runnymede Bulletin*, March, 1995). 'Nearly one in two of all stop and searches in Brent, Haringey, Hackney and Lambeth involved a black person' and almost a third of all stop and searches occurred in London boroughs where Asians form about 25% of the population (*Runnymede Bulletin,* March, 1995). Statistics show that black and Asian people are five times more likely than white people to be stopped and searched. The figures in the Bulletin also show that in London, black people are more likely to be targeted by the police than Asians, who comprise the larger population. In other words, Afro-Caribbeans are associated with public unrest and crime in a way that criminalises them and racialises poverty, unemployment, broken and single parent families.

They are seen as the 'enemy within' (Solomos, 1989:61). These statistics relate to police perceptions of criminality and not to actual evidence of crime. To this extent these figures are more a reflection of the attitude of the police and the state than evidence based on knowledge of crimes committed. This philosophy supports the state's perception of security.

Embodied within the state is a complex notion of security which has been constructed on the basis of Britain's past experiences of black people. From being in colonial times the 'enemy without', they have become both the 'enemy within and without'. Thus black communities remain the focus of the state's beliefs as being a source of urban unrest (Benyon and Solomos, 1988). Consequently, the unwillingness of the government to remove the element of doubt from the relationships between the police and ethnic minorities implies that full access to the rights and obligations of citizenship is racialised. Meanwhile, ethnic communities are left with the conviction that they continue to be disadvantaged compared to other citizens, and explain this in terms of their blackness (B.Gilroy, 1995). As once powerless immigrants, now they represent a force perceived to be able to destabilise society. This belief continues to drive the state and governments to employ prerogative measures to reinforce their concept of security, a concept which is buried deeply within the history and politics of the British state (for a comparable analysis of the USA state, see Campbell, 1990).

The British State exercises its power in relation to an ideology that associates racism with insecurity. Immigration in the post-war years brought this association into prominence again (earlier immigration of Jews had raised it in the past). The impact of the prerogative powers of the state is expressed through the implementation of immigration control and thus is best viewed from the control over the numbers of migrants entering Britain.

Bureaucratic dimension

Like the prerogative dimension, the bureaucratic dimension erodes the boundaries between the state and civil society: to some extent these two aspects of the state apparatus overlap in their functions. Before the 1980s, when concern was focused on immigration and the control of the flow of ethnic minorities into Britain, the implementation of decisions relating to immigration control could have an effect which was at once both local and national. Studies of the politics of race take for granted that the impact of politics on ethnic communities and their response to racism at the local and national levels will be similar; other studies suggest otherwise (Yancey *et al*, 1976:392-399; Ben-Tovim *et al*, 1989; Rex and Tomlinson, 1979). The implementation of bureaucratic measures to control black people range from the deportation of illegal immigrants to the allocation of housing, social benefits, access to the heath services and schools, control of fertility, and employment (Brah, 1992 a and b; Brown, 1992; Mama, 1992; Solomos, 1989; Benyon and Solomos, 1988; Smith, 1989). An extreme instance of the bureaucratic dimension eroding the boundaries between state and society was the deportation of Mrs Joy Gardner, which allegedly led to her death. The present government has used prerogative and bureaucratic powers effectively to control the allocation of housing, and to allow access to education, social benefits and the health service. Ferguson (1984) rightly observed that local education, health, social and housing policies 'create and colonise racial subjects' (also Brown, 1992). Smith (1989) demonstrated how the low social standing in which black people are held by the state is reflected in the low status and low value of housing available to them. The debate about the lower status of black women compared to that of white women was set in the context of the social devaluation of the migrant and immigration (Brah, 1992 a and b; Mama, 1992). The centralisation of power since the 1960s has shifted the power of local government into new areas, such as the targeting of development, giving the former greater power to control local communities financially and politically.

This process of the construction of racialised ideologies has reinforced the existence of a British cultural hegemony which dominates ethnic cultures (Ballard, 1994; Khan, 1982; and West for the U.S.A., 1994). The argument that is usually located within the two cultures debate claims that South Asians have moved from one place to another and from one culture to another. Implicit in this argument is a theory of social change (Ballard, 1994; Ballard R and C, 1977); the acceptance of British culture has formed a part of this debate, mainly because it raises issues such as assimilation and integration. On the one hand, these concepts have taken the form of political definitions (Roy Jenkins); on the other hand, they have been defined in terms of the acceptance of British values and beliefs (Robinson, 1986). An argument has been constructed which claims that by rejecting integration and by maintaining ethnic cultural identities, South Asians have resisted racism (Ballard, 1994). The domination of British culture over ethnic cultures has been translated into a political concern, which is expressed by a term such as 'valuing diversity'. This notion, which initially became embedded in educational debates about multicultural schools (Swann Report, 1985; Verma (ed.), 1989) has been extended to the context of the governing of a multicultural society (Parekh, 1991). Therefore, the logic would suggest that the maintenance of ethnic cultures is a form of anti-racism; but the difficulty with this argument is that this raises the question about how ethnic culture is being threatened. According to West (1994) African-American culture was deliberately eroded and destroyed by slavery and plantation cultures. He suggests that African-Americans will have to reconstruct a culture that will be theirs; this lack of a culture and reference to the dominating culture forms the basis for the debate in the Hill-Thomas hearings Hill and Jordan 1995. Khan (1982) drew attention to this debate, but it was not followed up. What Ballard's (1994) argument does raise is not only the question about the maintenance of cultures as an anti-racist strategy, but also the question of how racism is changing (also Miles, 1993) and ethnic forms of resistance to it. The influence of these changes has raised a wide range of issues. These include the position of women, and particularly black feminism in relation to white feminism (Mama, 1992; Brah, 1992 a and b; Knowles and Mercer, 1992), housing (Karn *et al*, 1985), education (Troyna, 1992; Troyna and Hatcher, 1994) and health (Pearson, 1986). All of these issues are generally related to the growth of a population whose access to these

29

scarce resources was not always foreseen, was not always taken into account and was not always reckoned to impose new demands of access.

Migration and settlement in Bolton

The arrival and settlement of South Asians between 1950 and the 1970s in Bolton was accompanied by public acts of hostility that matched those accorded to these migrants in other towns and cities in Britain. Some of these acts of racism are discussed elsewhere (Chapters Five and Six), but most are attributable to individuals' or media perceptions that gave a racist explanation for reduced access to scarce resources for the white community. The reactions of Boltonians to South Asians over this period were generated by similar concerns and were assimilated by politicians into the argument put to Parliament to encourage the government to control immigration. In a liberal capitalist country committed to a policy of full employment and high real growth policies, labour shortages are resolved by recruiting migrant workers who can fill the low-wage insecure jobs that require few skills (Bohning, 1981). The consequence of this policy is that it initiates an unending and self-feeding stream of migrants (Bohning, 1981:29-34). This polyannual model of migration can be used to explain Gujaratis' migration to Britain. The mechanics of chain migration are well established in the literature (Banton, 1972:128-131; MacDonald and MacDonald, 1964:82). Ties of kinship and marriage not only sustain the migration chain, but also define the extent of the pool of potential migrants. In theory, the chain ceases when there are no more kin to follow or kin choose not to follow; in practice, the chain is self-perpetuating. As Bohning (1981) observed, to control chain migration requires political means. Therefore, it is important to recognise some of the differences between the national and local scenes; one such difference lies in the impact of chain migration on the local Gujaratis. Continuing migration is taken by some Gujaratis to be a symbol of resistance to state control and therefore to racism.

Records of South Asian settlement in Bolton before 1950 are fragmentary. Some West Indians who fought for Britain in World War II settled here. One of the town's first South Asian families, the Deans, came in the early 1930s from what is now Pakistan. The majority of those who came around this time were Pakistanis. In the 1947 census a family with an Asian name is registered as living at 5 Henry Street, Bolton. Gujaratis began arriving in Bolton in the early 1950s along with other South Asian migrants seeking work in what was then a thriving textile industry. With white male and female workers leaving these jobs for better paid and more secure ones (Brah, 1982:13), these migrants had little difficulty finding work. Locally the textile industry had always been a large employer of women (Cohen and Jenner, 1981:112-113), but now as employers had to achieve higher rates of production in order to survive, they balanced their commitment to invest in improvements with the need to pay low wages. A solution was for them to employ migrants. Although I have no information on the jobs these migrants found, research suggests that they were no different from those found by immigrants elsewhere, that is, they were low skilled, worked unsociable hours on insecure terms for low paid with little training (Allen *et al*, 1977; Bohning, 1981:33). Such jobs were typical of a semi-automated manufacturing industry which was under pressure to modernise in order to compete successfully in developing globalised markets.

Initially, Asians settled in run-down and poor inner areas close to the textile mills where they worked. The 1961 census provides scant information on migrants, as data on country of birth was not recorded; according to it, the number of New Commonwealth immigrants living in Bolton comprised 534 men and 564 women (OPCS Census, 1961). Local Authority Housing Department information suggests that the immigrants had become part of a rapidly growing South Asian population community. This community grew from about 27 dwellings in 1956 to over a thousand by 1971. Although there is no way of knowing whether or not these Asians were Gujaratis, the sample suggests that some were living here at this time. The pattern of settlement of Gujaratis sampled reflects national trends, but there are a few differences. Some attribute their attraction to Bolton to its nineteenth and early twentieth century trading links with India, based upon the import of raw cotton and later leather, and the export of textiles and leather goods (Saxelby, 1971:97). However, it is more likely that it was the availability of work in the textile industry and their knowledge of this industry that drew them to the town. Before World War II the textile industry experienced a recession brought about by a growth in the manufacture of textiles in Britain's colonies. Locally, the industry experienced major changes; for instance, the closure of the coal mines forced mills to find alternative forms of power. Nevertheless, between 1956-1959 the textile industry enjoyed a revival which required a balance between modernising the industry while reducing labour costs. This change was evident in the rate of unemployment in the town, which rose from 1% to 2.5%; nationally, it was slightly higher (Ogden, 1966: Diagram 4). Towards the end of the 1950s the local textile industry experienced another and more sustained recession. The 1959 Cotton Act, which was intended to rationalise and revitalise this industry, set in motion the large scale closure of mills with outdated machinery (*Joint Working on Structure Plans in Greater Manchester Employment Sub Group*, 1972: Para. 2.2). The mills which survived this Act were encouraged to install new machinery but at considerable expense. The Act brought about the closure of over a fifth of the textile mills in Lancashire; Bolton's textile industry was affected particularly badly. Many engineering firms that produced textile machinery had to diversify. For the above reasons there was no shortage of jobs in the town (Ogden, 1966:4).

During the initial period of migration most migrants were single men, whose aim was to accumulate sufficient money to return home (Anwar, 1979). However, few achieved this aim and many who came alone soon brought over their wives and children. For those who came to save money, the difficulty of earning sufficient money to save some, the changing value of money both in Britain and India and the expense of living in Britain combined to change this ideal into a myth (Anwar, 1979). Most failed to reckon on the pressures that make short term plans of migration difficult to execute (Bohning, 1981:36-37). However, for those who lived here, the myth of return, far from being a temporary ideal associated with the early period of migration, became an important, achievable goal to be deferred till after retirement. By the 1960s these migrants were joined by their wives and families

(Ballard, R and C, 1977:35). The majority of Gujaratis sampled came here during the decades of the 1960s and 1970s (Table 2.1). There is a relationship between population growth and the emergence of ethnic identities (Ballard, R and C., 1977), which led to the emergence of factions, caste and sect communities. The majority of migrants found work in the mills, suggesting that employment was available well into the 1970s.

Table 2.1
Analysis of settlement of the sample

	Muslim	%	Hindu	%	Totals	%
1970-76	30	28.8	78	50.6	108	41.9
1960-69	71	68.3	73	47.4	144	55.8
1956-59	2	1.9	3	1.9	5	1.9
No Answer	1	1			1	0.4
Totals:	104	100	154	99.9	258	100

In the space of a relatively short period the South Asian population expanded from a few hundred to over 3050 (OPCS sample census, 1966). Between 1970 and 1977 some 3492 Asian migrants came to Bolton in a steady stream with two high points: one in 1972 and one in 1976. These figures for migrants who gave Bolton as their destination to immigration officials indicate that the numbers of male and female migrants rose slightly from 23% to 34% and from 35% to 51% respectively, but that the numbers of children declined from 43% to 15% (Table 2.2 see below). These fluctuations in local numbers of immigrants should be seen against a background of an overall drop in the numbers of South Asians entering Britain with a predicted rise in the number of wives and children (Bohning, 1981:37). South Asian migrants saw Bolton as a desirable location. Against an overall increase in the number of women and children entering the country, the number of men coming gradually declined. Where it is possible to distinguish between adults and children, the Table shows that at this time the pattern of men and women with dependants gave way to a pattern that comprised mainly single young men or women, who were either fiancées or wives coming to join their husbands/ partners.

Over 50% of migrants came here from the Indian subcontinent; most migrants who came from Uganda did so in 1972. Most of these migrants were Gujaratis; only a few were Pakistanis (Table 2.3). A number of those who came from Uganda and the rest of Africa included Pakistanis and Sikhs. An analysis of place of origin and name shows that 3422 (98%) migrants came directly from Gujarat, India. Gujaratis recognise a common social identity based upon a common origin, a common culture and language; to this extent they comprise an ethnic group (Wallman, 1979; Lyon, 1972/73; Desai, 1963). Though these data do not take account of internal migration of Asians within Britain, they provide evidence that Bolton's Asian population is predominantly of Indian Gujarati origin. Furthermore, the data also show that South Asian migration from Uganda tailed off dramatically after 1974, and from the rest of Africa decreased after 1977, but that the flow of migrants from Pakistan increased after 1976. Overall, the migration to Bolton did not reduce significantly in the 1970s.

Table 2.2
New migrants who gave Bolton as their destination*

Year of arrival	Males	%	Females	%	Children+	%	Totals	%
1970	78	22.6	119	34.5	148	42.9	345	100
1971	118	25	201	42.6	153	32.4	472	100
1972	239	39.2	272	44.7	98	16.1	609	100
1973	139	32.6	181	42.5	106	24.9	426	100
1974	101	33.8	124	41.5	74	24.7	299	100
1975	145	36.7	165	41.8	85	21.5	395	100
1976	227	42.3	229	42.6	81	15.1	537	100
1977	138	33.7	209	51.1	62	15.2	409	100
Totals	1185	33.9	1500	43.0	807	23.1	3492	100

*Data are drawn from lists of migrants who gave Bolton as their destination to immigration officials at Heathrow.
+ These lists identify children as being under ten years old. For children over ten years no age was specified, thus making it difficult to distinguish between them and adults. Some dependants over ten years are identified by sex and sometimes their ages are given. An adult's sex given, the sex of a child is not usually stated. Occasionally it is difficult to distinguish between an adult and a child/minor.

Table 2.3
Migration of Asians by country of last residence

Year of arrival	Uganda	Rest of Africa	Pakistan	India*	Totals
1970	9	50	81	205	345
1971	18	99	66	289	472
1972	333	64	51	161	609
1973	80	86	42	218	426
1974	6	90	17	186	299
1975	7	112	50	226	395
1976	1	148	113	275	537
Totals	454	649	420	1560	3083
%	14.7	21.1	13.6	50.6	100

*17 migrants came from Bangladesh and a few Gujarati Muslims came from Burma.

These data on migration give no indication of the religious composition of the immigrant population, but some indication of these differences of population can be gained from an analysis of the sample: the majority (60.4%) of Hindus came from Africa as compared to a minority (21.2%) of Muslims (Table 2.4). Although most of them came here between 1970 and 1976, it is difficult to separate those who came as refugees from Uganda in 1972 from others who fled that country either before or after this date. For those who came in 1972, the reception they received was hostile, with the local media reporting the fears of the white community expressed in terms of being swamped. These data suggest that Gujaratis and others who came here had a clear idea of where they intended to settle initially. Moreover, at the time, immigration procedures required that migrants gave addresses of houses to which they would go. As regards the Ugandan Gujaratis, this would appear to contradict the findings of Bristow (1979: 206), but an explanation for this may be that Bolton was not singled out for resettlement purposes (Ward, 1973: 374-376). With the economic recession deepening, a popular view claimed that the migrants took jobs away from white workers, were allocated housing intended for the needy, and their children in schools would adversely affect the level of educational attainment of white children (Brah, 1982: 20). Such beliefs served to support the level of racial hostility in the town which was typical of the country generally (Moore, 1975). From accounts in the national and local press, the white response to the arrival of South Asians here was little different from that which they received elsewhere. Locally, hostility was further exacerbated by the continuing recession in manufacturing generally and the textile industry in particular and other associated industries. Migrants and locals found themselves in competition for jobs and benefits. Two factors dominated this period: firstly, there was the emergence of a second generation in the Asian communities (Ballard. R, and C, 1977: 41), and secondly, a greater effort was made by the government to control immigration. This effort was associated with the use of virginity testing, surveillance of couples in their first year of marriage, and children being subjected to X-ray examinations to verify their ages (Brah, 1982). The sedulous application of immigration rules by the Home Office led to an increase in migrants being detained at detention centres, to the separation of families and to heart-rending cases of deportation. It also reinforced the fears amongst local Gujaratis that the government viewed them more as visitors than as settlers. With the politicians seeing the reduction in the numbers of immigrants entering the country as the key to controlling the vote and racism (Brah, 1982: 21; also Bohning, 1981), local Gujarati observers interpreted this as indicating that their position here was not as secure as they had believed. Politicians assumed that migrants such as Gujaratis would integrate. For instance, although Mr Jenkins, then Home Secretary, argued against the notion of 'assimilation' but in favour of 'integration' (Brah, 1982: 15), many South Asians were unsure that they could look upon Britain as their permanent home.

Table 2.4
Countries from which respondents came to the UK

	U.K	%	Indian subcontinent	%	Africa	%	No answer	%	Totals	%
Hindus	2	1.3	55	35.7	93	60.4	4	2.6	154	100
Muslim	13	12.5	68	65.4	22	21.2	1	1	104	100.1
Totals	15	5.8	123	47.7	115	44.6	5	19	258	100

Capitalist dimension

An economic relationship acts as an analogue of that between the state and its once colonised people (Phizacklea, 1990: 2-4). Like many other industrialised countries in post-war Europe, Britain needed cheap, flexible, relatively unskilled, low-cost and powerless labour. Again, in common with other countries, Britain turned to her ex-colonies and to black labour. Once the migration of this labour had been set in motion, it could not be stopped other than by political means (Bohning, 1981). The only other way in which this form of migration can be halted is by workers directing their migration away from Britain to other countries offering more attractive working environments. Other countries, such as Saudi Arabia, have encouraged migration, so as to utilise a cheap source of labour. The recent figures for migration (*Department of Immigration and Nationality Annual Report*, 1995) show that migration from the subcontinent and the Caribbean has dropped and that more migrants, refugees and asylum seekers are coming from Africa. This suggests that other markets in other countries are attracting these people. However, the chains that bind Gujarati families to their kin in Gujarat and elsewhere in the world have not been broken, thus ensuring that their migration to Britain cannot be easily stopped. A recent study of the need for an immigration service in Bolton shows that the majority of Gujaratis expressed their need for such a service, reflecting the continuing importance of migration. The demand in the past for immigration services suggested that labour control was an integral part of the Fordist state; but the transition to a post-Fordist state has separated immigration control from labour control.

Initially, migration to Britain was voluntary, whereas the organisation of migration of workers to West Germany was more closely linked to organised recruitment by the government (Layton-Henry, 1992: 12; Castles *et al*, 1984). In the latter instance, the conditions on which the relationship between immigration and employment were based were coterminous; that is, the conditions were built into the contract between government and migrant, which in turn imposed conditions upon contracts made between the immigrant and the employer. While in Britain this was not set out as clearly as this, nevertheless the contracts between migrant workers and employers are controlled by the state, that is the government can withhold permission to work from the immigrant. By drawing out the process of acquiring citizenship, the contracts between immigrants and employers could incorporate exploitative elements, which set the former at a disadvantage. Consequently, the state appears to South Asians people to be racialised. Supplementary and replacement labour needs to be seen against a background of white male and female workers moving out of less attractive work to more secure and better paying work, and industries replacing them with cheaper black labour to lower labour costs (Smith, 1989; Miles and Phizacklea, 1984; Castles *et al*, 1984; Miles, 1982). In Lancashire the textile industry was trying to survive not only because of foreign competition, which already threatened the industry in the pre-World War II years, but also because it had to come to terms with new Acts that required mills to modernise their system of production. In the 1970s Lancashire's textile employers looked upon South Asian migrants as labour that allowed those who could not afford to modernise to survive for a few more years, and others to modernise by lowering their production costs, freeing funds for investment (Hahlo, 1996). Thus employment of migrant labour by this industry delayed the inevitable: a collapse of an outdated industry in the face of failure to modernise, automate, and computerise, assisted by competition from foreign imported textiles, rising labour costs and the need to meet new anti-pollution legislation. The disappearance of this old industry is acknowledged physically by the disappearance of old mill chimneys and in labour terms by a shift to the production of modern textiles requiring automation, computerisation and a massively reduced but highly qualified work force. Therefore, the collapse of the industry that once needed migrant labour now has left most of the Gujarati men jobless.

Thus the work which was available to black people was shift-based, low paid, low skilled or requiring skills of limited value within labour intensive outdated industries, could be obtained through short term and low cost training programmes, and was open to exploitation by employers (Jenkins, 1992; Braham *et al*, 1981). With workers, men and women, from specific ethnic communities seeking work in particular industries, the fortunes of those industries and the work they provided became associated with the employment and careers of the ethnic communities. In addition to the low status of the industries that relied upon migrant labour, the dependence of migrants upon finding work through informed social networks, personal approaches and advertisements in conjunction with the racial and employment characteristics of the manufacturing, public sector and retailing industries reinforced entrenched disadvantages. (Jenkins, 1992). Furthermore, these disadvantages, in conjunction with the characteristics of these three industrial sectors and the recession, increased opportunities for employers to discriminate between applicants (Wrench, 1992; Jenkins, 1992; Solomos, 1991; Braham *et al*, 1982). The evidence on education and training of ethnic minorities, according to some research on job training, reinforces this picture of disadvantage (Wrench, 1992): according to others, it suggests that the ethnic minorities are not at the bottom of the occupational hierarchy (Ballard and Kalra, 1992). The contract between ethnic minority workers and employers complements that between the state and government and employee. While ethnic minorities have not found the social boundaries of their private space invaded by the state, what they have experienced is that their private activities have been moved into public space. Disadvantage derives not from the private sphere and associated activities but from ethnic minorities' participation in public and private activities, which are classed as public. Thus the capitalist dimension of the state both compliments relationships and contracts between employers and black workers and supports the state's notions of insecurity. While the state, government and employers regard these people as a potential threat to stability (Hall, 1981; *CCCS*, 1983), the conditions of their social contract with the state implicitly defines their powerlessness and rightlessness by incorporating the private sphere in the public one.

In addition to elements within the prerogative and bureaucratic dimensions acting as a form of control on South Asians in the 1970s, with the capitalist dimension they created a complex web of state control that affected their status as immigrants, members of families, the women and the children (Allen, 1982). Two decades later, control through capitalist relations impacts upon not only employment in a number of ways (Asylum Act 1996), but also upon immigrants' access to health services and housing. More importantly, the relationship between the migrant as a worker and the capitalist as an employer dominates the relationships between men and women within and without the ethnic family. Generally the distinction between the public and private domains explores the differences in the values attached to men and those that attach to women. It is argued that men receive some protection in the public sphere, while women within the private domain have to rely on the protection of their male partners. Racism and capitalism involved the employment and exploitation of men (Miles, 1982), but less mention is made of women. South Asian women have been working in the mills since the 1960s, but with the collapse of the textile industry in the 1970s many of these women took up home working (Allen and Wolkowitz, 1990).

The importance of this discussion lies in the low pay that they receive. In the context of the family and gender issues, the home worker employers are both white and South Asian men. Both offer the women lower pay than the women would receive if they worked at the workplace. The point is that within the relations of production, South Asian men are viewed by the capitalists as exploitable, because they do not have the protection afforded to white workers in the public domain. The position of South Asian women is more contentious: they are located in a private domain where they are beyond protection by the law. They are exploitable by white capitalists, South Asian capitalists and husbands. This hierarchy of exploitation, some black feminists argue, is located within the relations of production, and it creates a basis for black feminism which white feminists cannot share (Mama, 1992; Hill and Jordan, 1995). The capitalist dimension impacts on the work and the every day lives of South Asians. It is this hierarchy of inferiority that required the women to accept roles imposed by their men. One aspect of these roles was the maintenance of social networks which reinforced the positions of men and women. Thus this complex of domestic relationships, supported by racist relations of production in the public domain, is dependent for its formation and maintenance upon the structures in both the KWS and SWS.

The control of labour forms a central part of the Fordist and post-Fordist state. The 1970s was a critical period which witnessed the shift from the control of demand for labour to the control over the supply of labour. This raises the issue of chain migration as a system which delivers labour to a particular place virtually irrespective of changes in demand or supply. Moreover, the mechanics of chain migration with its attendant family, kinship and social commitments surround the migrant with a set of social obligations from which it is difficult to escape. On the one hand, it poses a political threat (Bohning, 1981), because it is both unselective and delivers labour to a location without any form of in-built control over the numbers of people who are drawn into the chains. On the other hand, it is both unselective and provides a range of labour, which is vulnerable to exploitation. This section analyses the position of Gujarati migrants in the occupational structure and argues that they were directed to what was a demand for labour in an industry which was under pressure to change to meet the demands of local, national and global markets. The consequences of these changes left these Gujaratis with skills that were to become obsolete; they became non-transferable. In addition to this, racism, the lack of spoken English, racial discrimination and lack of training have contributed to Gujaratis being contained within an occupation level. This was a typical experience and therefore, the purpose of this scenario is to establish the point of similarity between the local and the national.

The argument that chain migration perpetuates a self-feeding process is supported by evidence, which shows that Gujaratis continued to come here in the 1970s, even though the employment situation was worsening. The relationship between migration and unemployment is not as clear for Gujaratis as it is for West Indians (Peach, 1978/79: 40-44), although it has been argued that for Gujaratis living in neighbouring Blackburn an inverse relationship holds between in-migration and unemployment (Robinson, 1980). In Bolton the rise in the numbers of male migrants matched the rise in unemployment generally and particularly in the minority communities. With the recessions in the textile industry and a threat of larger recessions nationally, the attraction of potential job opportunities linked to a better style of life should have diminished. However, as Table 2.5 shows, the numbers of South Asians coming here between 1970-1977 matched the rise in the percentage of gross unemployed (Table 2.2 above). Though good employment prospects strengthen the attraction, poor prospects did not undermine it. Thus over a period of three years the self-feeding migration chains continued to draw people to Bolton, although the employment prospects for migrants worsened as unemployment became a feature of working life. This supports the argument that an existing Gujarati population attracts Gujaratis (Desai, 1963:17). Such communities still continue to attract migrants, though now these are not necessarily migrants seeking work (see Mulla, 1995, also Chapter Seven). This confirms Bohning's (1981) argument that only political legislation can stop the self-feeding processes of migration, since he could not foretell in the 1970s how the patterns of migration in the 1990s would shift with the political context of countries of origin and changing work prospects.

Table 2.5
Gujaratis who came Bolton in relation to unemployment

Year of arrival	Males	%	Gross unemployment* %	Ethnic unemployment+ No	%
1970	78	22.61	3.9		
1971	118	25.00	3.9		
1972	239	39.24	4.8		
1973	139	32.63	3.6		
1974	101	33.78	3.5	109	3.8
1975	145	36.71	5.3	232	6.0
1976	227	42.27	7.0	445	10.3

*These figures are based on Table 8.4, *Central Statistics Office*, No.13, HMSO, 1977.
+Data are drawn from *Manchester Council for Community Relations Report*, 1982.

The Gujarati population grew quickly from approximately 3050 people in 1966 to around 14,000 by 1977 (Table 2.6). By 1984, the ethnic population was estimated as 20,000 (*District Trends*, 1984: 0) with Gujaratis comprising the majority of the ethnic population (Hahlo, 1980: 296; Sherrington, n.d.; Hill, 1977:14, 54). Bolton became a recognised centre for Gujaratis. A breakdown of the religious composition of this population is possible only by referring to a number of diverse sources of evidence, i.e. census data, Heathrow immigration lists, BCCR area profiles, various surveys (Hahlo, 1983; Sherrington n.d; Hill 1977). Generally, observers agree that Muslims outnumber Hindus. During the 1970s the former were estimated as comprising about 7,000 and the latter 6,000 individuals. Since then these numbers have increased and at present these two communities are believed to number about 9,000 and 8,000 people respectively.

Table 2.6
Population of Bolton Metropolitan Borough*

	No.	%
British citizens (white)	250,950	93.99
Indians (primarily Gujarati)	13,000 ⎫	
Pakistanis	1,000 ⎪	
Bangladeshis	50 ⎬	6.72
West Indians	1,000 ⎭	
Others	1,000	
Totals:	267,000	100%

*Source *Area profile 1977*, BCCR.

The change in their status from migrants to settlers locally coincided with the emergence and development of community identities and with Gujaratis becoming the dominant minority. Some indication of the stability of Gujarati settlement can be gained from the length of time that some of those sampled had lived here;[1] five percent had lived here for over 14 years and 37% for nine or more years. This population comprised two religious communities whose members shared the experience of migration, a social identity as immigrant, and separate social identities as Gujaratis. These social identities provided the basis for translating ethnic politics into political realities (Chapters Five to Seven) through their search for work and housing (see below), facilities to practise their religions (Chapter Two), and the development of ethnic communities (Chapters Three and Four).

Employment

Any analysis of Gujarati employment (and housing) should be seen against a background of a rapidly expanding population. 'Over time, foreign workers become a more and more indispensable part of the labour force of post-industrial societies unless their employment is curtailed by political act' (Bohning, 1981: 34). Both Gujarati men and women formed an integral part of the local labour force; yet some 20 years later, these workers still depend upon low skilled, low-waged and undesirable jobs in a shrinking job market. After the 1970s, the government continued to introduce further legislation to control immigration and at the same time the recessions reduced employment opportunities in the manufacturing sector. Increasingly stringent controls, together with reduced employment opportunities, contributed to reducing the attractiveness of Britain for the South Asian migrant compared with other industrialising countries. When opportunities for employment decrease, other motivating reasons for migration may continue to attract prospective migrants, for instance keeping up links with family, and elderly parents coming to live with their children. These attractions have added to the imagery of opportunity over the years. The availability of jobs, an improved style of life and the attractions of a Gujarati community (Table 2.7 below) drew some 57% of Gujaratis sampled to Bolton. A survey in neighbouring Blackburn revealed that a predominantly Gujarati Muslim population migrated to improve their life-style and work opportunities. The main reason given for choosing to settle in Blackburn was to join their families (Townson and Moorhouse, 1979:13, Tables A2 and A3; Robinson, 1986). Some 76% of Gujaratis sampled came to Bolton to join family, friends and the community; only 19% came here to find work.

Joining family, friends and a Gujarati community was a greater priority than finding a job (19%), though one can lead to the other. Some 50% of the Blackburn sample heard about their present jobs through friends (Townson and Moorhouse, 1979: 21, Table A16) compared with 32% of Gujaratis sampled who heard about them from kin and friends. The majority (37%) of the sample (Hindu and Muslim) learnt about their present jobs through advertisements (Table 2.8 below) compared with 5% in the Blackburn sample. For Gujaratis there were attractions additional to employment, such as joining family and a growing Gujarati population. These Gujaratis were young with young families and therefore could look forward to a life with good job prospects; the average age for Hindu men was 32.6 years and for the Muslim men 38.6 years. Most of those sampled came already married and keen to find work, so that they could bring over their families.

Table 2.7
Reasons given by respondents for coming to Bolton

	Hindus No	Hindus %	Muslims No	Muslims %	Total	%
Kin and family	95	61.7	51	49.0	146	56.59
Friends	26	16.9	16	15.4	42	16.28
Gujarati Community	3	1.9	5	4.8	8	3.10
Job Opportunities	27	17.5	23	22.1	50	19.38
Religious Community			1	1.0	1	0.39
College Education	2	1.3	4	3.8	6	2.32
Housing			1	1.0	1	0.39
No reason	1	0.6	3	2.9	4	1.55
Totals:	154	99.9%	104	100%	258	100.1%

Table 2.8
How sample found their present jobs

	Hindus No	Hindus %	Muslims No	Muslims %	Total	%
Kin	17	11.0	14	13.5	31	12.0)
Close friends	16	10.4	5	4.8	21	8.1) 32.1%
Ordinary friends	13	8.4	18	17.3	31	12.0)
Advertisements	53	34.4	42	40.4	95	36.8
Promotion	1	0.6	4	3.8	5	1.9
Labour exchange	5	3.3	3	2.9	8	3.1
Went to door	1	0.7	1	1.0	2	0.8
No answer	48	31.2	17	16.3	65	25.2
Totals:	154	100%	104	100%	258	99.9%

Some arguments about employment of minorities claim that work is always available, however low-paid and insecure; others claim that migrants cannot obtain jobs commensurate with their skills and qualifications. Some question why, once they have lived here for some time, they cannot improve their job opportunities (Braham *et al*, 1981). Still others suggest that racism is part of the ideology of capitalism and that this accounts for these migrants being able to find only those jobs that are poorly paid, insecure and rejected by white indigenous workers (Miles, 1982). These explanations associate the low skills of these immigrants with the kind of jobs available to them. Most South Asians coming to Britain had few skills or qualifications (Wright, 1968: 34-5); and the Gujaratis who came here are no exception (Hahlo, 1980). Only 1.6% (4) Gujaratis sampled, all Hindus, claimed to have had no schooling. The majority of the sample (74%), that is 88.5% of Muslims and 64.3% of Hindus, had received some schooling but had no experience of education beyond secondary school level (Hahlo, 1980: 304). Any difficulties experienced by immigrants in finding jobs may be explained by models, such as the dual labour market model, which shows how racial discrimination can become a device for selecting on grounds of racial preference applicants for a reduced number of jobs (Blackburn and Mann, 1981). A line needs to be drawn between the 1950s, when there was full employment in Britain, and the availability of employment for migrants that extended into the 1970s. At this time Gujaratis still accepted jobs that others who were white or better qualified were not prepared to do. Better paying work was not available to them, as employers and the unions (Phizacklea and Miles, 1992) preferred to give this to white workers (Cohen and Jenner, 1981: 112-113, 122). Today these South Asian workers are still competing for similar jobs.

There is evidence to support these explanations. For instance, the textile industry was the largest employer of women in Bolton; some 38.4% of women were employed in textile mills in 1959. Though this figure was reduced in 1965 to 26% as a result of the closure of mills, this industry was still the largest employer of women. By 1971 the retail distributive business had become the biggest employer of women (19.4%) and only 15% were employed in the textile mills (Ogden, 1966: Tables 2 - 4). Over the same period of time, male employment in the mills was reduced from 19.9% in 1959 to 11.4% in 1965 and to 9.8% in 1971. By now the mills employed more women than men. Although the data does not distinguish between white and New Commonwealth women, it is reasonable to assume that most of these women were white. In the 1970s white women and Gujaratis, men and women, could still find employment in this industry, but the numbers of white male workers working in it had decreased, suggesting that the work was no longer considered desirable. In part, an explanation for this can be attributed to people's perceptions of the industry: the monotony of the work, the conditions in which people worked, the poor pay and the increasing vulnerability of the industry to the effects of the local and national recessions. An explanation for the reduction in the numbers of women workers a decade later can be explained by the closure of mills and by a change of attitude which suggested that mill work for women was no longer seen as desirable. Thus, to a limited extent, opportunities increased for Gujaratis to find unskilled and low skilled work in the mills. As women become less dependent upon this industry for employment, they began to find work in an expanding service sector. Thus the offering of these jobs by employers to Gujaratis can be explained in terms of their exercising a preference for the next available source of reserve labour. An analysis of the occupations of respondents reflects the range of occupations they held (Table 2.9 below). The majority of the sample held jobs in the textile industry (49%); this being the industry that first offered them jobs and it was also the industry with which they were most familiar. Gujarat had, and has, a developing textile industry. Five of those sampled who held professional jobs were not Gujaratis: one was a Sikh, a lecturer; four who came from other states in India included three doctors and an engineer. Generally this pattern of employment is typical of Asian workers in other textile towns, for instance Bradford (Allen *et al*, 1977: 58, Table 2.14).

For Gujaratis the mills offered day and night shift work, with some offering multi-shift and continental shift work. Apart from the possible familiarity of Gujaratis with this industry prior to their leaving India, millwork offered some positive advantages. Firstly, night shift work was better paid than day shift work. Secondly, Gujaratis could work with mainly Gujaratis and other Asians, such as Pakistanis, which meant that the majority of the workers could speak languages with which they were familiar. Thirdly, they did not need to interact at work with white workers, with the result that the most socially important interactions occurred outside work. Fourthly, the work itself required only minimal commitment, and finally, the work contracts were sufficiently simple and immediate that to break a contract was as easy for the employer as it was for the employee. The combination of these features of work in this industry appealed to the Gujaratis' work ethic. Millwork allowed them to maintain their social ties with kin and friends in Bolton, Britain and India. White workers regarded such work as undesirable, because it was associated historically with the working class work, long hours, poor conditions of work, low pay, little job security and few transferable skills. However, for Gujaratis its advantages balanced, if not outweighed, its disadvantages, the greatest of which was that they could continue to maintain strong ties with their family and friends in Bolton and abroad. Arguably, this commitment to their communities overrode any incentive on their part to improve their job prospects. The experience of racial discrimination possibly also accounted for such a commitment, since it provided Gujaratis with a way of coping with racism. When Gujaratis sampled were questioned about their job prospects, they showed little inclination to seek promotion, or to change their jobs for better ones. Some 60% of the sample did not wish to change their jobs, even though many claimed that they experienced racism at work. Only 21.3% expressed a wish to change their jobs and a further 12% said that they would like better jobs, but did not specify what these might be. An explanation for a large percentage of Gujaratis who expressed a preference to remain in their jobs can be explained by the conditions of employment. They had freedom to maintain their ties with kin and community ties and they had learnt to avoid the worst effects of racism.

Table 2.9
Occupations of respondents

Occupational category	Total	%
Professional	9	3.5
Self-employed	22	8.5
Clerical	10	3.9
Textiles	126	48.8
Engineering	25	9.7
Transport	15	5.8
Other	14	5.4
Students/apprentices	23	8.9
Unemployed/retired	13	5.0
No answer	1	0.4
Total:	258	99.9%

Importantly, Cohen and Jenner's (1981: 122) prediction that South Asians who favoured work in the textile industry might transfer to alternative but similar work in other industries, were it available, is unconvincing. While transferring was difficult, it later proved to be impossible, as a result of the massive closure of mills in the 1980s with the disappearance of similar work. This served to underline the lack of transferable skills from the old textile to the new textile industry and service industries in the 1980s and 1990s. More importantly, the Gujaratis did not favour the work but favoured the conditions of work. Explanations such as those offered by Cohen and Jenner take insufficient account of the abilities of individuals to make decisions within the context of their own cultural values (Kosmin, 1979; Allen et al, 1977). A possible consequence of valuing the characteristics of the job more than the job itself ensured that Gujaratis would be the first to lose their jobs in a recession. By 1976 Gujarati men were experiencing increasingly high levels of unemployment as the availability of work declined in what now became a declining industry. Their own preferred work ethic was best suited to a situation where redundancies and unemployment were rare occurrences for low paid unskilled workers, thus the recession did not encourage them to acquire new skills. Rather the reverse; the trend amongst those sampled was to remain in the same job (60%). Only 12% indicated a wish to move to another job, and they could not think of a job to which they would like to move. This suggested apathy and a sense of loss of control over their lives. Those who expressed a desire to change their jobs were asked to explain why they thought that they would not find a new job. They attributed their believed lack of success to a lack of training and racial discrimination (Table 2.10 below). A further 18% believed that racism in some combination with a lack of training, spoken English or work experience explained their lack of success. A further 11% indicated that a lack of training in conjunction with a lack of experience or spoken English accounted for their lack of success. This shows that Gujaratis were well aware of racism and were also aware of their own skill deficiencies in the job market. However, they committed themselves to an industry that was vulnerable to modernisation and to economic recessions, to jobs that remained low-paid and insecure, to a style of work that did not enhance their employment prospects or careers, and, if anything, made them even more vulnerable to unemployment and poverty.

Once unemployed, they became dependent upon the welfare system for support. As employment opportunities declined in the Northwest of England, poverty and unemployment became common experiences for them. Unemployment ensured that they became major competitors for welfare benefits along with the growing numbers of indigenous workers and school leavers. Thus by 1976 Gujarati communities had become familiar with the politics of poverty and powerlessness. Within the next decade they began experiencing particularly high rates of unemployment: for instance, by August 1982 25% were registered as unemployed (*District Trends*, 1987:13), but in some wards this figure reached 40%. Their social identity as immigrants and their place within the local social class structure was defined by their occupations. Thus Gujaratis had a place within Bolton society. They were defined as a community requiring financial support rather than as a community of consumers; that is, they could not buy their way to a better situation (Rex and Tomlinson, 1979).

Table 2.10
Reasons given for being unable to obtain the jobs they desired

	Totals	%
Lack of training	14	23.0
Spoken English	9	14.8
Experience	6	9.8
Education	1	1.6
Racial discrimination	13	21.3
Lack of training,experience and spoken English	7	11.5
Lack of training,spoken English,experience and racial discrimination	11	18.0
Totals	61	100%

Liberal dimension

This dimension of power depends upon the division of the polity into autonomous domains of the family, civil society and the state (Brown, W 1992:17). The state supports the gendered division between the public and private domain, which has disadvantaged women by associating them in the family and unwaged labour. This disadvantage formed part of the process of immigration; as Phizacklea observes, 'racism and sexism have been enshrined in immigration legislation institutionally relegating women to the position of chattels of men' (1990:4). The pattern of social control that the State exercises through prerogative, bureaucratic and capitalist dimensions of power is concerned with the control of labour, that is male labour, with women relegated to an invisible role as wives and mothers (Allen, 1982). To an extent the attitudes of the British state and governments towards black people are located in the history of labour relationships from slavery and colonialism to the present day (Fryer, 1984; Walvin, 1984; also Jordan, 1971). Men were associated with production; women were associated with production and particularly reproduction (Mama, 1992; Brah, 1992 a and b; also for the USA Hill and Jordan, 1995). A number of writers have made the point that the state is more concerned with controlling the fertility of black women than with establishing their rights vis-à-vis those of black men and white women. For instance, South Asian women, who worked day shifts in the textile mills, earned less than did their husbands who worked night shifts. As migrant South Asian men were at a disadvantage as targets of exploitation and racism, they were not recognised as having equal status to other workers within the public sphere (Castles and Kosack, 1973). With the collapse of the textile industry in the 1970s both the men and women lost opportunities for work. However, a recent survey found that in 1 in 10 households there was a homeworker, and in the past the figure was even higher (*An Economic (and Social) Audit of the 3Ds Area of Bolton*, 1996). Most of these workers were in the age range 22-48 years old. The survey also found that these women workers' earnings were low and that they recognised that they were being exploited. In comparison with men, the women have even lower status in the public sphere and this is reflected in the private sphere.

In the 1970s women were to a large extent still hidden within the private domain of the home. Their contact with the wider society was mainly through home based activities, such as child bearing and rearing which brought them into contact with the health services (Mama, 1992; Brah, 1992 a and b; Pearson, 1986). Their roles within social networks that linked them to their families in countries of origin served to remove the opportunity for them to enter the public sphere. Through these dimensions of power the state reinforced the inferior position of women in the public and private spheres by extending its control over men to women by virtually making the private as accessible to control as the public sphere. Locally, the geographical location of Gujaratis public and private spheres in Bolton symbolised their relational position to the white community and wider society. Therefore, in this next and final section, I shall analyse the residential settlement patterns of Gujaratis. These patterns share similarities with settlement patterns elsewhere, but there are some differences and I shall return to these in the conclusion.

Residential settlement patterns of Gujaratis

The aim of this section is to identify those factors affecting the Gujaratis' patterns of settlement. Their pattern of settlement increased their visible association with certain social and economic disadvantages and linked them to ungoverned space in Bolton. Initially Gujaratis moved into inner town houses vacated by white owners, who wisely moved to better housing further out of town. In response to the growing demand from these immigrants for housing, the owners could rent or sell them at inflated prices. Gujaratis' demand for housing, combined with its availability in the inner urban areas and their preference to purchase, contributed to their clustering in certain neighbourhoods. Although as new arrivals they had to purchase property from white owners, those who came later preferred to buy or rent houses from Gujaratis (Desai, 1963:17,34). Convenience and immigration rules ensured that newly arrived immigrants went to houses owned by kin. Thus kinship obligations and social necessity contributed both to the clustering of Gujaratis in particular areas, and also to their pooling resources to purchase the next family owned home. As more members of the chain arrived, the process was repeated, thus extending their ownership of property as a family, and the size of the population. Tables 2.11 and 2.12 (below) show how Gujaratis responded to need to extend their home ownership in a housing area characterised by the lack of access to financial resources and the pressures of racism (Smith, 1989). This expansion led to Gujaratis, like other South Asians, becoming the main inner town residents and homeowners (Saunders, 1990).

Initially, Gujaratis acquired property as tenants or lodgers, but ownership was the preferred form of occupation (Dahya, 1974). The pattern of occupation shows how strong was the desire of Gujaratis to possess their own homes. By the time the respondents had moved to the houses in which they were interviewed, a space of

46

four to five years, the number of tenants/lodgers had dropped from 37.99% (Table 2.11) to 10.86% (Table 2.12) and owner occupiers had increased from 32.56% to 63.95%. The rise of 5% of Hindus and 9% of Muslims living with their families to 34% (Hindus) and 12% (Muslims) can be accounted for by the rising numbers of new migrants coming here. More Hindus (42.9%) were still tenants/lodgers compared to Muslims (30.8%). A possible explanation for this difference might be that the latter recognise their obligations to a wider group of kin than do the former.

Table 2.11
Previous type of occupancy of Gujaratis

Status	Hindus No.	Hindus %	Muslims No.	Muslims %	Totals No.	Totals %
Owner	43	27.9	41	39.4	84	32.6
Member of family	8	5.2	9	8.6	17	6.6
Relative	7	4.5	1	1.0	8	3.1
Lodger/tenant	66	42.9	32	30.8	98	38.0
Respondent not in UK*	21	13.6	11	10.6	32	12.4
No answer	9	5.8	10	9.6	19	7.4
Totals	154	99.9%	104	100%	258	100.1%

*These Gujaratis were first time residents in Britain.

Table 2.12
Present type of occupancy of Gujaratis

Status	Hindus No.	Hindus %	Muslims No.	Muslims %	Totals No.	Totals %
Owner	84	54.5	81	77.9	165	63.9
Owner's family	52	33.8	13	12.5	65	25.2
Lodger/tenant (not Council)	18	11.7	8	7.7	26	10.1
Tenant-Council			2	1.9	2	0.8
Totals	154	100%	104	100%	258	100%

A survey by Bolton Planning Department (1976) ranked wards in the Metropolitan Borough in terms of nine broad indicators: housing, health, race, education, culture, social crises, age structures, employment and mobility. On the basis of these, the wards of the town can be compared and ranked into three categories: 'average and above', 'below average', and 'poor'. When the locations of the minority communities generally and the sample in particular were plotted, the Gujaratis sampled had settled in the poor inner city wards. In addition to a high ethnic minority population, these wards included high numbers of single parents, the elderly, and the unemployed. Furthermore, more of these houses lacked facilities like baths, there was a higher proportion of rented property, and a higher number of non-car owners and TB sufferers than in better areas.[2] According to the

1974 Electoral Register Gujaratis were concentrated in a few wards.[3] Little was known about their distribution other than that Muslims favoured some wards, Hindus favoured others, and that some wards were favoured by both Hindus and Muslims. If wards are classified according to the findings of the Planning Department survey, then it is possible to identify their pattern of settlement. Table 2.13 presents the wards into which and from which those sampled moved until they established themselves in the homes where they were interviewed. It also shows how the majority of them lived and continued to live in the 'poor' and the 'below average' wards. Additionally, it demonstrates how incoming Gujaratis moved into these same 'poor' wards.

The map of Bolton (page 49) shows how Gujaratis clustered in the inner urban areas. Today they are still resident in these same areas, although they have gradually extended their ownership of housing, moving progressively outwards (Chapter Seven). Fact coincides with folklore: Gujaratis first settled in the Derby and Bradford wards in the 1950s and 1960s, a triangular area bounded by two major thoroughfares, Derby Street and Deane Road. From this area they extended their area of settlement in a circular fashion southeastwards and northeastwards around the town centre; by the 1970s they had surrounded the town centre. In the course of settlement they established businesses, shops, temples, mosques and community centres which became recognised as symbols of their presence and social identities in the ungoverned inner urban spaces. Underlying this expansion is a pattern of residential mobility that enabled Gujaratis to select houses next to others belonging to their caste and religious community,[4] thus creating a pattern of ethnic clusters. Exceptions to this settlement pattern are the Gujaratis and other Asian professionals who moved into middle class white areas.

Table 2.13
Bolton wards in which respondents lived and live now

	Ward of first residence		Ward of second residence		Ward of present residence	
Poorest	27	55.1%	141	71.2%	183	70.9%
Below average	15	30.6%	32	16.2%	70	27.1%
Average and above			1	0.5%	5	1.9%
Bolton (unspecified)	7	14.3%	24	12.1%		
Totals	49	100%	198	100%	258	99.9%

The expansion of Gujaratis' occupation and ownership of houses from one small area to surrounding the town centre can be explained by their commitment to home ownership (Dahya, 1974), and the availability of poor quality and council housing (Smith, 1989). At one level, racism allowed landlords in these areas to find a ready market prepared to pay over the odds for poor quality housing (Smith, 1989; Rex and Tomlinson, 1979; Rex and Moore, 1971). At another level, racism, by reducing access to mortgages and loans, reduced Gujaratis' options to buy or rent property in

MAP 1
METROPOLITAN BOROUGH OF BOLTON 1976

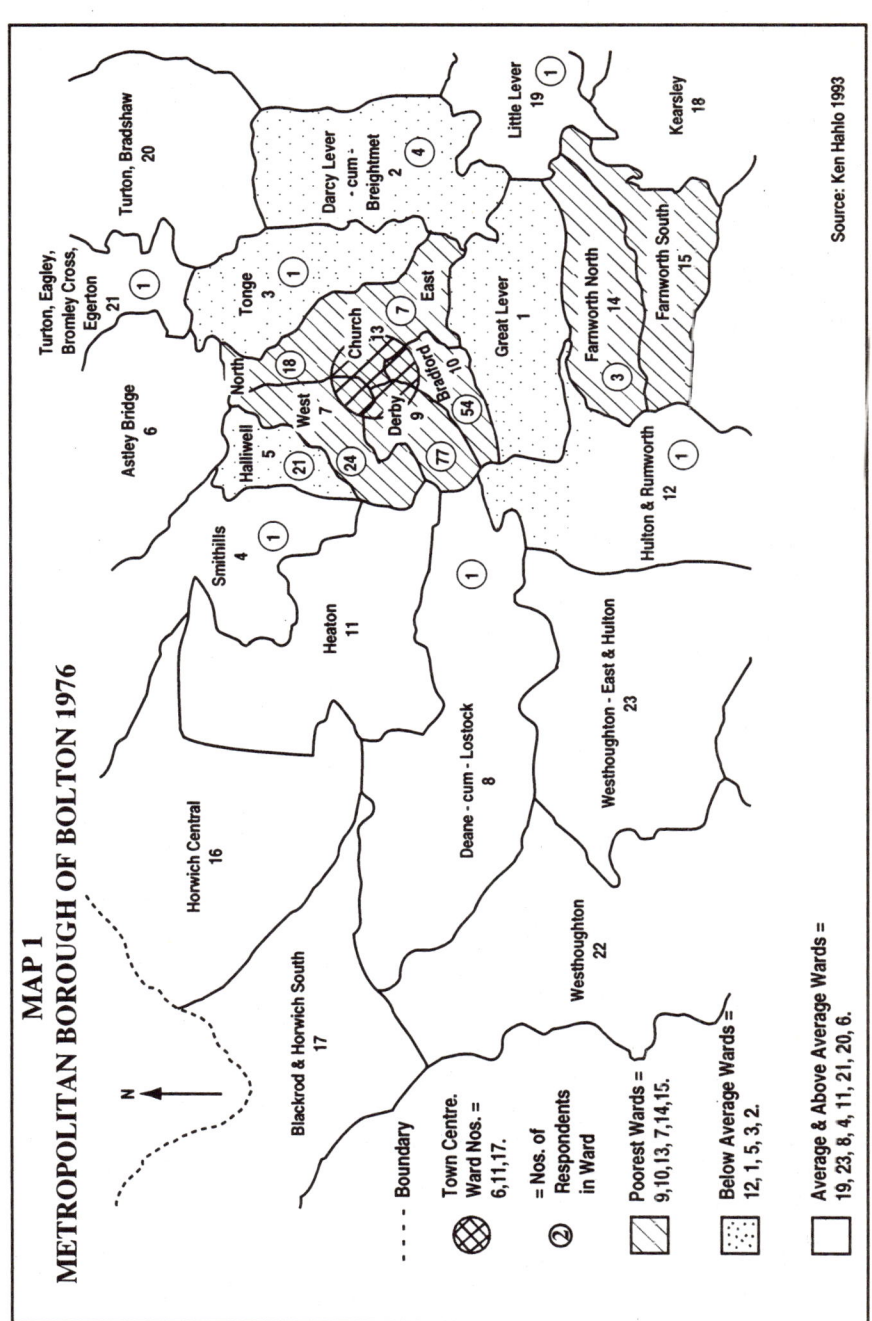

N

Turton, Bradshaw
20

Turton, Eagley,
Bromley Cross,
Egerton
21

Astley Bridge
6

Smithills
4

Horwich Central
16

Blackrod & Horwich South
17

Heaton
11

Deane - cum - Lostock
8

Westhoughton
22

Westhoughton - East & Hulton
23

North

Halliwell
5

West
7

Derby
9

Church
13

Bradford
10

Tonge
3

Darcy Lever
- cum -
Breightmet
2

East

Great Lever
1

Farnworth North
14

Farnworth South
15

Hulton & Rumworth
12

Little Lever
19

Kearsley
18

Source: Ken Hahlo 1993

- - - - Boundary

⊕ Town Centre.
Ward Nos. =
6,11,17.

② = Nos. of
Respondents
in Ward

Poorest Wards =
9,10,13, 7,14,15.

Below Average Wards =
12, 1, 5, 3, 2.

Average & Above Average Wards =
19, 23, 8, 4, 11, 21, 20, 6.

other areas of the town. This lends support to the notion of choice and constraint (Robinson, 1979:390-396) which stresses five factors: firstly, the high social value Gujaratis, like other Asians (Dahya, 1974), place upon home ownership. Secondly, there was a lack of competition for this housing. Thirdly, housing further out of town was expensive, and competition favoured those who were better off. Fourthly, the loans they received from the Local Authority extended their home ownership only within the inner urban area (Smith, 1989). Finally, the value of the houses they owned was too low to enable them to generate sufficient funds to purchase housing in better areas (Smith, 1989). The pattern of clustering allowed Gujaratis to establish ethnic owned and managed shops. which specialised in commodities ranging from clothes and food to musical instruments, records to videos and electronic goods. Firstly, it enabled Gujaratis to create their own cultural and secure environment (Phillips, 1981; Smith, 1984; Desai, 1963). Secondly, it encouraged them to make demands for ownership of property. Thirdly, it increased their political visibility. It ensured that they could lay claim to a socio-geographical area that politically symbolises poverty, deprivation and dependence, that is, it was ungoverned (Lash and Urry, 1994). By purchasing the houses in these areas, Gujaratis placed themselves in the centre of an urban social, economic and political system. On the one hand, their position symbolised their powerlessness, while defining them as a potential threat to law and order. On the other hand, it placed them at the centre of a politico- economic system of resources.

Clustering brought out the social and cultural differences between Gujaratis that allowed for the development of their social identities in relation to the pattern of settlement in these inner urban areas and thus laid the basis for emergence of ethnic organisations and ethnic politics.

Ethnic identities of Gujaratis

One characteristic of chain migration is that it links a specific site of origin with another elsewhere; another lies in its flexibility, that is, the ease with which people who are related to members of the chain, irrespective of where they are located, are drawn into its stream. Thus each chain has the potential to gather and disperse its members according to economic fortunes and social dreams that determine points of deposition. A chain that brings individuals to Bolton may take some living in Africa to Canada and bring others from Burma back to Gujarat. Wherever the chain collects or deposits members, the identity of the members of the chain remains specific. A consequence of this form of migration is the formation of cohorts of Gujaratis, who came from the same village, belonged to the same caste, accepted the same religion and belonged to the same sect, and who chose to live close together. Each chain in the collection of chains that comprises the Gujarati population is an embryonic community (Table 2.14). By virtue of the fact that some chains are larger than others, the larger ones can assert their superiority over others by generating sufficient funds to purchase property for use as religious or community centres, just as the Kutchis, Surtis and Baruchis have done. The overwhelming majority of the sample of 258 respondents traced their origins to districts in Gujarat, spoke Gujarati, patronised Gujarati owned shops and chose to live in areas where Gujaratis had settled.

Hindus traced their origins to four main areas in Gujarat, namely Kutch, Kathiawar, Surat and Navsari: only four Patel families came from Petlad and Nadiad, and they describe themselves as Charotar Patels - the original elite group of Patels (Pocock, 1972:2). The few Hindu respondents (3%) who came from other states in India were educated and thus marginal men who avoided involvement in the Gujarati communities. One of them, a Sikh, became involved with the development of the largest local Hindu organisation, the Vishwa Hindu Parishad (VHP) (Chapters Two, Five, Six). By contrast the Muslims trace their origins primarily to two districts, Broach and Surat, with a few coming from Kathiawar (Table 2.14, page 52). One Gujarati Muslim traced his origins to South Africa, claiming to be a Turk. The Table identifies the districts of origin of the sample, which form the basis of Gujarati ethnic identities. Each district represents the origin of one or more migration chains. The Gujarati population comprises a collection of people who came from different districts, each seeking to establish their community identity. At one extreme Muslims and Hindus are divided by the social identities that link them to villages and districts, and at the other extreme are divided and united by social identities, such as Muslim or Hindu, Gujaratis, Indian, and immigrant. Their identity as Gujaratis acts as a collective identity. Desai remarked upon the strength of the linguistic regional identity that unites Gujaratis (1963:10-18,34,56). Recently Ballard (1994) has drawn attention to the strength of a shared identity based upon language, culture and religion. It is these social identities which emerge through the pattern of Gujaratis' settlement. The consequences of shallow or deep chains are not only important for the analysis of settlement patterns (see below), but they are important for the analysis of Gujaratis' social networks (Chapter Four), since the former determine the social boundaries of the latter.

A consequence of the process of social identification on residential mobility is that Gujaratis sharing the same ethnic identity formed residential enclaves which became the basis for the formation of factions that in turn influenced the location of mosques and temples.[5] An analysis of the residential movements of Gujaratis sampled gives some indication of how clustering occurred along factional and religious lines. The pattern of settlement shows that the majority of Muslims (Table 2.15, page 53) and Hindus (Table 2.16, page 53) lived on the southern side of the town with 38% Muslims (mainly from Broach) and 25% of Hindus living on the northern side. Since the 1970s the number of Hindus living on the northern side has grown and extended their area of residence into Deane-cum-Heaton. Derby and what was then Bradford wards are mixed wards; Gujaratis settled here when they first came to the town. Initially, Muslims established more mosques in the northern than in the southern part, but this pattern has changed recently with the establishment of a number of new mosques in the south. An enclave of Muslims from Broach district became established on the north side, while the majority of those from Surat district live on the south side (Table 2.15). This residential separation is not only given symbolic expression in the perceptions Surtis and Baruchis have of each other in daily life, but it also reflects a power struggle between these factions for control of the mosques. Likewise, the Hindus have moved around the town centre, establishing themselves on the western side (Map 1). Those from the south of Gujarat tend to live on the south and west and those from elsewhere on the south and east of the town. There are a few temples, which generally are caste- or sect-based. The link between Hindus' places of residence and places of worship is less well defined than that between Muslims and their mosques. While Muslims established themselves in streets and wards in relation to their faction and sect allegiances (Chapter Two), the pattern of settlement of Hindus was slightly different. Hindus have spread across the town, with most living in four wards. In terms of their places of origin, the greatest proportion of Hindus sampled trace their origins to Surat and Navsari districts in south central Gujarat, and Kutch and Kathiawar districts in northwestern Gujarat. If Bolton is divided into a northern and a southern section, the majority of Hindu respondents (75.3%) lives in the southern section of the town and a minority (25.7%) lives in the northern section (Table 2.16). Unlike the Muslims, the Hindus have contained their expansion to the western and eastern areas of the southern half of the town, thus creating social and geographical distance between themselves and the Muslims.

Table 2.14
The Indian origins of respondents

State	District	Hindu	Muslim	Total
Gujarat	Kutch	49		49
	Kathiawar	14	7	21
	Ahmadabad	2		2
	Nadiad	2		2
	Petlad	2		2
	Broach		48	96
	Surat	33	48	81
	Navsari	42		42
	Daman	1		1
	Gujarat (unspecified)	1		1
Mombasa		1		1
Other states+		7	1	8
Totals:		154	104	258
%		59.7%	40.3%	100%

+Maharastra (Hindu, 2), Sholapur (Hindu, 1), Madya Pradesh (Hindu, 1), Andra Pradesh (Hindu, 1), Bengal (Hindu, 1), Bihar (Hindu, 1) and Punjab (Sikh, 1).

Table 2.15
Residence pattern of Muslim respondents by ward

Wards:	Broach*	District of origin Surat+	Kathiawar	Andra Pradesh	Totals	
North	30	7	2		39	37.5%
South	18	41	5	1	65	62.5%
Totals:	48	48	7	1	104	100%

*A Muslim who gave Uganda as his place of origin later identified himself as a Baruchi Vohra.
+Another Muslim, who gave his place of origin as Uganda, is a Memon from Kathiawar.

Table 2.16
Residence pattern of Hindu respondents by ward

Wards	Surat	Districts of origin Navsari	Bhuj	Kutch	Kathiawar	Other	Total	
North	6	14	8	1	2	7*	38	24.7%
South	25	28	38	6	9	10*	116	75.3%
Totals	31	42	46	7	11	17	154	100%

* Others trace origins to: Ahmadabad 2, Petlad 2, Nadiad 2, Gujarat 1, Daman 1, Patna (Bihar) 1, Calcutta (Bengal) 1, Indore (Andra Pradesh) 1, Bombay 2, Maharastra 1, Punjab 1, Mombasa 1, and 'not stated' 1.

The debate about housing restricting people's access to scarce resources, such as health and education, does have bearing upon the geographical position of the Gujaratis. Although in 1973 many Gujaratis purchased their first homes, a few were purchasing additional houses for the purposes of generating wealth (Saunders, 1989:208; Hamnett, 1989; Werbner, 1989). When in the 1980s local authorities offered council houses for sale, Gujaratis purchased them. Whenever the opportunity presented, they purchased additional council houses. Their desire for houses went beyond simple pride in ownership (Dahya, 1974): it suggested that they regarded purchasing houses as a way to generate wealth (Werbner, 1989). Their selling or renting these houses to kin, friends, other Gujaratis or, if the houses were in demolition areas, obtaining compensation from the local authority, allowed them to generate wealth. For Gujaratis, home ownership became a means of accumulating capital in an environment in which obtaining access to an income and wealth through employment was more difficult. The preference to purchase homes from Gujaratis gave them a ready housing market which was protected from intrusion by white housing agents. The effect of this on Gujaratis' settlement is that they occupy a distinct and visible space within Bolton, which gives them a social and economic base within their communities.

In a Fordist state, the producer and the market have power over the consumer; in a post-Fordist state, the consumer has power over the producer and the market (Urry, 1990a). In a Fordist state, control over labour amounted to control over black workers. By using these controls to construct their private life in the public domain, the state not only controlled their labour, but also their women and children. The transition to post-Fordism has given these workers and their families a degree of wealth, and with it they have become consumers. It is as consumers that they share power with other consumers over producers and markets. The contradiction here lies in that as consumers they can again become targets of racism in a fickle white-dominated consumerist world. Racism has become dissipated within an ideology of choice and subcontracting. Only the consumer can initiate action against racism. In response to the efforts by the state to control migration, the migration flow diminished, but not before a sizeable Gujarati population had established itself. The emergence of ethnic communities and organisations with a hierarchy of social identities should be seen as a direct response to state control and to racism. It also enabled these migrants to change their status from exploitable and dependent to consumers, in which role they can actively respond to racism. Arguably the link between a national and a local identity lies in the formation of ethnic enclaves and the construction of ethnic identities. Freedom lies in employing these identities to make the shift to becoming consumers and this was made possible through the development of ethnic politics.

This Chapter has set out the way in which the state expressed itself through four dimensions of control and deployed these to control Gujarati migrants and their social lives, thus ensuring that they remained poor, powerless and rightless. However, the interface between the national and local allowed them to develop, through employment and the purchase of housing, an ethnic formation that in turn allowed for the development of a structure that could bring political awareness. Faction, caste, and sect divisions enabled Gujarati organisations to mobilise support for community grassroots movements. The subject of the next Chapter is to identify the main organisations that participated in local ethnic political activities and analyse their structures. The only bases on which Gujarati social identities could develop were in religious organisations (Chapter Three) and communities and social networks (Chapter Four). These provide Gujaratis with social and spatial identities that allow community differences to become the bases for the mobilisation of support, the development of ethnic identities within a racial context (Chapter Five) and structures of political leadership outside formal political party structures (Chapters Six and Seven).

Notes

1. At the time this survey was carried out, Gujaratis felt insecure answering questions on their length of stay in Britain. In some instances this could be calculated, in others it was impossible to establish.

2. These wards and residents shared the social characteristics that were typical of those living in inner city areas (Rex and Tomlinson, 1979:127-157; Gerrard, 1981:641-644; Rex and Moore, 1971). After 1976 large areas were demolished, thus reducing the availability of poor quality old housing. The building of new council housing led to inner city residents becoming dependent upon this kind of housing.

3. According to the 1974 Electoral Register, Gujaratis were concentrated in a few wards. After the reorganisation of local authority boundaries in 1974, Farnworth, Little Lever, Egerton, Westhoughton and a number of other wards were incorporated into the Metropolitan Borough of Bolton. Since this research was completed, a further reorganisation of the local ward boundaries reduced the number of wards by merging some of them.

4. Gujaratis could have moved to better areas of the town, but they preferred to live close to other Gujaratis.

5. I use faction in a slightly different way from its usage in the literature. Nicholas (1965:28-29) identifies five characteristics as typical of factions. These include conflict groups, political groups, and corporate groups recruited either by a leader or on the basis of diverse principles. The groups I describe as factions can become corporate under certain circumstances, for instance, if they acquire property for community or religious purposes. The politicians saw them as potentially destructive.

3 Religious organisations: structures of leadership and support

The next five Chapters present a case study of a Gujarati population in the 1970s, which were crucial years in the formation of the development of a consumerist South Asian community. This development took place within a context of in-migration, a rapidly expanding ethnic population, racism, a medium sized sunset town, a situation of increasing shortage of housing and rising unemployment. The political situation provided the dynamic, which allowed ethnic minorities the freedom to participate in local politics in terms of ethnic politics. They were able to compete for physical, social, economical, and political space in a post-Fordist society, which was beginning to recognise the importance of the power of consumerism. Therefore, the case study which follows is not an analysis of individual caste communities and their efforts to improve their standing within a caste system particular to one town. It is an analysis of how caste communities with their own particular perceptions of their positions within a relocated social system that enabled them to meet their social, religious and political needs (Ballard, 1994; Nesbitt, 1994; Knott, 1994) and as such is relevant to their standing in British society. What is important for those living in Britain is how they can integrate socially, economically and politically and how they as a cohort can oppose racism. Much of the literature makes attributes an anti-racist function to ethnic and black organisations without spelling how it occurs (Layton-Henry, 1984; Solomos, 1989; Parekh, 1991). The emphasis is not on ties with Gujarat, but rather on how a collection of caste communities, some Hindu and some Muslim, made use of ethnic social identities to create a political Gujarati community in Bolton.

An analysis of the formation of a political Gujarati community forms the case study. I shall begin by looking at migration and internal community divisions (Chapter Two), then at religious organisations which mesh the general with the specific allowing for localisation and globalisation (Chapter Three), the formation of communities based upon friendship (Chapter Four), the political deployment of social identities (Chapter Five), the political position of Gujarati communities (Chapter Six), and ethnic politics (Chapter Seven). Ethnic politics facilitated the process that led to ethnic political participation, and acted as a catalyst uniting disparate Gujarati communities - Hindu and Muslim - into a coherent whole. Finally I shall consider how the Gujarati communities have developed since the 1970s and 1980s and how they have responded to post-Fordism in a sunset town (Chapter Eight). Although gender is a fundamental division within these communities, and impacts upon the organisation of the family, the caste and the sect, in the 1970s, however, it was men who were most active in ethnic political activities. Consequently, the analysis focuses on men, but reference will be made also to women.

Based upon the origins of the migration chains, Chapter Three sets the scene locally with an analysis of the structures of communities within a Gujarati community; I shall argue that the Gujaratis comprise two large religious groups, which in turn are made up of a number of smaller communities. These tend to be mainly caste-based, but may include village communities. Faction- and sect-groups cannot be strictly described as communities; they have different forms of recruitment, different bases for formation, and different structures of membership. Larger religious groups who share the same beliefs, such as Hindus or Muslims, or followers of Swaminarayan or Saibaba, comprise either a complex collection of individuals, or castes or families. The latter two sects share a corporate-like character which stems from their ownership of property and wealth and/or other assets; for the former there is a community only in so far as individual mosques can combine to form a united front in response to conflict. This Chapter shifts the emphasis from the macro-theory to the micro-ethnographic. The debate about ethnic communities is blurred by a tendency not to define what comprises an ethnic community in Britain. The tendency is to regard Pakistanis as a community on the grounds that social exchange of women through marriage, culture and a common religion (Islam) and language unite it (Werbner, 1989; Shaw, 1988), whereas those who have studied Gujaratis emphasise the social divisions in the community. Some regard Gujarati communities as comprising two communities - one Hindu and one Muslim (Brooks and Singh, 1978/79), while others analyse Gujarati communities at the level of the caste community (Nesbitt, 1994; Dwyer, 1994; Warrier, 1994; Knott, 1994). There is a confusion of analysis over the level of community between the observer and observed. The former stresses the obvious difference in religious belief without providing a more structured analysis of why Gujarati communities seem to be different in an industrial society in which such differences are not reinforced in everyday life. The difficulty with the latter approach, a two cultures thesis (Ballard, 1994:30), is that it also does not explain why an ethnic group should be reduced to a collection of caste communities. Yet its supporters claim that these communities are resisting racism by adhering to caste values, accepting them or through caste members challenging the position of their caste in the wider caste system (Ballard, 1994). On the one hand, not all castes are attempting to maintain their caste boundaries; those that are, are doing so with differing degrees of commitment. On the other hand, Ballard argues that maintenance of a culture that is not British is a form of cultural resistance and as such is a form of anti-racism. I would argue that this line of argument needs further development possibly drawing upon West (1994) and Khan (1982). Their approaches to the destruction of black culture by hegemonic cultures of the USA and Britain respectively attempt to construct a thesis of oppression. Otherwise there is a risk that by concentrating upon castes, anti-racism is reduced to a cataloguing of cultural differences (Miles, 1982:46) and associating these uncritically with the social values and norms of South Asians in the subcontinent or in a South Asian diaspora.

How caste associations are using the situation in Britain to promote their members to attain greater heights in education, finance and politics, cannot escape the structure of social mobility in the caste system and the process of sanskritization (Ballard, 1994; Nesbitt, 1994; Knott, 1994). The British context acts only as a catalyst for caste mobility; caste mobility as such is largely irrelevant within British society. However, I shall argue that what is important is not caste mobility, but how caste communities work together to develop new community identities and a new hierarchical structure to meet the concerns of those living here. Opportunities for such developments range from social to political ones. Because they are responses to British situations, they may involve different castes and different religious groups; where they involve or require different Hindu castes, or different religious groups (Hindu and/or Muslim) to make political decisions, they can be reasonably described as ethnic politics.

Sivanandan's (1990) claim that ethnicity is divisive in a racial situation is tenable, but it is not a reason for dismissing ethnicity. Similarly, Miles (1982) argues that racism is a form of labour exploitation in a capitalist-led society and that the ethnic argument is irrelevant in this context. Prior to both of these arguments being put, Heineman (1972) had already demonstrated that a black movement against racism in the 1960s (CARD) failed, because the South Asian communities had separated themselves from the Afro-Caribbeans on the grounds that they were not black. Modood (1988; 1992) has taken up these debates arguing that South Asians prefer not be labelled or label themselves as black, but this does not prevent them from being anti-racist. The point is that there was and is still no political platform on which those labelled black can achieve unity against racism. I shall argue that within the parameters set by the local capitalist exploitation of labour, Gujaratis could express their opposition to racism through their involvement in ethnic politics. Possibly the fact that Bolton is a town, rather than a city, has meant that its smaller size has brought Gujaratis, Muslim and Hindu, together through their common experiences of migration, racism, housing, working conditions and a lack of access to scarce resources, such as health, education, benefits. More importantly they have had to share the experience of racism, because as a visible minority they are perceived as comprising a single black group. Their reaction to racism was as a cohesive community, irrespective of religious differences. For these communities to react in terms of caste differences or even broad religious communities would have undermined their opposition to racism. To have done so would have attracted the argument that they are only representing a minority view and that it has no place within the local or national political system. The argument about the politicised ethnic community can be traced back from Parekh (1991) to Solomos (1989) and Layton-Henry (1984). The arguments can be summarised simply as follows.

Layton-Henry suggests that ethnic communities can act politically through withdrawal of political participation. Solomos suggests that there may be a place for a regional or national ethnic political community. Parekh argues for the political recognition of the notion of an ethnic community in such a culturally diverse society as that in Britain. The tendency to distinguish between South Asian communities on the grounds of ethnic differences has obscured any attempt to focus on how these communities have tried to control and reduce their differences, successfully or otherwise, in order to present politically a common front to racism.

The argument claims that the development of Gujarati ethnic communities as political entities was made possible by a number of factors. These include the relatively small size of Bolton, a rapidly expanding Gujarati population, and the general experience of racism by all Gujaratis and the recognition that they, as Muslims and Hindus, were united in their opposition to racism. The importance, therefore, of the divisions between these two religious groups is social and cultural, although it may be translated into intra-community antagonism. In political situations this antagonism may be overridden in an effort to present a united front. The local or national political system does not recognise religious or ethnic groups as political units. Although the political participation of an ethnic community as a political unit has been recognised as a form of minority participation, what has been less certain is the form this activity might take. It could involve the withdrawal of political participation or participation in and through so-called buffer organisations (Layton-Henry, 1984), or in some form of ethnic community (Solomos, 1989; Parekh, 1991). Katznelson (1973) did not distinguish between organisations which were buffers and organisations which others tried to use as buffers. Thus one can recognise why he attributed such a role to the Community Relations Commission, but local CRCs were not buffers. Having said this, local politicians and local authorities may have tried to use them as buffers. However, CRCs developed a political role (Ben-Tovim *et al*, 1986), which set them apart from buffer organisations. By taking on such a role they supported antiracism by supporting ethnic organisations in their efforts to participate in the wider political processes rather than blocking their efforts to participate. Within CRC ethnic communities developed ethnic politics, which reached its peak of development in the 1970s and 1980s. Then it gradually disappeared partly because of the change in the role of CRCs as a consequence of the 1988 review (Gay and Young, 1988), and partly because of political party resistance to religious or ethnic community political participation.

While ethnic politics was allowed to flourish, the competition for space lay at the centre of the process of the formation of a political ethnic community. This case study begins by looking at the fundamental differences between Gujarati Hindu and Muslim religious organisations, arguing that Hinduism encourages differences through the caste system, whereas Islam promotes unity through religious commitment. In a situation in which scarce resources, such as land, buildings and finances, are shared across religions and castes, the importance of co-operation can override these differences, allowing for the sharing of facilities and thus providing grounds for political co-operation. The new structures that have been created in the Gujarati community involving either Hindus or Muslims or both in response to a political situation in Britain generally and Bolton in particular, are not reflections of those in Gujarat or in a diasporic ideology, but rather new structures that are British.

Religious organisations and social identities

Having considered how the state and its expression through four dimensions of control impacts upon migrants and ethnic communities at a theoretical level, the aim of this Chapter is to set the scene locally. Control is one side of a relationship between the state and the migrant; the other side is the reaction of migrants to this control. The formation of ethnic organisations in conjunction with the expansion of ethnic populations provided symbolically and actually a form of resistance to racism, that is, to a wide range of activities - social, economic, political, local governmental - which were interpreted by Gujaratis as being racist. Therefore, ethnic communities formed the basis for the emergence of ethnic organisations, the production of social identities and their involvement in ethnic politics. These organisations made possible the generation of ethnic identities, which played a central part in ethnic politics. This production of identities allowed for inter-ethnic competition and opened the way for the gradual shift towards consumerism in a post-Fordist state. This Chapter lays the ethnographic basis for the development of ethnic organisations, arguing that it was the emergence of religious identities which acted as catalysts to the emergence of ethnic organisations and ethnic politics. It was the demands made by the religious organisations that gave ethnic communities a religious and political presence in the town.   In the 1970s Gujaratis' ethnicity was dependent upon the social networks that linked those living here with those in India. The migration chains that brought them to Britain and Bolton formed a part of these social networks and as such helped maintain the link between those living here and their recreated culture and those living there and their existent culture (Werbner, 1989). A consequence of this form of migration is that each chain draws into a globalised web individuals who are linked by marriage and kinship.   Thus the structure of the Gujarati population in Bolton consists of collections of members of chains of varying sizes, from various places of origin, and with greater or lesser links with members of other chains. By virtue of its specificity, members of each chain have social identities which are definable in terms of family, caste, sect, religious group and ultimately as Gujaratis. The experiences, which they share as members in a migration chain, include the process of migration, settlement, and racism. Therefore, the social identities migrants brought to these chains that both separated them from or united them with other South Asians were first and foremost religious identities. This Chapter is divided into two parts: the first looks at the development of Gujarati Muslim religious identities and the second focuses on the Hindu religious organisations. This Chapter sets the scene for the development of ethnic communities, ethnic identities and ethnic politics.

'Weber's approach conceived of society as an arena of competing status groups, each with its own economic interests, status honour, and orientation toward the world and man' (Bendix, 1966:262). Weber recognised the importance of a religious organisation providing its believers with a church and shared social and moral values. To this degree religion shapes and articulates a worldview for its adherents. In this Chapter I shall argue that the formation of religious organisations provided the basis for the development of ethnic status groups and that through them Gujaratis' response to racism has been shaped and articulated and the concept of consumer has been moulded. Only in this context can religious communities (status groups) also take on a political role (Chapters Five and Six) and in the course of exercising their political support they become communities of resistance (Ballard, 1994). In developing this dynamic aspect, these organisations are new: they are located 'in-between' the society of origin and the society of domination (Bhabha, 1990). They are new organisations which in the competition for funds, space, buildings and support drew upon a reservoir of social identities to establish their differences in a social situation in which, from the outside, they were seen to be the same or similar.

Muslims

The specific villages of origin from which these Muslims were drawn into migration chains provide each migrant with a set of social identities - memberships of a village exchange circle (*ekada*), a district, faction and caste community - centred on a mosque (*jamatbandi*). By definition they also share acceptance of the social and religious values of an Islamic school, pathway, and social identities as Gujaratis, Indians and Muslims. The specificity of membership of a migration chain provides Muslim migrants with a link into a general set of social identities through membership of a mosque, district of origin, and the caste community (a term used by Misra, 1964). Thus the mosque becomes a political symbol of the wealth and influence of a caste community within a Gujarati Islamic world. At the root of local British Gujarati Muslim communities are three crosscutting allegiances which separate or unite their members: these are firstly, acceptance of a particular Islamic pathway (Christopher, 1972), secondly, adherence to an Islamic school and thirdly, membership of a caste community. These identities link the ideological and social to the geographical; they provide a structure within which the family, village, caste community, mosque, and religion are connected through social, economic, marital and religious exchanges, thus creating an ideological link between the specific and the general.

Islamic pathway

The majority of the sample accepted the Sunni Hanafi pathway (93.3%) with three who stated that they were Shia (2.88%), three who were Shafii (2.88%) and one Christian (0.96%). Being such a small minority, the Shia and Shafii Muslims attended Sunni Hanafi mosques. The Shias left Bolton soon after 1976 and moved to Birmingham, where there was a large number of their caste community (Daudi Bohra). In a local situation such as Bolton the acceptance of an Islamic pathway has little meaning, as the majority of Gujaratis are Sunni Hanafi Muslims [at Bolton Institute, where students come from Iran, Iraq, Egypt, Turkey and Malaysia, these differences are more obvious. At one time graffiti in the lifts gave some indication of latent hostility between Sunnis and Shias, but these Muslim students were not really part of the wider Gujarati population]. The link between the village of origin and the acceptance of an Islamic pathway creates a structure through which the specific (concrete entity of a village) can be related to the general and global (ideological).

Islamic school

Membership of Islamic schools forms the basis for one of the most enduring social identities within the Gujarati Muslim population. Excluding Shia and Shafii Muslims who play a minor role in community affairs, the majority of Muslims belong to either the Deobandi (79.8%) or Berelewi (9.6%) schools [local Pakistanis belong to the Berelewi School]. The history and background of these schools show that they share a number of similarities. These include their origins at a time when many Muslims in colonial India expressed their antagonism towards British rule through their interpretation of certain Islamic procedures and prayer (Hardy, 1972: 170, 242, 277-278; Faruqi, 1963: vii, 75, 96, 170-171). Both schools established centres in the 1800s in Gujarat with the result that many Muslims who lived there accepted their teachings. Although today there is a degree of consensus on religious practices and preaching between the followers of these schools, there are some minor differences. I was informed that a difference between them is that Berelewi *imams* read out salutations to the Prophet, whereas in Deobandi mosques Muslim worshippers recite them out.

In terms of generality, pathway and then school are the two most widely applicable sets of social identities; there is no tangible group or organisation which is Sunni or Deobandi. These identities impinge upon all the more specific social identities and communities. The identities of schools allow for the process of filling in the gap in the structure between the local and the global; this process regionalises the ideological at one extreme and localises it at the other extreme.

Caste community

Membership of a caste community does not determine acceptance of the teachings of a pathway or school. Within the Muslim population in Bolton it is unclear as to what determines or determined membership of a pathway or school. What is important is the degree to which members of a caste community who espouse the teachings of a pathway and school are prepared to express their differences publicly. As opposed to sharing an ideological identity, membership of a caste community provides a social and ideological identity. The caste community is the organisation which is recognised by Muslims as comprising social equals,[1] therefore intermarriage between members is possible and, more importantly, desirable. Although there is no hierarchical caste structure, there is a common sense social perception of prestige, which uses ideas based upon an urban-rural dimension to establish caste ranking. There seemed to be little general agreement about this, and few Muslims could define criteria that underpinned this ranking system. There was no religious element in this ranking system as there seems to be in Pakistan with some caste communities claiming a closer link with the Prophet (*peace be unto him*) than others. The caste community provides for the religious and social welfare of its members (Misra, 1964:143) through its role as the basic organisation which links its members directly to a local mosque. This community traces its origins to one or a number of different villages within the same district in Gujarat. Through caste community membership a Muslim can express particular social identities in a way that potentially globalises them. A local narrative can be transformed into a global meaning and a global meaning can be translated into a local identity. Thus a structure exists which relates actual membership of a group to a religious ideology; it exemplifies what Weber (Bendix 1966:262) recognised in religious organisations providing the basis for ethnic status groups.

These Muslims accept the teachings of the Sunni and Hanafi pathway and the Deobandi school within it and a minority following the Berelewi school (Table 3.1:64 below). Those sampled represented only seven castes out of over a hundred different Muslim caste communities (Misra, 1964). The majority recognise the teachings of the Deobandi school and belong to one of two caste communities, namely Surti or Baruchi Vohras. Incorporated in caste community membership is a further set of social identities based on districts of origin. Vohras trace their origins to Surat or Broach districts (Table 3.2:64 below). The sample suggests that these two caste communities are roughly similar size and that they form two antagonistic factions in the community. Although Broach and Surat provinces share a boundary, the individuals resident here may come from villages that are geographically distant. The stereotypical views these Muslims hold of each other are used to form factions that compete for the same living space and for control of local mosques. From the Surti Vohra point of view, a Baruchi is regarded as dull, narrow-minded, poorly educated, rigid in religious beliefs, aggressive and 'they carry knives even in the mosque'. Surtis see themselves as enlightened, educationally progressive, flexible in their approach to Islam, reasonable and peaceful. Thus Surtis believe that they have a worldliness which their neighbouring Baruchis do not share. Meanwhile, Baruchis see themselves as the 'pious ones', and see Surtis as a people who flout the strict principles of Islam. These stereotypes point to the depth of the social division between these two communities and to clear and separate social identities.

The importance of these stereotypes is that they have led to each faction competing for control of the Islamic Culture Centre (ICC), which is located at Zakariah Mosque. This was Bolton's first mosque. By virtue of it being the first Islamic committee to exercise control over all Muslims in the town, this body has remained in control to the present day, even though the Muslim population has grown considerably and not all mosque communities choose to recognise its authority. In the 1970s it still had control of most Deobandi mosques and was in the act of not being recognised as an authority by a newly establishing Berelewi group who fought for permission to build their own mosque. Thus in the 1970s the majority of mosques were Deobandi with some being controlled by Surtis and others by Baruchis, but control of the ICC was open to competition. Therefore control over this body meant control over the form of Islam practised, control over a major ethnic and religious community, control over considerable financial resources and influence over a potentially powerful political source of support. It also provided each faction with the impetus to develop its own mosques to meet the needs of particular caste communities. Most importantly, control over the community gave control over sufficient financial resources for Muslim communities to move from being supported and exploited by a white community and wider society to becoming consumers of space - land, buildings and financiers of new ventures.

Table 3.1
Caste community membership of Islamic schools

Islamic schools:

Caste community	Deobandi		Berelewi		Others		Don't know		No answer	
Surti Vohra	46	97.9%					1	2.1%		
Baruchi Vohra	36	76.6%	8	17%	2*	4.3%	1	2.1%		
Memon			1		1*				2	
Nagori			1							
Miabhai	1									
Khojah					2+					
Daudi Bohra					1+					
Muslim					1@					
Totals	83		10		7		2		2	104
%	79.8		9.6		6.7		1.9		1.9	100

* Shafii; + Shia; @ Christian.

Table 3.2
Caste communities and districts of origin

Caste communities	Districts of origin				Totals	%	
	Surat	Broach	Kutch & Kathiawar	Andra Pradesh			
Sunni Vohra	47	47			94	90.6	Sunni
Memon			4		4	3.9	
Nagori		1			1	0.9	
Miabhai	1				1	0.9	
Khojah			2		2	1.9	
Daudi Bohra			1		1	0.9	Shia
Other				1	1	0.9	
Totals	48	48	7	1	104		
%	46.2	46.2	6.7	0.9		100%	

These stereotypical beliefs had some foundation when Surtis and Baruchis sampled were asked for their views on a number of different aspects of Islam and Islamic practices which these Muslims considered to be important. These were expressed in the form of demands for more facilities, such as single sex schools, facilities to bury the dead within 24 hours, *halal* meat in schools, access to the coroner over weekends and holidays, and the right of Muslim children to wear Islamic clothing in school. Indications of commitment include observing the taboo on the eating of pork, attendance at prayers on Fridays, the need to pray fives times a day, the burial of the dead within 24 hours, and marriage to cousins. These six observances have become recognised as symbols which 'stand for' the social identity of Islam and more specifically are values on which the commitment of Surti and Baruchi Vohra Muslims differ. When Muslim respondents ranked these observances in terms of their importance, that is, as very important, important and unimportant, the differences between these two factions became clearer (Table 3.3:66 below). The data in this Table are arranged by caste community, faction, sect and respondent's ranking in order of importance of six religious commitments. Findings show that Deobandi Surti Vohras regarded attendance at Friday prayers, burial within 24 hours and the taboo on pork as more important for Muslims than did the Baruchi Vohras, although the latter considered praying five times a day as more important than did the former. Only the Baruchi Vohra Berelewis claimed total commitment to the taboo on pork, Friday prayers and burial within 24 hours. Although there is very little difference between these religious communities, it is significant that the stereotypes held by Surtis of Baruchis being rigidly zealous does not hold up to scrutiny. If anything the reverse holds, namely that the Surtis are more committed to these aspects of Islam than are the Baruchis. The opinions held by Surtis are stereotypes: based on suppositions rather than actual knowledge.

The conflict between these social and religious identities becomes apparent when it is translated into political demands that impinge on the space controlled by the white community. While such demands give the impression that these Muslims are deeply committed to Islam, for them to be met requires space and recognition. Analysis of these observances show that the Surti Vohras are more committed than the Baruchi Vohras to upholding symbols of Islam. This is a reversal of the stereotypes each faction has of the other. The divide between these factions is further reinforced by the practice of *tabligh*,[2] an evangelistic exercise that is intended to convert Hindus to Islam and to persuade lax Muslims to return to the fold. Almost half of the Muslims interviewed (49%) participate in *tabligh* and most of them (55.6%) were Vohra Baruchis. This is a public commitment, which endorses the stereotype of Baruchis as being more pious than Surtis. The view that the most committed should control the mosques encourages the Baruchis to believe that they are the right people to do so and they have the will to do so. Though the Surtis would like to control the mosques and particularly their own mosques, they do not seem to have the conviction to do so. This may hide a difference in the size of these two groups; the impression gained is that the Surtis are the larger group. Lines of cleavage between Gujarati Muslims are reflected in their stereotypes and their battling for control of the Islamic community. Control includes not only decisions taken within the Islamic community, but also their reactions as an Islamic community to decisions taken by local politicians. This conflict between the Baruchis and Surtis dominates the social interaction between Muslims and also wider community affairs.

Table 3.3
Ranking of selected religious observances by Muslim respondents

Observances ranked as: very important

	Taboo on pork	Attend Friday prayers	Cousin marriage	Pray 5/day	Grow a beard	Burial within 24 hrs	Single sex school	Total Nos.
	%	%	%	%	%	%	%	
Deobandi Surti Vohra Baruchi	95.8	97.9	40.4	89.4	25.5	97.9	57.4	(47)
Berelewi Baruchi Vohra	88.9	91.7	36.1	94.4	44.4	75	58.3	(36)
Berelewi Baruchi Vohra	100	100	44.4	100	22.2	66.7	44.4	(9)
Memon	75	75	25	25		50	25	(4)
Baruchi Vohra*	100	100	25	75	25	100	25	(4)
Shia Khojah & Daudi Bohra	100	66.7	66.7	66.7				(3)
								(103)+

*Includes two Baruchi Vohras, a Miabhai and a Nagori.
+ A Muslim who converted to Christianity is excluded giving a total of 103.

These internal differences are partly submerged when there is a threat to the Islamic community from the non-Muslim communities. For instance, when Muslims were informed that they could not have 24 hour and seven days a week access to the cemetery to bury their dead, they united in their protest. However, when one Baruchi leader attempted to gain a position of influence by exploiting a political situation involving the white community, the Surtis refused to support him (Chapter Seven). At another level, members of both religious communities accept the Sunni Hanafi pathway and follow the teachings of the *Sunna*, *Shariah* and *Hadiths*. Thus, they share a common and overriding religious identity irrespective of their place of origin: they are all Sunni Hanafi Muslims. Commitment to these observances is called into question only when Islam or the social identity of Muslims is under threat or when the mere expression of it reinforces the identities of the believers as Muslims. They adhere to these observances in word and deed, as they confirm their commitment to Islam. At the centre of this active Muslim community is the rivalry for control of mosques, which are a public and private expression of Islam acting as symbols of both Gujarati Islam as well as membership of the wider Muslim brotherhood. Thus, the Gujarati Muslims, both Sunni and Shia, are united in their acknowledgement of their religious identity. I was told that this identity is given expression at funerals of fellow Gujarati Muslims and Pakistanis, all of whom are expected to attend and thereby to demonstrate their respect for the Islamic brotherhood.

Caste communities and marriage

The association between caste community and religious observances is not an exclusive one. For instance members of the same caste community may espouse different forms of Islam. Marriage preferences ideally confine people's choices to within their caste community and to those of the caste living in particular villages. From what is potentially a wide set of approved choices for marriage, that is anyone who is a Muslim, the majority of the Muslims sampled selected wives from their caste communities (95.9%) and a third of them were cousins (29.6%) and of these 80% were first cousins.[3] The differences between Surti and Baruchi Muslims was reinforced by the former marrying cousins who came from different villages in the exchange circle and the latter marrying women who came from the same villages as they did. Generally, marriage with women who come from outside the *ekada* is frowned upon, as the following anecdote shows. A Vohra Baruchi, who arranged the marriages of his eldest son and daughter, said: 'I wrote to my relatives in five villages: Kapodra, Kosamri, Kandh, Mangrol, Dhamrod. They selected a brother and a sister and both marriages were celebrated in Bolton'. A few years later both ended in divorce. He blamed his kin for having chosen a brother and a sister whose mother came from the city of Surat and not from the five villages in his *ekada*. Because of this, he said of his daughter-in-law: 'She cooks differently, the food doesn't taste the same as ours, and for this reason the marriage could never work'. Apart from distrust being expressed in terms of 'cooking' (Mayer, 1973:33-52; Dubois, 1959:183-186), this man committed himself to social and religious isolation to show his disgust for his kin who arranged these marriages.

Members of the *ekada* expect to be invited to the weddings of their members and they know the value of the presents they are expected to give them. This discussion illustrates the strength of the *ekada* and the caste community as the fundamental form of social organisation within the wider local Islamic community. When asked about the continuation of their marriage patterns, most Baruchis (81%) and Surtis (64%) were of the opinion that their children should marry in-caste. Few Muslims interviewed recognised that their children might and could choose to marry anyone. The differences between Surtis' and Baruchis' attitudes to marriage also underpin deeper divisions of social identities as reflected in the geographical separation in Bolton: Surtis favour the southern wards of the town, while the Baruchis have settled in the northern wards. Their opposition is translated into struggles for the control of mosques and the Islamic Culture Centre (ICC); four years ago these struggles brought the ICC into ruin. It has been replaced now by the Bolton Mosque Community Care Centre, which organisation is responsible for all ten local mosques. This factional conflict is embodied in stereotypes each holds of themselves and others, and their differences are now expressed in terms of hostilities between young Muslims; the Baruchis from Bolton and Blackburn are involved in drug peddling and gang fights in which they attack Bolton Surtis. The social importance of caste community social identities is that they provide individuals with more concrete social positions within firstly the structure that links together their villages with globalised Islamic ideologies, and secondly locates them in well-defined structures of social networks. Thus the link in the structure between the local and concrete and the global and ideological is rendered complete. On the one hand, marriage serves to embed Muslims within a circle of exchanges - through friendship and marriage - with other members of their caste community irrespective of geographical distances (Shaw, 1988); on the other hand, these exchanges reinforce and help to maintain wider cultural exchanges (Werbner, 1989).

Mosques offer not only visible confirmation of a potential political Islamic presence, a presence to which the local politicians and local authority responds but more importantly they provide a visible symbol of a caste community's financial, political and numerical strength. By 1976 there were five Gujarati Muslim mosques and one Pakistani mosque; twenty years later the former had established seven mosques and the latter three. Almost half of the mosques are situated in the north and the others in the south of the town. As mosque communities (jamatbandi) expanded, new mosques were established and the control and management of mosques became a major battle ground between Baruchis and Surtis for overall control of Islamic affairs. Responsibility for the former devolved upon the local communities, who supported, lived close to and prayed at their mosques. Responsibility for the latter, however, was located at the Islamic Cultural Centre (ICC) whose headquarters were at Zahariah Mosque. The first mosque to be established in Bolton was also the site at which Baruchis and Surtis struggled for control of the ICC. In the 70s a further split between Baruchis belonging to the Deobandi and Berelewi schools occurred with the latter separating from the larger group of Deobandis - Surti and Baruchi - and refusing to recognise the authority of the ICC. Four years ago this came to a head with the demise of the ICC as a controlling body, and its replacement being the Bolton Mosque Community Care organisation which has representatives from all ten mosques, irrespective of their districts of origin and recognition of Islamic schools.

Control of a mosque is central to the control of faction and caste community members and their affairs. This means control over often community resources, funds and donations, applications for public funds, religious teaching syllabuses, and appointments of imams. Therefore, from the point of view of members control by their caste community is regarded as not only desirable, but also essential. Without a dominant caste community, its members would have to accept the social and religious dictates of some other caste community, and by implication faction, and possibly another Islamic school. Since these members of two factions live together in some wards and separately in others, competition for control of individual mosques and the ICC in the 1970s was not a foregone conclusion. It left the control of the ICC open to take-overs by politically active members, which lay at the root of Muslim ethnic politics. Although the Surti-Baruchi divide forms such an integral part of Muslim social and religious life, as a group they have built up an image which emphasises their commitment to Islam compared with that of the Surtis, which stresses flexibility and understanding.

On the one hand, when there is a threat to the Islamic community from the non-Muslim communities, these internal differences are submerged. For instance, when Muslims were informed that they could not have 24 hour and seven days a week access to the cemetery to bury their dead, they united in their protest. A recent instance of such an expression of unity occurred when the Muslims in Bolton, one of only two Muslim communities - the other being in Bradford - burnt Salman Rushdie's *Satanic Verses*. On the other hand, when the threat is located within the Islamic community, schisms occur along faction and caste community lines. For instance, as one Baruchi influential man tried to gain influence without ICC support by exploiting a political situation involving the white community, the Surtis refused to support him (see bearded school boy, Chapter Seven). At another level, members of the larger caste communities accept the Sunni Hanafi pathway and follow the teachings of the *Sunna*, *Shariah* and *Hadiths*. Thus, they share a common and overriding religious identity irrespective of their place of origin, they are all Sunni Hanafi Muslims. Commitment to these identities is called into question when Islam generally is under threat. In Britain, where Muslims are regarded with suspicion, if not some degree of fear (Modood, 1992, Said, 1981), they publicly claim their commit-ment to Islam through adhere to their religious observances in word and deed.

The Gujarati Muslim population interacts at three levels: firstly at the level of villages, in terms of district factions and caste communities (Diagram 1); secondly at the level of Islamic schools, namely as Deobandis or Berelewis; thirdly at the level of a united Sunni Hanafi Islamic community. These three levels of interaction give Muslims the potential to unite or divide according to which social identity is appropriate to a social situation. At one level opposition can take the form of village or faction identities; at another it can unite all Muslims in opposition to all non-Muslims. It is this facility to detach and reattach within a structure that allows the local to be linked to the global, which sets the Muslims apart from the Gujarati Hindus. This facility to unite and divide may explain why the Muslim candidates in local elections have unnerved white candidates who opposed them. The communities represent power bases and as such have no place in the British political system.

At the centre of this Gujaratis Muslim community lie struggles for control over mosques. These mosques act as 'symbols and what they symbolise is fused' into complex Islamic social identity (Evans-Pritchard, 1967:245-247; Firth, 1973:415). The public expression of beliefs in Islam provides the Muslims with both a symbol of Gujarati Islam as well as membership of wider Muslim brotherhood. Thus, Gujarati Muslims, both Sunni and Shia, are united in their acknowledgement of their religious identity which is given expression on ritual occasions, such as at funerals of fellow Muslims, Gujarati and Pakistani. All Muslims are expected to attend them and thereby they symbolically demonstrate their membership of the Islamic brotherhood. The interconnection between these social and religious identities becomes apparent when the conflict between factions, castes and Islamic schools is translated into demands that impinge upon the white community.

Gujarati Muslims share with Gujarati Hindus the same period of migration, similar experiences of migration, similar experiences of settlement and racism and a

69

sharing of the politics of coping with racism in Bolton and Britain. The next section will focus attention on the Hindu communities within a community. Thus the over-riding notion is that the Muslim and Hindu communities form a Gujarati community, although at times they will act separately and at other times together.

Diagram 1
Model of social, residential and religious allegiances in Muslim communities

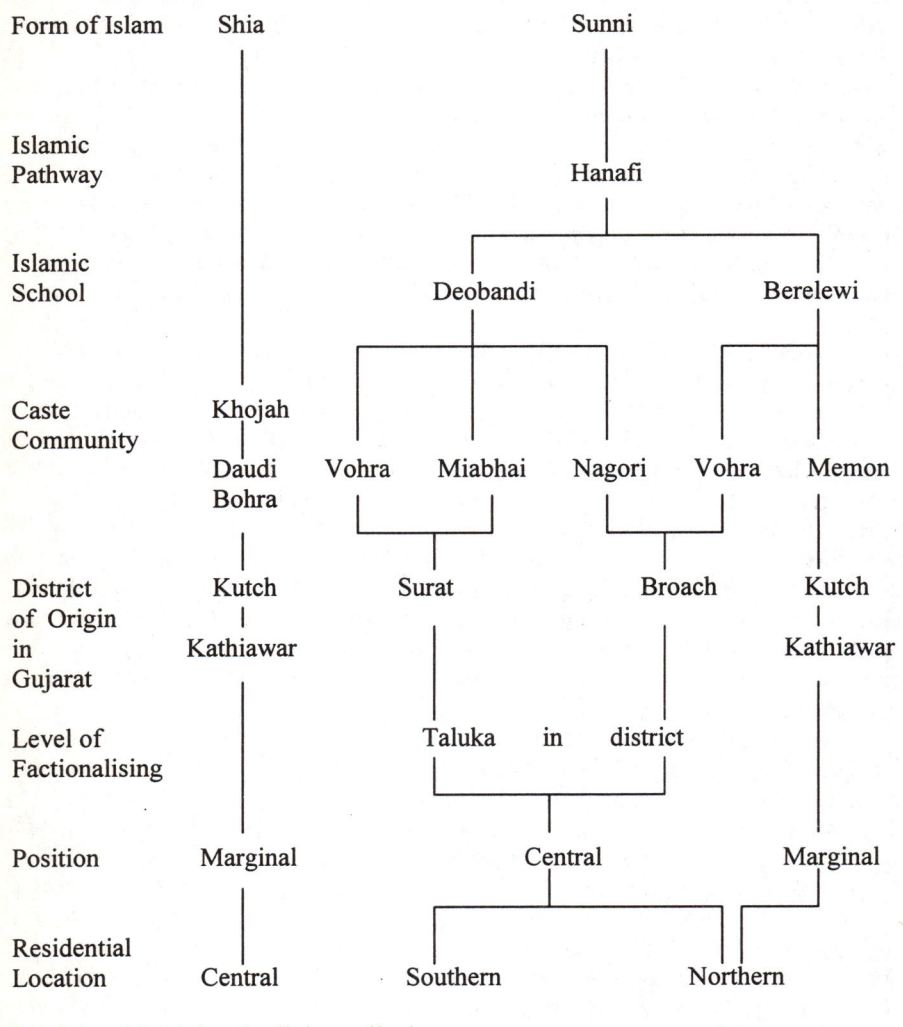

Spatial, residential and religious allegiances = ——————

70

Hindus

This section will argue that although in theory the link between groups on the ground and an overall ideology provides a structure for Hindus to unite and divide, in practice this process is hindered by a number of conflicting social processes. Firstly, some caste organisations are using migration to elevate their status within the caste system; secondly, some are developing new forms of social control to maintain the welfare of their members and extend their power; and thirdly, some are modifying their commitment to caste rules and norms. While the former processes seek to maintain caste boundaries, the latter undermine them. Although there is no clear relationship between the groups on the ground and Hindu ideology, the Hindu population comprises a collection or bricolage of castes whose members cannot work together but who therefore are able to participate politically in the local political system without conflicting with it. The development of caste and sect organisations facilitated the development of socio-religious communities. However, the absence of a structure or ideology, which allows the local to be translated into the global, ensures that caste communities are concerned with the maintenance of caste relationships and little else (Nesbitt, 1994; Knott, 1994).

Again chain migration has shaped the chains in terms of their villages of origin and the caste membership of the migrants. A large number of Hindu migrants who came here also know Muslim migrants who came from their villages, but the chains that brought Hindus to Bolton also separate them by origin, caste and sect. Thus each chain forms the basis of an embryonic community within a larger Hindu community; origins, caste and sect memberships serve to differentiate those in one chain from those in other chains. Undoubtedly the close relationship between caste position, occupation and the idea of pollution as features that form an integral part of the caste system could not be sustained by migrants who came here, since the working environment could not sustain such relationships, although they may exert an influence over them. Unlike Muslims, migration gave Hindus opportunities to achieve caste social mobility through either changing their occupations, freeing themselves of social disadvantages, and collectively seeking out new life styles. With few exceptions, identities based upon the association between caste position and occupation have little meaning here, giving rise to opportunities for upward social mobility.[4] What is particularly important is that such mobility can bring as great rewards in the wider society as it can within the Hindu communities; upward social mobility is seen as important by parents, their children and caste communities (Ballard *et al*, 1994). The experience of migration with the social situation in Britain has placed new demands upon caste organisations, with the aim of maintaining existing systems of social exchange and exploiting new opportunities to enhance caste status.

Reasons for Hindus migrating were similar to those that motivated Muslims, but in addition they possibly included a wish to escape from some of the constraints imposed by the caste system. The effect of chain migration on the Hindu population led to the development of a collection of large and small caste communities, whose members trace their origins to particular districts and towns or cities in Gujarat. Unlike Muslims, shared origins have not led to emergence of factions, because

71

those from the same areas do not necessarily belong to the same caste. Although they too confine the selection of spouses to *ekadas*, they avoid cousin marriages. Thus the link between chains whose members look for spouses from an *ekada* does not lead to the formation of strong kinship based groups, as it does for Muslims.

Consequently caste membership takes precedence over membership of migration chains and their places of origin; thus the group to which Hindus attribute their membership is not the village or district of origin but their caste.

Caste system

Although caste is one of the most precise forms of identification available to Hindus, there are changes to caste values, which point to its weakening. Traditionally this system of social stratification is based on four ranked *varnas* in a hierarchy based upon notions of pollution and occupation. 'The principle of hierarchy is attribution of rank to each element in relation to the whole' (Dumont, 1972:131). It is based upon a complex relationship between specialisation and interdependence of constituent groups. At one level specialisation entails separation of them, at another it demands co-operation if the needs of the whole are to be met. This relation to the whole links the division of labour to the hierarchy (Dumont, 1972:133). What appears to be happening to Hindus in Bolton is that they are losing sight of the relationship between the structure of the *varnas* and the castes that are ranked within them. Whether or not this is intentional or otherwise is difficult to ascertain, but the outcome is similar, namely that the sharpness of the process of identification once provided by the system has become blunted through possibly its inapplicability to aspects of life in Britain. For instance, when Hindus sampled were asked to identify their *varnas*, the majority (67.5%) could not or chose not to do so; only 32.5% of them identified a *varna*. Although they show that they are aware of the hierarchy of *varnas*, they give the impression that they possess an imprecise idea of the ranking position of their caste in relation to other castes. Therefore, the misidentification of caste position can be explained as either an attempt to reduce the importance of caste ranking to outsiders, or as evidence of the diminished importance of caste as a form of social stratification. Whether or not it can be taken as a sign of the separation of castes whose members intend to operate as self-contained communities irrespective of the caste system is unclear. However, in certain circumstances Hindus show an awareness of *varna* membership, such as when they refer to the social distance between themselves and their doctors, many of who belong to castes within the Brahmin *varna*. From discussions with Hindus and the questionnaire, a hierarchy of caste and *varnas* was constructed (Table 3.4).

The majority (92.8%) of the Hindus sampled belonged to castes within Vaishya *varna*. Six respondents belonged to Solanki, Rohit Chauhan and Dhobi Rajput castes in the Shudra *varna*. Most of the Hindus I spoke to looked down upon these Hindus, thus making it apparent that they were perceived to be of lower status than those in the Vaishya *varna*. None of these six Hindus placed their caste in the Shudra *varna* or gave it a position in the caste system. Possibly, an effect of chain migration has been to accentuate the caste identities of those in a chain at the expense of the total caste society. Though there is little evidence of the interdependence that might be associated with those living in a caste society, there are examples of inter-caste relationships that echo those described in the literature on India (Mayer, 1973). For instance, a Mandhata Patel who worked for a water authority told how he had instructed a Kutchi builder, whom he employed, to bring his own flask of water. The explanation he gave was that he did not want this Kutchi, whom he regarded as being of a lower caste, to pollute his supply of water. Another Hindu who is a Patidar Patel claimed that if his friends knew that he ate and liked chicken, he would be outcaste. These examples suggest that caste identity has remained important and that it generally remains latent until some situation forces it to become manifest. Table 3.4 sets out the probable caste rankings of the Hindus sampled.

Table 3.4
Caste identities of Hindus

Vaishya Caste:			Brahmin Caste:		
Mistry	14		Brahmin	2	
Kumbar	1		Lingayat	1	
Parjapati Kumbar	5		Bawa	1	
Rajput Rana	1		Total	4	2.6%
Rajput	1				
Katri	2		Kshatriya Caste:		
Luhar	4		Kshatriya	1	
Lohana	1		Total	1	
0.65%					
Bania1					
Zarola Bania	1		Shudra Caste:		
Koli	11)		Solanki	2	
Mandhata Patel	14)		Rohit Chauhan	3	
Matia Patel	1)		Rajput Dhobi	1	
Leva Patel	44)	Patels	Total	6	3.9%
Patidar Patel	7)	111			
Kadva Patel	4)	72.08%	Ramgharia Sikh		
Kanbi Patel	18)		Sikh	1	
Leva Patidar Patel	6)		Total	1	
0.65%					
Leva Kanbi Patel	5)				
Kadva Patidar Patel	1)				
Total	142	92.2%			
Overall Total =	154	100.01%			

Some 92% of Hindus belonged to Vaishya *varna*; the remainder included Brahmins, Kshatriyas, Shudras and Sikhs, which shows that it was mainly Vaishyas who migrated from India to Africa and elsewhere including Britain. Although twenty-eight different castes are represented in the sample, some castes were not represented, for instance Soni, Mochi, Darji, Halpati, Thakkar, Tailor, Parmar,

Gohil and Valand. The majority (72%) of Hindus sampled not only belonged to the Vaishya *varna*, but also were members of one of the seven 'Patel' castes who do not regard each other as equals. Although the common title of Patel superficially confers a degree of homogeneity on this group, they comprise a diverse collection of unrelated caste communities tracing their origins to different parts of Gujarat (see below).[5] One group of Patels who are not clearly identified as Patels is Koli; they are included with the Patels, because most of them are now known as Mandhata Patels. Locally the Leva and Mandhata Patels comprise the largest of the caste communities.

The combination of occupation with notions of purity and pollution form the basis of the caste hierarchy. Hindus who came to Britain had to accept jobs which often bore no relation to their position in the caste system. In this way migration created opportunities for Hindus to achieve upward social mobility by abandoning their caste-defined occupations for new ones or, more likely, encouraging their children to achieve qualifications at school and university. These opportunities would give them access to prestigious occupations in the professions (Ballard, 1994; Penn and Scattergood, 1991). If anything, migration has made it difficult for Hindus to establish occupational relationships with members of castes with a few exceptions, such as *jajman-kamin* (Desai, 1963:57-60). Observation suggests that similar relationships may exist between doctors and shopkeepers, between Asian doctors and Asian patients, and between Asians who in the early years helped Asians who could not speak much English to communicate with their kin in the subcontinent. The majority of Hindus sampled abandoned their caste-related occupations in favour of typical urban-industrial jobs; however, some Hindus, such as jewellers and carpenters, manage to practise their caste-related occupations. For instance, Sonis manage much of the trade in jewellery in Bolton and the Northwest of England. Two Brahmins performed the appropriate ritual roles at weddings, cremations and in the temples over and above their full-time jobs in mills.

The pattern of employment of Hindus differed from that of the Muslims; for instance only 35.7% compared to 68.3% of Muslims were textile workers, the remainder of Hindus (64.3%) working in other jobs some of which could be in textile mills compared with 31.7% of Muslims. The Hindus and Muslims in other employment included electricians, bus drivers, washing machine mechanics, builders, and joiners. The doctors belonged to Brahmin and Kshatriya castes who traced there origins to Calcutta (Bengal), Indore (Madya Pradesh), Maharastra and Patna (Bihar) respectively. Three others, a Sikh, a Mistry and a Zarola Bania held jobs which placed them in Class I, namely lecturer, tax officer and accountant respectively. The latter two were Gujarati; the Sikh traced his origins to the Punjab in Pakistan. No Muslims sampled matched these Hindus in occupation or social class. Thus, most Hindus accepted low-paying and often insecure jobs, which placed them in the semiskilled and unskilled manual Class (Class VII), while those who came from other states in India held jobs which were better paid and professional. The modern work environment has brought together members of different castes requiring them to work together. Outside the work situation, they can maintain separation as defined by their caste within certain limits. Thus they can attempt to pressure their children into marrying spouses from the appropriate castes;

74

they can maintain caste values pertaining to the cooking and eating of food. For the majority, however, the work situation threatens to undermine traditional caste relationships, while their social time allows them to stress the importance of caste relationships through social exchange of wives, gifts, kinship obligation and rituals (Werbner, 1989). Consequently, caste identities have remained important, since they unite those who share them, and separate those who do not. Most importantly of all, castes and caste organisations have become reservoirs of scarce resources, funds, support, social and religious rituals, knowledge, and friendship to which only members have access.

Caste, district of origin and social mobility

Although there is a link between district of origin and caste, this is not expressed in terms of faction membership and to a limited extent it is expressed through sect membership. The castes represented in the Bolton Hindu population came from certain districts in Gujarat: for instance, a large number of Hindus sampled came from Surat district excluding the Navsari region, they comprised seven different Patel castes and 11 Leva Patels (Table 3.5, page 75). Another set, consisting of 12 Mistrys and 12 Mandhata Patels, came from the Navsari region. The largest set came from Kutch and included 31 Leva Patels and 10 Kanbi Patels; with smaller sets coming from Kathiawar, which included 5 Parjapati Kumbars, and the Ahmadabad district which included four different Patels castes. The remainder included 5 Hindus who came from other areas of India and the Sikh who came from Pakistan. Most of the nine Patel communities share three districts or regions of origin; they are known loosely as the Kutchi (32.5%), the Surti (27.3%), and the Mandhata Patels (21.4%). Within each set members perceive of each other as roughly socially equal and they have developed organisations to serve their social and religious needs. For instance, the Kutchi Patels shared in the emergence of the Swaminarayan sects - the new face of Hinduism (Williams, 1984; Barot, 1980) - with the establishment of temples, burial societies and their support of visiting leaders and priests. The Surti Patels share in the older face of Hinduism and support the Vishwa Hindu Parishad. The Mandhata Patels come from the Navsari region and shared in their move to elevate their caste status from Koli to Mandhata Patel (discussed below). Geographical identities provide Hindus with a ready-made guide to a common sense model of a caste hierarchy based upon perceived social distance, which they express in terms of status differences. This enables them to separate those who are socially equal from those who are unequal.

Without a common geographical base or a common diasporic identity,[6] Gujarati Hindus give the impression that they share little in common with each other, and even less with Gujarati Muslims. Migration provided Hindus with opportunities to alter their social position within the caste system through the process of social mobility (Ballard, 1994; Knott, 1994; Nesbitt, 1994). In addition to changing their status as a group, individual caste members could modify their commitment to their caste values. I have selected a number of instances of castes and members of castes who used migration to elevate the position of their caste or to modify caste behaviour with the effect of undermining caste boundaries. Firstly, Kolis changed the ranking of their caste by their own efforts; secondly, another caste outcaste a member for behaving in a way they deemed detrimental to the caste. Thirdly, Kutchi Patels changed their status through the Swaminarayan movement and now espouse a life style that is more akin to that of high caste Brahmins than to Vaishyas. The fourth instance involves the Mistry caste.

Table 3.5
Origin of Hindu respondents by district

Districts	Castes		
Surat (includes 7 Patel castes,11 Leva Patels)		42	27.27%
Navsari in Surat (includes 12 Mistrys,12 Mandhata Patels)		33	21.43%
Kathiawar (includes 5 Parjapati Kumbars)		13	8.44%
Kutch (includes 31 Leva Patels and 10 Kanbi Patels)		50	32.47%
Ahmadabad (includes 4 Patel castes)		6	3.9%
Gujarat		1	0.65%
Other* (included 5 from outside Gujarat)		9	5.84%
Total		154	100%

*Four Gujaratis described themselves as Gujaratis. The Rajput Rana came from Daman.

Firstly, the Koli Patels used migration to improve their caste position and took on the name of Mandhata Patel. When asked to identify their caste, some Mandhata Patels referred to themselves as Koli Mandhata Patels; some professed to not knowing the name Koli, and others referred to themselves as Koli.[7] The chairperson of the Mandhata Patel Caste Association explained this as follows: 'In Gujarat our caste name was Koli. Migration to East Africa gave us the opportunity to improve ourselves, and many became successful businessmen, teachers and doctors. The caste association established a fund to assist their children to obtain an education, training and members to establish businesses. With the success of their members, they decided to change their caste name to Mandhata Patel'. Today he asserts that his caste is the largest in Bolton, with high caste status and the caste organisation is located in Birmingham. They have also established a separate temple in Beverley Road where they can hold their various social and religious ceremonies. Their stay in East Africa gave them the opportunity to elevate their caste status signified by a change in their name and the establishment of a strong caste organisation with large financial resources.

The second instance of a caste using migration to establish itself involved a lower caste Hindu, a Parmir, who chose to act in a way that the caste disapproved of to protect its members. In the 1970s such decisions by caste associations illustrated their concern to protect their caste position by changing names allied to bargaining of new and higher status, to controlling the size of dowry payments and to outcasteing errant members. The maintenance of caste rules by members brings caste approval; the breaking of caste rules brings opprobrium and sometimes punishment. The decision to outcaste and to administer the decision is an indication of the strength of a caste. In 1975 a Hindu and his children were outcaste by their caste association, the Shree Sarvodaya Samaj (UK). His outcasteing revolved around his indecision to marry a third wife. After his first wife's death, his relatives helped him select a second wife, whom he probably married in Gujarat. Having lived with her for a year, he sent her back to Gujarat to manage as best she could without him. It was reported that her family in Gujarat refused to look after her, because they were too poor and she was no longer their responsibility as they had paid her dowry. As a result of the shock at being sent back to India, she is reported to have become mentally ill and she died five years later.

This man decided to marry for a third time and his kin found him another possible partner. Having arranged the marriage, he discovered that the woman had two sons by a previous marriage. On learning of their existence his two sons objected to the marriage on the grounds that, according to Hindu custom, her two sons as males would gain rights to property to which they had never contributed. They got their father drunk one night and persuaded him to sign a change of deeds to the house. Having lost control over the family property and sharing access to the bank account with his sons, he had in effect lost his position as the head of the family. His sons threatened to make this public if he chose to marry this woman and to conceal it if he did not. He decided to withdraw from the marriage, and by coincidence this decision was followed by a Home Office order on his 'wife-to-be' to leave the country. The caste committee wanted this woman and her children to have the opportunity to live in Britain and so to improve her social position; they were prepared to support her even if she lived in Leicester and her husband lived in Bolton. His decision not to proceed with the marriage destroyed her chances of living here. Consequently, separate committees for men and women in the caste association decided to outcaste him and his family. A letter from the association was sent to all caste members instructing them not to socialise with any member of his family, unless they too wished to be outcaste. The outcasteing had other consequences: his daughter's marriage was to take place about the same time. Few of the invited guests attended the wedding, because they had received the letter threatening them with outcasteing if they associated with the family. The bridegroom, who came from Gujarat, only heard about the decision of the association after the wedding and took his frustration and anger out by battering his wife and then divorcing her.

The elevation of the Swaminarayans is well known (Williams, 1984; Barot, 1980); I shall discuss the Swaminarayans later, but they uphold caste values with a fervour that matches their belief in their caste superiority. However, another caste whose members claim to have used a similar process to alter their caste status are Mistrys. In Gujarat they claim that they were known as Kumbars. Though I did not pursue the explanation for this change of caste name, it is interesting to note that both Mistry and Koli established strong caste associations in East Africa, which they brought to Britain. Both caste associations took decisions to limit the amount of dowry to be paid, because members of both became aware of the large amounts of money that the grooms' families are expecting to have spent on them in the form of presents. A consequence of this expenditure was that the brides' families were often crippled financially, leading to the impoverishment of the caste.[8]

Instances of the weakening of the caste boundary point to a process which is both a consequence of migration as well as a reaction against the caste system. The first of these examples concerns reactions to marriage within caste generally.

While opinion reflects an ideal, reality demands that these Hindus continue to adhere to their caste values and rules. Thus the divide between the castes is maintained by in-caste marriages. Of those Hindu respondents who were married, some 95% married in-caste; and their wives traced their origins to villages which were part of *ekadas* that included the villages of their husbands. Only 5% of the married respondents married wives who either did not belong to the same caste as them or were not Hindus. Existing marriages provide little indication of any change in the overall pattern of marriage, although it is commonly believed by parents and the white community that Hindu (and Muslim) youth who grow up in Britain will set aside their 'traditional' acceptance of arranged marriages and will adopt more Western attitudes. An analysis of Hindu marriage preferences provides an indication of changing attitudes. It was respondents in higher castes, rather than those in the lower castes, who claimed to accept the notion of free choice of spouse for their children. Recognition of the possibility of marriage to any Hindu implies that caste is no longer considered to be socially important, which is an indication of caste breakdown. Some 18% (28) of Hindus sampled recognised the former possibility and 11% (17) the latter. However, the majority of Hindus interviewed (68% - 105) preferred their children to marry in-caste.[9]

The second instance of a weakening of caste boundaries became apparent when the reactions of different caste members are analysed in regard to the social values that in discussion Hindus had singled out as very important. On the one hand, caste organisations take it upon themselves to act as monitors of social behaviour; on the other hand they are a resource offering their members a wide range of benefits, which include financial, social and psychological support. Efforts by caste communities to maintain what their members believe to be appropriate behaviour reinforce their social importance within the caste system. As reservoirs of scarce resources, caste communities have authority to demand, if not command, the appropriate behaviour from their members. Any commitment to caste values serves to divide rather than unite them (Ballard *et al*, 1994). To obtain some indication of the strength of commitment to caste customs, those from the three Patel castes were asked to rank seven customs regarded as being important. These were the avoidance of meat, endogamous marriage, cremation of dead within 24 hours, eating food prepared by caste members only, arrangement of marriage of daughters at sixteen years of age, maintaining caste position vis-à-vis other castes and membership of one's caste association.

Patels

The title 'Patel' was used by Hindus to separate themselves from other castes. It is often used *as if* it is a caste name by Gujaratis speaking to white people or Muslims speaking of Hindus and the white community often uses it, erroneously, to describe Hindus. No Hindu normally would refer to his/her caste solely as Patel (see Pocock, 1972:56); generally, some other appellation is attached, such as Leva, Patidar,[10] or

Kanbi. I have separated the Hindu Patels sampled into three sets: namely the Kutchi Patels, who comprise Leva, Patidar, Kadva, Kanbi including combinations e.g. Leva Patidar Patel, the Surti Patels who also include Leva Patidar Patels and the Mandhata Patels.[11]

The Kutchi castes included Leva Patels, Kanbi Patels and Leva Kanbi Patels (Pocock, 1972, 1973), who perceived themselves as social equals, if not superiors, to Patels from Charotar and Surat districts. When they were asked to rank seven caste-related values and customs in order of importance (Table 3.6), they ranked as being very important the cremation of the dead within twenty-four hours (85%), 61% the avoidance of meat, and 48% marriage in-caste. Belonging to a caste association, eating food cooked only by members of the caste and the maintenance of superior position of the caste were considered to be of lesser importance. Yet it was a disagreement over preparation of food that led to some of these Patels refusing hospital food unless it was prepared by their own caste. The avoidance of meat for these Patels can be explained in terms of the rise of the new face of Hinduism (cf. Williams, 1984), as well as their strict adherence to a vegetarian diet as a sign of upward social mobility, namely sanskritization (Mandelbaum, 1972). These Patels are the most committed of all the Patels to maintaining their exclusivity. The social boundaries between district, caste and sect are coterminous.

Table 3.6
Caste-related customs ranked as very important by Patels*

	Kutchi		Surti		Mandhata	
	No	%	No	%	No	%
Cremate dead within 24 hrs.	39	84.8	11	40.7	8	32
Avoid eating meat	28	60.9	7	25.9		
Marry in-caste	22	47.8	11	40.7	6	24
Caste association	9	19.6				
Eat food cooked by own caste	5	10.9				

* Where less than 10% have ranked a custom as very important, it is not recorded.

For most Hindus there would appear to be a declining commitment to maintaining all aspects of caste behaviour and Surti Patels are good example of such behaviour. Few of these Patels considered as very important in-caste marriage (41%), the avoidance of eating meat (26%), and none regarded eating food cooked by caste members as very important. The majority of them rated membership of their caste association, eating food cooked by caste members, and the maintenance of the caste's position as unimportant. The order in which they ranked caste customs and values as being important reflects a less positive attitude to the maintenance of caste status. Many of them eat meat and eat with friends who belong to other castes. They are widening the range of people with whom they associate, but by doing so they are losing their social basis for developing a distinctive caste identity and are in danger of separating themselves from the caste system. Today they form the largest group of supporters of the VHP, a multi-caste based religious organisation. Only in-caste marriage provides a form of social change, which gives castes a degree of caste exclusiveness. An explanation for this loss of commitment to caste values can be explained partly by the lack of involvement of caste members in either a religious experience, such as the rise of the new face of Hinduism, or a commitment to the process of sanskritization.

The third set of Patels, Mandhata Patels, achieved upward mobility through success in East Africa (see above). Initially having a lower caste position than other Patels, their success, according to their caste representative, was in a western style economy. Thus their success has little to do with caste values and this is reflected in their low commitment those values which others consider important, that is the cremation of the dead within 24 hours and marriage in caste. With less commitment to their caste, these members are ready to reduce their recognition of caste-appropriate behaviour. From the data collected only a third ranked cremation of the dead within 24 hours as important and in-caste marriage attracted even less commitment. As a caste who are elevating themselves from low caste status to a higher position in terms of the achievements of their members, recognition of caste values is of lesser importance.

These three groups of Patels present a contrast between Kutchi Patels, who believe in their established high status within the caste system, and the Surti and Mandhata Patels. The commitment of the Surti Patels to upholding the caste system is diminishing and that of the Mandhata Patels is minimal. A consequence of such varying patterns of commitment to caste values is that Hindus, already separated by caste commitments, are being driven further apart by them in terms of their commitment to achievement in a society which does not recognise the caste system. These two processes of separation serve to undermine the dominance of the high status castes and to encourage their participation in a political environment that is not based on established caste, sect or ethnic identities. The shared title of 'Patel' barely provides them with an identity; to all intents and purposes they comprise three disparate communities. These changes signal a breakdown in the caste and a greater dependence on intra-caste exchange to maintain caste identities, while also freeing them to participate politically within their caste organisations and outside them without any allegiance to a social identity. The divisions between castes or caste communities are exemplified by their commitment to different aspects of Hinduism and different Hindu religious organisations.

Religious organisations

Under the umbrella of religious organisations Hindus developed political structures of leadership and support. On the basis of a shared identity based on a district of origin and a recognition of caste equality Hindus developed shared aims, such as the establishment of religious and community centres. The growth and establishment of Hinduism in Bolton can be linked to the development of religious organisations. Recruitment to these religious organisations is based either on common geographical origins, or to caste membership or to merely a commitment to a particular religious leader. Some Hindus belonged to two organisations, such as a Swaminarayan sect and the VHP. This pattern of membership suggests a sharing of structures of leadership and support.

The religious organisations can be arranged on the basis of those which attract Hindus from a wide range of castes and districts of origin to those which attract those from specific castes and one district in Gujarat (Table 3.7 below). The most specific association of district of origin, caste and sect can be found exemplified by the Swaminarayan movement. The combination of a shared district of origin and the maintenance of caste exclusiveness through a reinforcing set of religious beliefs led to the development of the two Swaminarayan sects in Gujarat (Williams, 1984). These Hindus distinguish between those who belong to the Shree Kutch Satsang Swaminarayan and the Shree Swaminarayan Sects. Both draw followers primarily from Kutchi Patel castes (Williams, 1984; Barot: 1980, 1972/73; Chaudhuri, 1979), although according to Williams (1984) their influence extends to members of castes living elsewhere in Gujarat. Over 80% of Hindus sampled who traced their origins to Kutch belonged to one or other of these sects. Furthermore, the majority of them are also members of the Shree Kutch Leva Patel Burial Society, which exclusively manages their cremations. Swaminarayan beliefs allied to social ideology of reform supported by values relating to caste exclusiveness make for a clear structure of leadership (Barot, 1980), although in the 1970s this leadership survived by non-contact with other Hindus and Muslims and non-participation in local CRC and those in the wider political arena. Though this may give members of both Swaminarayan sects distinctive social identities, it also separated them from the other Gujarati communities.

Table 3.7
Religious affiliations of Hindus by district of origin

District/ city of origin	Shree Swami-narayan Mandir no. %	Shree Kutch Swami-narayan no. %	Saibaba no. %	VHP no. %	Hindu no. %	Others no.
Kutch	13 81.3	19 82.6	2 10.5	13 18.3	3 13.6	1
Kathiawar	1 6.3	2 8.7	2 10.5	6 8.5	2 9.1	
Nadiad	2 12.5					
Petlad			1 5.3	1 1.4		
Ahmadabad				1 1.4	1 4.6	
Surat		2 8.7	5 26.3	18 25.4	6 27.3	1
Navsari			8 42.1	27 38	6 27.3	1
Other			1[$] 5.3	5[**] 7	4[+] 18.2	
Totals 154:	16	23	19	71	22	3
% 100:	100.1	100	100	100	100.1	100

Gujarat (1)[**], Punjab (1)[**], Bombay (2)[**], Mombasa (1)[**], Maharastra (1)[+], Calcutta (1)[+], Indore (1)[+], Patna (1)[+], Daman (1)[$].

The history of both Swaminarayan sects is documented (Williams, 1984); they share the same founder, recruit adherents from the same districts in Gujarat, same castes and even from same families. Relations between their followers are occasionally marked by aggression, supported by tales of inhumanity related by members of one sect about the behaviour of those in the other. Stories are told of how children were enticed away from their families and taken by a Swami in the other sect to his temple in Gujarat, where they are trained as *sadhus*. Their families, the tale goes, never see them again. Although I came across no evidence of a kidnapping, these stories confirm adherents in their conviction that their own sect is superior to the other and that members of the other sect are prepared to descend to any depths to ensure the continuity of their sect. The present-day leaders of both sects have made a number of visits to Bolton, usually paid for by their followers here and in other British towns and cities, making public appearances before Hindu and white audiences.

Both sects demand that their members are committed to the beliefs and precepts, which are set out in the *Shikshapatri*, which is regarded as 'a representative of his very self, Svarupa' (Pocock, 1973:141). Pocock sums up the philosophy behind this work as follows: 'there is, in other words, a tendency ... towards a kind of exclusivism, an absolutism which seems to me to mark a radical innovation' (1973:142). Three issues are pertinent to influence the process of the separation of Swaminarayans from other Hindus and from a British way of life: these are the Gujarati language, Gujarati cuisine and the traditional position of women. They pursue through their beliefs a degree of exclusiveness, which is based upon codes of behaviour: they must not eat meat, avoid alcohol and avoid food prepared by people who are not Swaminarayans. These codes also provide detailed rules about how women should behave.[12]

Some sects were led by a religious leader who had an established a reputation which has spread beyond local district boundaries. Saibaba is such a person and he is based in Southern India. He argues that his message should have universal appeal across continents, religion, nations, and races. His fame is international today and so his rallies attract people from all over India and the world to his movement. His form of belief is most accurately described as eclectic and, according to his adherents here, invites people to pray to their god(s) through him. Although the Hindus sampled came from mainly the Surat area, his followers in Bolton include not only South Asians, but also white people. When his followers in Bolton celebrated the birth of Krishna, the worshippers included both Hindu and white believers. This same scene was repeated recently when this sect celebrated a festival. His claims to miraculous cures have added to the appeal of his movement. By establishing their independence through renting halls not owned or controlled by other Hindus, the followers of Saibaba have developed their own social identity.

Although Hinduism is caste based, the VHP is a multi-caste organisation with members who are drawn from across the caste system. It is an international organisation whose aim is the promotion of Hinduism. In the 1970s Hindus here claimed that the Bolton branch was the largest branch organisation in Britain (*Hindu Vishwa*, October 1974:21). With the building of the new temple in Neasden, London, the London branch is probably the largest. As a registered charity, the

VHP endeavours to provide for both the religious and community needs of all Hindus and its local membership reflects this wide appeal. Its membership is drawn from a wide range of states, districts and castes, although most of the Hindus sampled came from Kutch and the Surat district. The emergence of the VHP exemplifies how a local South Asian Hindu organisation changed from being dependent upon the local white community for its accommodation to becoming a consumer.

Initially the VHP had no place of its own and its members hired halls to celebrate their festivals. Early in 1973 a Sikh from East Africa, who was also a member of the local CRC, was elected chairperson. Before taking up the position of chairperson, his predecessor had unsuccessfully attempted to unite the membership. However, in the face of opposition from the Mandhata Patel members, who belonged to the largest caste in Bolton, he made little progress. Conflicts over the control of money and decisions about the timing of festivals led to his being replaced by the Sikh. The Mandhata Patels separated and bought an unused church in Beverley road, which they have converted into a temple, dedicated to serving their social and religious needs. Meanwhile members of smaller castes in the VHP argued that all castes should participate equally, since they were too small to establish their own temples. In 1972 the VHP recognised that it required its own building, while its members could not decide whether or not caste allegiance was more or less important than the establishment of a united Hindu membership. Against this background of inter-caste rivalry, the Sikh was elected chairperson. As one of the relatively few Sikhs in Bolton, he was seen by VHP members to have no significant caste power base and therefore, posed no threat to other caste representatives.

Under his leadership, conflicts between caste representatives were shelved and he launched the VHP on a campaign to raise £25,000 from the local Indian population for the purchase of a building for use as a community centre. In 1974 he began the negotiations for the purchase of St. Barnabas Church, which belonged to the Church of England. The negotiations were successful and the local and national media claimed, rightly or wrongly, that this marked the first sale by the Church of England to members of a non-Christian faith in England (*BEN*, 6/5/75, 13/5/75; *Guardian*, 7/5/75). Under his leadership, the VHP established a community and religious centres in the building and Hindus of every persuasion were encouraged to join the VHP to participate in community activities and religious festivals. Undoubtedly, the VHP was, and still is, the most popular organisation if the responses of the Hindus sampled taken as a guide; some 46% of the Hindus are members of the VHP with the largest proportion of these coming from the Surat district. Under the leadership of the Sikh the VHP also became a major participant in ethnic politics and, had the Sikh not resigned, he and the VHP might have become major participants in local politics.

Finally, those respondents who did not belong to any religious organisations can be divided into two categories: firstly, those who accept the general principles of Hinduism but who do not wish to be associated with any religious organisations; secondly, those who were antagonistic to the VHP. Generally doctors, like many other professional Indians, declared their belief in Hinduism to be a general one.

Although they generally show little public commitment to caste values, they may show some commitment in the company of other Hindus. They may attend religious ceremonies at the VHP, but they rarely become involved in the organisation's activities. Quite a few of them regarded the VHP as still a supporter of the caste system through its commitment to Hindu ideology. Others, who are no longer socially and residentially linked to the Gujaratis, made similar claims. There were no social links between these individuals. While they might support, with donations, the VHP as a provider of facilities which they used they were located on the margins of the Hindu communities.

The pattern of development from a dependent organisation to one that becomes independent with the purchase of a building or the construction of a new purpose-built building marks the change to consumerism. Both Hindu and Muslim sects in the town have followed this line of development and thus have established themselves in the town, but more importantly their buildings represent signs of their presence in the urban space of the town. They are a recognised part of the town. Such development in the Hindu communities was bedevilled usually by inter-caste conflicts. An instance of such conflict is the antagonism between those who were intent upon developing the VHP and the Mandhata Patels, who appeared to undermine such development. As they were the largest caste represented in town and as members of the VHP at one time, they had the power to oppose the management over decisions about the timing and place for holding festivals. When they separated from the VHP, they temporarily impeded the efforts of the VHP to become independent. Later on, once the VHP had established itself and applied for a grant of £40,000 to improve the centre, the Mandhata Patels argued publicly that the VHP should not be given the grant, because it would be detrimental to the interests of the whole 'Indian' population. This opposition within the Hindu community and more publicly stopped in 1980 only when the Mandhata Patels bought their own property which they converted into a temple. Both the VHP and the Mandhata Patels suffered a series of arson attacks, but these were attributed to racist groups and not to opposing Hindu communities.

Inter-caste rivalry is deeply embedded in the Hindu population. Further evidence of this conflict is apparent from the commitments of Hindus to other religious organisations in addition to the VHP. While members of the VHP made regular donations to it, this did not prevent them from making donations to the other religious organisations. It was not the commitment of Hindus to the VHP that is in question, but the commitment of those who belonged to other religious organisations that is in question. Some 54% of respondents who belonged to other religious organisations also made regular donations to the VHP. The majority of those sampled, who did not contribute to the VHP, included most of those who belonged to Shree Swaminarayan sect or declared themselves to be just Hindus. They gave the least to the VHP when it most needed support. By contrast, over 80% of the respondents who were members of the Shree Kutch Swaminarayan and Saibaba sect donated money to the VHP. In a sense, by supporting the VHP and a separate sect, these Hindus supported caste values, while also supporting a multi-caste organisation. With the VHP having the most politically effective leaders of all minority organisations, Hindus from other castes and sects were attracted to it.

Nevertheless, the link between various Hindu organisations was tenuous and when the Sikh resigned from the leadership of the VHP in 1980, the link between the VHP and other castes broke. The Mandhata Patels and the Parjapati Kumbars broke away, both established their own organisations, and although the latter does not own a building of its own it does support and take pride in the academic and business achievements of its members.

To conclude this section, the Hindus were divided at one level by caste and at another by religious commitment; the Hindu population comprises a bricolage of castes, tracing their origins to various districts in Gujarat. With no unifying structure they experience some difficulty in developing a pan-Hindu social identity. Some sought to maintain both by attitude and belief the exclusiveness of their castes; others were prepared to ignore caste values and began developing roles freer of caste commitments. Within Bolton's Hindu population, the old and the new faces of Hinduism clash with those of the old and the new Hindu on the streets, in the temples, in community centres and in the political arena. Initially, these religious organisations had no bases from which they could launch a social movement or develop as a status group. Of the four which established separate temples, namely the two Swaminarayan sects, the Mandhata Patels and the VHP, only the latter two have used the political arena of the CRC and ethnic politics to mount a protest or campaign to influence local politicians. The crux of the problem for the Hindus in their search for common identity is that 'religion … was never separated from their general life' (Chaudhuri, 1979:299). Once the step has been taken to colonise space, then the temple becomes a symbol of a shift to consumerism and to the construction of a social identity that has both a private and a public impact on the Hindu population and the town as a whole.

In conclusion, the Hindu community is segmented by food rules, which stress comparative hierarchy, pollution and division. By contrast, Islam stresses the unity of Islam versus the rest of the world. Pork for Muslims is forbidden, for Hindus polluting. Commensality is a religious prescription for Muslims. Among Hindus the caste that handles pollutes rather than the food being polluting. Pollution is cumulative, that is cooked food, faeces, beef, blood and the castes associated with them are increasingly polluting. Commensality divides Hindus and unites Muslims. Where close friendship is reinforced by commensality, the development of structures of support follows lines of commensality. Where commensality divides individuals, structures of support follow lines of social and religious equality. Unity and commensality for Hindus are in opposition to inequality and close friendship. Unity and commensality for Muslims support equality and close friendship. These issues underpinned the social life of the Gujarati communities and the pattern of close friendships marked lines of social cleavage, which is the subject of the following Chapter. Underlying the community structures of both Muslims and Hindus are social networks which provide the social relationships that link members of both religious communities across organisational divides. Social networks allow members of organisations to unite or fragment into social and religious communities, allow organisations to amass resources - financial, political, religious and social - and provide the links between structures of leadership and support that are an essential part of a political community. These organisations provided the basis for the development of a consumer culture in an ethnic population with a small middle class that enabled these minorities to purchase space in Bolton, thus creating a symbol of belonging and making a political statement. Some of these issues are addressed in the following Chapters.

Notes

1. See Barth in E.R.Leach (ed.), *Aspects of Caste in South India, Ceylon and Northwest Pakistan*, 1960. Although this may be typical of Islam in Gujarat, in West Africa Islam has not been found to be compatible with caste-like hereditary craft groups elsewhere (S.F.Nadel, *A Black Byzantium,* IAI, OUP, London, 1969, Chaps. 14-16; also J.S.Trimingham, 'The Phases of Islamic Expansion and Islamic Culture Zones in Africa', in I.M.Lewis (ed), *Islam in Tropical Africa*, IAI, OUP, London, 1966:135).

2. As a movement, *tabligh* originated in India in 1924, when the Deobandi *Ulami* were looking for greater political support from the Muslim community. This movement provided a way to increase the size and the political commitment of the community (Hardy, 1972: 208).

3. Although the preference for cousin marriage is of cultural origin, Baruchis regard it as a measure of religiosity. I am indebted to the late Prof. E.L. Peters for drawing my attention to his paper on 'Aspects of Affinity in a Lebanese Maronite Village', in J.G.Peristiany (ed) *Mediterranean Family Structures*, Cambridge, Cambridge Univ. Press. 1976.

4. Hindus who migrated first to Africa or elsewhere in the Pacific and Indian oceans have had two opportunities to elevate their caste positions (Bhachu, 1980).

5. According to Pocock (1972:57) and Misra (1964: 170) the origin of the title Patel goes back to Mogul times, when those appointed to administrative positions in villages to collect taxes were known by their titles as Desai, Amin and Patel. Desai ranked highest, the Amin second, the Patel third. The Patel was the headman of a village, who carried out the assessment of taxes, their collection and administered justice. This means that both Hindus and Muslims could become 'patels'.

6. Parekh (1994) argues for the existence of a Hindu diaspora on the grounds of a shared culture of origin. This is more specific than the argument put forward for an Indian diaspora (Clarke *et al*, 1990). However, both of these arguments lack a dynamic that is present, for instance in Gilroy (1993) and Hall (1990). Furthermore Parekh's notion of a Hindu diaspora raises the issue of the existence of many diasporas, namely Muslim, Sikh, Hindu and other religion-based diasporas. This suggests that a distinction needs to be made between migrants whose beliefs point to the existence of a diaspora and those whose beliefs do not.

7. 'The term Koli...refers to an assortment of people who owned little land and who were presumably of tribal origin' (Pocock, 1972:30; Mandelbaum, 1972:462). Mandelbaum describes them as low caste agriculturalists, or agricultural labourers who have Sanskritized and Rajputized themselves

(1972:462-463). However, neither Mandelbaum (1972) nor Pocock (1972) make reference to a Mandhata Patel caste; and Morris (1968) does not mention Mandhata Patels living in Uganda.

8. The Mistry caste also used a similar process to alter its status. In Gujarat those I spoke to claimed that they were known as Kumbar. While in East Africa, they established a strong and successful caste association that they brought to Britain. Here the caste association took a decision to limit the amount of dowry to be paid, because excessively high dowries were crippling their members financially. Nevertheless high dowries are still being paid by fathers of brides to protect them from abuse by husbands and other members of their families.

9. I spoke only to the Hindu youth but did not formally interview them. My impression was that their attitudes varied from acceptance of arranged marriages in some form to a brave rejection.

10. Pocock has given one explanation for the origin of the caste term *patidar* (1972:1,52,69ff). Leva Patidar Patel informants told me that the name was given to Patels whose job it was to weigh grain; it means 'weigher of grain'.

11. I came across no Charotar Patels (Pocock, 1972:52).

12. As these rules apply to women, they give the impression of restriction and domination (Williams, 1984: 142-146).

4 Close friends and communities

In the previous Chapter I argued that without the formation of ethnic religious organisations, ethnic communities would have been unable to amass scarce resources, in particular financial, to purchase space within the town. The recognition of the existence of such resources forced the town, local authority and local politicians into recognising Gujaratis as consumers, that is, as people who are free to claim space that others are equally free to claim (Bauman, 1988). In some instances they were hindered by opposing claims based on racism or confronted by racialised barriers, which is evidence of the existence and presence of the exercise of social control by those with power, that is, freedom. Whether or not the Gujaratis perceive themselves as one community, as two religious communities or as a collection of multiple caste and sect communities is of lesser importance than whether or not the white community and politicians perceive them as a single community. The reason for this argument is that to perceive them as a single community is to pre-empt their selection of an appropriate social identity, that is, stereotype. Therefore, it is important to recognise these identities representing social, economic and political communities, which are committed to the regeneration of culture.

Underlying the formation of communities, which provide the raw resources namely people and finance, are religious organisations. Therefore, any analysis of the structure of these communities will show how these organisations developed structures of leadership and support, how the structure of these communities contributed towards the formation of ethnic communities with the aim of husbanding scarce resources. I shall argue that a community consists of a web of social exchanges between members which, when taken as whole, leads to the social construction of a community as a reservoir of scarce resources. This includes the maintenance of ties between groups based on marriage, and allows for the maintenance of culture, social values and attitudes, structures of political support, and a range of social relationships including kinship and friendship. Social networks link a community to a set of markets, culture and hierarchies (Thompson et al, 1993) that define a community.[1] The concept of markets used here is different from that considered by Thompson et al; the markets that are of concern here give the ethnic community an identity that is social and religious. The ethnic community can be regarded as a form of status group (Weber, Vol. I and II, 1978). The community is defined not simply by territory, identity and interaction, but also by its capacity to impose itself upon external markets, and more importantly its capacity to maintain and develop its internal markets (Weber, Vol. I and II, 1978). In terms of its capacity to maintain these markets the ethnic community itself is shaped by internal and external pressures. Freedom in a capitalist society is embedded in the capacity of ethnic members and their communities to act without experiencing social constraints imposed by a racialised state. The internal structure of an ethnic community is a reflection of its capacity (freedom from social control) to participate in markets. To unravel this argument I shall firstly address the concept of social control and freedom, then I shall focus attention on internal and external markets, and finally I shall consider the notion of networks.

In our society, individual freedom is constituted as, first and foremost, freedom of the consumer; it hangs upon the presence of an effective market, and in its turn assures the conditions of such a presence (Bauman, 1988:7-8). Taking this argument further, the market capacity of a community is also reflected in the freedom of its members to have access to markets that will enable them to improve their social, economic and political condition. The argument that black people could not gain access to that sector of the housing market which might have given them access to improved opportunities for themselves and their children is well made (Rex and Tomlinson, 1979; Rex and Moore, 1971). It is not just the lack of resources that restricted ethnic communities to inner urban areas (Rex and Tomlinson, 1979; Rex and Moore, 1971), but also the form of social control that a racialised state exercised over ethnic minorities that limited them to low value housing (Smith, 1989). These two theoretical arguments focus on the external market. Weber identified two markets, an internal and external market (Vol. I and II, 1978). The ethnic community controls access over the former, but the latter is controlled by the state. While an ethnic community has access to an internal market, it has limited access to the external market to which its members seek equal access. Although in the 1970s South Asians were confined to low value inner urban housing with associated poor facilities, there were always some individuals who, through their success in business or management of property, accumulated sufficient resources to move to better areas (Werbner, 1989). Such movement does not imply integration, but does suggest equality for some in external markets. However, these individuals remained members of a community that is racialised.

Another dimension of this argument concerns not just the inability of South Asians as a whole to compete for better housing, but, more importantly, the perception of those outside it that minority communities are in some way disadvantaged and so should become the target of improvement policies. It is not only the view that South Asians as individual consumers could not compete successfully for scarce resources, but also the impression that a community was disadvantaged because of their shared social identity based upon a political notion of visibility. This notion of visibility underpinned much of local authority and government policy: the funding of inner urban housing areas, the improvement of schools, health services and other local services. The conditions attached to local and national government funding, such as section 11 funding, housing and improvement grants, have contributed to South Asian communities being seen by local and national government as a totality whose circumstances can be improved (Smith, 1989) by targeting resources (Hay, 1994). This approach highlights the distinction Bauman (1988:10) draws between different aspects of social control: 'to put people in a situation which prevents them from doing things, or putting them in situations which encourage them to do things one wishes them to do'. The target of much of local and national governmental support has been to place the South Asian community in a particular position from which their access to external markets can be controlled as individuals and as a totality.

It is not just placing an ethnic community in a situation which is not shared by other communities that distinguishes them from other urban communities, but also the fact that the ethnic community is perceived as one whose social and economic conditions can be improved as a totality. This difference separates the ethnic community from the caring community, the latter becoming regarded as an administrative and political construct. An ethnic community can also be a caring community. Although some of the assumptions embedded in the concept of community form part of the notion of community in community care, the caring community is constructed differently from the racialised community. An important difference is that the racialised community is perceived as a social, cultural, economic and political unit. As a target for economic improvement, local and national governmental support often aims to bring a range of improvements from housing to education and health to the whole community. In a post-Fordist state, the community is seen as a consumer in the wider context of consumerism, particularly as part of a hierarchy of consumers, some of whom are freer than others. The local and national government views the ethnic community as a consumer whose access to markets can be controlled. By restricting ethnic communities to low value housing and disadvantaged inner urban areas, the access of its members to external markets was racialised by the state (Smith, 1989). If 'freedom is privilege and power' (Bauman, 1988:27), then racialisation or the erection of racialised barriers (Small, 1994) implies a curtailment to a greater or lesser degree of freedom of access to external markets.

If the social structure of a community is defined 'as a persisting pattern of social relationships among social positions' (Laumann, 1973:3-4), then the position of an ethnic community in a hierarchy of communities should be reflected in terms of their access to markets. The social characteristics of this access are reflected in their transparency and opacity, predictability and unpredictability, and power and subordination (Bauman, 1988:24). The ethnic community can be gazed upon and is a gazer; it can see without being seen. The response of an ethnic community to a restriction on its access to external markets is to restrict access of others to its internal markets. It achieves this through controlling recruitment to social networks which are characterised by their close-knittedness. The closure of internal markets to outsiders is a process by which ethnic communities reinforce their culture by focusing attention and resources on what they consider to be culturally important social exchanges, such as marriage, kinship and close friendship, a shared morality, and a shared world view (Weber, Vol. I and II, 1978). This allows a community to develop a common culture and 'sentiments of likeness' through which its members can maintain their 'conduct of everyday life' (Weber, 1978:390). Through language, culture, and everyday life a belief in a common ethnicity is forged in the form of social opposition. As a basis for social action the development of an ethnic identity becomes a reaction to racism; in this sense it is anti-racist, a point made but not explored by Ballard (1994). The social construction of community boundaries implies a construction of notions of social identity concerning access to internal ethnic markets. This construction can change with situations and with membership (Cohen, 1985).

Studies of the poor point to their having less access to scarce resources, such as political and economic power, wealth and information, than those who are better off (Goldthorpe, 1980; Miles, 1982; Townsend, 1979). One characteristic of such studies is that they stress the absence of social relationships between those in power and those without it (Lin, 1982; Laumann and Pappi, 1976). Without any clear power base within the formal white political power structure in the 1970s (Rex and Tomlinson, 1979), Gujaratis had two options. They could develop their social networks into structures of support within their communities or they could extend their friendship to those with power belonging to other communities, namely the white politicians and businessmen. One explanation is that they chose egocentred close-knit social networks, because the structure of these networks enabled them to strengthen their existing power bases and to best amass resources in their communities. Whereas to extend their networks to others might also strengthen them, but it would expose them to racism. The location of Gujaratis within the local and national black community hierarchy means that those experiencing the greatest degree of racism will have the least access to scarce resources. Therefore, the formation of close-knit egocentred social networks was a response to a situation in which resources had to be protected and the maximum political support generated to make the optimum of a limited degree of power.

Community

'The structure of relations among actors and the location of individual actors in the network have important behavioural, perceptual and attitudinal consequences both for the individual units and for the system as a whole' (Knoke and Kuklinski, 1993:175-76). A distinction is being drawn here between community as an objective group with social rules, values, and attitudes and community as a subjective mental construct (Cohen, 1985). The social characteristics of social networks anchored to members of a religious status group and the community in which they are located demonstrate a sharing of social values and attitudes. This sharing is embedded in the social composition of the networks, that is, who are selected as close friends and the social interaction between them and others within the networks. The extent to which Gujaratis interact with other Gujaratis and/or with members of other communities, ethnic and white, will provide some indication of how closed or open they are as a community. Therefore, the social relationships that are important are those which involve a major social commitment, such as

91

kinship or close friendship, because they form the basis of the social exchanges in the internal markets, which contribute to the maintenance or breakdown of the ethnic culture. Therefore, this analysis will focus on close friendship. In Granovetter (1973) terms they are strong ties and are seen to be such by Gujaratis. Close friends form only a part of an egocentred network; the other parts comprise social relationships with other categories of people. For this reason, this analysis will be concerned only with the primary zone, that is, the one in which relations and close friends and their relationships with one another are located. Network analysis forms the subject of this Chapter. An analysis of the structure of these zones and the relationships between close friendship adds to the analysis of the social characteristics of these network zones. The pattern of selection of close friends influences the characteristics of the structure of the zone and the social perceptions of ethnic communities based upon it. These social perceptions developed into symbolic markers that were used to define social boundaries of communities by Gujaratis in different political situations (see Chapter Five).

When attributing a social identity to themselves, people describe themselves as being part of a community; this implies a sharing of cultural background, social relations and the process of identifying social boundaries (Cohen, 1982: 3-7, 9-11; 1985). A shared identity as reflected in this use of the term community also implies that those who recognise it do so because either they can define it or they are excluded from defining it (Emmett, 1982:207). The extent to which people can share in the defining process of a social identity is dependent upon the perceived social distance between themselves and those who identify or give expression to it in a social situation. If social identities are arranged in order of their exclusiveness/ inclusiveness, Cohen argues that the arrangement provides a deceptively simple structure of social identities (Cohen, 1982:10; 1985). Although Britons define their belongingness in terms of social identities (Cohen, 1982), the degree of exclusive- ness or inclusiveness of these social identities gives some indication of the extent to which they are shared by others. This structure tacitly allows for the recognition of multiple social identities.

At levels of ascending social interaction (inclusiveness) the definition of community becomes increasingly simplified and generalised; whereas at levels of descending interaction (exclusiveness) the definition of community increases in specificity (Cohen, 1985 1982). When Gujaratis refer to themselves as Gujaratis, as Hindus or Muslims, as members of a caste, as members of a village or faction, they speak of themselves as belonging to a community (*kom*) in relation to a social situation. Gujaratis speak of being part of a community at a number of different levels ranging from the ideological to the concrete. For instance, in relation to other ethnic communities or the white community, Gujaratis often describe themselves as Gujaratis. However, when differentiating between themselves and other Gujaratis they distinguish between belonging to a community, such as a caste community, and others belonging to other caste communities. These distinctions are part of the social language of everyday life. When they establish businesses, their success depends as much upon the support of their caste or sect community as it does upon knowledge of the business and the market. Thus those who choose to establish businesses without community support risk failure. Shia Daudi Bohra and Khojah and Sunni Memon respondents all spoke of 'not having' a large local community to support them.

For instance, an increase in the number of Gujarati and Pakistani driving schools in the middle 1970s was a response partly to workers preferring to have their own business and partly to the approaching recession that reduced the old textile industry to a handful of mills a decade later. It was also partly a reflection of growing resources in these communities which enabled more individuals to buy cars and therefore to have a need to learn to drive them. Furthermore, this encouraged the growth of a business which could be managed by one person or a family, and therefore costs could be kept down, while profits could be high. Another instance, which highlighted this point, arose in the context of competition between driving schools for customers. By 1974 some Gujaratis who looked for jobs outside the textile industry chose to establish driving schools, which gave them the opportunity to become self-employed and to respond to a new and growing demand for driving lessons from Gujaratis. A Memon who established a driving school believed that he was supported by a clientele, which included Muslim, Hindu and white pupils, based on past pupil recommendations. When his business experienced a decline towards the end of 1979, he attributed this to the inability of a small Memon community to support him, and to competition from an increasing number of caste community supported Gujarati and Pakistani driving schools which sprang into existence. Shortly after his business collapsed, he moved to Glasgow where there is a large Memon community. By contrast, a Mandhata Patel's driving school business, which was established soon after that of the Memon, survived and prospered because he could draw on the support of his own large caste community. In other words, communities look after their members.

An instance, which supports the argument, involves a Leva Patel and member of the Parjapati Kumbar caste community from Kutch who came to Bolton from Uganda, where he lost his business, house and his personal fortune to Idi Amin. He started a small family business, which he called the 'penny profit' shop, selling vegetables and groceries to a particular clientele, namely others from Kutch, that is, Leva, Kanbi and Patidar Patels, who belonged to a branch of the Swaminarayan movement. Their women, he claimed, had a reputation for being discerning buyers. His reasoning was that by attracting these customers, he acquired a name for selling good quality vegetables and spices and that this would help spread his reputation and thus enlarged his clientele. Once he established a clientele, his success was assured. His reasoning proved sound and his business expanded and is still expanding with the result that today his family manages one of the town's most successful businesses.

The development of members of caste and sect communities into a consumer role depends upon their ability to acquire property, the accumulation of skills, the development of a social identity, a style of life supported by education/training, connubial, commensality and status conventions. To this extent the development of communities is arguably a form of anti-racism, because they are a consequence of and a reaction to a racist situation. More importantly, they symbolise the change from an ethnic community that is constrained to one which is unconstrained and can develop into a free consumer. In a sense the social process of becoming a consumer is a relational one, that is, ethnicity becomes the mechanism for separating consumers and their ability to gain access to external markets. To achieve this end in a racialised situation depends, in turn, upon the power of a community to protect its access to its internal markets in relation to others by enhancing its differences from other communities. The social construction of ethnic communities is an exercise in the construction of ethnic space in relation to other ethnic communities and to the white community. The hierarchy freedom comprises an intermeshing of the horizontal and vertical relations between those who have more power and privilege (freedom) than others do and those that have similarly less freedom (Bauman, 1988). These different castes, sect and ethnic communities combine or separate according to the inclusiveness or exclusiveness of their social identities; and the context in which this is most likely to occur is a political one.

Thus the space over which caste communities have the greatest control is the internal market or private domain and the social exchange of language, women, finances, friendships, support, gifts, and ultimately culture. This space is in opposition to the space they have to share with other communities, namely public (external) space, and in particular with the white community whose members have comparably more power and privilege. The social relationships that are fundamental to ethnic communities are those of kinship and friendship (Werbner, 1989), because it is through them that social exchanges take place.

I shall focus mainly on those of friendship and in particular close friendship, because they are the fundamental relationships which facilitate the social exchange of women, gifts, language, scarce resources and culture. Close friendship implies social equality. Therefore, it provides the social relationships which structure the internal markets that provide the medium through which members can maintain 'their conduct of everyday life' (Weber, 1978: 390).

Close friendship: a strong tie

Many social relationships link Gujaratis to each other and to members of other communities; some of these are based upon social equality. One such is friendship. It is important to separate the role from the social characteristics of the relationship. In terms of the former, by the term friendship I mean individuals who are paired in the same role (friend/friend). Friendship is a voluntary role. As a voluntary role its affective content is dependent upon a 'sense of worth' (Briggs in Paine, 1969). The implication is that friendships can cross social divides between social class and race. Friendship occurs within an ascribed role such as a kinship relationship: in other words, kin can be friends. An assumption that underlies this argument is that those who share a similar set of deeply held social attitudes, values and beliefs are also those who share similar social positions in a society. 'Similarities in status, attitudes, beliefs, and behaviour facilitate the formation of intimate (or consensual) relationships among incumbents of social positions' (Laumann, 1979:386); stated simply, 'like attracts like'.

Close friendship overrides differences of social inequality. It differs from other social relationships in terms of four social characteristics. These, Paine (1969:519) suggested, are autonomy (as opposed to ascription), unpredictability (as opposed to routinisation) and terminality (as opposed to open-endedness). By comparison a kinship relationship differs from that of friendship in that it is ascribed, routinised, open-ended and public. Though friendship relationships share these social characteristics, it is necessary to distinguish between categories of friendship: close friendship differs from acquaintanceship on the grounds that the latter is regarded as neither a relationship of confidence or intimacy but is terminal, private, unpredictable and autonomous. It may develop into close friendship, but it also may not. There is a category of friendship which lies in between these two extremes; I shall refer to it as ordinary friendship. An egocentred social network is defined as one which comprises all those people to whom ego refers as his/her friends, that is, people ranging from close friend to acquaintance. An egocentred social network can be regarded as being socially constructed in terms of a number of separate zones each comprising different categories of friends. It is possible for an individual to have as close friends two individuals who dislike or even hate one another. What is important to this model of a network is ego's decision to have them as close friends, not their decisions not to have each other as close friends. Most of the sample organised their friendships according to these social categories (Chapter Five).

Friendship differs from other relationships such as that of colleague in that relationships between colleagues are structured first and foremost by the organisation for which they work. Thus the formation of friendship assumes that a work-based relationship, or any other form of relationship, could develop into a friendship. Friendship is not easily distinguishable from kinship using the above mentioned social characteristics, but more simply implies that social interaction in the privacy of homes exposes individuals in a way that is not characteristic of more public relationships. What is important to friendships, particularly close friendships, are the number of friends, their social identities, their geographical accessibility, the frequency of contact, the places where they meet, and their social standing. In addition to these characteristics which derive from friendship as opposed to some other relationship, the structural characteristics of the organisation of these friendships impose certain characteristics upon the network. This implies that it is possible to organise friendships in different ways. The analysis of social networks needs to take account of the social characteristics of the friends and the characteristics of the way in which they are organised.

Form this point of view a social network is 'a specific set of linkages among a defined set of persons, with the additional property that the characteristics of these linkages as a whole may be used to interpret the social behaviour of the persons involved' (Mitchell, 1971:2). From the point of view of the network anchorperson (ego) the individuals in the social network are definable in such a manner that they are not confused with persons who lie outside it. It is this information that enables the actor to make abstractions about his (her) network as compared with the networks of others (Niemeijer, 1973:50). An egocentred social network is one in which social relations are organised around an anchorperson (Boissevain, 1974; 1968). Radiating out from the actor are direct, reciprocal relationships with a unique set of individuals whom he refers to as kin, close friends and friends of lesser degree, such as ordinary friends and acquaintances. As an actor creates his (her) own social network, both actor and observer can regard it as being a bounded group.[2] A social network is an organisation which is structured by an individual to provide access to resources, which include friendship, social belonging, a social identity, a channel for controlling incoming and outgoing information, and ideas about what are appropriate attitudes, values, beliefs and forms of social behaviour.

An egocentred network comprises ideally a model consisting of a structure of layers of friends who are similarly linked to ego (the anchor point), but who are also linked into other similar social networks. Furthermore, in the model, each layer separates one form of friends from another; so kin who are close friends are separated from close friends, ordinary friends and acquaintances. This analysis will concentrate mainly on egocentred social networks and in particular on the layer or zone, which is referred to here as the primary zone, in which are to be found close friends. Therefore, social networks need to be analysed in terms of social and structural characteristics; the former includes size and reachability, the latter includes network density, intensity of relationships and network connectedness. The analysis will begin with the former and then progress to the latter.

A social network is a structured system by which and through which people can either influence ego, the anchor point, or ego can reach people, or information or resources held by people. Reachability is a social process by which individuals influence or are influenced by members of their social networks (P.Mayer, 1962; to an extent Bott, 1971), or control or open their access to new ideas and assistance provided by others (Lin *et al,* 1982; Granovetter, 1973; Erbe, 1977; Coleman, Katz and Menzel, 1977; Laumann, 1973; Laumann and Pappi, 1976). This analysis of social networks is concerned with how others promote or control access of anchor points (individuals) to others or to information. These social networks are egocentred. This usage of reachability refers to the overall effects of the social and structural characteristics of a social network. It differs from that defined by Mitchell (1971:15-17) on the grounds that it separates the social characteristics of network participants from the structural relationships that connect them. Consequently, Mitchell's use of the term reachability is akin to my usage of the notion of connectedness, which he defines as the number of steps an anchor point has to take to reach his close friends. Therefore, reachability, as used here, refers to the overall social characteristics of those who comprise the network and the social relationships which link or tie them together in helping or hindering the anchor points in their reaching others or being reached by others. In an ethnic context, reachability is concerned with the accessibility of Gujaratis to influences and information and to those outside who control scarce resources. The first part of this analysis will focus on the social characteristics of close friends, namely ethnic identity, geographical proximity, frequency of contact, places of contact (multilocality), and social standing, and the second part will concentrate on the structural characteristics, that is density, intensity and connectedness.

Reachability is a complex concept comprising a number of elements, which facilitate or impede access to resources through others.

In his seminal analysis of the social exchange of power, Blau (1967) observed that those in power are unlikely to form relationships with those who are powerless on the grounds that such a relationship would jeopardise the power base of the former. The issue raised is whether it would enhance the position of the powerless to unite with others who are powerless, or to establish ties with the powerful? Lin (1982) argues that the former would strengthen the position of the weak, because they could concentrate their strength through controlling social exchanges. Much of the 'politics' of immigration was concerned with integration, which implies uniting with the strong. The fact that such a relationship is unacceptable to the powerful, as Blau (1967) argued, is overlooked. What is accepted superficially is that friendship with white people can be interpreted as a sign of such integration. However, this line of argument overlooks the class differences between those in power and those who labour under them. Furthermore, what is critical to this analysis is the degree of friendship: a relationship based upon acquaintanceship carries very different demands from that imposed by close friendship. Therefore, I shall argue that by establishing close friendships with Gujaratis, Gujaratis could form a closed community, and by doing this were able to offer some resistance to racism and racialisation. In the political climate of the 1970s, Gujaratis transformed religious organisations into power bases by becoming consumers as opposed to the exploitable by investing in close friendships with Gujaratis. While residential proximity gave them the opportunity for frequent and intense social contact, it was done at the expense of overriding the social rewards that might be brought by the freedom to associate with close friends belonging to different ethnic groups and different social classes. An analysis of reachability depends upon the ethnic identity of close friends, their places of residence, frequency and places of contact and freedom of association.

Size impinges upon all aspects of network analysis. Not all those sampled had or chose to identify their close friends. These individuals are excluded from this part of the analysis. A more detailed discussion of size is to be found in the following Chapter. What is important about close friends is how they can help one another gain access to information, support, opportunities or resources. To analyse these social characteristics of networks, I shall employ the concept of reachability (see above).

Ethnic identity

An individual's ethnic identity is defined in terms of the identity which they recognise as most important to them. They define themselves first and foremost as Gujaratis, and then as Muslims or Hindus. For the purposes of this analysis, where all a Gujaratis's close friends are Gujaratis, irrespective of whether they are Hindu or Muslim, I shall describe the zone as being homogeneous. However, where a zone includes one or more close friend(s) who are either white, Sikh, Parsee, Pakistani or West Indian, I shall describe the zone as being heterogeneous.

Overall, ninety Muslim respondents identified 530 Muslim close friends and 145 Hindus identified 857 Hindu close friends. An analysis of close friends in primary zones showed that the majority of close friends of Gujarati respondents belonged to the same ethnic and generally to the same religious groups as they did (Table 4.1). As a percentage of the total number of zones, 76.7% (69) of Muslim and 71.7%

(104) of Hindu zones were homogeneous. Only five of these Muslims included a Hindu amongst their close friends (one had two Hindu close friends). Only eight Hindus included a Muslim close friend amongst their close friends. The majority of Gujaratis sampled anchored homogeneous zones. The sparseness of Muslim close friends in Hindu anchored zones and vice versa points to the strength of Gujaratis' commitment to their religious groups. It is this commitment which gives these religious groups the properties of status groups. The remaining zones comprised heterogeneous zones with close friends belonging to the same and different communities to the anchor points. These close friends are to be found in 21 (23.2%) of Muslim and 41 (28.3%) of Hindu anchored zones, thus accounting for 30.8% of Muslim and 35.1% of Hindu close friends. At first sight this analysis suggests that almost a third of Gujaratis sampled established close friendships across ethnic communities, and that Hindus are more prepared to accept into close friendship members of other communities than are Muslims.

Table 4.1
Close friends in homogeneous and heterogeneous network zones*

Muslim anchored zones:

	Homogeneous		Heterogeneous		Totals	
Respondents	69	76.7%	21	23.2%	90	100%
Close friends	367	69.2%	163	30.8%	530	100%

Hindu anchored zones:

	Homogeneous		Heterogeneous		Totals	
Respondents	104	71.7%	41	28.3	145	100%
Close friends	556	64.9%	301	35.1%	857	100%

* Muslims (14) and Hindus (9) who have no close friends have been excluded.

Frequency of contact

The frequency of contact between close friends is influenced by their geographical proximity and the places where they meet. Two models of such networks are recognised. The first suggests that where close friends share the same geographical environment they increase their opportunities for social contact while decreasing their range of access to scarce resources. By living in the same environment, they share similar social experiences. Thus they disadvantage themselves, since those contributing to a shared pool of knowledge bring nothing new to it. When this is taken together with a high frequency of contact, the combination creates a social environment in which close friends exert a conforming influence upon one another (Hart, 1970/71:84-87; also Mayer, 1962). The second model suggests that where close friends are spread over a wide geographical area they have opportunities to draw on a wider range of social experiences arising from different social environments (Erbe, 1977). This allows individuals to become receptive to new influences and ideas. A strategy, arguably, which would advantage members of a minority community, would be to invest in social relationships within their community, thereby increasing the strength of their ties to it and to the resources in them (Lin, 1982: 134-135). By living in relatively close proximity, Gujaratis strengthen their social, economic and political commitment to each other, and in so doing they create a safe environment (Smith, 1984:360). Thus the community becomes physically, socially, and ideologically closed, secure and ethnic supportive.

An analysis of the geographical locations of close friends of those sampled reveals that the majority resides in the same town and ward as the respondents. The majority of close friends of Muslims (75%) and Hindus (76%) live in Bolton; a minority of 22% are resident elsewhere in Britain and the remaining 2%-3% live overseas (Tables 4.2 and 4.3). Excluding the close friends who live outside the Bolton Metropolitan boundary, the pattern of residence of close friends who live in Bolton matches the pattern of residence of those sampled (Chapter Two). Some 65% of close friends of Hindus live in poor wards, 17% in below average wards and 5% in average and above wards. The close friends of Muslims live in similar areas: 73% in poor wards, 17% in below average wards and 4% in average and above wards. As Gujaratis live in similar socio-economic areas to their close friends, the social process of sharing experiences serves to strengthen their view of their disadvantaged position. This concentration of people whose close friends live around them was a consequence of chain migration, which delivered members of a family and locally based caste to a particular place in Britain. Thus, it is not surprising that only 22% of close friends of these Gujaratis lived in towns and cities elsewhere in Britain. Although there has been some movement of the population since the 1970s, it is not as great as might be expected; where it has taken place it seems to have been from members of a chain located in one place to members of the same chain residing elsewhere. No analysis of the ethnic populations in the five large conurbations reflects the kind of detail that would show how chain migration has created a bricolage of caste communities which from the outside appear to be relatively homogeneous, aside from religious differences. Social relationships between caste members are maintained through social and religious occasions, such as naming ceremonies, weddings, funerals and other major religious festivals, most of which involve some form of gift giving (Werbner, 1989).

Although relatively recent settlers might be expected to maintain relationships with kin living overseas, only a minority of respondents mentioned having close friends who lived overseas. Virtually as many close friends of Hindus (2.2%) as Muslims (2.8%) live overseas. Of these, the majority live in India with smaller numbers living in Canada and the USA. Irrespective of the ethnic community to which they belong, their presence has little effect on a person's close friends here. Analysis showed that few kin were included amongst the close friends of those sampled (Chapter Five). One explanation might be that in the urban industrial context an immigrant's dependence upon friends increases with the time they have lived here and as the differences between kin and friends becomes more apparent. There is also the matter of the need to be literate to keep in touch with people and much of this sample have difficulty reading and writing Gujarati. In a way, the fact that most close friends are locally-based and that only a few live overseas supports the argument that 'like attracts like'. Furthermore, by recruiting their close friends locally, the Gujaratis ensured that they all shared to a greater degree a common knowledge of the local situation and this contributed to their use of ethnic politics to exploit the local political situation.

Table 4.2
Frequency of contact between Muslims and their close friends

Frequency of contact	Residence of close friends miles from Bolton							
	Bolton	10	25	50	100	150+	Overseas	Totals
once/week:	380	16	22	4	3	2		427
	71.7%							80.6%
once/month:	3	10	1	2		12		28
								5.3%
once a year	13	9	9	1	11	17	15	75
								14.1%
Total:	396	35	32	7	14	31	15	530
	74.7%							100%

Table 4.3
Frequency of contact between Hindus and their close friends

Frequency of contact	Residence of close friends miles from Bolton							
	Bolton	10	25	50	100	150+	Overseas	Totals
once/week:	603	19	2	1	1			626
	70.4%							73%
once/month:	22	7	2	1	19	18		69
								8.1%
once a year	22	7	10	2	35	67	19	162
								18.9%
Total:	647	33	14	4	55	85	19	857
	75.5%							100%

Geographical proximity influences frequency of contact: undoubtedly, frequent meetings help friends exchange ideas, information and support. Frequency of contact should be separated into two elements; the first concerns the number of times close friends meet and the second concerns the places where close friends meet (multilocality). Contact between friends can either stifle change (Hart, 1970/71; Mayer, 1962) or promote change (Lin, 1982; Erbe, 1977; Bott, 1971). One of the difficulties with these analyses of contact is that often it is unclear what the precise social relationships are between the respondents and those with whom they interact. Granovetter's (1973) now classic analysis of strong and weak ties demonstrated the importance of this distinction. In the present analysis of social networks I have made it clear that I am mainly concerned with strong ties, such as close friendship. Close friendship can develop in a wide variety of social situations allowing, in theory, for a range of personal preferences.

Some 75% of close friends of Muslim respondents are Bolton residents; of these they meet 72% at least once week (Table 4.2) and 3% less often. They meet their remaining close friends, who live outside the town, less often. Muslims, belonging to the same caste community, belonging to the same Islamic sect, and sharing the same areas of residence as their close friends, are likely to meet them frequently in the streets, shops, mosque(s) and on a variety of social and religious occasions. This is a typical pattern of contact for a Muslim community notwithstanding their strong ties with other similar communities elsewhere in Britain and overseas. It points to the formation of a close, if not closed, community.

Although the opportunity for Hindus to share in religious festivals and rituals as a single community is available, the emphasis on caste differences (Ballard *et al*, 1994) should make participation in communal social activities difficult. It might be expected that Hindus might not have the same high degree of frequency of contact with their close friends, because not all members of castes migrated in the same numbers to Britain. Thus some castes are better represented here than are others. Consequently, they will either confine their friendships to kin or establish relationships with non-kin who belong to other castes. Across-caste friendships threaten caste relationships, since Hindus may choose to see such relationships as relationships that may bring them into conflict with their caste commitments. These in-built tensions add to the difficulty of across caste friendships.

Despite these potential difficulties, most (73%) close friends of Hindus meet weekly of whom 71% are Bolton residents (Table 4.3). Some 6% of close friends resident in Bolton and the remaining 24% of friends, who live outside Bolton, meet less often. Although Hindus are divided by caste in a way that Muslims are not, they (Hindus) still meet their close friends as frequently as do Muslims. The Hindu pattern of contact points to close friendships across caste communities, which suggests that social relationships which underpin caste differences are separated from those of close friendship. Since they do not recognise a single community centre, this implies that they meet at work, at home or in some other less public situation, that is, in locations and situations where they are less likely to breach their caste rulings, such as public houses and the cinema. As with Muslims (14%), only a few close friends (19%) were seen once a year and most of these live outside Bolton. This pattern of contact amongst Hindus suggests that they too form a close, if not closed, community.

As Brooks and Singh (1978/79) argued, Gujarati communities separate most easily and publicly into two large but closed religious and social communities. The roles of the Hindu and Muslim social and religious institutions that form a central part of their lives are dissimilar and contrasting. The mosque holds a key position in the social, cultural and political life of the Islamic community. Muslims go to mosque to pray, to pay dues, to bring the dead for preparation for the burial, to hear pronouncements on what is or is not appropriate behaviour, and to debate political decisions on issues affecting the mosque and its community. In contrast to the central role of the mosque, the role of the temple among Hindus is peripheral to their lives. With no overall religious structure to unite them, most temples serve the socio-religious needs of the members of specific castes and sects. They enhance rather than diminish caste differences. Members of a temple have frequent contact with members of their own castes and sects, but they have less contact with members of the wider Hindu community. Arguably this pattern of social contact intensifies the social control that members of castes and sects exercise over their members at the expense of the development of some form of wider unity. Though the aim of the founders of the VHP was to create a multi-caste facility, the strength of the commitment of Hindus to their caste identities prevented it from becoming a focal point for its members.

An analysis of the places where people meet (multilocality) illustrates the importance of the mosque and temple in the daily lives of these Gujaratis. An analysis of the places where respondents meet their close friends (Table 4.4) shows that there are more places outside their homes where Muslims could meet their close friends than seemed to be possible for Hindus to meet their close friends. When asked where they meet, most of the Muslims sampled quickly pointed to the mosque as one of the obvious places where they meet friends. Hindus who belonged to different caste communities also often attended different temples and belonged to different sects. For them to find places to meet was more difficult, because the places either had to be more public for Hindus or had to be more private, that is, where the Hindu clientele might be more restricted. Having said this, a number of Hindus went to public houses in the evenings and they were drawn from different castes. This pattern of contact suggests that Muslims have the infrastructure to support a more public and community orientated life than do Hindus. The data supported this view; the most significant difference between these two religious communities is that a third (30) Muslims meet their close friends between 4 - 6.69 times/places/week as compared to only 9 Hindus. The majority of Hindus (117, 80.7%) of Hindus meet their close friends between 1 to 2.29 times/places/week compared with 43.3% (39). The data would seem to support the argument that close friendships across castes were in the 1970s relatively uncommon. It did point to Muslims having a higher degree of contact with their close friends and therefore providing a social basis for a socially close community. Generally most of the more public places, like public houses, attract disapproval from Muslims, because they regard them as places where they are tempted to drink and gamble, that is, to break with some of the rules of Islam. The general expression of disapproval by Muslims of such places does not mean that individuals will not visit them and other public places of entertainment. On the one hand, this analysis supports the view that at one level the Gujaratis separate along religious lines in their everyday life; on the other hand, there are opportunities for Hindus and Muslims to meet and also to meet members of other ethnic and white communities. For Muslims to meet close friends so frequently suggests that the social and religious activities of this community, its members and their families are closely enmeshed in close and overlapping social networks. Community social control and conformity can only be strengthened by such frequent contact. In comparison, Hindu respondents have less contact with their close friends. Caste differences and to a lesser extent religious differences contribute to the few places where they can meet socially without jeopardising their caste status. This pattern of contact suggests that the social control by caste communities remains untouched, or if anything, it may be strengthened, by Hindus not admitting to meeting members of other castes in private or public places. In a negative sense this suggests that there is no united Hindu community.

Table 4.4
Degree of multilocality among Muslim and Hindu close friends

Muslims zones	Number of places where close friends meet						
	0-0.9	1-1.9	2-2.9	3-3.9	4-4.9	5-5.9	6-6.9	Total
No.		10	29	21	18	10	2	90
%		11.1	32.2	23.3	20	11.1	2.2	100

Hindus Zones	Number of places where close friends meet						
	0-0.9	1-1.9	2-2.9	3-3.9	4-4.9	5-5.9	6-6.9	Total
No.	1	60	57	18	6	2	1	145
%	0.7	41.4	39.3	12.4	4.1	1.4	0.7	100

Social standing and freedom of association

The high frequency of contact between close friends who belong to the same castes or sects in a range of different places suggests that they should have a wide range of friends from different walks of life within the Gujarati population. The reverse implies that where Gujaratis have a limited range of places for meeting and conform to principles of their castes and sects, they should meet friends from a narrow range of social backgrounds. What is also possible is that a social class effect will influence the selection of close friends, 'like attracting like', and that Gujaratis will befriend those Gujaratis who belong to the same social classes as they do. The analysis has already demonstrated that the majority of close friends of Gujaratis are Gujaratis. In the 1970s most Gujaratis were encapsulated within the working class, disadvantaged by their racial visibility, their inability to communicate, their lack of qualifications, their low position in the class structure and their lack of formal political power (Solomos, 1989; Miles, 1982; Rex and Tomlinson, 1979:120-126; Banton, 1972:72). To improve their access to better jobs and to politically influential people, close friendship provided them with a social bridge between themselves and those in occupations of high social standing within their own communities. As an aspect of reachability, social association provides a measure of social class mobility within the Gujarati population. On the one hand, the higher an individual's position within the social class system, the higher are the social positions of their friends and therefore the easier is their access to information, power and wealth (Lin, 1982:132-135; Blau, 1967:133-140). On the other hand, Gujaratis at the bottom of the social class structure have as Gujarati close friends those who are in the same class position as themselves. They have little access to information that might lead to changes in their social positions.

Furthermore, the social class position of Gujaratis could have changed in a number of ways since their arrival in the early 1950s. For instance, the first jobs available to them were of low status, little skill and low pay (Castles *et al*, 1984; Miles and Phizacklea, 1984; Constantinides, 1977:279-282). Much of immigrant folklore is built around the notion of starting low and being able and free to rise to the top in the adopted society (Dorson, 1959:135-165). Thus occupations held by Gujaratis by the 1970s, some ten to fifteen years after coming here, provide a useful indication of their social standing in British society (Goldthorpe, 1981/82; 1980).[3] An analysis of the social standing of Gujaratis sampled and their close friends provides a pattern of social association that shows the extent to which close friendships cross social class boundaries. It provides a measure of social mobility.

As first generation migrants, the Gujaratis sampled achieved limited access to jobs of high social standing; the majority held jobs as manual waged workers employed mainly in the textile industry in semi- and unskilled grades (Chapter Two above, also Golden, 1996). Using Goldthorpe's classification of occupations, the social standing of Muslims' and Hindus' close friends are analysed in relation to those sampled (Tables 4.5a and b; 4.6a and b). Generally Gujaratis sampled have close friends who are of similar social standing. An analysis of Muslims' anchored homogeneous zones shows that overall a similar percentage of respondents hold jobs in social class VII and Other (78.3%) as do their close friends (84.5%). However, the distribution of close friends across the sample shows that 55.3% had only close friends who belonged to the same social classes as they do. Some 30% of close friends belonged to social classes higher than those sampled and only 15% belonged to lower social classes. Overall, this points to some social mobility within the Muslim community. Since so few Hindus were identified as close friends, this pattern of friendship across social classes points to the closeness of this religious community.

A different pattern of friendship holds for the Hindu sample. More respondents belonged to Social Class VII and Other (74%) than did their close friends (68.7%) (Table 4.6a). This difference between the social standing of Hindus and their close Hindu friends points to a hint of social mobility within castes. An analysis of social standing of respondents in relation to all their close friends shows that the pattern of friendships is spread more evenly across the social class spectrum than for Muslims. A third of their close friends belonged to social classes higher than the sample, almost 40% belonged to social classes of similar social standing and just under a third belonged to social classes below those of the sample. This suggests that there is considerable social mobility within the Hindu community. An explanation for this might point to a changing association between caste and social class. Caste is still important. This importance holds not only for the arrangement of marriages, but also for friendships. By befriending those within the same caste, Hindus are establishing close friendships with Hindus belonging to the same caste but to different social classes. The homogeneity of these zones points to Hindus having only Hindu or Muslim close friends in these zones. Because they have so few Muslims as close friends, the majority of their close friends are Hindus.

Table 4.5a
Social standing of Muslims' close friends in homogeneous zones*

Social standing of respondents

Classes	respondents		I	II	III	IV	VI	VII	Other	Total
							close friends			
I	1		4	-	-	-	-	-	-	4
II	1		-	-	1	1	-	7	1	10
III	4		-	-	1	3	-	24	2	30
IV	8		1	1	1	8	-	33	10	54
VI	1		1	-	-	-	-	4	-	5
VII	50⌉	78.3%	4	3	4	21	-	190	23	245
Other	4⌋		-	-	-	-	3	16	-	19
Total	69		10	4	7	33	3	274	36	367
								84.5%		

*Classes IVa to IVc are combined into one class in both Tables following Goldthorpe, 1980, and no one had a friend in Social Class V, so this category has been omitted.

Table 4.5b
Summary of Table 4.5a

	Total	above	equal	below
Nos. of close friends:	367	109	203	55
%	100	29.7	55.3	15

Table 4.6a
Social standing of Hindus' close friends in homogeneous zones*

Social standing of: respondents

classes	respondents		I	II	III	IV	V	VI	VII	Other	Total
								close friends			
I	2		7	5	-	-	-	-	-	-	12
II	3		-	3	6	1	-	1	10	1	22
III	8		1	6	8	5	-	5	22	11	58
IV	4		1	1	-	-	-	3	7	8	20
VI	10		-	3	4	8	-	7	28	14	6
VII	62⌉	74%	3	5	16	30	3	26	171	52	306
Other	15⌋		-	1	6	6	-	3	34	24	74
Total	104		12	24	40	50	3	45	272	110	556
									68.7%		

*Classes IVa to IVc are combined into one class in both Tables following Goldthorpe, 1980, and no one had a friend in Social Class V, so this category has been omitted.

Table 4.6b
Summary of Table 4.6a

	Total	above	equal	below
No. of close friends:	556	179	220	157
%	100	32.2	39.6	28.2

A number of further explanations can be offered for these trends. Generally, in what are relatively closed communities, people establish close friendships with others regardless of their social standing. With kinship relationships to support relationships that cross differences in social standing in a social situation that is constrained (racialised), the pressure to overlook class differences is considerable. Moreover, caste and sect relationships provide a supportive social environment for the establishment of friendships within these groups and their organisations. While these patterns of friendship militate against the formation of relationships across caste and sect, they enhance and encourage relationships across social class divisions. Though this pattern of social relationships is becoming increasingly apparent in Hindu caste communities, for Muslims the emphasis is on Islam rather than social class differences. The often-quoted adage states that 'all Muslims are brothers'; Islam lays stress on social equality. Though there is some evidence which points to a belief that Islam can overcome class differences between fellow Muslims, class divisions in contemporary Islam are becoming, if anything, stronger rather than weaker (Gilsenan, 1979: 265). As yet, there is little evidence to support the argument that there is social mobility in these ethnic communities, but this could be explained by their relative youthfulness in the 1970s.

These data point to Gujaratis befriending. There is persuasive evidence which points to Hindu castes investing resources in promoting educational and business opportunities for their members (Ballard et al, 1994) and to the high aspirations held by young Asians (Penn and Scattergood, 1991). Both of the arguments suggest that the potential for social mobility is considerable, but it is unclear how this will affect social relationships between parents and children and between Asian and white. Furthermore, on the one hand, there are documented instances of kin who have acted as patrons controlling access to employment in textile mills; on the other hand there are instances of Gujaratis and other South Asians who have made their fortunes working alone since arriving here as penniless immigrants.

An occupation favoured by Gujaratis is that of becoming self-employed. Both Hindus and Muslims aspire to owning a business, believing that it can bring them wealth and independence without the disadvantages of working with or being employed by people belonging to their own or other communities. In the 1970s it was difficult to estimate the total number of Gujarati businesses in Bolton. The most prominent self-employed people were shopkeepers, providing a wide range of foodstuffs, and there were a number of small Asian businesses both selling and producing household textiles - curtains, bedding, and clothing. There was also a number of Gujaratis who owned shops and factories in Manchester; possibly some of these could be described as being wealthy. It was difficult to identify these people, because as they achieved success, they become increasingly invisible. The success of Asian businesses is itself mercurial and interesting, but it is not relevant to this book.

The presence of close friends from other communities, excluding Gujarati Hindu or Muslim ones, suggests that at this time a limited degree of social association was occurring. This can be confirmed by an analysis of the social standing of the few close friends who belonged to other communities. If social networks facilitate or restrict access of anchor points to information, power and influence, then the presence of close friends belonging to other communities provides an indication of social association across ethnic and the white communities. The above analysis of social standing suggests that close friends who belong to other communities generally do not belong to different social classes from those of their Gujarati close friends. There are at least three patterns of accessibility that can be related to close friendship: firstly, investment in Gujarati close friends; secondly, investment in close friends belonging to other black minority communities; and thirdly, investment in close friends belonging to the white community (see above). As regards the second and third options, only 21 Muslims sampled included one or more close friends who belonged to an ethnic (not Gujarati) or white community.

An analysis of the social standing of the sub-sample of Muslims (Tables 4.7a and b) and Hindus (Tables 4.8a and b) anchoring heterogeneous zones shows marked differences in the structuring of close friendships. Overall the percentages of Muslim respondents (38.1%) and their close friends (54.6%) in Social Classes VII and Other were markedly lower than were those in the same classes anchoring homogeneous zones (Table 4.5a above). This suggests that close friendships with people from other ethnic and the white communities provided social relationships with people of a greater range of social standing than is shown by the analysis of homogeneous zones. This conclusion is supported by an analysis of the social standing of respondents and their close friends, which shows that more of their close friends had higher social standing than those sampled. The presence of a few non-Muslim close friends are not seen to pose a threat to the Gujarati or Islamic social values of these Muslims. None mentioned any such conflict when they were interviewed. However, the extent to which these friendships give Gujaratis access to much sought after resources is more difficult to access.

More importantly, this pattern of close friendship provides one avenue to social mobility. If close friendships with members of other communities are taken as an indication of their potential access to public resources, then these data remain limited. Observation indicates that friendships of lower social intensity, such as acquaintanceship, are used for achieving access to resources. They provide the same opportunity for access with less likelihood of the social identity of the anchor point being compromised. If anything, this pattern of close friendship suggests dissociation rather than association with any community that does not share an Islamic identity, irrespective of whether or not they share similar immigration, racial, social, economic or political experiences. This pattern of dissociation echoes the explanation given for the collapse of CARD (Heineman, 1972), which highlighted the divisiveness of ethnic identity. However, it points to a potential benefit, namely the political power that is generated by a shared Islamic identity, which emerges on occasions, e.g. when Muslims demonstrated against the publication of *Satanic Verses* and their more recent opposition to the film *Border*. The trend amongst Muslims to establish close friendships with Muslims of similar social standing leads to the development of strong social networks based upon shared Islamic social identity. Thus the Muslims form a strong and cohesive community.

Table 4.7a
Social standing of Muslims's close friends in heterogeneous zones*

Social standing of respondents		close friends						
Classes		I	II	III	IV	VII	Other	Total
I	1							
II	-	2	10	7	4	2	11	36
III	4	-	1	9	11	21	7	49
IV	6	-	-	5	6	16	2	29
V	2							
VII	7⎤ 38.1%	3	1	6	6	17	13	46
Other	1⎦	3						3
Total	21	8	12	27	27	56	33	163
						54.6%		

*Both Muslims and Hindus sampled had no close friends in Social Classes V and VI.

Table 4.7b
Summary of Table 4.7a

	Total	above	equal	below
No. of close friends:	163	94	42	27
%	100.1	57.7	25.8	16.6

An analysis of the overall social standing of respondents to close friends shows that 65.9% of Hindus sampled hold jobs that would place them in Social Class VII or Other (Table 4.8a) and that an identical percentage of the their close friends (65.8%) are of similar social standing. This suggests that Hindus have not profited by the establishment of close friendships (strong ties) with people belonging to other ethnic and the white communities. This suggests that some degree of caution needs to be considered when associating social heterogeneity with social diversity in social relationships. Heterogeneity of close friends does not always open access to new social resources. It may do the reverse. Further analysis associating the social standing of respondents with their close friends shows that the majority have the same social standing and that a quarter have a higher social standing and a similar percentage a lower social standing than the respondents. There is much less evidence of social mobility in these Hindu-anchored heterogeneous zones than might be anticipated. The differences between the Muslims and the Hindus, given the relatively small numbers of their ethnically different close friends, emphasises the degree of social mobility amongst the former. A possible explanation for these differences is that Hindus, who have close friends belonging to other ethnic communities, are placing themselves at risk of having to reconcile commitments to their caste values with those of close friendship. While this may not pose any difficulty, in practice community pressure may persuade them to believe that they are marginal men. Gilsenan's observation about social class divides amongst Muslims does not emerge in this study; rather, what does emerge is the notion of Muslims being social equals. Possibly time will change this pattern of social relationships. Amongst the Hindus, caste divisions still seem to be more important than social class differences. An exception is the Sikh leader of the VHP: his occupation placed him in Social Class I. Two of his Hindu and Sikh close friends are in class I, the other Sikh close friends are in class II and the remaining four Sikh close friends are in class IV. This evidence points to a social class divide within the Hindu communities.

Table 4.8a
Social standing of Hindus's close friends in heterogeneous zones*

Social standing of respondents		close friends								
Classes		I	II	III	IV	V	VI	VII	Other	Total
I	4	13	3	-	7	-	-	1	-	24
III	2	-	3	1	-	-	-	4	4	12
IV	2	3	1	4	8	-	-	18	20	54
V	1									
VI	5	1	-	1	1	-	1	2	-	6
VII	18 ⎱ 65.9%	2	1	14	27	-	5	57	26	132
Other	9 ⎰	-	-	5	1	1	-	7	59	73
Total	41	19	8	25	44	1	6	89	109	301
							65.8%			

*Both Muslims and Hindus sampled had no close friends in Social Classes V and VI.

Table 4.8b
Summary of Table 4.8a

	Total	above	equal	below
No. of close friends:	301	88	139	74
%	100	29.2	46.2	24.6

An analysis of the ethnic composition of heterogeneous zones shows how few non-Gujarati close friends were included in close friendships by Gujaratis, thus suggesting that the Gujarati community is a closed one. A detailed analysis of the heterogeneous zones shows that about half of their close friends are Gujaratis who belong to the same religious communities as the respondents and a few belong to the other major religious community (Table 4.9). Half (50.9%) of the close friends of Muslims are Muslims and 65% of close friends of Hindus are Hindus. These data contradict the impression that Hindus are more likely than Muslims to accept

109

as close friends members of other communities. An analysis of the ethnic identities of the remaining close friends of Muslims shows that 17.2% of Muslim close friends are Hindu, 17.8% are white people and a further 14.1% include friends belonging to other ethnic groups. In addition to the 64.8% of Hindus in Hindu anchored heterogeneous zones, 1.3% are Muslim, 22.6% are white friends, and 11.3% are friends who belong to other ethnic communities. Both Muslims and Hindus appear reluctant to accept as close friends people who are not like themselves. Furthermore, the analysis suggests that both are more ready to have white people than Muslims as close friends, and that Muslims are more prepared to have Hindus as close friends than are Hindus to accept Muslims as close friends. Although the VHP had a Sikh as chairperson, only one Hindu respondent had a Sikh as a close friend. Most of the close friends of the Sikh were Sikhs, and he also had two Hindu close friends. It is their presence which makes his zone of close friendship heterogeneous in character. These patterns of friendship suggest that this generation was unwilling to commit itself to establishing strong ties, like that of close friendship, with members of other communities.

Table 4.9
Community identities of close friends in heterogeneous zones

Nos. of: respondents:	Gujarati Muslim	Hindu	White	Pakistani (21) West Indian (1) African (1)	Total
Muslim (21)	83	28	29	23	163
	50.9%	17.2%	17.8%	14.1%	100%
	Gujarati Muslim	Hindu	White	Pakistani (22) West Indian (2) Parsee (1) Sikh (9)	Total
Hindu (41)	4	195	68	34	301
	1.3%	64.8%	22.6%	11.3%	100%

Gujaratis are committed to close friendships with Gujaratis. The data appear to lend support to the argument that Gujaratis comprise two religious communities (Brooks and Singh, 1978/79:22). An analysis shows that there is an even greater reluctance on the part of Gujaratis to establish strong ties with members of other minorities who share similar social disadvantages, which supports the view that Gujaratis comprise one community. Although the apparent probabilities of Gujaratis befriending white people are high, the actual chances of their doing so are low. This analysis suggests that Gujaratis avoid strong ties with white people, possibly with the intention of avoiding relationships which are likely to make them vulnerable to racial harassment and discrimination (Smith, 1976:185). Only two Hindu zones are totally heterogeneous: one anchored to a doctor comprises only one close friend, a white shopkeeper; and the other is that of a student. Neither offers convincing support for an argument that their Gujarati ethnic identities are fragmenting. Only two Muslims have a majority of close friends who are not Gujaratis; these close friends comprise 90% and 70% of their primary zones. One is a qualified chemical engineer and his close friends belong to the same social class as he does. At the time of the survey the other had no job. If anything, these two individuals show that it is difficult for Gujaratis to establish close friendships with people who hold different beliefs and/or belong to different ethnic communities.

Although the heterogeneous zones arguably give these Gujaratis greater access to resources and information by including individuals belonging to ethnic and white communities, an analysis of the social standing of the Muslim anchored zones shows that these close friends were generally of similar and lower social standing than the Muslim and Hindu anchor points (Tables 4.7b and 4.8b above). The social standing of these close friends in Muslim anchored zones is contrary to the high social standing of their Muslim close friends. This supports the explanations that point to the existence social buffers separating Asians from white people (Goldthorpe, 1980: 46ff). These patterns of social association point to an order of social investment. The preference of Muslims and Hindus is to establish strong ties with members of their own communities, then with members of the white community, and only then with members of other minority communities (see Chapter Five). What also is apparent is a strong disinclination on the part of Muslims and Hindus to welcome friendships with Gujaratis who do not share their religious beliefs. Although the high social standing of some Gujarati Hindu respondents and their close friends in Class I, II and III may be interpreted as pointing to the construction of a social class buffer within the ethnic community, the opposite holds for Muslims whose friendships with Muslims cross social class divides. Close friendships with members of other communities point to the possible existence of social buffers, leading to Gujaratis establishing close friendships with people who are of similar or lower social standing to them. These patterns of contact between Muslims and Hindus and their close friends conform to an ideal model of zone characteristics associated with one form of accessibility, namely, investment in social relationships of high intensity within their own communities. These data show that leaders, who act as entrepreneurs or brokers, rely on strong relationships such as close friendships with members of their own community, and by implication establish weak relationships with members of other racial, ethnic and political groups. This supports the argument that those with power and/or wealth are unlikely to commit themselves to a relationship, such as close friendship, with people who do not share similar social standing (Lin, 1982: 132-135; Blau, 1967: 133-140). Generally, members of the white community with power are unlikely to establish close friendships with Gujaratis. The argument is that where like attracts like, the pattern of social relationships that develops out of such interaction will form the basis of a strong and cohesive community structure. Gujaratis prefer to establish close friendships with those with whom they share most in common, that is, those who belong to the same community, accept similar religious beliefs, live close to them and hold jobs of similar social standing. These social characteristics point to an exclusiveness of these Gujaratis and to the exclusiveness of the two religious communities within the larger one.

Within the wider context of Bolton, Gujaratis account for 5.2% of the total population, with Muslims accounting for about 3% and Hindus about 2.2%, and with smaller ethnic minorities, such as the Pakistanis and West Indians, comprising less than 0.3% of the total population. By choosing to invest in close friendships with those most like themselves, Gujaratis separated themselves from the white community and the other ethnic minority groups. Observation suggests that West Indians, who form one of the smallest communities in the town, also have the closest and highest number of affinal relationships and close friendships with members of the white community. Although this has not impeded their access to funds for a community centre and cricket ground, they shifted their argument from the needs of their ethnic community to those of black people. By socially separating themselves from other ethnic communities, Gujaratis believed that they could control who had access to social information about themselves, that is, they can see without being seen. In a racialised society, heterogeneity of friends is not always advantageous and may even act as an impediment to the attempts of a community to improve their opportunities to access scarce resources.

The next Chapter will concentrate on the structural and perceptual aspects of these social networks. It will focus on how Gujaratis organise their close friendships and therefore influence the social relationships between close friends. The analysis will begin by considering Gujarati definitions of friendship.

Notes

1. For a recent updated summary of network analysis, see Knoke and Kuklinski, 1993.
2. This is a crucial definition. I use the term bounded in the sense that the actor perceives his close friends to form a bounded/ exclusive group. The intensity of close friendships marks off close friend from less intense forms of acquaintanceship, such as ordinary friendship, and acquaintanceship.
3. This version of the Hope-Goldthorpe scale is based upon a collapsed version of their more elaborate 36 class categories of 'Social Standing' or 'General Desirability of Occupations' (Goldthorpe, 1981/82:9).

   I   Professional, administrative and managerial, higher.
   II   Professional, administrative and managerial, lower.
   III   Routine non-manual.
   IVa   Proprietors & self-employed with employees.
   IVb   Proprietors & self-employed without employees.
   IVc   Farmers & smallholders.
   V   Lower & technical supervisory.
   VI   Skilled non-manual.
   VII   Semi-skilled & unskilled manual.
   Other unemployed, apprentices, students, retired.

5 Social perceptions and common-sense racism

The analysis of close friendship and social network zones showed the complexity of close friendship amongst Gujaratis (Chapter Four). While there is some indication of social mobility across social class in the Muslim anchored zones, there is much less evidence to support such a conclusion for the Hindu anchored zones. The conclusion drawn was that the Muslim community could sustain social mobility within itself and even the few close friends who were not Muslims belonged to higher social classes than did most Muslims themselves. However, for Hindus the conclusion drawn is that caste acts as a containing factor; thus Hindus tend to establish close friendships with Hindus of similar social standing. If anything, it is possible that class formations are developing within castes. Generally, the principle that like-attracts-like holds.

Furthermore, the analysis reveals a contradiction that is, present in racial situations. The pattern is for Gujaratis, who are disadvantaged, to befriend those in the white community who are often of similarly low social standing. The social selection of close friends is reflected in the structural characteristics of social networks and in their perceptions of the social distances that separate them from others. The social characteristics of close friends, the construction of social distances between communities, and the structural characteristics of the social networks together form the basis for the social construction of a hierarchy of social identities. This hierarchy provides a social map of social relationships that connect Gujaratis to their families, castes, sects, religious and ethnic communities and ultimately to British citizenship. It is an idealised construction that maps ranging from the most specific social identity to the most general, that is, from the ethnic world of the exploited to that of the globalised consumerism.

The aim of this Chapter is to explore the space, in particular the ethnic political space, that separates some communities within the Gujaratis population on the basis of their perceptions of social distances. The identification and definition of this space is symbolised by labels, which when taken together provide common sense explanations for racism (defined below). The spaces between Gujaratis and the white community physically, socially and politically separate the constrained from the free, the exploited from the consumer, the racialised from the racialiser. The bridging of these spaces imply that the exploited becomes consumer. Living within a defined area of the town and defined as at one-time immigrants and later as ethnic minority and/or black, they are visible to the state (Chapter One). Therefore, for those held up by racialised barriers, whatever can be hidden from sight enhances their perception of power, while that which can be seen, reduces their freedom (Bauman, 1988:41-48). In an all-seeing world, power and freedom lie with those who have privacy; for those who cannot hide, there is little privacy and freedom. Consumerism is a course of action, which allows the powerful to buy out the exceptional from the lower echelons of the constrained. However, as Bauman notes, individuals in a racial or ethnic group cannot be bought out (Bauman, 1988:98; Dench in Baumann, 1986). The logic of this argument leads one to suggest then that if an individual member of such a group cannot be freed by consumerism, then the group as a whole have to buy themselves out of a constrained state. To achieve this end, an ethnic community (group) has to establish itself as a consumer; this means that it has to achieve privacy. In Chapters One and Two the argument is made that the racialised state is one which seeks to control all aspects of migrant labour. To this extent state power is all seeing but not seen. This Chapter argues that with the formation of status groups within the ethnic community the Gujaratis had the resources to begin to oppose racism by contesting their status through the use of labels used to redefine space that separates the constrained consumer from the unconstrained consumer.

The first step for Gujaratis to challenge these constraints was to conceal knowledge about themselves. They did this by recognising the existence of two bodies of social knowledge that bridge this space. Firstly, I refer to knowledge about them as private, because it is the part of ethnic everyday life that Gujaratis could conceal. Secondly, I describe shared knowledge as public and this includes racist ideologies. The hierarchy of Gujarati social identities forms a continuum that can be arranged in terms of those which are perceived by Gujaratis as being socially close and specific (private), and those which are perceived as socially distant and more generalised (public). The former include ideas about the social distances between kin, close friends, and friendships of lesser intensity, and the latter include ideas about distances between Hindus and Muslims, between Hindus or Muslims and Pakistanis, white people, West Indians and Sikhs. These two notions of social distances underlie Gujarati ideas about what is private and public knowledge, and they are underpinned by a structure of social networks which form the basis of these communities (Laumann, 1973). These two dimensions of social interaction come together in social situations enabling Gujaratis to define social identities. This Chapter explores the social construction of a Gujarati hierarchy of social identities.

Common-sense racism is a set of recipes, embedded in an ideology of the state, which act as explanations for social behaviour, resulting in discrimination against certain others on the grounds of colour, culture and race. Discrimination deprives those being discriminated against in varying degrees of their freedom. While committed members of an ethnic or racial community 'cannot 'buy themselves out' of the group burdened with deprivations' (Bauman, 1988:98), those in other less privileged communities may be able to do so. Opposition to racism implies that, if individuals cannot buy themselves out or be bought out, then group as a whole has to buy itself out. Until it achieves new status as a consumer and producer, the group is not only unable to have equal access to scarce resources, but also its members have to consume the products produced by the more advantaged groups. This requires that they develop a body of knowledge based upon past and present experiences of racism, which enables the group to establish a social identity with or without the support of other disadvantaged communities. These differences are not only made explicit through social relationships, as the analysis of social network relationships demonstrates, but they are also made explicit through the construction of social identities. The pattern of the hierarchy of social identities is an arrangement based upon notions of power, and not always hidden power (Willis, 1979).

To develop privacy an ethnic community has to contain knowledge about itself; the first step is the social construction of perceptions, which define social distances between their members and those of other communities, and the second step is to embed this social construction in social relationships. The structure of social network zones should reflect these characteristics. If, as Laumann observes, the social structure of a community is defined 'as a persisting pattern of social relationships among social positions' (1973:3-4), then the social structure of Gujarati communities can be conceived as incorporating the construction of a private domain. This Chapter is divided into three sections. The first will analyse Gujaratis' social perceptions of kinship and friendship; the second section will analyse the structural characteristics of the primary zones of their social networks and the final section will consider the social construction of a hierarchy of social identities.

Social perceptions of kin, caste and community

Most people differentiate between three categories of friends, namely best or close friends, ordinary friends and acquaintances (La Gaipa, 1977). In urban contexts what changes are the social values that are placed upon these categories of friendship, that is, they become increasingly seen as negotiable. Gujaratis refer to these friends as *kas dost* (close friend), *dost* (ordinary friend) and *aurkhan* or *pichan* (acquaintance). With the addition of kin, Gujaratis distinguish between these relationships in terms of five social attributes, namely: can rely on, can trust, can obtain help from, receive respect from, and receive sympathy from. Although kin have separate roles from those of friends, as Gluckman (1971: xxv) reminds us, 'blood is thicker than water'. Hindus perceive kin and close friends as sharing most of the attributes of reliability, help, trust, respect and sympathy (80%). Both can be almost equally relied upon, with kin being regarded as trustworthy but less helpful than close friends (Table 5.1). They expect kin to show more respect and sympathy than close friends. What is striking about these perceptions is the dramatic distinction Hindus draw between, on the one hand, kin and close friends and, on the other hand, ordinary friends and acquaintances. Less than 15% considered ordinary friends as reliable and trustworthy, although 40% thought that they could be helpful and over 60% believed that they would offer respect and sympathy. The distinction Hindus draw between ordinary friends and acquaintances shows that such relationships carry little immediate social value; they are weak ties. An explanation for this pattern of perceptions lies in the social structure of caste communities. If caste members are the people with whom a Hindu can interact as a social equal, that is, accept food, then it stands to reason that most of their friendships will be with members of this group. It comprises kin, affines and people who are unrelated by blood or marriage with whom a Hindu can establish friendships (Mayer, 1973a: 4). A close friend is a logical extension of existing relationships in a caste community.

Table 5.1
Social attributes of friendship

Muslim respondents

	rely %	trust %	help %	respect %	sympathy %
Kin	79	83	84	95	94
Close friend	78	81	80	90	91
Ordinary friend	33	30	48	82	83
Acquaintance	22	21	28	72	74

Hindu respondents

	rely %	trust %	help %	respect %	sympathy %
Kin	81	90	90	98	98
Close friend	80	85	92	97	97
Ordinary friend	14	13	39	65	72
Acquaintance	5	5	18	31	45

Amongst Hindus, kin help arrange marriages and, if they are able, contribute financial help to the wedding. Although most Gujaratis rely on kin in Britain and Gujarat to find them or their children acceptable partners, it is the caste that has the power to divide kin from kin through exercising its power to outcasteing members. The Parmir caste association outcaste a member, thereby severing his and his immediate family's relationships with their kin, and destroying the imminent marriage of his daughter (see Chapter Seven). In Britain parents choose not to impress on their children the social importance of caste relations until they reach marriageable age. Then they sometimes use it to impose their authority on their children by introducing new constraints on choice of partners and by submerging their children in a state of dependence on kin from which it is difficult for them to escape (Taylor, 1976). Thus kin are used as a form of social control in a way that close friends cannot be used. An anecdote that illustrates this point concerned a Hindu who needed money to buy a public house. He approached kin on both sides of his family for financial support to buy the rights to the management of a public house. As his own brother earned too little to help, he asked his maternal cousin for support, as he always seemed to have money. He also approached his uncles and paternal cousins, who lived in Bolton, Bilston in the Midlands and London. He told me that, only if he could not raise sufficient money from them, would he turn to his close friends for help. On two occasions he referred to me as a close friend and then asked me if I could lend him a couple of hundred pounds. On a previous occasion he had borrowed £500 from a maternal cousin, which replicated a similar transaction between their fathers in Gujarat. When this man negotiated the purchase of a post office (prior to his purchase of a public house), he again asked his cousin for money. On this occasion the maternal cousin said that his father would first collect the money owed him by the father of his cousin. Both were aware that he was unable to pay back the money. By doing this, the maternal cousin threatened the social status of his cousin's father, and thus put pressure on his cousin to return the money that he and his father owed them. Kin exercise social control over kin; these elements of social control are not part of friendship relationships. Hindus are more dependent upon kin than close friends.

Such negotiations are everyday occurrences. Furthermore, as these Gujaratis prefer to buy their homes outright and could not expect and preferred not to receive support from banks and building societies, such transactions between kin · formed the principal means by which they could amass sufficient resources. Such complex negotiations can only exist in a society where kinship relationships are well defined. The only major difference is that kin are considered to be more likely to offer help than are close friends, because kinship carries sanctions, reciprocal and moral, that friendship does not (Fortes, 1970). Friendship is utilised where kinship is not available or to supplement it. While this example may show that Hindus perceive of an overlap between the social obligations and expectations of kin and close friends, this should not be taken as evidence that they confuse the roles of these two categories of people. Analysis of those they define as close friends shows that Hindus include more kin as close friends than Muslims. Furthermore, these examples demonstrate that Hindus can have pressure placed on them through the mobilisation of kin, but this pressure cannot be extended to close friends. Consequently, no Hindu can afford to risk alienating kin.

An indication of the differences in social values attached to kinship and close friendship is illustrated by the following anecdote told by a Mandhata Patel, who attended the wedding in West Bromwich of a son of a member of his caste association. Kin of both the bride and bridegroom's families received invitations to the wedding. However Mandhata Patels, who were not invited to the wedding, but who came from villages linked by *ekadas* to those of the young couple, attended the occasion. They were expected to give the newly wedded couple a gift, but it was formalised, that is, they gave a token gift of one pound, and their names were written down in a book containing the names of all the guests. A distinction is drawn between close kin and not so close kin. The perceived overlap between kin and close friend relationships may incorporate more distant kin as well as non-kin, consequently one might not expect to find many of them having close friends of whom their kin disapproved. The perceived social closeness between kin and close friend points to members of caste communities seeing each other as socially close, that is, close enough for social relationships between members to act as a form of social control. However, there are no similar social controls between people who are not caste members, that is, they are not necessarily perceived as social equals, nor can they exert any form of social control as close friends. The expectations and obligations associated with ordinary friends and acquaintances is low and reflects a high degree of social distance separating them from kin and close friends within the caste or between castes.

Muslims' perceptions of kinship and friendship differ from those of Hindus on at least two points. Firstly, the Muslim caste organisation is significantly different from that of Hindus and secondly, they prefer to marry cousins. Muslim caste communities are not bound by the social constraints that underpin the classic Hindu caste system. Muslim caste communities have social ideas about their differences, such as being urban or rural, which are used to rank them. Ideologically Islam claims that all members are 'brothers'; however, they draw a clearer distinction between kin and close friends than do Hindus. The data show that the majority of Muslims, unlike Hindus, draw a clear distinction between kin and close friends, the former being perceived as more reliable, trustworthy, helpful, respectful and sympathetic than the latter. Although men expect kin to help them find partners for their children, the importance difference is that Muslim men expect that preferred partner to be a first cousin. Kin negotiate with kin when arranging a marriage; thus kin are allies. This gives added meaning to an often quoted adage: 'Those whom we marry are those with whom we fight'. However, this dependence on kin separates kin clearly from close friends. It also separates Muslims from Hindus, since the latter do not marry kin or distinguish as clearly between kin and close friendship. Though close friends of Muslims may, and usually do, belong to the same factions, caste communities and sects, they are not regarded as potential affines. Close friends are expected to provide social and political support, occasionally to help with financial transactions, to relay information and to give advice. Probably their most important social role is to act as go-betweens in family feuds.

Although Muslims drew a sharper distinction than Hindus did between expectations and obligations linked to kinship, close friendship, ordinary friends and acquaintances, they placed a higher value on friendship than did the Hindus. An explanation for this might be that as all Muslims are 'brothers', they are obliged to help fellow Muslims. This philosophy is in accord with their social perceptions; this has enabled them to develop a community that is, united ideologically by belief and perception. This makes for a close, if not closed, community. Two anecdotes illustrate this. On one occasion, attending the wedding of the son of a teacher in Blackburn, the host referred to his guests as close friends. Many of the guests were members of the *ekada* to which the fathers of the bride and bridegroom belonged. The term 'close friend' was used here as a polite blanket term to describe the relationship between the host, his kin, his potential affines and his friends. As used here it is synonymous with one meaning of the word for cousin (Peters, 1976). The wedding guests included unrelated friends from other parts of Gujarat, Pakistan, and white friends. The distinction between kin, close friends and other friends was clear. Kin were invited to stay for the full three days duration of the wedding; friends were invited for a meal. The second anecdote relates to a funeral of a Muslim girl who had committed suicide. Only men attended the burial at the cemetery. Some of them knew the girl and her family, some knew of them and some knew only how she had died. It was explained to me that Muslim men have a duty to attend funerals of members of the Muslim community. For Muslims a funeral, irrespective of how the deceased died, provides an opportunity for a public expression of unity.

Social perceptions of Hindus and Muslims structure a cognitive map of social relationships, from kinship to friendship, and their associated expectations and obligations. As 99% of the sample married Gujaratis, it is friends who are likely to provide the links between Gujaratis and members of other groups and communities, ethnic and white. Friendships depend upon the freedom of association. Kin are not chosen; friends are chosen. Therefore, this analysis is concerned with friendships and close friendships in particular. Close friendships carry high social expectations and obligations that separate them from other forms of friendship. The extent to which non-Gujaratis are admitted into close friendship provides a measure of their closeness. These perceptions influence the recruitment of friends by separating those who share similar social values from those who do not. Thus kin are separated from non-kin, caste members from those belonging to other castes, those who accept the same religious beliefs from those who do not, and Gujaratis from those who belong to other communities. Gujaratis are linked into a web of social relationships that underpins their community. This comprises a range of social relationships from kinship to acquaintanceship. Through these relationships Gujaratis share a common social identity and a degree of access to the scarce resources controlled by those sharing this identity. To some extent estimates of how many friends they have gives an indication of how they perceive their community. The assumption made is that from an egocentred point of view the relationships which link an individual to the community radiate outwards through zones comprising kin and various forms of friendship, to relations with strangers. Unlike Barnes (1971:55-57), rather than looking from the community inwards to individuals, the individual is used to looking outwards to the community. The model of social networks developed here implies that individuals are surrounded by relationships of different levels of social intensity of decreasing social expectations and obligations.[1]

One model of an egocentred social network is of an anchor point surrounded by kin and close and ordinary friends and acquaintances. Hindu and Muslim estimates of the numbers of close and ordinary friends provide some idea of how these social networks are structured (Table 5.2 below). The majority (70%) of those sampled had between one and ten close friends, and slightly more Hindus (25%) than Muslims (20%) estimated that they had more than ten close friends. Sample estimates of the numbers of ordinary friends show that most had over ten such friends. Half of the Muslims compared to a third of Hindus estimated that they had hundreds of such friends. Notions of social equality form an ideology that unites the Muslim community, while caste differences divide the Hindu communities. The zone of close friendship comprises fewer friends than does the zone of ordinary friends. When asked, both Muslims and Hindus claimed that they had hundreds of acquaintances.

On the basis of these perceived differences between various categories of friendship, it is possible to construct a model of a social network comprising a set of inter-related zones of friendship distinguished by differing expectations and obligations. An individual can be visualised as being at the centre of a social network surrounded firstly by kin, then close friends, ordinary friends, acquaintances and categories of people of lesser acquaintance and strangers. In theory a zone incorporates more people as the social obligations and expectations connecting them directly with ego become weaker. Excluding kin, the primary zone contains the individuals upon whom ego can rely, trust, seek help from, obtain sympathy from and be given respect. The key to this model of zones in social networks lies in perceptions of social distances between kin and categories of friends.

Table 5.2
Estimated numbers of close and ordinary friends

Hindus	No. of	close friends		ordinary friends	
	friends	No.	%	No.	%
	0	7	4.6	9	5.8
	1 - 10	108	70.1	34	22.1
	11 - 20	12	7.8	24	15.6
	21 - 30	2	1.3	6	3.9
	31 - 90	15	9.7	31	20.1
	100s	10	6.5	50	32.5
	Totals	154	100%	154	100%

Muslims	No. of	close friends		ordinary friends	
	friends	No.	%	No.	%
	0	11	10.6	8	7.7
	1 - 10	72	69.2	20	19.2
	11 - 20	9	8.7	9	8.7
	21 - 30	6	5.8	5	4.8
	31 - 90	1	1	5	4.8
	100s	5	4.8	57	54.8
	Totals	104	100.1%	104	100%

Social distances and social boundaries

Observation and evidence suggests that generally people have fewer close friends than ordinary friends and fewer ordinary friends than acquaintances. An analysis of who Gujaratis befriend and the perceived intensity of the friendship contributes to a shared community mental construction of social boundaries (Cohen, 1985). Social network analysis will not only reflect differences in the intensity of friendships, but will also show with whom differing forms of friendship are considered to be appropriate. To reiterate a point made earlier, if Gujaratis are in a socially disadvantaged position, then theory suggests that they should develop ties with those whom they perceive to be socially closest. Gujaratis share the same social niche as members of other disadvantaged minorities.[2] In the circumstances, two arguments have been put forward. Firstly, ethnic minority communities will perceive members of other minority communities to be socially close, and therefore friendships will develop on the basis of a wide range of experiences. Secondly, these communities will perceive of white people as being desirable partners and allies, since they have both the political power and are numerically the largest community (Blau, 1967; Lin, 1982; Granovetter, 1973). Embedded in Gujaratis' cognitive maps of their social relationships are notions of social distance and power relationships and imbalances.

To obtain some impression of this cognitive map, Gujaratis were asked whom they were prepared to accept as kin, close friends, ordinary friends and acquaintances. This included considering befriending people from other minority communities (Table 5.3). Such commitment amongst Muslims is reflected both in the preference for first cousin marriage and in their hostile reaction to any member who might choose to marry a non-Muslim. During 1976 two cases of Muslims marrying non-Muslims were reported in the Press; in one case a Muslim married a Sikh in Huddersfield, Yorkshire, and in another case in Nelson, Lancashire, a Muslim girl brought home her white boyfriend. In the former instance, the Muslim community forced the couple to separate by threatening to kill the Sikh; and in the latter case, the girl's father shot and wounded the boy. When I asked a past president of the ICC and president of Tayaibah Mosque Committee what their reaction would be if one of their members married a non-Muslim, he replied, 'We would force them to separate, and kill them if necessary'. Two further instances illustrate the divide between the two religious communities. Firstly, Hindu parents married their 16 year old daughter to a 45 year old man. After he had battered her, her parents refused to accept that the husband they had chosen for her was to blame. Eventually after being injured by him she took him to court, where he was found guilty of assault. She obtained a divorce, married a Muslim, and now lives in Blackburn. Her move to the Muslim community was uneventful and she was accepted as a Muslim. However, her family severed all ties with her and she is no longer considered by them to be their daughter. Similarly a Leva Patidar Patel, who embraced the Islamic faith, was ostracised by his kin. When they were asked to name kin with whom they kept in touch in Bolton, this man was never mentioned. Both Hindus and Muslims are prepared to accept people of their own background and religious persuasion in all forms of kinship and friendship. With the remaining forms of friendship carrying lower obligations and expectations, both Hindus and Muslims were ready to accept one another in them. These data provide support for the view that Gujaratis comprise two religious communities. Although some have argued that these two religious groups comprise ethnic groups (Brooks and Singh, 1978/79; Robinson, 1979; Banton, 1972), it is not a common religion alone that underpins their ethnic identity, but a culture, language and origin. It is important to separate religious identity from ethnic one. The Rushdie incident demonstrated the importance of this distinction. Gujaratis refer to themselves as belonging to one community, namely Gujaratis, and then they refer to their family, village, caste, faction, sect and religious groups as communities.

Perceived relations with other communities are revealing (Tables 5.3a and b). Over 97% of Hindus and Muslims perceived members of their own groups to be acceptable as kin. Only 4% of Hindus (Table 5.3a) were prepared to accept Muslims as kin; perceived acceptance rose with close friendship to 34%, to 63% for ordinary friends and 77% for acquaintances. Muslims appeared to be more accepting of Hindus, 13% would accept a Hindu as kin, 56% as a close friend and 85% and over in other forms of friendship (Table 5.3b). This bears out the anecdote cited above regarding a Hindu woman who married a Muslim. Acceptance of white people by Hindus and Muslims was similar. Some 16% of Hindus and 18% of Muslims said they would accept them as kin; both samples of respondents said that they would accept them as close friends (57% and 58%). The responses suggested that fewer Hindus (77%) than Muslims were prepared to accept white people in lesser forms of friendship. More revealing are the attitudes of Hindus and Muslims to other ethnic minorities. Hindus were more ready to accept West Indians, Pakistanis and particularly Sikhs in most forms of relationships than were Gujarati Muslims. Their dislike of Pakistanis was similar to that of Gujarati Muslims. Muslims' dislike of Sikhs set them apart from all others. While these data may provide a simplified social map, the map provides a guide to daily social interaction. The analysis points to a perceived divide between Hindus and Muslims, between Muslims and Sikhs, and between Gujarati Hindus and Muslims and Pakistanis. Most importantly, it shows how in the 1970s there was little chance of any coherence between those ethnic minorities who were labelled black people. The break-up of the communities that formed CARD in the late 1960s came as no surprise.

Table 5.3a
Hindu perceptions of social distances

Accept as:	Gujaratis		White Person	West Indian	Paki-stani	Sikh
	Hindu	Muslim				
	%	%	%	%	%	%
Kin	97.4	3.9	16.2	8.4	5.2	16.2
Close friend	99.4	34.4	57.8	37	26	50.6
Ordinary friend	99.4	63.6	77.3	60.4	49.4	75.3
Acquaintance	99.4	76.6	83.8	68.2	61	84.4
Don't know	0.7	23.4	16.2	31.8	39	15.6

N=154   Percentages total = 100%

Table 5.3b
Muslim perceptions of social distance

Accept as:	Gujaratis		White Person	West Indian	Paki-stani	Sikh
	Hindu	Muslim				
	%	%	%	%	%	%
Kinsman:	12.5	97.1	18.3	9.6	37.5	8.7
Close friend	55.8	98.1	56.7	38.5	58.7	34.6
Ordinary friend	84.6	98.1	84.6	66.3	86.5	65.4
Acquaintance	94.2	98.1	93.3	80.8	93.3	77.9
Don't know	5.8	1.9	6.7	19.2	6.7	22.1

N=104   Percentages total = 100%

A number of anecdotes illustrate some of the intricacies of the perceptions of social distances between these communities. One incident involves a Hindu Kutchi family. The couple had separated; the husband lived alone, while his wife had gone to live with her parents and close relatives. The husband asked me to force them to release her. When told that I had no power to do this, he said, 'You can ask the police to go with you and then they will let my wife go.' Implicit in this request was an assumption that a white person could use the police to put pressure on individuals in a minority community. This suggests that there existed a perceived power gap between what Asians thought that they could do and what they thought white people could do. I learnt later that the families involved in this dispute had a 'bad' reputation amongst other Kutchis. A number of instances came to light of social situations over which nobody, Hindu, Muslim or white, had social, economic, legal or political control. Into these, Gujaratis tried to draw others who were not Gujaratis, so that the blame for failure could be placed upon them (Frankenberg, 1957:19, 43-44, 66, 98).

An incident that occurred in 1972 demonstrates the complexity of social distance as perceived by a Muslim and a Pakistani. A Pakistani took charge of a bus trip organised by the BCCR. He arranged the seating so that Hindus sat on one side and Muslims on the other. A Gujarati Muslim passenger suggested that people should be allowed to sit wherever they chose. If Muslims sat next to Hindus, then the aim of the trip to improve Hindu-Muslim relations might be achieved. However, the Pakistani insisted on separating the trippers. Later the Muslim argued that the Pakistani had acted against the aims of the BCCR and therefore should resign (which he did soon afterwards). The social distance that separates these communities was supported by memories of years of bitterness associated with Indo-Pakistani wars and the partitioning of India. In response to a question about young Asians learning about other Asian religions at a BCCR meeting (24/3/77), a young Pakistani said 'Pakistanis could not mix with Indians in religious places'. The label Pakistani was used by this young man to mean Muslim and by Indian he meant Hindu.

A third anecdote concerns differences between Sikhs, Hindus and Muslims that were expressed when the Sikh chairperson of the VHP at a BCCR meeting mentioned his intention to sell liquor in his shop. He stated that Hindus and Muslims had indicated their willingness to support him. Both Hindu and Muslim representatives at the meeting took him to task for making such a claim, as he had never sought their opinion. A Muslim asked the Sikh if he was a Muslim or a Hindu. When he said no to both questions, the Muslim told him that as a Sikh he could not assume that he shared a common identity with these communities. For the Muslims this incident confirmed their distrust of Sikhs.

Still another anecdote points to the tensions between Muslims and Afro-Caribbeans. In 1979 a seven-year-old West African Muslim child, whose father came to Bolton to study, joined a class of Muslim children in a local primary school. She was labelled a West Indian. Even though she and her parents were Muslims, none of the Gujarati Muslim children would play with her at school or in the street. When the children were asked why they did not play with her, they replied, 'West Indians are black and dirty; we are not black, we are white'.[3] Her parents likewise experienced racial discrimination from the local Muslims with the result that in the end they left the area and the town. In this instance 'brother Muslims' are Asian and not Afro-Caribbean Muslims.

Although exchange theory suggests that weaker members of communities should befriend those in stronger ones, this analysis of social of distances shows that firstly, the weak prefer to select close friends from a weak community, while recruiting those from other weak and the stronger communities to lesser forms of friendship. In other words, the strength of weak ties lies not in only their linking the weak to the stronger, but also in protecting the weak from racism, exploitation and from increasing the power of those with power. Gujaratis prefer Gujaratis, or 'like attracts like'.

Structural characteristics of social networks

The structural characteristics of the relationships between close friends suggests a closeness or close-knittedness that supports and is supported by the narrow social characteristics of close friends and the perceptions of social distances separating Gujaratis from others. The most obvious structural characteristic is size; it is also the least susceptible to other influences. The other structural characteristics treat the zone in the social network as a total social unit.

Size

To avoid the problem of overloading a few ties, the number of possible close friends were restricted to ten, excluding anchorpersons. This was originally done for the following reasons: (a) to avoid the lack of analytical continuity associated with too low numbers - such as in the case of three close friendships; (b) to recognise that people draw a distinction between their 'best' and 'close' friends;[4] (c) to allow for a variation in the number of close friendships between one and ten,[5] and (d) to recognise that these close friends are the most likely of all friends to exercise control over an anchor point. Though the number of close friends was limited to ten, most of the respondents (70%) identified only ten or fewer close friends. Analysis of the mean size of the network zones showed that close friends ranged from 5.56 (Hindus) to 5.1 close friends (Muslims). While 5.8% of Hindus and 13.5% of Muslims claimed to have no close friends,[6] 20% of the former and 25% of the latter identified ten close friends. The high percentages of respondents claiming to have no close friends could possibly be explained by the degree of suspicion that Gujaratis had of anyone asking such questions. The similarities in sizes of zones allow for the comparative analysis of the structural characteristics of the relationships between close friends.

Three ideal types of social networks are identified in the literature. There are those which are characterised by social closeness and are described as close-knit (Bott, 1971; Mayer, 1962) or completely interlocking (Laumann, 1973:113). Then there are those which are loosely knit (Bott, 1971; Mayer, 1962) or radial (Laumann, 1973:113). Some of the social consequences for anchor points of these different network structures have been analysed showing how they have become more or less receptive to new ideas (Leinhardt *et al*, 1977; McKinlay, 1973:275-292; Hart, 1970/71:84-87); have gained access to scarce resources or been prevented from obtaining them. In this section the aim is to examine the notions of close-knit and loosely knit in relation to density, intensity and connectedness of the structures of the primary zones of networks and secondly to draw from this conclusions about the pattern of social relationships which underlie the Gujarati community.

On the basis of the principle of homophily, that is, 'like attracting like', people who share social characteristics are more likely to be acquainted with those who share similar social characteristics than with those who do not. Gujaratis are likely to have as close friends people who share their social activities and social values, that is, are Gujaratis, are either Muslims or Hindus, and have the same or higher social standing. To analyse the structural characteristics of these primary zones of networks, I shall begin by analysing density/completeness. Density is defined as the extent to which all close friends in a zone are acquainted with each other. Then I shall consider the degree of intensity, which I define as the level of friendship that links close friends in a zone, and finally I shall look at the internal mesh of these zones, that is, the degree of connectedness.

Density/completeness

Density/completeness is the degree to which close friends in a zone are perceived to be acquainted by the anchor person.[7] Where all close friends of an anchor point are perceived to be friends of one another, the density will be 100%. Where none are acquainted, the density will be 0%. The data show that Muslims (72.6%) anchor a greater number of zones that are 100% complete compared to only half of the zones anchored by Hindus (Table 5.4 below). A primary zone, which is 100% dense, is bounded, that is, those within it recognise a social boundary that separates them from others. The zone encapsulates the anchorperson shielding him/her from the social influences that might arise from their less intense social relationships (Mayer, 1962). Zones of social networks that have a high social density are associated with a high level of social conformity (Bott, 1971: 208-210; Mayer, 1962: Chapters 5 and 6). In this social situation this means that Gujaratis will accept the social norms and values of the community. Outsiders who gaze in (Foucault, 1991) cannot see what is happening. Density is an indication of the strength of Gujarati resistance to intrusion by the local political community and the national state.

Less dense loose-knit networks provide greater social advantages to those anchoring them (Lin, 1982:134; Rushing, 1978; McKinlay, 1973; Bott, 1971:60), because they increase the dependence of a couple upon one another and upon their friends (Bott, 1971:60; Mayer 1962). This shifts the onus of communication onto friends and therefore onto their social location relative to the anchor point. If they reside within the same locality, the anchor point gains little, since they all share the same social, political and economic environment. If close friends are widespread, then the anchor point can benefit from access to information from a wide range of situations, experiences and knowledge sources. In the latter instance, the zone is loose knit by virtue of close friends living elsewhere. While some have argued that for a person to be enmeshed in a close-knit zone can be socially disadvantageous (Hart, 1970/71; Bott, 1971; Mayer, 1962) others have pointed to its strengths. For instance, Rex and Moore (1971) argue that it was close-knit relationships that gave migrants social and psychological support when resisting racism. In comparison the characteristics of a low-density zone include a greater dependence upon individuals to find solutions to their problems, and a greater dependence upon non-kin, with greater access to ideas and sources. Thus the pressure from close friends on an anchor person in such a zone to conform is reduced, freeing social relationships to become a resource for gaining access to new ideas (Erbe, 1977). What the analysis of the social characteristics of close friends revealed was that most of the close friends of the Muslims sampled lived in Bolton or close by and that the close friends of the Hindus were more widespread (Chapter Four). The analysis of the densities of Hindu and Muslim zones suggests that the zones of the former are less dense than those of the latter. This difference points to a more loosely knit community of Hindus and a more tightly knit community of Muslims.

Table 5.4
Degrees of density/ completeness of anchored zones*

No. of close friends	Muslims				Hindus			
Density:	0	1- 99	100%	Totals	0	1- 99	100%	Totals
2+	1		6	7	4		3	7
3			12	12		3	14	17
4			11	11	1	3	18	22
5		5	8	13		15	14	29
6		4	2	6		14	7	21
7			4	4		3		3
8		3		3		6	3	9
9		2		2		2	1	3
10		8	18	26	2+	12	17	31
Totals	1	22	61	84	7	58	77	142
%	1.2	26.2	72.6	100	4.9	40.8	54.2	100

*Respondents with no close friends are excluded, and two person zones, whose density is either 0% or 100%.
+ One of these zones had zero density and one had a density of 6.67%.

The interrelationship between homophily and density of the primary zones shows that zones which are 100% dense tend to be homogeneous and zones which are heterogeneous tend to have a low density, that is, are incomplete (not all close friends are acquainted with one another) (Table 5.5). A comparison of Muslims and Hindus sampled shows that the majority of Muslims (85.7%) anchor 100% dense homogeneous zones compared to 63.7% of Hindus. In general like attracts like. Similarities in the pattern of Hindus (71.4%) and Muslims (72.2%) to include non-

Gujarati close friends in heterogeneous zones that are incomplete is also striking. This means that close friends who are not Gujarati Hindu or Muslim respectively are to be found in zones where one or more close friends are likely to be unknown to the others. In other words, if an individual is going to have a close friend who belongs to a different ethnic community, it is socially 'safer' to ensure that the fewer the close friends who know of the relationship the better. Generally, the higher number of Hindu (45.3%) as compared with Muslim (27.2%) incomplete zones supports the view that Hindu close friends, who may or may not belong to other castes, are treated little differently from close friends who are not Hindu. Arguably, this structure of Hindu anchored zones may make it easier for them to establish close friendships with people who either belong to different castes or are not Hindu. It also may account for an observation, that is, both superficial and inaccurate, which has gained acceptance in Bolton amongst those who work with the Gujaratis, namely, that Hindus appear to be more ready than Muslims to accept the values of the white community. Though this conclusion may be unjustified, the fact that Hindu close friends are more often less well acquainted with each other than are Muslim close friends lends some support to it.

Table 5.5
Association between zone density and heterogeneity across zones*

Homogeneous zones

	Muslim				Hindu	
Incomplete	Complete	Totals		Incomplete	Complete	Totals
9	54	63		37	65	102
14.3%	85.7%	100%		36.3%	63.7%	100%

Heterogeneous zones

	Muslim				Hindu	
Incomplete	Complete	Totals		Incomplete	Complete	Totals
13	5	18		25	10	35
72.2%	27.8%	100%		71.4%	28.6%	100%

Overall totals

Incomplete	Complete	Totals		Incomplete	Complete	Totals
22	59	81		62	75	137
27.2%	72.8%	100%		45.3%	54.7%	100%

* 9 Muslim and 8 Hindu zones with less than 5 persons are excluded, as they are too small to produce significant measurements.

Intensity of relationships in primary zones

Density is a measure of acquaintanceship, which does not allow for distinctions to be made between different forms of friendships. For this purpose I use the notion of intensity. Respondents were asked according to their knowledge whether or not their close friends were kin, close friends, ordinary friends, acquaintances and strangers to one another. Levels of acquaintanceship are ranked above that of stranger. If all of the relationships linking close friends in a zone are described as being similar, for instance close friends, then this set of similar relationships forms a level of intensity. Where relationships between close friends are described as comprising close friendships and acquaintanceships, then the zone has two levels of intensity.

Table 5.6a
Levels of intensity in Muslim anchored zones*

		Homogeneous			Heterogeneous	
		No.	%		No.	%
Levels	1	43	68.2		5	23.8
of	2	11	17.5)		4	19.1
intensity	3	4	6.4)	31.8%	7	33.3
	4	4	6.4)		5	23.8
	5	1	1.6)			
Totals:		63	100.1		21	100	84

*Excluded are 14 respondents who have no close friends and 6 who have one close friend. In the former instance there are no levels of intensity and in the latter there is one.

Table 5.6b
Levels of intensity in Hindu anchored zones*

		Homogeneous			Heterogeneous	
		No.	%		No.	%
Levels	1	40	39.2		11	27.5
of	2	23	22.6)		4	10.3
intensity	3	15	14.7)	60.8%	13	32.5
	4	16	15.7)		7	17.5
	5	8	7.8)		5	12.5
Totals:		102	100		40	100	142

* 9 respondents who have no close friends and 3 who have only one close friend are excluded for the reasons given above.

A difference in the structure of relationships between close friends in 100% dense Muslim and Hindu anchored homogeneous zones is that more of the former (68%) claimed that their close friends shared one form of friendship (intensity) as compared with the latter (39%), whose close friends were linked by multiple forms of friendship (Table 5.6 a and b above). The more complex organisation of Hindu zones of close friendship points to a fragmented Hindu community structure, which undermines the idea of there being a united Hindu community. However, the greater unity across Muslim anchored zones suggests that the Muslims share a greater degree of cohesion, which has been a factor on certain occasions, such as their

128

reaction to the publication of *Satanic Verses*. In comparison with homogeneous zones, Muslims (76%) and Hindus (73%) who anchored heterogeneous zones perceive friendships between their close friends as comprising multiple levels of intensity. The presence of different levels of intensity of friendships suggests that people band together friends who share certain social characteristics, like religious beliefs and ethnic identity, and separate those who do not share them. A quarter cf the Muslims (24%) and Hindus (28%) sampled who anchored heterogeneous zones perceived their close friends to share a single form of friendship.

This pattern of friendship suggests that it is difficult for Muslims particularly to integrate their close friends who are Muslim with those who belong to other communities, whereas this would seem to be superficially easier for Hindus. Further analysis of relationships within single level intensity zones shows that 84% of Muslim and 65% of Hindu anchored zones comprised close friends. Two Muslim and one Hindu anchored zone consisted only of kin. Of the remaining single intensity zones, 9% of Muslim and 20% of Hindu anchored ones comprised ordinary friends. This analysis points to an ideological unity that is, shared by Muslims as compared to Hindus, who seem to share little in common. Muslims see their close friends as uniting them, while Hindus perceive of social differences dividing them and their close friends.

Connectedness

The connectedness of primary zones of the Hindus and Muslims provides a further measurement for comparing the structural characteristics of network zones. Connectedness of a zone is defined in terms of the ease with which one close friend in a zone can, theoretically, contact another. This concept of connectedness is similar to that of reachability (Mitchell, 1971:15-17), but the difference is that here connectedness or connectability is treated as a characteristic of the structure of the zone as a whole and not as a characteristic of the individuals who comprise it. To derive a measure of connectability, I use the notion of an optimum spanning tree (Deo, 1974:39). This measure of connectedness relates the size, density and intensity of the relationships between close friends in a zone. An optimum spanning tree (OST) is the sum of the lowest number of relationships of highest intensity which link all close friends together.[8]

To establish a measure of connectedness, the size of the primary zones of networks is plotted against the total weight of the OST. An analysis of the connectedness of Muslim (Table 5.7a) and Hindu (Table 5.7b) anchored zones shows that those of the former are more closely connected than those anchored to the latter. Slightly more Muslim than Hindu anchored zones are connected by ties of the highest level of intensity, that is, kin who are regarded as close friends and regard one another as close friends. Over 60% of Muslim zones are connected by OST weights that fall within the close friend/kinship range as compared with 42% of Hindu zones. Higher numbers of Hindu than Muslim zones are more loosely connected by OST links of lower social intensity, that is, close friends who are perceived to be connected by ties of ordinary friendship, acquaintanceship and/or are strangers. Only one (1%) Muslim anchored zone comprises close friends all of whom are perceived to be unacquainted with one another as compared with seven (5%) Hindu anchored zones. Five of these Hindu zones include some close friends who are perceived to be strangers and in two zones all close friends are perceived to be strangers, that is, they are totally unconnected. These are exceptional, since network theory argues that where three or more individuals are close friends (friendly), then the close friends are also likely to be acquainted. Generally, overall the Muslim anchored zones of close friends are more strongly connected than are Hindu anchored ones.

Table 5.7a
Extent of connectedness in Muslim anchored zones*

No. of friends in zones	Weights of optimum spanning trees					zones
	2-9	4-18	6-27	8-36	10-45	
3		10		2		12
4	1	7	3			11
5		7	3	2	1	13
6		2	2	2		6
7		4				4
8			2	2		4
9			1			1
10	1	16	7	2		26
Total	2	46	18	10	1	77
%	2.6	59.7	23.4	13	1.3	100

Close ———— Connectedness ———— Loose

Table 5.7
Extent of connectedness in Hindu anchored zones*

No. of friends in zones	Weights of optimum spanning trees					zones
	2-9	4-18	6-27	8-36	10-45	
3		20	6	3		29
4	1	13	6		2	22
5	2	9	11	5	2	29
6		6	12	2	1	21
7			2	1		3
8		1	4	4		9
9		1		2		3
10		9	17	3	2	31
Total	3	59	58	20	7	147
%	2	40.1	39.5	13.6	4.8	100

Close ———— Connectedness ———— Loose

*Zones with two or fewer people have no spanning tree and are excluded.

If the structure of a community is a 'persisting pattern of social relationships' (Laumann, 1973:3-4), then on the basis of the analysis of the structural characteristics of these network zones, Muslims form a more closely connected community than do the Hindus. The inclusion of close friends from other communities in Muslim anchored zones has not altered appreciably the degree of connectedness of the zones. They remain closely connected. Hindu anchored zones are more loosely connected than are the Muslim ones. The inclusion of close friends from other communities may have contributed further to the already low degree of connectedness. These characteristics have made it easier for Hindus to include members of other communities amongst their close friends.

To summarise the analysis, perceptions of social distances between communities and the structural characteristics of the primary zones show that a social boundary based upon strong social ties of kinship and close friendship separates the Gujaratis as a whole from other communities, ethnic and white. Gujaratis establish weaker social ties of ordinary friendship or acquaintanceship with members of these other communities. Gujaratis invest in strong ties with Gujaratis and reserve weaker ties for non-Gujaratis. This provides them with a degree of protection from racism, it insulates them to an extent from exploitation, and it enables them to develop from a position of weakness by concealing their social world from those who can exploit them. Thus they can strengthen their position by husbanding their own scarce resources and use them to develop their claims to social, economic and political space as consumers. This pattern of development became associated with a collection of labels that were in common use in the 1970s. An analysis of these labels supports the argument that to achieve freedom as a consumer implies achieving power and this means that a distinction needs to be drawn and more importantly maintained between the state and the black person in private and in public.

Common-sense racism and labelling

Gujaratis' daily lives require them to manage their social interactions through a range of social situations, some of which involve Gujaratis alone, and others which involve members of other communities. In other words, Gujaratis find themselves acting the roles of insiders and outsiders. In this section I shall concentrate attention upon the social meanings attached to commonly used labels that define the social boundaries of Gujarati communities within a community. Some social meanings of the labels are 'private' and are understood by Gujaratis, and some are public, and are understood by Gujaratis and members of other communities. Everyday social interaction is guided by history, experiences, social norms and values of Gujaratis and British society which are embedded in common sense racism (Brewer, 1984:71-72; Lawrence, 1983:48-50; Hall et al, 1981; Hall, 1978). Common sense racism is a body of knowledge which both white and Gujaratis (and other ethnic minorities) employ to guide them in their everyday social interaction: to this extent it is an empirical issue (Brewer, 1984:71) and it is based on received knowledge. It comprises recipes or 'precepts for action', 'schemes of expression', and 'schemes of interpretation' (Schutz, 1976: 103; Barth, 1970:15ff; Goffman, 1970:64ff). In racial situations recipes, through usage, become associated with trigger words that function as labels. At a cognitive level, labels mark social boundaries between communities. These labels are used by labellers and labelled to indicate what is believed to be knowledge about social relationships between racial groups, but which may signal knowledge or ignorance to those in the situation. They function as if they are symbols associated with some key characteristic, often of a discrediting nature (Goffman, 1970:14) of which the labelled are aware (Goffman, 1970:64ff). Gujaratis and white participants use labels to describe one another, but their meanings and appropriateness are open to negotiation and debate. What studies of labelling make clear, and particularly secondary labelling (Lemert, 1972), is how labellers impose a label on a person or group of people, often choosing to ignore the labelled's interpretation of the label and the applicability of the label.

As if they are symbols, analysing labels can show them to be associated with Gujarati ideas about how to manage their social relationships within and without their communities. If this system of labels is taken to represent a symbolic order of social identities, it is possible to analyse the social positions of the labelled by virtue of their perceived position in relation to the labellers. It is possible to conceive of a hierarchy of social identities comprising labels ranging from those defining the specific at one extreme to the general at the other. From the point of view of this analysis the former are perceived to be socially closer to the labelled and the latter to be more distant. The Gujaratis (the labelled) and white people (the labellers) have each developed a set of labels, some of which they share and whose meanings are recognised (public) and some of which are not shared and are not known (private). Continual public usage of these labels ensures their survival. As such labels are not fixed, their positions in the hierarchy of social identities are flexible. Labels have three purposes: firstly, they act as 'precepts for action'. Secondly, they are directional, that is, they act as a guide to the status positions in which the labelled perceive them to be in relation to the labellers and vice versa. Thirdly, they and their meaning are subject to negotiation by labellers and labelled in public situations.

As a consequence of their origins in India, the Gujaratis are associated with a group of people with a history that embodies a particular set of social characteristics (Lawrence, 1983:57-66; Rex and Tomlinson, 1979). Evidence of this is provided by the labels which the media and people generally used during the 1970s to describe Asians and black people. The most well known label that was used to identify these people is 'immigrant'. If the ideology embedded in a label reflects socially approved power relations between groups, the label 'immigrant' categorises the Gujaratis along with other Asian and black people as visually identifiable newcomers. Furthermore, it also invests them with a social identity that signifies their social position as people with unequal rights to public resources. Implicit in the usage of the label is a range of meanings, some of which are public and some of which are private. The usage of this label provides an illustration of the social boundary between Gujaratis and white. One of the definitive characteristics of such labels is their polysemous nature (Turner, 1962: 125), which the analysis that follows shows.

People who were labelled immigrant were regarded as a threat by white labellers, and the threat was access to public resources. However, from the side of the labelled the label indicates a vulnerability and lack of access to resources. This label is used by white people to describe any person who is identifiable as foreign born by virtue of their having a darker skin colour, wearing a different style of clothing, having obvious difficulties with spoken English, and possessing certain diacritical cosmetic marks (Brah, 1982). For instance when that late Enoch Powell MP talked about the 'invisible enemy within' in his speech at Northfield during the 1970 election, the label immigrant identified the highly visible 'enemy' within British society. The context in which the 'enemy within' is debated is an historical one associated with the 1970s and to the moral panic that characterised the implementation of often ill considered solutions to inner city problems (Hall, 1981: 32-33) and law and order (Solomos *et al*, 1983:21-26). The notion of a moral panic adequately conveys the idea of an establishment which was experiencing difficulties coping with and controlling immigration and maintaining law and order in those areas in which black people settled. For the labellers the label immigrant reduced a complex of social and ethnic identities to a visible other that was seen as a threat to society.

Bolton textile mill employers used the label to describe workers who had dark skins, were Asian, and favoured night shift work. Employers divided them into Pakistanis and Indians. One employer said: 'I prefer to employ Indian immigrants, as Pakistanis cause too much trouble wanting time off to attend their religious festivals'. The label Indian identified the Hindus and Pakistani described all Muslims. These labels were partially correct and reflected a partial awareness of the social and religious differences between these Asian workers. These labels were used by this employer to identify workers in terms of a white common sense understanding of the Asian communities in Bolton. Of itself this misunderstanding is important, because it illustrates how a white employer had the authority to impose an interpretation of the label upon his workers irrespective of inaccuracies. The Gujaratis had to accept this usage, and as such it became part of their body of common sense knowledge. It became public knowledge. They met fewer white people on night shift work than they would have on day shifts and those they met were employed in supervisory positions. This formalised but limited contact meant that reliance on visible characteristics was at a premium, and for the sake of identifying who worked where, when and in what position with what skills, the skin colour of Gujaratis became an essential sign. White workers use the label immigrant to describe their Asian co-workers, thereby conflating social identities of Gujarati Hindus and Muslims, Pakistanis, Bangladeshis and Sikhs into one single identity - immigrant - Indian and Muslim.

On the basis of misconceptions held by employers of the differences between Indians and Muslims, Gujaratis gained an advantage by being classified as Indian rather than Pakistani. The latter were people who became identified with those who put their faith before their jobs. For instance, there is no general agreement between the members of the two Muslim sects, Deobandis and Berelewis, and between them and Pakistanis, on which day *eid* falls, heralding the start and end of Ramadan. The decision on which day Ramadan begins and ends rests with each group. Deobandis accept decisions made by Islamic authorities in Morocco, while the Berelewis and Pakistanis prefer to wait twelve hours. The former chose to take one day off work to celebrate the end of Ramadan and the latter choose to take the following day. With little understanding of how there could be debate about the beginning and end of a major fast and with little knowledge of these sects, employers had to negotiate directly with the workers, which they did not like to do. The workers were left to make their own arrangements and the employers were left to cope with an insufficient labour force without advance warning.

Another factor which encouraged these employers to rely on a simple identification was that Gujaratis gave an impression of being more committed to their families and religion than to their work in a way that the employers found difficult to associate with their own career values. Hindu and Muslim workers just walked out of their jobs and went to India or Pakistan for holidays that lasted for months. Then they returned looking for work. This work behaviour reinforced the impression held by employers that these immigrants were not committed to their jobs. This apparent indifference to their jobs separated Asian workers from their white co-workers. It convinced the employers and white workers of the soundness of their belief in the inadequacy and unreliability of their Asian co-workers. As the white union managers recognised the same body of common sense knowledge, they were reluctant to support their Gujarati members' calls for strikes. The result of this was that the Gujarati workers accused the unions of racism.

For Gujaratis the application of the label immigrant in the work situation implied little chance of promotion, job security, day shift work, and the possibility of co-operation with white co-workers. The kind of issues which arose in the work situation centred on promotion, pay, and religious holidays, issues which, with the general problem of language (Braham and Rhodes, 1985:24-31; Brown, 1984) became specific to immigrants. A typical comment made by a Hindu engineering mill worker was: 'When we attend union meetings to discuss promotion, the white workers speak with a broad Lancashire accent. We cannot understand and then a white man gets promotion'. As few employers choose to antagonise the union to which the majority of their white workers belonged for the sake of a worker from a minority, they turned a blind eye to racism at work (Phizacklea and Miles, 1992). Responses of employers were directed towards the label rather than the workers.

At this time most white Boltonians described black people as immigrants, that is, people who dressed differently, had different customs, lived in certain areas of the town, could not speak English, and worked in the mills. Many local councillors spoke of helping immigrants. At local elections, politicians spoke of capturing the immigrant vote. For instance, before the Derby Ward local election in 1974, a Conservative councillor, who had helped many Indians settle in Bolton, went out to capture the immigrant vote. This meant going from door to door until an Indian was found who had received help in the past. The councillor argued that in return for this past favour he, a Hindu, should vote Conservative and persuade his friends to do likewise. After all, if the councillor and family, who had the interests of Indians at heart, could vote for the Conservatives, it showed that the Conservative Party was aware of and working towards recognising the interests of Indians. The councillor

134

informed party colleagues that all Asians in the Deane Road area of Derby ward would vote Conservative. As it happened, most of this man's Hindu friends lived in Bradford ward and those Asians who lived in Deane ward never received the message. Moreover, at least half of those living in the ward were Muslims and therefore did not know the Hindu. Most of the Muslims at this time supported the Labour Party, which won the seat. What is interesting about the event is that, again, the inaccurate usage of the label Indian by a local politician separated him from the Gujaratis whose vote was sought.

The label immigrant implied that those so labelled deviate in certain respects from what the labellers, white people, perceive to be English or British. By referring to them as immigrants, white people show that they perceived Gujaratis as different and the label encouraged them to maintain a social distance between themselves and Gujaratis. As for the Gujaratis, this only reinforced their belief in the insecurity of their position in Bolton and Britain. An aspect of this distance was expressed in terms of a status difference, almost a form of colonialist behaviour. Under certain circumstances white Boltonians responded to the label immigrant as they would respond to those who need help but whose help was not wanted or expected in return. White people could adopt the role of a patron. Once aware of this meaning, Gujaratis used it to their advantage when they required help or made a mistake. For instance, a successful Muslim butcher who owned two large businesses in Bolton, said to me, 'When I need help, I tell people (white people) that I am an immigrant. Then they help me'. Generally Gujaratis' response to being called an immigrant was to ignore it, reject it as inappropriate or even insulting, or turn it to their advantage. On one occasion at an annual general meeting of the BCCR held during Ramadan, the Chief Constable rose to speak, when a Muslim (who held two degrees from British universities stood up and asked the guest speaker to excuse his poor English. As an immigrant he explained it was not his first language. He then proceeded in flawless English to explain why all the Muslims present had to leave the meeting to attend to their prayers. For those present who knew him, he quite deliberately took everybody to task for having held the AGM during Ramadan. For those who did not know him, his speech could be taken at face value for providing a genuine explanation for why the Muslims had to leave.

When Gujaratis went to the local authority for help with housing, educational, social welfare or employment matters, they provided as much information as they believed necessary. Often this was inadequate. White officials refrained from inquiring too deeply into Gujarati affairs. They took this view because partly they were convinced that Gujaratis could not understand or speak English, partly that they would be unable to select the relevant details, and partly that they believed that Gujaratis were unable to comprehend the complexities of local issues. This gap in communication serves only to bolster stereotyped attitudes, such as 'they never tell you the whole story', that were associated with the label immigrant. For Gujaratis the label immigrant not only allowed them to plead ignorance, but also it implied that their status here was insecure, that is, those in power could require them to leave. Thus Gujaratis took the view that the less white people knew about them and their social, religious, economic and political affairs, the better they could protect themselves against this insecurity. Most Gujaratis observed during the research that

135

they had noticed an increase in the level of racial discrimination against Asian and black people. They controlled information about themselves, which was the only information that they could control. This information comprised the personal side of their lives, their village relationships, village factions, caste associations and communities, sects and some aspects of Islam and Hinduism. This became an area of 'private knowledge' that was accessible only to those who knew and were part of its creation (Emmett, 1982:207-209). [9]

Immigrant: a positional label

The label immigrant is part of a complex of symbols used by various groups of people to describe Gujaratis and other minority communities. Other labels in common usage included foreigner, Indian, Asian, Paki, Coloured and Blackie. Occasionally the labels migrant, Hindu and Muslim were used by white people or the media; rarely was the label Gujarati used. It is not the labels that are inaccurate or insulting, it is the inaccurate usage of them that causes offence. When those sampled were asked to comment on whether or not they found them acceptable, unacceptable and insulting, all were are in general agreement on most of them. The labels Indian and Asian were considered to be acceptable; Paki and Coloured were unacceptable and Black and Blackie were regarded as insulting. The labels Asian, Indian and Pakistani were acceptable and any misapplication was not taken as an insult; it was just seen as misidentification. The neutrality of these labels became apparent when I asked Hindus and Muslims what they thought of the label Paki. A number replied, 'I am not a Pakistani, so why should I be insulted?' Then they usually add, 'When I am called Paki by a white person, I feel insulted.' All agreed that labels like Blackie and Coloured were insulting. Gujaratis did not normally use labels like Paki, Coloured or Blackie when speaking to other Gujaratis; however, young Hindus called Muslims Pakis. The responses to the labels foreigner and immigrant showed that Hindus regarded the former as unacceptable and the latter as insulting, while the Muslims accepted both. Possibly Hindus believed themselves to be closer to Britain and part of the Commonwealth therefore they did not regard themselves as foreigners, even while living in East Africa, but as British. The Muslims saw themselves in the 1970s as being less British on two grounds. Firstly, they were regarded as immigrants, and this underlined their insecurity. Secondly, they were Muslims living in a non-Islamic or anti-Islamic country. In other words, generally, immigrants were people whose stay could not be made secure, because they were regarded as untrustworthy.

By the middle 1970s the label immigrant was losing ground to the label black, as people became increasingly aware that many immigrants had lived here for over 15 years; in other words, they were no longer immigrants. Reliance on visible identification remained. A chairperson of BCCR in his parting speech posed the question: 'When we speak of immigrants, we mean black or dark-skinned people, so why not say black people?' (*Minutes of BCCR Annual General Meeting*, 1976). The question of whether to acknowledge immigrants as black and therefore as different from white, or to say that they are the same as everyone else, but are recognised as immigrants, is still unanswered. Black has become a label of convenience, which has continued to allow the state and others to separate Asians and other ethnic minority communities from those who are not black, irrespective of their status as citizens. It has become a sign of the presence of racism. Black symbolises racialisation. Modood (1992; 1988) argues vigorously that South Asians are not black, but others treat black as a category that identifies those who experience and oppose racism. Its misapplication points to deeper issues. Firstly, it allowed some to perpetuate a misunderstanding about racial inferiority. Secondly, it acted as a politically emotive label for Asians and black people when used in a political context. Thirdly, when used by white people in a political context, it pointed to the political space between communities within a community. The 1991 Census places as much value, if not more, on skin colour in the question on ethnicity than any census did previously (Census 1991: User Consultation, Topic Statistics, March 1990, *Ethnic Group and Country of Birth Proposals*, OPCS, Paper TS4).

In the public arena, where informal labelling is a daily occurrence, the usage of inaccurate labels by those who are seen to represent the power group not only serves to reinforce inaccuracies, and so confirms their meanings, but also their meanings become part of white and Gujarati common sense knowledge. When Gujaratis choose to conceal their differences, they use labels whose meanings are understood only by others like themselves. Although the usefulness of certain commonly accepted labels, such as black or immigrant, as devices for recruiting black political support at a national level has failed (Heineman, 1972:79ff, 136-137), these labels were used with some success by local Gujarati leaders to recruit support on local issues (Chapter Seven). An anecdote shows how those in authority chose to misuse a label, and how those labelled, knowing it to be inaccurate, chose to accept it. Misuse and acceptance form part of a process of social negotiation. Attended a hearing at an Industrial Tribunal Court in Manchester in 1975, I heard a manager and two foremen from a local textile mill refer to Gujarati Muslim employees as Pakistanis. The court accepted the label as correct. Although a couple of Muslims in court spoke and understood English, none made any attempt to correct their employers. When asked why they did not correct their employers, they said, 'Why bother; there is no need for them to know.' Although the label Paki is recognised to be an insult, the label Pakistani was perceived by these Muslims to be inaccurate but not an insult.

Labels and some hidden identities

Participants in a social situation can negotiate the appropriateness of labels used as part of the social process of interaction. Both the meaning given and the directional characteristics are open to dispute by the participants. One individual's common sense perception of social position is not that possessed by another. 'The actor within the social world, however, experiences it primarily as a field of his actual and possible acts and only secondly as an object of his thinking' (Schutz, 1976:101). Agreement between participants on the appropriateness of a label implies that they also accept and recognise a meaning as well as the implied relationship. Gujaratis avoid using the label immigrant, but when they do use it, it means 'illegal immigrant'. By the 1970s many Gujaratis considered that they were no longer immigrants, they were British citizens. For instance, a Muslim friend and I met another Muslim friend in the town precinct. My friend's opening words to the other Muslim were 'Let us talk to this immigrant'. As all three of us were friends, this form of address was accepted as a joke. However, another Muslim I interviewed asked me if the purpose of my research was to obtain the addresses of immigrants; by this he meant 'illegal immigrants'. I later learnt that a number of his close friends were illegal immigrants, so he had reason to fear my questions about his close friends. When Muslims used immigrant publicly amongst themselves, they used it jokingly to imply that some person was an 'illegal immigrant'. If they used it in a public context in which white people were present, then they usually knew or had good reason to believe that a person was an illegal immigrant. The consequences of such a revelation could be enormous, therefore most Muslims rarely admitted to knowing the identities or whereabouts of illegal immigrants; apart from anything else they would be undermining their own insecure position.

Once I was accepted by these Muslims, this meant that I could not refer to them as immigrants, jokingly or otherwise, without insulting them. As I was regarded as sharing some access to their 'private' social world, I did have a deeper knowledge of their situation. However, I was white and therefore was not in the same insecure position as many of them. So to joke about insecurity would have undermined my position of trust. I could use the word immigrant without causing offence, just like any other white person, when I spoke to Gujaratis, Pakistanis and Sikhs, whom I did not know personally and had not heard of me. Thus, the term immigrant as used by Gujaratis is rich in social meanings, meanings that are different from those given to it by white people who are outside these communities.

There is a wealth of labels used by Gujaratis within the context of their own communities to describe social relationships between and within them. The most obvious of these is that between Hindus and Muslims. Members of these two religious groups mingle in daily life, but they rarely went into each other' homes unless they were close friends. Hindus referred to Muslims and Pakistanis as *Musula* (Muslims). This label carried no insult, but when a Hindu wished to insult a Muslim, he addressed him as *bandia* (circumcised). Likewise, Muslims referred to Hindus as *Patels* or *Kutchis*; again these labels were not regarded as insulting. If insult was intended, then Muslims addressed a Hindu as *kanda* (onions). Reference was made here to the bad smell onions give off. Those Hindus who choose not eat onions for religious reasons can still be said to smell as bad as onions, then the insult becomes even more pointed. Reference has been made to the use of the labels Baruchi and Surti (Chapter Three); they may be used by Muslims to insult fellow Muslims. Few people know what the labels really mean to consider using them. Though most Hindus know that Muslims come from two different districts in Gujarat, they cannot identify them visually and therefore they tend not to use such labels. The Sikh chairperson of the VHP, when speaking jokingly to a Muslim whom he had known for a long time said, 'You Baruchi or Surti or whatever...' This was the exception rather than the rule. Similarly, Muslims rarely used caste names when addressing a Hindu. One Muslim shopkeeper allowed a Hindu lady to take some goods she wanted, but for which she had insufficient money to pay. When I asked him how he could be sure that she would return with the money, he said, 'I can trust her; her caste are honest'. The woman was a Mandhata Patel. He believed that she was honest, although he, being a Baruchi, would be less willing to trust a Surti Muslim.

Hindus use caste names as labels when they refer to Mandhatas, Mistrys, Levas and Kanbis. Caste labels are in a general sense neutral; it is their usage in exceptional situations that is, of interest. I came across two such situations. The first was when a Hindu of higher caste implied that a Hindu of lower caste was untrustworthy. A Leva Patidar Patel complained to his Hindu drinking companions in a public house that, on the previous day he had lent a Valand (barber), an inferior caste, money to buy bottles of whisky and rum. The man promised to repay the money the next day; however, he did not appear. Turning to some Leva Patidar Patel friends, he said, 'What can you expect of a Valand?' On another occasion a Leva Patidar Patel pointed to a Mandhata Patel in a public house and said that the Mandhatas were really Kolis, implying that they were just labourers (Chapter Three). When I asked the Mandhata Patel if he was a Koli, he said that he had never heard of them. Some Mandhata Patels are aware that their caste name was once Koli, but they would never admit to this publicly. The application of a low caste name to Hindus whose caste has achieved higher status is a form of insult.

To quote 'these identities are categorical and are in fact a labelling process which relates primarily to expectations of behaviour in the public place rather than to basic customs, beliefs and practices' (Mitchell, 1974:19). The importance of the label immigrant is that it comprises a range of social identities that only become apparent in social situations, when participants debate and negotiate the meaning they are prepared to recognise. The complexity of meanings associated with such a label goes far beyond its superficial meaning and usage by white people, by Gujaratis and by other ethnic minority peoples. Most white people are unaware of the meanings that Gujaratis attach to it, but Gujaratis are aware of the meanings that white people associate with it. The perceived social distance between participants to some extent determined which range of meanings might be appropriate in a situation. The use of labels again makes apparent the social boundaries that separate private knowledge from public knowledge. The way in which people use labels and the meanings attached to them that others in a situation understand identifies their position. The labels, their meanings, and their usage also clarifies the positions of Gujaratis and white people in power terms within the Gujarati community and within the wider local society. The use of more specific labels with which white people and members of other ethnic communities are unfamiliar allows Gujaratis to manipulate social boundaries. The reason for doing this was for ethnic political purposes, namely to increase their access to scarce resources by identifying a change in their role from exploited to consumer. These cultural symbols are located within Gujarati experiences of white racism and incorporate ideas about how they manage their social relationships with other Gujaratis as well as with white people. Taken together they represent a socially constructed cognitive map of Gujarati political attempts to gain control of the space between their communities, the white community and wider British society. This body of knowledge provides them with a guide to and explanations for the appropriate social behaviour in intra- and inter-community situations. Their construction is a 'field of actual and possible acts' (Schutz, 1976: 101). This is the subject of the next two Chapters.

Notes

1. In a social network, a first order star, an individual is surrounded, metaphorically, by a set of dyadic relationships which can be arranged in terms of levels of intensity into a number of zones (Barnes, 1971:58-60).

2. By the 1970s there was no simple relationship between the social standing of Gujaratis and social classes. They can not be collectively assigned a class position.

3. In Milner's analysis of children's misidentification of colour (1975, Chap.4), he argues that 92 per cent of Asian children said that they 'would rather be white' than black (1975:135). Although only 24 per cent of Asian children chose the white doll in an actual identity test, some 65% did so in a theoretical situation (1975: 134). On the basis of this, he suggests that Asian and West Indian children have to resolve a conflict between their own identity, as black people, and a social reality in which white people have power. I would argue that Milner seems to be unaware that Asian children do not think of themselves as being black; they think of themselves as being white or brown. For them, the obvious choice is the white doll.

4. La Gaipa distinguishes between best friends, close friends, good friends, social acquaintances and casual acquaintances (1977: 251). These distinctions between friends were generally used by Gujaratis (see Chapter Three).

5. I restricted the number of close friends to ten, as this not only met La Gaipa's estimated number of best/close friends, but it also was a convenient number with which to work. Any larger number would have increased the complexity of the calculations considerably.

6. I had to accept their answers as they were given. In other circumstances I might have delved more deeply into their reasons for having no close friends.

7. To determine completeness I asked respondents to define the relationships between their close friends. Then I used the formula for the calculation of density for undirected networks where Density = $100 \times Na / \frac{1}{2} N(N-1)$ where Na stand for the actual relations between close friends in the primary zone, excluding those between the respondent and his close friends; N stands for the number of close friends (Kapferer, 1973:96; Niemeijer, 1973:46).

8. 'In its simplest form, a spanning tree algorithm yields one spanning tree in a given connected graph' (Deo, 1974:277). It is the weight of one, and only one, tree that I have plotted against the size of the zone. As the number of people in a zone decreases, so too does the possible number of spanning trees that link them. Zones comprising less than three people have one spanning tree. Wherever a zone includes relationships of different intensity, the algorithm will select a tree with the highest values (Appendix II). The weightings given to the different relationships are: kin = 1, close friend = 2, ordinary friend = 3, acquaintance = 4 and not known = 5. These are arbitrarily attached weightings.

9. To some extent sociologists and social anthropologists have shown that it is possible to penetrate such social barriers with the support of the participant actors (see Drucker-Brown, 1984; Goode and Hatt, 1952).

140

6 Leaders and politics

Although throughout the 1970s the politicians spoke of integration, the state was (and is), concerned with control of migrants, and particularly black migrants, whose labour was (and is still) exploitable. In Chapter Two I argued how the process of state control identified the space between black and white, between the exploited and the consumer. The pattern of settlement of Gujaratis and their employment in Bolton was typical of a sunset town whose industry had become dependent upon cheap labour for survival. The development of ethnic social and religious organisations was a response to a fast growing ethnic population to state control and to racism generally (Chapter Three). An important aspect of this response was the emergence of ethnic communities with an investment in strong ties, making for dependence upon friendships with Gujaratis to resist racism and recreate a culture that drew on both their origins and their new environment. This enabled them potentially to control the flow of information about themselves to others (Chapter Four). Network analysis such as this was typical of the 1970s. While this approach has been criticised (Troyna and Hatcher, 1992), it does serve the purpose of delineating a general pattern of association. In Chapter Five Gujaratis' commitment to controlling the flow of information is reflected not only in their perceptions of social distances between themselves and other ethnic minorities and the white community, but also in the social characteristics of the structures of their social networks.

In this Chapter I shall look at competition between Gujarati communities for control of ungoverned political space, the formal political system and at the politicisation of Gujarati communities. This space was perceived by those in authority, such as the police and local authority, as being ungoverned, suggesting that they were less concerned about conflict between and within ethnic communities than about conflicts between the ethnic and white communities. The politicisation of ethnic communities and organisations within a haven provided by CRCs and their predecessor organisations provided the space for them to develop ethnic politics. Alongside these developments, the focused concern of political parties on black votes encouraged the formation of community identities by attributing to elected officers' influence over the voting behaviour of their members. This newly found authority encouraged many ethnic officers to take on political functions in addition to their existing community ones and to present themselves as leaders. A consequence of this process was to intensify competition between leaders or persons of influence for positions of leadership and for support through competition to expand the domains of their ethnic organisations. Such competition led to the political development of relationships between ethnic communities that was, and still is, characterised fragile alliances which are established and broken (Werbner and Anwar, 1991). The literature has generally ignored this space (Rex and Moore, 1971:117), and has focused on cultural relationships between the communities here and in South Asia (Shaw, 1988; Werbner, 1989; Ballard *et al*, 1994), or shifted the analysis to a postmodernist perspective (Hall, 1990; 1992; Gilroy, 1993; Rattansi and Westwood, 1994). These approaches avoid considering how those living in Britain establish social relationships with members of other ethnic communities, and by whom and how the space between them is governed. This opens up the debate of whether or ethnic communities could ever unite politically as a black opposition or as members of CARD (Heineman, 1972).

A tendency has been to dismiss as irrelevant issues which do impinge upon intra- and inter-ethnic community conflicts until relatively recently (Werbner and Anwar, 1991). What ungoverned space does highlight is a relationship between the perception of ethnic minorities as comprising communities and the concept of multiculturalism (Rex, 1986). This raises the issue of power between the 'ethnic minorities' and the majority community (Modood, 1996; Ben-Tovim *et al*, 1986, 1992; Solomos *et al*, 1983:13; Lawrence, 1983: 115). Any analysis of local power relations needs to include not only ethnic communities and organisations, but also the role of political parties, and CRCs. What is often absent from the debate are the issues that illuminate the relationships between these organisations. These issues form the substance of this and the next Chapters. This chapter sets the political scene by so-called ethnic leadership. The next chapter will explore some of the issues that enabled ethnic organisations to compete for ungoverned space.

Since the arrival of first West Indians in 1948 and later South Asians, at the end of the 1960s welfare-orientated organisations were replaced by CRCs. Their tasks included assisting refugees, helping immigrants with language, nationality, and immigration difficulties, and also performing a raft of social welfare-type work. This role existed into the 1980s. The effect of this has been to focus attention upon the ethnic community. Together with the South Asian commitment to their communities here and abroad, the social, economic and political importance of the community has dominated much of the thinking about race relations. However, it sits uneasily in debates about politics and leadership (Josephides, 1991:253; Goulbourne, 1991:297; Eade, 1991; Kakla, 1991; Banks, 1991). Although most of the contributors to Werbner and Anwar (1991) discuss these concepts, few address the implications of ethnic communities as political entities. Goulbourne (1991:317) recognises this difficulty in his reference to Dench (1986) when he refers to the 'communal cul-de-sac' (p.317) and his observation that West Indians have not sought to use ethnicity as a basis for political action. The deployment of ethnicity as a basis for social action is taken for granted by most of the remaining contributors. This suggests that any community action is political, from the election to and in a CRC (Werbner, 1991) to the collection for a temple (Banks, 1991). Yet it was Rex and Moore (1971) who dismissed such activity as factionalism and thus as not relevant to the responses of black communities to racism. What is missing from some of the accounts in Werbner and Anwar (1991) is a firm view of the role of CRCs, the role of ethnic communities and organisations and therefore of how they relate to issues of leadership and politics.

In Chapters Three and Four I argued that the Gujarati population comprises a collection of socio-religious communities bound by the social networks of their members into two major religious communities, Hindus and Muslims (Brooks and Singh, 1978/79). The situation in Bolton typical of many Gujaratis populations and highlights some of the complexities of the notion of community and leadership. What the analysis in the above Chapters showed is that it is difficult to speak of a Muslim community, unless there is some issue against which all Muslims can unite and so override their intra-ethnic differences. The same applies to the Hindu community. This adds to the argument that ethnicity should be seen as a mental construct employed to redefine social boundaries in changing social situations (Cohen, 1985:97ff.). As a totality, an ethnic community only forms an ethnic boundary when (a) its members choose to see it as such, or (b) when it is treated analytically as such by an observer. At other times, the ethnic community is seen as a collection of ethnic communities, many represented by mosque or temple organisations, and/or village or burial societies. Although Gujaratis refer to their kin as a community, they are organised into communities. This suggests that observers define community differently (Cohen, 1985). In this sense, kin-based communities may have traditional structures associated with kin-based leadership, while mosque and temple and other community organisations have more bureaucratically organised structures and the appropriate forms of leadership. This is the kind of distinction made by Anwar (1991; 1979); and it also integral to Goulbourne's discussion of Weberian ideal types of leadership (1991). It is necessary to recognise how ethnicity and race are important influences in political situations. There is a possibility that the relationship between ethnic organisations and political parties becomes blurred and that the relationship between these organisations is reduced to a racist dimension alone.

At one extreme Layton-Henry (1984: Chap.11) identified five different forms of black political participation, none involved ethnic community organisations. At the other extreme Rex and Tomlinson's (1979) argued that frustrated ethnic communities would become militant which proved to be untrue. Political integration of ethnic minorities into a political system, which is controlled by political parties, lies at the heart of a dilemma: to what extent are political parties prepared to embrace ethnic communities or organisations? For any political party to admit a community as a totality would conflict with the concept of a democracy. Much of the debate about black sections in political parties supports this argument: it could only lead to a conflict of racial versus political interests (Jeffers, 1991; Fitzgerald, 1984; Hall, 1985). This conceals a number of important issues: for instance, the conflict between the support accorded to an ethnic leader and political support. Goulbourne's argument about West Indians being concerned with engagement and participation and not disengagement and separation (1991:297) applies to other ethnic minorities (as he himself observes). Anwar's work since the 1970s has shown consistently how South Asian communities have sought engagement and participation, but have consistently experienced rejection and obstruction (Anwar, 1994). In Bolton the political parties have assiduously controlled black attempts to achieve candidacy in local and national elections. Such has been the control that only two black people achieved success as Labour Party candidates in local elections: one was a South Asian and the other a West Indian in the late 1960s. While the former eventually dropped out of politics, the latter continued to be involved even in the face of racist opposition from within his political party (see Solomos and Back, 1994). No other black person has been offered a safe or a winnable seat in any election since the 1970s. The result is that today Bolton has only one ethnic minority councillor. However, while consistently supporting the notion of equal opportunities, he gives the impression of putting party politics before ethnic interests. On the one hand, he has experienced racism in his party; on the other hand, he has been criticised and virtually disowned by other black people and South Asians in particular.

Since the 1970s two factors have contributed to the development of ethnic communities in their development from being nationalistic and welfare-oriented to becoming ethnically focused ones with multi-response interests. The first factor was the role of the local CRC, and the second was the relationship between CRCs and local political parties (Ben-Tovim *et al*, 1986). Ethnic leadership and ethnic politics were partly responses to changes in the relationship between CRCs and the CRE, and partly to political parties which sought to attract ethnic votes while discouraging their development as political organisations. I shall begin by looking at the former and then moving to a consideration of the latter. This Chapter sets the political scene by analysing the role of the local CRC, namely the BCCR, then analyses the political participation of Gujaratis in the local political system and concludes with an analysis of the social characteristics of Muslim and Hindu leaders.

Community Relations Councils (CRCs)

In the late 1960s the BCCR emerged as the principal local organisation whose concern was the welfare of immigrants. In its 27 year history all directors (once referred to as chief officers) have been white, and with the exception of one West Indian chairperson, all have been white. Recently, an ethnic member has acted as a joint chairperson. Vice-chairpersons have included members of ethnic communities. The structure of a CRC takes the form of a council membership from which the membership of the executive committee is selected by election. However, the composition of membership of the executive committee is open to influence and it is these aspects of CRCs that contribute to its vulnerability (*The nature and structure of local work for racial equality*, CRE, 1978: 14, para. 4.17;

144

Hill and Issacharoff, 1971). Although Katznelson's (1973) analysis of race relations in Britain gave the appearance of looking at all levels of organisations concerned with black people, a careful reading shows that he overlooked local CRCs and did not consult available literature on them (e.g. Hill and Issacharoff, 1971). His reference to CRCs is to the Community Relations Commission and not to local Community Relations Councils. The difference between these two organisations is considerable: the former was a national body and predecessor of the CRE, while the latter are local organisations that became the responsibility of the CRE. Katznelson's knowledge of local CRCs is scanty and he shows little evidence of knowing how they operate. However, his claim that the CRC is a buffer organisation has become associated with local Community Relations Councils in error. Hill and Issacharoff (1971: 203) argue that by the development of their role as welfare agencies, CRCs became organisations providing indirect social control. Hill and Issacharoff do not identify how this control operates and who operates it. By the early 1970s CRCs had not way of exercising such control and their vulnerability to take-overs removed and opportunity to develop such control. Far from acting as buffer organisations, local CRCs became the facilitators in bringing ethnic leaders into contact with elected politicians and the political system to overcome buffer organisations. For local CRCs this has resulted in their role being examined on a number of occasions (CRE, 1978; Gay and Young, 1988; CRE 1997) in order to make them more accountable to the CRE, more responsive to their clients and more modern in their approach to their role.

What is at issue is political participation. Over the past 30 years various efforts have been made to address the issue of ethnic political participation in British politics. Some have argued that ethnic politics and its impact on local politics is important (Scott, 1972/73; Bentley, 1972/72; John, 1969, Solomon, 1983; 1989, Solomon and Back, 1995 Parekh, 1991; Ben-Tovim et al, 1986, 1992; Heineman, 1972; Beetham, 1970). Others have argued that political participation involves voting for political parties and election to formal positions, such as councillors and MPs (Anwar, 1994; 1984; 1986; 1979; 1980; Rex and Moore, 1971; Anwar and Kohler, 1975; Le Lohe, 1983; 76). An explanation for why political participation should involve only mainstream political processes is left unexplained. A few have attempted to demonstrate how voluntary organisations, such as CRCs, can form the link between the political parties and ethnic communities (Ben-Tovim et al, 1986, 1992; Ball and Solomos, 1990; Hahlo, 1993). Although few have expressed the central issues, such as how can an ethnic group, community or organisation can participate in politics within the political party system (Modood, 1996; Parekh, 1991). This debate has been informed by reference to black sections and forms of participation within political parties (Fitzgerald, 1984; Hall, 1985; Goulbourne, 1991; Jeffers, 1991). The form of democracy that exists in Britain is political party controlled. Therefore, what is at issue is whether or not political parties can accommodate representation from ethnic groups, communities or organisations. There is no mechanism for such participation and the above commentators on black sections have shown that there is a fundamental conflict between black and party interests. From this debate a number of arguments have become clearer: firstly, there is an argument that ideologically there is a place for ethnic communities or organisations within the political system (Parekh, 1991; Solomos, 1992). Secondly, there is no place for ethnic organisations within the political system, but political parties need to provide more support for ethnic candidates. Thirdly, buffer organisations no longer have a part to play in hindering the political participation of ethnic communities (Solomos, 1989). Fourthly, political parties can accommodate black sections only with difficulty (Jeffers, 1991; Hall, 1985). With a political system that lays stress upon individual participation, there is no place for group participation in political parties. This means that minority participation at any level above that of the individual implies some form of anti-party structure, which has no place in the British political system or lobbying or interest group opposition.

Prior to the merging of the Community Relations Commission and Race Relations Board to form the Commission for Racial Equality, local CRCs provided a wide range of services that duplicated and replicated those provided by local authorities and voluntary organisations. What distinguished CRCs was their commitment to working with ethnic minorities and to do race related work and the reluctance of the latter to do such work. As noted above CRCs also provided an informal political platform for ethnic minorities. CRCs responded to the needs of their clients but in the process became vulnerable to take-overs by ethnic sections. Since 1973 a number of CRCs have experienced such disruption as a result of factions take control by establishing their domination of executive committees, and thus gaining majority control of councils. Some CRCs that were disrupted included Rochdale, Sheffield and Brent. Others, funding like Liverpool, Scunthorpe, Tower Hamlets and Cleveland, that were fully or partly funded by local authorities were threatened with a withdrawal of their unless particular ethnic organisations ceased attempting to dominate the CRC. The proposed new partnership between the CRE and CRCs sidestepped this issue by placing the onus on political parties to give minorities greater opportunities for political participation. It did this by making CRCs responsible for monitoring this involvement (CRE, Community Relations Group of MSF and National Association of Community Relations Councils, *A New Partnership for Racial Equality*, 1989). Evidence that the new partnership has avoided this issue is to be found in Bury, Lancashire, where a chairperson has refused to stand down, having been voted off the committee. For a time Bury REC has two chairpersons and two executive committees. The CRE threatened to withhold the funding for this REC, but in the event this proved to be unnecessary. Recently Oldham REC was closed down by inter-ethnic conflict that destroyed the executive committee (*Oldham Chronicle*, 30/7/97: p.9).

Furthermore, their accountability to the CRE and its predecessor organisations was often unclear. These issues were to be remedied in the 1988 review of their role (Gay and Young, 1988). In the decade between the early 1970s and the review in 1988 local CRCs had the freedom to become facilitators in linking ethnic organisations to the local political system through executive committee meetings. Politicians who were seeking ethnic votes found this arena particularly useful for making contact with leaders of ethnic organisations. CRCs developed these informal political arenas in which ethnic leaders and politicians debated a wide range of issues, some of which highlighted the ungoverned space between ethnic communities and ethnic organisations. This evolution enabled ethnic leaders to

146

politicise social, religious, economic and political issues within an ethnic political context. This also provided ethnic representatives with a political platform that legitimised these representatives in the role of leaders; that is, they were expected on the grounds of their claims of support to be able to take decisions and to seek decisions on behalf of their supporters.

The role of local CRCs was flawed in a number of ways: firstly, this development was not a planned one within the relationship between CRCs and the CRE (or its predecessor organisations). Secondly, it encouraged ethnic organisational participation in the local situation in which there was no role for ethnic group/ community/ organisational involvement. This opened local CRCs to the danger of being taken over by ethnic sections as well as to becoming the channels linking ethnic communities to local political parties (Ben-Tovim et al, 1986). Thirdly, by association local CRCs became linked to the buffer role attributed to the Community Relations Commission. Fourthly, CRCs were absorbed into the social construction of the race relations industry. The insistence upon ethnic community and/or ethnic organisational representation became the key to selection of members to CRC councils and executive committees. The achievement of a balanced executive committee remains an idealistic goal for CRCs. The onus to achieve this end is placed upon CRC directors without their having any acceptable or publicly approved mechanism for achieving such a distribution of members. This is attempted by allocating a larger number of places to ethnic organisations and a smaller number to individual members. The paradox is that, as Miles (1982) noted some years ago, race related issues became linked to ethnic cultural interpretations and vice versa. Local authorities by accepted this form of representation and definition of business endorsed this way of working with ethnic communities.

For a South Asian population, such as that in Bolton, the structure of CRCs matched their potential for schism, what is referred here to as detachment. In the decade of the 1960s the development of ethnic organisations and ethnic communities was a response to the rapid growth in the South Asian population in Britain (Ballard R and C, 1977), to racism (Rex and Moore, 1971), and to the recreation of ethnic culture (Werbner, 1996a, 1989b). By the 1970s maintenance of the ethnic community as a social, economic, political and cultural unit had become paramount. With competing interests based on faction, caste, sect and religious grounds, ethnic communities emerged organised around temples, mosques, burial or village societies. By politicising an arena in which ethnic minorities had access, these competing interests were set in the context of members' experiences of racism and local government. To their surprise elected representatives of ethnic organisations found themselves able to politicise their demands and those of their members in an informal political arena. In an atmosphere of fragile alliances ethnic leaders found that advantages were to be gained from treating their membership as if it was a structure of support. Furthermore, politicisation gave a new impetus to the development of ethnic identities and belonging in a situation that allowed for detachment and unification of organisations. Unintentionally, political competition for ungoverned space became central to CRC business. At the same time this competition assisted the development of ethnic organisations and the maintenance of ethnic culture. It was the combination of factors which included the need for

CRCs to get closer to their grassroots membership, the politicisation of their activities, at a time of the rapid growth of ethnic communities and emergence of community/religious organisations, that contributed to development of social identities.

Even though CRCs have had the greatest impact on local race relations nationally since their establishment in the late 1960s, they have received remarkably little attention with a few exceptions (Hill and Issacharoff, 1971; Gay and Young, 1988; CRE, 1997). Ben-Tovim *et al* (1986) observed that apart from the Labour Party in Liverpool, the local CRC was the only organisation which attempted to give some political recognition to ethnic organisations and their members. With over a hundred CRCs in British towns and cities, they have had more direct and closer contact with, and a greater impact on, ethnic communities over a greater length of time than any other organisation. Interestingly, most of the major reviews of the CRE are not of this body but of its management of local CRCs and their accountability. The CRE has never quite dealt a criticism made of it, that it is a white and government dependent organisation (Solomos, 1989). Reviews of the CRE have concentrated on making CRCs more accountable and more responsive to the CRE, their clients, and the public (CRE, 1997; Gay and Young, 1988; CRE, 1978; Hill and Issacharoff, 1971). However, each review has resulted in reducing the contact between CRCs and the communities they serve, while making them more accountable to the CRE.

The aim of two recent reviews has been to raise race relations to the level of a public debate by shifting the responsibility of recognising their role in opposing racial discrimination on to other voluntary organisations. The response of the CRE to state pressure to remove immigration and nationality issues from their agenda culminated in the delegation of such work to organisations specialising in immigration work and solutions. This redefinition of role was accompanied by another shift in the work of CRCs to provide a more public oriented service. The responsibility for the work they had done on behalf of a range of voluntary organisations, such as Citizens' Advice Bureau, Community Voluntary Services, Victim Support etc., has been shifted back to these organisations. This has focused the role of CRCs on the public aspects of racism and made them financially even more aware of their dependence on the CRE. As ethnic organisations are being persuaded to recognise that their role as voluntary organisations, the CRE is pushing CRCs towards becoming financially dependent on service level contracts as opposed to an annual grant from the CRE. These changes have not only opened CRCs to change, but have also shifted the onus of ethnic representation away from ethnic communities and organisations to individual members of the ethnic community. However, these changes are in their early stages and the dilemma between seeking the involvement of ethnic organisations and shifting the onus of response to racial discrimination onto voluntary organisations has been bedevilled by the notion that ethnic participation has to take the form of community representation. Ethnic organisations are now recognising that they, like other voluntary organisations, have to act on behalf of their members. The depoliticisation of competition for space is complete. Now the CRE has responded to the criticism that ethnic organisations received more favourable treatment than did white organisations by having access to an informal political arena to which other voluntary organisations had no access (Solomos, 1989). The depoliticisation of ethnic politics has met this criticism fully.

In contrast to a focus on ethnicity, debates about black sections have attempted to give priority to the notion of black as a political grouping) and thus see ethnicity as counterproductive in the reduction of racism (Modood, 1992; 1988; Sivanandan, 1990; Gilroy, 1993; 1987. However, ethnicity underpins community identities, which lie at the centre of South Asian culture. The ethnic community is not a political community, because its members are not by their membership of it committed to a single political view (Goulbourne, 1991). In the same paper Goulbourne notes that West Indians chose not to employ ethnicity as an organising factor in their efforts to improve their access to political participation. This is a critical observation, because earlier commentators on West Indians (Philpott, 1977) have spoken of those from different islands having distinct social identities. This observation is borne out by the activities of the West Indian community in Bolton. If West Indians have chosen not to employ their social identity to assist their participation in politics, then, in contrast, South Asians have chosen the community and its identity as a way of organising their participation in local politics (see Chapters Three and Four). The level of concerted action, as will become apparent in Chapter Seven, is that of the religious community, which is comprised of factions, castes and sects. These differences alone ensure that the politicisation of ethnic communities would complicate the political party system and the development of black sections in parties were seen by the parties to be unproductive (Hall, 1985). The changes to CRCs in the 1990s (CRE, 1997) resulted initially in a drop in ethnic commitment to supporting CRCs. This forced South Asians to recognise that their organisations no longer had a political role. Rather, they had to recognise that their roles as like those of other voluntary organisations having charitable status. Now they have to develop their role as social and welfare organisations to meet the needs of their members. This has brought to CRCs members from a range of community backgrounds who were committed to fight racism.

In the twilight period of CRCs in the 1990s ethnic communities, whether or organised around ethnicities or blackness, have been stripped of any opportunity to politicise as organisations outside the party structure. Instead, their members have to compete for political party support which is predominantly white controlled. Thus, the politicisation of ethnic issues and cultural diversity is dependent upon a minority of ethnic and black MPs in Parliament and a minority of councillors in local politics. Parekh (1991) rightly wonder who might raise such issues for national debate.

Bolton Council for Community Relations

The BCCR is a typical example of a CRC whose activities in the 1970s provided ethnic communities with an informal political forum that encouraged the development of leadership. Like others, it provided an opportunity for the development of ethnic politics as a way to challenge control of ungoverned space between the ethnic and white communities. It is one of the earliest surviving CRCs in Britain and today has to confront the changes in its relationship with the CRE and will have to face new ways of finding funding through service level agreements.

In most respects the racism experienced by Asian and black people elsewhere in Britain is no different from that experienced by Gujaratis here. Initially the role of the local CRC was to promote harmony and goodwill. The CRC could achieve this in a number of ways through three broad but interrelated, policies: integration (Hill and Issacharoff, 1971:164), equality (Gay and Young, 1988:17) and the elimination of racial discrimination. The first was a development from the work of the welfare oriented organisations established to care for refugees and immigrants who came to settle in Britain in the decade after the war (Hill and Issacharoff, 1971: 1). At the time, ethnic organisation benefited from joining the BCCR. They could bid for funds allocated by the CRE for special projects; make contact with local authorities, political parties, and elected politicians; and work with an organisation whose aims are to eliminate racial discrimination and promote equality of opportunity.[1] The issues described above that beset CRCs, including that in Bolton, are well-documented (CRE, 1978; Hill and Issacharoff, 1971). The key one which was identified and which has persisted to the present day concerns a balanced membership. Any ethnic organisation could become an affiliated member of a CRC Council if it could produce a constitution, an annual report and a written undertaking to support the objects of the Council (Hill and Issacharoff, 1971: 86). Not all members of the Council could become members of the CRC executive committee. Initially, the number of places on this committee was fixed by locally determined constitutions; later on this was fixed by a nationally determined constitution. The chief weakness of the BCCR (now Racial Equality Council) was: how can a representative cross section of ethnic community interests be established from an arbitrary selection of organisations ranging from ethnic community and religious organisations to individuals committed to opposing racism?

In the 1970s most, though not all, representatives of ethnic organisations wanted representation on the BCCR executive committee, because it provided political opportunities that these men would not have had. The BCCR was a good example of a CRC that provided an arena in which leaders of organisations and communities could meet with elected political representatives and officers of the local authority as well as with each other. These men had the opportunity to represent the interests of their organisations with a view to influencing political decisions. Control of ethnic organisations was, if anything, supposed to be exercised through the selection of members.

One form of control was achieved through a balanced ethnic composition of the executive committee. The key to achieving a balance was placed in the hands of the director of the local CRC. For instance, between 1970 and 1975, two Hindus and two Muslims represented 13,000 Gujaratis on the CRC executive committee. Two small communities, one Pakistani and one West Indian, representing populations of 1000 members each were represented by three members - an organisational representative, an elected officer and by an additional member elected or co-opted to the Council. This bias in representation, in conjunction with no recognised or accepted system for election/selection of ethnic representatives led to growing ethnic dissatisfaction with the representation of organisations and communities on the Council and its committees. The profile of membership changed drastically in the following years, when the representation of these small communities was reduced as the Gujarati Muslim communities flooded the BCCR with their representatives and the Gujarati Hindus increased their representation. Over the next few years the population rose to 20,000 and the number of ethnic organisations almost doubled. Efforts to reduce the Muslim representatives until they no longer threatened the future of the CRC raised questions about the extent to which Gujarati executive members were representative of their communities.[2]

Unable to cope with the sudden appearance of competing Muslim and Hindu leaders by 1976, the BCCR experienced persistent attacks on its existence. There were as many Muslim and Hindu leaders as there were organisations and associations in the Gujarati communities, let alone the representatives of smaller communities, like the Pakistanis and West Indians. Each organisation had elected officers who competed to perform the functions of leadership. Most of them sought membership on the BCCR, but did not always obtain it. This competition served to increase the demand for places on the council and executive committees and increased the political importance of membership. Consequently, the selection of organisations into membership on the BCCR became a critical issue with those who were accepted, but they were not always recognised as leaders by those inside or outside their organisations. While the BCCR recognised all the organisational members as representatives, the local politicians were trying to establish who were and who were not leaders, so that they could target them for recruiting votes. Since most Muslim and Hindu organisations chose to seek membership on the executive committee of the BCCR, there were always some leaders whose organisations were not represented on the BCCR.

After 1988 when the BCCR became known as Bolton Racial Equality Council (BREC), it experienced a decline in membership, a lack of recognition by the formal political hierarchy and a continuing difficulty in having to cope with a selection process that was never effective. Its effectiveness depended upon objectives which combined a mix of vagueness and precision (Hill and Issacharoff, 1971:163-164), and which could not and still cannot be translated easily into practical action (John, 1969: 37-38). This served to reinforce the importance of the role of RECs in dealing with individual cases arising from racial discrimination. One review of their role claimed that detracted from their ability to 'conduct arguments about policy and practice' (Gay and Young, 1988:117) and a need for them to evaluate their role within the 'framework of local voluntary social action' (Gay and Young, 1988:121). These difficulties were attributed to the imbalance between the work CRCs had to conduct through the medium of meetings and that which had to be done outside meetings. This gave rise to a view that the subject matter of meetings which involved decision-making and procedural matters could be best coped with by those members who were 'educated, confident and urbane' (Hill and Issacharoff, 1971:283). However, it was during the early 1970s that the representatives of communities, such as the Indian and Pakistani societies, rather than ethnic organisations, withdrew from participation in the BCCR in the face of growing dissatisfaction from their members. This opened the way for the development of religious and social organisations, with representatives committed to anti-racism and the maintenance of their ethnic identities, to demand political recognition. Although some directors of CRCs chose not to lose sight of issues connected with immigration and nationality, they were now required to consider issues that were at the forefront of race relations. These included unemployment, poverty, racism, crime, homelessness, underachievement in education, health and the role of the police (Howe, 1988; Whitehead, 1987; Dalton and Daghlian, 1989; Hann, 1988; 1987; Scarman, 1981). On the one hand, they served to highlight the importance of ethnic involvement in local issues and local politics, on the other hand, served to stress the importance of ethnic political participation (Layton-Henry, 1984: 148; Anwar, 1984; 1980; Anwar and Kohler, 1975).

Since the 1960s ethnic community representation in politics has attracted attention. The history of politicians and political parties seeking the ethnic vote has been an exercise made all the more attractive by the possibility of capturing a block vote in the form of members of an ethnic community. Scott (1972/73) was one of the first to show how local politicians established relationships with ethnic communities to recruit ethnic votes; this has been more recently demonstrated in a Pakistani community in the East End of London (Eade, 1989). The importance of this is that it shows how the expectation of local politicians has accorded ethnic organisation representatives status as individuals who represent their members. Recently, in an analysis of local development, Hay (1994) notes how both ethnic communities and the areas in which they live may become targets for redevelopment. To persist with the notion of ethnic community arguably is a form of political racism, because politically they are not recognised as political bodies by political parties. Nevertheless, targeting ethnic communities remains the way favoured by local authorities and these other organisations for involving ethnic communities in debates about development and representation. On the one hand, local CRCs, rather than functioning as buffer organisations, acted as promoters of the social, economic and political interests of ethnic communities. On the other hand, by promoting organisational involvement, they and the CRE have persisted in supporting a form of participation that is unacceptable in formal political interaction. It is this dual role which has led to the CRE attempting consistently to re-assess the role of CRCs and to ethnic communities having to reconsider the role of their organisations in the context of local organisations generally and in the context of the CRCs. This support for ethnic organisations and their role in representing ethnic communities encouraged the development of ethnic leadership.

Leadership

The development of ethnic leadership is a function of the changing relationships within and between ethnic organisations and local white organisations. On the one hand, ethnic representatives accepted that their organisations were voluntary; on the other hand, local politicians accorded elected officers of these organisations a political status that acknowledged their political responsibilities. A number of processes have contributed to the social construction of ethnic representatives as leaders. Firstly, competition between the Gujarati leaders for a place on the executive committee and an opportunity to achieve political influence over the white politicians contributed to the emergence of individuals who claimed allegiance to particular ethnic identities. This often fierce exposure of ethnic interests led to the emergence within the BCCR of a group of members who were assumed to support the policies of the establishment, and an opposition group who were committed to Gujarati and minority representation in all spheres of local government. This set the scene for the BCCR to provide a forum in which these leaders could compete with each other for funds and support for their organisations, could debate local and national government policies and could assert their ethnic identities within a political context. The key issues that faced the Muslim and Hindu communities, BCCR and politicians are 'who are the leaders? Who has control over the ungoverned space between these communities? How could the politicians make political space for demands from the Gujarati leaders for political representation?'

To understand the emergence of ethnic leaders, one needs to understand the background of racism in the 1970s, which has been described as 'the result of the combined effect of economic, political, ideological and cultural processes' (Solomos *et al*, 1983: 11) in Britain generally. '... indigenous racism of the 60s and 70s is significantly different, in form and effect, from the racism of the "high" colonial period. It is racism "at home", not abroad; it is racism, not of a dominant but of a declining social formation' (Hall, 1981: 26). This is symptomatic of the crisis arising from the reaction to the shift by the state from its emphasis on integration and more indirect forms of control to more direct forms of state control (Solomos *et al*, 1983: 17). For instance the emphasis in race relations legislation changed from integration to control (Solomos *et al*, 1983: 17-21). Against the background of the 1970s the emergence of Gujarati leaders seeking participation in local government amounted to another crisis to which local and national politicians reacted as if it was not a policy of integration but a problem of control. For analytical purposes I shall separate leadership from decision-making, discussing the former in this Chapter and the latter in the next.

The racism of the 1960s and early 1970s was marked by debates about the status of immigrants, repatriation, control of immigration from New Commonwealth countries to Britain, and their access to public resources, namely housing, employment, schooling for their children, health services and political participation. These issues may be seen as precursors to the riots and disturbances of the early 1980s in Brixton and Toxteth. The development of grassroots urban social movements within the minority communities has been ignored in favour of grounding explanations for unrest in poverty and urban renewal and the lack of access to public resources. For instance, many pay lip service to the importance of ethnic political participation in local and national government, but few concentrate on the political exclusion or marginalisation of ethnic leaders (Benyon and Solomos, (eds.) 1987: Chaps. 1-3,15,19 and 20). Most of the contributors to this debate explain the riots in terms of unemployment, poverty, housing, policing, racial disadvantage and discrimination rather than in terms of a lack of political access to decision-making arenas.

Therefore, my aim is to concentrate on the importance of grassroots politics, which some have rather derogatorily described as factionalism (Rex and Moore, 1971: 117). The argument offered is that the decade of the 1970s witnessed an emergence of micro-social movements associated with events that provided opportunities for the development of ethnic leadership. Without any formalised structures of support, social networks functioned as the vehicles of social communication between supporters and leaders. The development of a view of the quality of living as part of Gujaratis' urban experiences led to leaders protesting about the social disadvantages that they claimed existed for Asians and black people resident in Bolton. Without any access to the formal political hierarchy other than through a white controlled political party system, Gujarati leaders expressed the view that white politicians, whose knowledge of the Gujarati communities was minimal, could not represent their supporters. With no connection with the political party system, these leaders emerged as spokesmen for their community organisations. They came to be regarded and often were treated as leaders by the white politicians, officers and members of organisations who worked with members of these communities. The scene is defined by the dilemma that faced the local (and other) CRCs, which was that as the main organisation offering ethnic minorities participation, its remit was concerned with their social, religious and welfare needs.

Leadership in the Gujarati communities

Much of the literature on leadership focuses attention on professional, business oriented, educated middle-class individuals or MPs and councillors (Werbner and Anwar, 1991; Anwar, 1979; Werbner, 1979; Hill and Issacharoff, 1971).

To gain an understanding of Gujarati leadership and its relationship with local politicians, it is necessary to recognise that a transformation took place amongst the Gujarati leadership as the political arena provided by the BCCR increased in importance. This saw the removal of three kinds of leaders, namely, those who were 'confident, educated and urbane', those who had the support of a kin-group and those who held high status occupations. They were replaced by men who had jobs, often of low social standing, if they had jobs at all, lived amongst their people, and above all placed great importance upon social friendship, religious and ethnic identities.

Anwar distinguishes between three types of leaders: formal, integrationist and traditional. Formal leaders depend 'upon their occupation and status in British society' and 'their role is mainly in inter-ethnic situations' (Anwar, 1979: 172,183). Integrationists are men mainly involved in forms of community work, have often experienced a longer period of education, have an urban background and wish to integrate with the white community (Anwar, 1979: 173). Traditional leaders are the *biraderi* elders who depend for their support upon 'age, length of stay in Britain, and the number of relatives sponsored and patronised' (Anwar, 1979: 173-174).

Their power derives from their kinship groups. Anwar notes 'the question of leadership cannot be understood unless the divisions within the Pakistani population are grasped' (1979: 171). This observation needs to be treated with caution. The social divisions within the Gujarati population need to be understood, in order to recognise that Gujarati leadership evolved through these three forms of leadership into a fourth form and much later in the 1990s into another form. Before the 1970s kinship group leaders and the integrationists comprised the majority of so-called leaders. These men were not political leaders, as they held no politically recognised office. A few held positions in national organisations, such as the local Indian or Pakistani Society, but the majority developed influence through the assistance they rendered to those who required help but often spoke little English. The formal leader also existed using, usually, his knowledge and status to unite disparate ethnic communities and individuals into some cohesive group or assisting an existing organisation to achieve some end (Werbner, 1991). However, these social characteristics are not typical of the 1970s Gujarati leaders. The pattern of Gujarati leadership, which became apparent in the 1970s, was similar to that described for the Pakistanis. The Gujaratis' leaders opposed integration and were enmeshed within kin and community social networks. The strength of these social networks came not from kin but from faction, caste and sect-based membership. The development of ethnic leadership reflects a shift away from political leadership towards the qualities associated with chairpersons of voluntary organisations.

The debate about styles of leadership (Werbner, 1991) does not apply to this Gujarati population, because style cannot become a substitute for the functions of leadership. Furthermore, the ethnic organisations vary in their recruitment from faction to caste, sect and religious organisation. Leadership of these organisations comes from external recognition rather than from internal acceptance. The performance of ethnic representatives varies with personality and political acumen, but hardly warrants classification by style. Leadership is a function amongst other functions performed by the elected representatives of ethnic organisations. Without an understanding of the monolithic structure of the Islamic Culture Centre and Islam generally, compared with the more fragmentary, divided structure of the Hindu communities, it is difficult to understand the positions leaders occupy and their relationships within and without ethnic organisations. Therefore, any analysis of Gujarati leadership needs to take account of the social identities of each community. To understand the change in the character of ethnic leaders of organisations, it makes sense to review briefly the evolution of ethnic leadership from the 1950s onwards.

Men of influence or integrationists (1950-1960)

Gujaratis came to Bolton seeking a better life. Linked by their membership of particular communities, they supported each other in what was an alien environment. Initially, individuals who had abilities to communicate with these settlers and those in official positions quickly rose to positions of influence, since the people looked to them for help with finding accommodation, jobs and dealing with local authority departments, the Home Office and the police. These people were often prominent doctors, teachers and businessmen. By social standing many were middle class or adopted the social trappings of a middle class life style (Anwar, 1979:173; Hill and Issacharoff, 1971: 146). Those who were prominent became men of influence by virtue of the respect they received from their fellow Gujaratis and white colleagues. Others achieved positions of high standing by establishing businesses upon which many Gujaratis depended for essential ethnic items, like food and clothing. Some of the more prominent of these men included an eye specialist, a teacher, two businessmen, and an Acting Community Relations Officer. Not only did Gujaratis seek help from them, but also Asians belonging to other minority communities sought their help, advice and support. The eye specialist chaired the first Indian Association, whose members were mainly Hindus. Since they were able to speak English and claimed to speak for Asians, they were treated by white Boltonians as if they were leaders.

These men shared the view that most Asians experienced similar disadvantages, that is, they lacked essential information about the society they had just joined, they could not speak English adequately and their support for their ethnic and religious identities would only impede their absorption into British society. Furthermore, they also held the opinion that Gujaratis coming to or already living in Bolton should and would become increasingly integrated with the passage of time. They interpreted their role of leadership in terms of assisting other migrants by helping them to find jobs, send money home, and to cope with problems of communication and settlement. In this spirit they devoted time, effort and money to establish associations like the Pakistani and Indian Associations. They did not regard it as necessary to be informed about the opinions of the people whose support they claimed, nor were they interested in finding out what these were. Their main and overriding aim was to promote integration. Whether or not they were structurally in the most effective positions to do so is not relevant or important (Anwar, 1979: 171). There is no evidence that they believed themselves able to do this and it was not their aim. The answer to the question: did they assist the process of integration of individual immigrants, is in the affirmative. Paradoxically, they proved to be unable to perform or even to convince the members of the organisations they represented that integration was a useful goal, if a goal at all. Dissatisfaction with these leaders grew as the supporters rejected the philosophy of integration, which most Gujaratis began to recognise as involving unrealistic aims, because it failed to convey the problems and difficulties that they faced in their everyday lives. Most Gujaratis shared little in common with these so-called leaders. The personal difficulties which led to the development of relationships of dependence of Gujaratis upon them have been likened to that of patron or broker, reminiscent of that between *jajman* and *kamin* (Desai, 1963: 57-60). Generally, few of these old style leaders chose to concentrate on issues that emphasised ethnic identities, such as *halal* food in the schools, or cremation or burial of the dead within 24 hours. However, it was these issues which became increasingly important to these Gujaratis once they no longer saw their future here in terms of a return to 'home'. Home was Britain.

Alternative leaders: *imams* and priests

The consolidation of the local Gujarati population was accompanied by the emergence and establishment of religious organisations (Ballard, R. and C, 1977:35ff) that did not represent the interests of a single Islamic community, but rather of one of a number of Islamic communities. A parallel process took place amongst the Hindu organisations. Now the Muslim community and Hindu community became multiple communities based upon recruitment from different factions, castes and sects (Chapters Three and Four). Within a relatively short time a number of the Hindu and Muslim communities were looking for suitable buildings to use as temples or mosques. The Muslims had established their first mosque, Zakariah Mosque, at Peace Street; now they began establishing other mosques. Although *imamship* potentially incorporates some aspects of leadership, they are employees of mosque committees. Unless they have exceptional ability, they cannot override their relationship as employees and take on the functions of community leadership, which are vested in the mosque committee. Mosque committees can pay their *imams* a bare minimum and had the power to obtain Home Office approval for the entry into Britain of an *imam* of their choice, and so also came to believe that they had power to prolong or terminate this permission to stay. The effect of this form of contract is that *imams* are at the mercy of their mosque committees. Consequently, there is little opportunity for them to rise to positions of leadership outside their rigorously defined roles as prayer leaders. Only one *imam* in Bolton succeeded in rising to a position of leadership: he achieved this through becoming the founder and principal of the *darul-ul-loom* at Ramsbottom.

In contrast to the Muslims, the Hindus struggled to find suitable places. When suitable places could not be found, religious worship took place in private homes or rented halls. Priests who held positions of authority by virtue of their religious qualifications in theory had the potential to fulfil the functions of leadership. For instance, a Brahmin doctor might seem to be an obvious choice as a leader, but none took on this role, since the eye specialist had done so in the 1950s and 1960s. A reason for their lack of involvement most likely is that they are in a similar position to imams: they are employed by particular temple communities to perform ritual roles. Thus they could not be both employee and leader. During the period of research no full-time priests were resident in town. A few years later a number of priests came to Bolton. One priest to whom I spoke worked in a local paper mill and performed the appropriate rituals for a fee when called upon to do so.

Emergence of the ethnic leader

The emergence of grassroots ethnic leaders in the Hindu and Muslim communities owes much to the proliferation and consolidation of socio-religious organisations. Men were elected to positions in these organisations which gave them power to employ priests or *imams*, to influence the attitudes and social values of their members, and to take on some of the functions of leadership. Since they achieved their positions by election, they were expected by their supporters to perform a range of functions, one of which included leadership. Not all leaders did. The political functions of leadership became a simple extension to their existing offices. The informal political arena provided by the CRC, to which the elected organisational representatives had access, supported the assumption that this political function was part of their role. When I use the term leader I shall mean an officer of an ethnic organisation who, in addition to his other responsibilities, has taken on some of the functions of leadership. Most leaders of these ethnic organisations in the 1970s were ready to assume this political function. However, the Swaminarayans and the followers of Saibaba chose neither to seek positions on the BCCR nor to participate in political debates. They chose to commit their time to the development of a community/religious centre for their respective communities. Since the CRC had at that time access to funds for which ethnic organisations could apply, and through membership of its executive committee ethnic leaders could establish personal relationships with elected politicians, competition for places on the executive committee was keen. The number of places was defined by a constitution approved by the Community Relations Commission and Race Relations Board and, with the replacement of these two, the CRE. To keep their positions and to control the executive, leaders established a web of fragile alliances (Kalka, 1991) between ethnic organisations. These shifted frequently thus providing an underlying dynamic that matched the competition between factions, mosques, sects and caste organisations for control of the ungoverned space between them. Representation on CRCs, which was critical before 1970 (Hill and Issacharoff, 1971: Chapter 6), became more contentious afterwards (CRE, 1978). Not only were the majorities of Gujarati Hindu and Muslim organisations seeking representation on the BCCR, but also the Bolton West Indian Society, Bangladeshis, Pakistani Association, Somalis and Kashmiri Workers Association were demanding places. The decision on whom to admit was left to the judgement of the CRO and the existing members of the CRC, whose knowledge of ethnic organisations varied greatly. This dilemma over selection or election of representatives and organisations ensured that Gujarati leaders would become committed to competing for influence in the BCCR, with its members and with one another.

To reiterate, elected representatives of ethnic organisations considered membership of the BCCR as desirable for at least four reasons: firstly, it could help them obtain funding, directly or indirectly, for community projects. Secondly, it could provide them with access to a sought after resource - a political arena. Thirdly, recognition by the BCCR implied recognition by other organisations, such as the local authority. Fourthly, it provided them with a source of advice and help for a wide range of problems. Representatives of different factions, castes or sects belonging to the same religious community could swamp the CRC and thus take control of it. Being aware of this, it made it all the more important for those who had representatives to win places for more representatives from their religious community. Since no one organisation could have more than two representatives, the way to increase representatives was to create new organisations whose officers owed allegiance to the umbrella organisation. The Gujarati Muslim leaders understand these dynamics and deploy them with consummate skill. Already existing factions, caste communities and sects under the umbrella of the ICC have separated into smaller units, a process that I describe as detachment or proliferation. This is a process by which a larger organisation splits into a number of smaller ones whose relationship to the larger one can range from co-operation to competition. At one level these organisations share a common social/religious identity; at another they have their own identities. Depending upon a situation, leaders established or demolished the fragile alliances that once united them and now divide them (Kalka, 1991:216-217, 220). The structure of the Islamic community (Chapter Three) allows for such restructuring. As the officers in charge of each mosque demanded representation on the BCCR, a situation developed in which there were more mosque representatives looking for more places on the BCCR than existed. In other words, the Muslims could have taken over the CRC. Within the monolithic structure of the ICC the facility of detachment allows for the proliferation of mosques without endangering the unity of the host organisation. If anything, this process strengthened the position of the ICC.

Although this process of detachment could be seen to operate in other communities, such as the Hindu community, they made little use of it. An explanation for this is that there is no central structure around which the Hindus could unite. Another is that they had a strong outsider leader of the VHP, who dominated Hindu participation in the CRC without seemingly having to look for support from smaller Hindu organisations. For small communities, such as the Pakistanis and West Indians, the process of detachment was of little use, but there is evidence that, for instance, the Pakistanis used it (Kalka, 1991:216-217). In Bolton the Pakistanis and other small Islamic communities were drawn into the process of detachment or unification through their shared allegiance to Islam. On the one hand, the weakness of this form of representation is that it provides an opportunity for a leader to become a 'big man', an idea which all Gujaratis found unacceptable. On the other hand, detachment is a particularly suitable form of representation for the Muslim and Hindu communities, since as a process it opens the way for a religious community to segment into many parts and thereby exploit the process of democracy by swamping the CRC with their men.

Social characteristics of Gujarati leaders

In the course of the survey, I collected completed schedules from forty men who had been or were officers in Gujarati organisations. Twenty-five of them were Hindu and fifteen were Muslim. The majority of them had acted as representatives for their organisations on the Executive Committee of the BCCR.

In an urban society, race provides a way of expressing ideologies about economic and political relationships in such a way that they encapsulate a self justifying circle of explanations about conditions, problems and contradictions faced by Asian, black and white people (Hall, 1981: 35). In the 1970s the recession in the textile and related industries on which most Gujaratis and other ethnic communities depended for livelihoods was experiencing a crisis, and so each community began to establish a visible symbol of their social identity; this generally took the form of a mosque or temple. Competition for space and signs to demonstrate ownership became as intense as competition for jobs. Not only did this mean finding funds to purchase land and buildings, leading to a greater demand for representation on the BCCR, but also it was evidence of emergence of consumerism. 'This involves a dual focus: firstly, on the cultural dimension of the economy, the symbolisation and use of material goods as "communicators" not just utilities; and secondly, on the economy of cultural goods, the market principles of supply, demand, capital accumulation, competition, and monopolisation which operate *within* the sphere of life-styles, cultural goods and commodities' (Featherstone, 1996:84). Gujarati leaders were required by their supporters to demonstrate their leadership by meeting their cultural needs, which at this time took the form of a need for mosques and temples. It also proved to the immediate social world that they were part of it, as success demonstrated that they had competed successfully for space, property and established a symbol of cultural identity in which all could share.

The aim of Hindu and Muslim leaders to establish the ethnic identities of their communities in a wider urban arena became an exercise in exchanging ethnic cultural symbols for white ones. The leaders of ethnic organisations who saw this as their task derived their authority neither from kin groups, a commitment to tradition, nor integration. These were men who were steeped in the ethnic, racial and to some extent class conflicts of life in British cities. Although there is a variation in their social characteristics, they all were bent on the task of creating an ethnic area demarcated by cultural symbols that reflected their dominance of it. This defined the ungoverned space between the Gujaratis and the white political hierarchy. It was into this space that these ethnic leaders stepped, and the arena in which they could contest their claims was that provided by the local CRC. Thus the ethnic leaders found themselves in a new political environment which militated against the philosophy and policy of integration, but which allowed ethnic politics to flourish. While the integrationists stood outside the communities they represented, these ethnic leaders had to be deeply embedded in the social, economic and religious fabric of their communities in order to understand the needs and ethnic identities of their supporters. These men were responsible for property and funds owned by their community, for any employees, and for decisions on local services upon which a religious community depended. These issues included the quick release of a body by the coroner, the preparation of bodies for burial, the burial or cremation itself, access to burial grounds, religious tuition for children of members, the provision of *halal* meat in schools, and at this time facilities for community gatherings. Competition for public resources and for political support through lobbying politicians placed these leaders in positions where they had to become political to achieve the results they wanted for their members.

These Gujarati leaders were enmeshed within the social fabric of their communities but they owed their positions as representatives of organisations not to their kin or traditional qualities but to their aggression and defence of their culture. An analysis of their social characteristics shows that most of them are employed in jobs that fall within Class VII, that is, 'semiskilled and unskilled manual'. Further analysis shows that the majority (60%) of them (Table 6.1a) are employed in similar occupations to those of their close friends (81%). Compared with the

Muslims, slightly more Hindu leaders (64%) belong to lower social classes than do their close friends (57%) (Table 6.1b).

Table 6.1a
Social standing of Muslim leaders and their close friends

Social standing of respondents			Class of close friends					
Class	no.	%	I	III	IV	VI	VII	total
II	1	6.67		1	1	7	1	
III	2	13.33		1	1	17	1	
IV	3	20		4	8	16		
VII	9	60	3		2	47	2	
Totals	15		3	6	12	87	4	112
%			2.7	5.4	10.7	77.7	3.6	100%

Summary of Table 6.1a

Close friends	Above	Equal	Below
Totals	112	9	56	47
%	100	8	50	42

Table 6.1b
Social standing of Hindu leaders and their close friends

Social standing of respondents			Class of close friends						
Class	no.	%	I	II	III	IV	VI	VII	total
I	2	8	5	3		6	1		
III	2	8		2	3	4	6		
IV	5	20	2	3	3	5	12	14	
VII	15	60	1	4	11	22	45	15	
Other	1	4			3			7	
Total:	25	100	8	12	20	37	64	36	177
%			4.5	6.8	11.3	20.9	36.2	20.3	100%

Summary of Table 6.1b

Close friends	Above	Equal	Below
Totals	177	51	65	61
%	100	28.8	36.7	34.5

These leaders share with their close friends similar social standing within and without their communities. They are not seeking to join the white middle class; rather they are rejecting such aims in favour of aligning themselves with the

161

grassroots in their own communities. This pattern of turning to grassroots support to awaken religious and ethnic identities conflicts with the pattern of leadership between the 1960s and 1970s. From this analysis the social characteristics of the Sikh leader of the VHP are different from those of the other ethnic leaders. Of all the leaders, he held the most formal educational qualifications and his wife was as well qualified as he was. At the time he was the only outsider leader (I discuss him in more detail below).

Evidence that leaders' immediate support did not come from kin is provided by an analysis of the connectedness of the primary zones of their social networks. This analysis also shows that their primary zones, the strong ties within their networks, are similar to those of the people to whom they look for support. The average numbers of close friends of the Muslim and Hindu leaders are larger (7.6 and 7.1) than those of the total sample of Muslims and Hindus (Chapter Four). A higher percentage (87%) of the zones of Muslim leaders are complete compared to those of Muslim respondents (73%) generally, whereas slightly fewer Hindu leaders' zones are complete (48%) as compared with those of the Hindu sample (54%) as a whole. Hindu leaders' zones include fewer (68%) homogeneous close friends than do those of the Hindus sampled, suggesting that they are more prepared than their supporters to include friends who belong to other ethnic or white communities. However, Muslim leaders anchored more homogeneous zones (80%) than are anchored by the Muslim sample (76.6%). Arguably, the characteristics of these zones of Muslim and Hindu leaders enabled them to utilise ties better between their members or across caste and ethnic boundaries than can their respective supporters. These social characteristics of the Muslim leaders' zones suggest that they may be at least as deeply entrenched, if not more so, than those of their Muslim members. In other words they are in good positions to benefit most from the ideology that reminds all Muslims that they are brothers. In a different way the Hindu leaders, given the loose-knittedness of their primary zones, can establish more wide-ranging and stronger relationships with Hindus across caste boundaries than could their members.

To maintain strong relationships with supporters, leaders have to meet them frequently. The average number of places where Hindu leaders meet their close friends (2.49) is above the average for that of the Hindu sample (2.12), and the same holds for the Muslim leaders (3.3 for leaders and 2.84 for the sample). A comparison of levels of intensity of zones of close friends of leaders shows that the proportion of Muslim leaders (73%) anchoring zones comprising a single level relationship is markedly higher than that for the Muslim sample as a whole (57%). However, only 36% of Hindu leaders anchored such zones, which is about identical to that of the sample as a whole (36%). Further analysis of leaders shows that all Muslim leaders interviewed perceived their close friends being linked by ties of close friendship (93%); only one Muslim included a kinsman amongst his close friends (Table 6.2a) compared to the total Muslim sample (87.5%). Most of these zones comprise one level of intensity. No Hindu leader included kin amongst their close friends (Table 6.2b). A higher proportion of Hindu leaders anchored strong zones in which all friends are close friends of one another (56%) compared with a lower proportion of Hindus sampled (53%). The degrees of connectedness of

162

leaders' zones, as measured by the weight of the optimum spanning trees, indicated that more Muslim leaders' zones are closely connected than are those of the Muslim sample as a whole (Chapter Four). Generally the connectedness of the Hindu leaders' zones is similar to that of the Hindu sample as a whole, except that more zones anchored by them are more loosely connected than those anchored by the sample.

Table 6.2a
Degree of connectedness of Muslim leaders' zones

Total no. of friends in zones	Weights of optimum spanning trees					zones
	2-9	10-18	19-27	28-36	37-45	
3		2				2
4	1	1				2.
5		1				1
7		1				1
8			1			1
10		6	1	1		8
Totals:	1	11	2	1		15
%:	6.7	73.3	13.3	6.7		100

Close ——————— Connectedness ——————— Loose

Table 6.2b
Degree of connectedness of Hindu leaders' zones

Total no. of friends in zones	Weights of optimum spanning trees					zones
	2-9	10-18	19-27	28-36	37-45	
4		2	1		1	4
5		3		1	1	5
6		2	2	1	1	6
10		3	5	1	1	10
Totals:		10	8	3	4	25
%		40	32	12	16	100

Close ——————— Connectedness ——————— Loose

Outsider as leader

The search for cultural symbols that could be transformed into a concrete entity, such as a mosque or temple, gave rise to the emergence of a variety of ethnic organisations, whose members supported individuals who would perform the functions of leadership without becoming 'big men'. The majority of Muslim and Hindu leaders were not 'big men', although some aspired to being such leaders. It is feasible to distinguish between two extreme types of leaders as opposed to the function and style of leadership: the one is the insider who is elected to leadership; the other is the outsider who is recruited to leadership. Most Gujarati Muslim and Hindu organisations can accommodate such individuals, but some can accommodate them more easily than others. It fell to the VHP to elect one such person to a position of leadership. Under his leadership the VHP became a high profile consumer of local culture and producer of its own culture.

For some years before 1972, a Sikh member of the BCCR had spoken on behalf of the Hindus. He was the most prominent Punjabi Sikh from a largely hidden small group of Sikhs. Although he lectured at a Manchester college, he lived in Bolton. Unlike most leaders of the day, who lived in the Gujarati area of the town, he moved from a Gujarati area to a white area. His occupation gave him high social standing and as an articulate, urbane and educated man, he was accepted as a leader by the BCCR, leaders of other Asian and black communities, local councillors and MPs. He was quickly elected vice-chairperson of BCCR. In this position he rose to prominence through his involvement in helping Ugandan Asian refugees settle in Bolton. In 1973 he was invited to join the VHP, where he was soon elected to the position of chairperson; a position he held until 1979. His election brought a temporary cessation to the inter-caste rivalry that had bedevilled relationships between VHP members. As a Sikh, he could not be identified with a particular Hindu caste. Of his ten close friends, only two were Hindus, the remaining eight being Sikhs, whom he maintained were unacquainted with each other. In terms of connectedness, the primary zone he anchored was exceptional: it had an optimum spanning tree weight of 45. This made it the largest and most loosely connected zone in the sample. Although he quickly established working relationships with the white politicians, he found it more difficult to associate himself with caste issues. Some of those who elected him, such as the Mandhata Patels, found it difficult to reconcile his general approach to supporting the VHP with his inability to identify with caste issues. To the white politicians, he fitted their notion of what a leader should be, well spoken, politically acute, tactful and hostile as appropriate.

As chairperson of the VHP, this Sikh was called upon to play a prominent part in many activities and projects. One of his most notable achievements was to unite members from different castes to raise funds for the purchase of a community centre. The demand of this large organisation was for a leader who could handle the complex negotiations between themselves and whoever had property to sell which might meet their needs for a community centre. As events transpired, one building they favoured was St. Barnabas Church, owned by the Church of England. These negotiations brought this leader into contact with representatives of the church, the Charity Commission and also brought him face-to-face with the public face of racism. Through public opposition to the purchase of the building from local people including a local vicar, he experienced public and private criticism from both his own members and ardent racists (see Chapter Seven). In 1976 when the Church of England sold St. Barnabas to the VHP, the Press claimed that it was the first consecrated building ever sold to Hindus by the Church of England. A few years later, it was opened with due pomp and circumstance before invited guests, who included local MPs, the Mayor, councillors and many other prominent people. During this time, he probably received more publicity in the local press than any other Asian or black leader before or after him. Consequently, he became the most respected and widely known Asian leader in Bolton.

Of all the Hindu organisations in Bolton, the VHP is the one which could accept most easily an outsider as a leader. It claims to be a multi-caste organisation. The Sikh and his wife had friends who were members of the VHP, and they were able to provide him with the kind of support he required to overcome the inter-caste disputes that existed. He was fortunate in having the support and close friendship of a number of the prominent members, who were also well educated and held jobs of high social standing as well as belonging to two of the largest castes in Bolton. They made a good team. There were advantages and disadvantages to be gained by the VHP electing an outsider as chairperson. The main advantage was that they could handpick their leader; the main disadvantage was that without being tied to a caste he could develop the role of leadership into something greater than that linked to one ethnic organisation. This is precisely what he achieved. The position of leader of all Gujaratis or all Muslims or Hindus is one to which some leaders aspire. However, such a leader would attract criticism and hostility on the grounds that he wanted to be a 'big man'. In this respect the Sikh was no exception: he wanted to be recognised as a 'big man'. Eventually, some influential members of the VHP turned caste support away from him by criticising his handling of certain VHP matters, such as difficulties linked to a visit the VHP members made to the Isle of Man (Chapter Seven). This event also gave some members the opportunity to allege that he misappropriated funds, an accusation that was never proved. He alone of all the minority leaders tried to form an association of leaders - a forerunner of the Minorities Joint Consultative Committee (MJCC), but they were suspicious of his motives and failed to give him the support he required to become a leader of leaders. In 1979 he severed his links with the VHP and moved away. Under his leadership the VHP made claims on the space and time of most prominent people in the town, it surpassed the Islamic community in the publicity it received, and also it attracted considerable racist aggression, which took the form of arson and structural damage. However, the VHP became, with the exception of the Swaminarayan temples, the centre of Hindu cultural activities. Likewise the VHP also endeavoured to offer a similarly large range of facilities and services, including a library, at one time certain health services for women and children, a place where its members could hold private functions, and employed a priest to look after the religious needs of the community. Thus elected leaders had considerable influence over the lives of their members and it became both a consumer and producer of culture.

The Muslim organisations could also have chosen an outsider as a leader, but in practice they were reluctant to do so. When they do accept advice from an outsider, they are quick to disown or blame him for their misfortunes. Although during the period of research no such person emerged as a leader, in 1983 a Bangladeshi doctor, a prominent member of the Bangladeshi Association and of the Labour Party, was elected as a member of the BCCR and chose to speak for all Muslims.

165

However, at the 1989 annual general meeting of the BCCR he lost his seat, because the Gujarati Muslim representatives voted against him. He believed that as a Muslim and a doctor holding a respected position in Bolton, his quest for overall leadership of the Muslim community would be unopposed.

For men, like the Sikh and the Muslim doctor, who set out to be leaders without ties other than those that bind a voter to his/her supporter, support is determined solely by a tenuous thread which supporters can recognise or break at will. For leaders with ties in their communities the freedom to achieve success is limited by the constraints exercised by supporters through these same ties. In the 1970s the adage that most Gujarati leaders quoted was that big men are bad. It revealed their deep distrust of ethnic leaders and recognition of the temptation to be drawn away from their communities towards the white community. To some extent these attitudes are supported by an analysis of the relationships between leaders and some of their supporters.

Leadership in the Gujarati population

Although leadership of ethnic organisations can take a number of forms, three kinds of leaders predominate. These are firstly, a pan-Gujarati leader, secondly, a leader of Muslims or Hindus, and thirdly, leaders of community organisations. In 1970 only one kind of leader existed. This was the leader of ethnic organisations. An explanation for this is that offered by Gujaratis themselves, namely that 'big men' are untrustworthy. Another explanation is reflected in the attitudes of supporters who stated that they could not accept a leader who does not accept their religious beliefs and/or come from their community. Therefore, before analysing the wider relationships between leaders and supporters, I shall briefly discuss these other forms of leadership.

When those sampled were asked whether they would be prepared to accept a leader from one of the four ethnic minority communities, most respondents expressed a preference for a member of their religious community. Thus the majority of Muslim respondents expressed a clear preference for a Gujarati Muslim as a leader as opposed to a Pakistani leader. Their lack of willingness to accept a Hindu was matched by an equally great reluctance to accept a Pakistani. Gujarati Muslims perceive themselves as being different from Pakistanis (see Chapter Five). The Muslims gave the impression that they would rather have anyone but a Sikh. Those who knew the Sikh considered him to be anti-Muslim, a reputation he acquired when he expressed his opinion in the BCCR on how the Lena Street Mosque community should view the local authority's order to close their mosque (Chapter Seven). Even those Muslims who did not support the chairperson of Lena Street Mosque regarded his behaviour as evidence of his duplicity and were not prepared to accept him as a leader. Although the idea of a pan-Gujarati leader is theoretically possible, there is little opportunity for such a leader to emerge. A reason is that the fragmented nature of the Gujarati population by religion, faction, caste and sect would probably make such a position untenable. Without a reason for Gujaratis acting as Gujaratis, there is no call for such a leader. The skills of leadership rested with the ability of a leader to meet the needs of his supporters and to perform the function of leader within the wider arena of the BCCR and the local political community. Implicit in the reasoning of these Gujaratis is the argument that they can control leaders through social relationships and this implies that successful leaders or 'big men' cannot be controlled through them. When asked, few Gujarati Hindus or Muslims were prepared to accept as a leader a person who did not accept their religious beliefs. No Hindu was prepared to accept a Muslim or vice versa as a leader. Consequently, Gujarati leadership is characterised by the rapid turnover of leaders. A number of the leaders who were in positions of leadership in 1976 disappeared, but later returned to prominence. In this sense this minority group is hydra-headed; there is no single identifiable structure of leadership, but rather there are a number of leaders of ethnic organisations with the majority competing for recognition by politicians and white organisations as leaders. Thus leaders came and went, each one hoping that events might bring them into prominence.

As the political arena in which they strove for influence over the white politicians was an informal and developing one, their strength lay in the 'fragile alliances' which they established between themselves and their supporters, between each other, and between themselves and the formally elected white politicians. Two factors increased their chances of becoming known: firstly, their ability to turn their organisation into a consumer and producer of cultural symbols, and secondly, their presence on the BCCR. The larger the organisation and the broader its basis for recruitment, the more opportunity its leader had to raise issues of political interest to supporters and politicians. Competition between Muslim and Hindu organisations for public resources implied competition between these leaders for political influence. Since the organisations developed initially in response to the social, cultural and religious needs of their members, the tasks of these officers were to establish their cultural symbols in a competing urban environment. For their time in office these men had considerable influence over their members and the organisations' resources. All ethnic organisations in Bolton were branch organisations and so had to accept the decisions of their head organisations, which tended to be based in the Midlands or London. For instance, the head organisation of the Mistry caste tried to reduce the size of dowry payments by caste members, while another Hindu caste organisation outcaste a member (Chapter Seven). A local difference between Hindu and Muslim organisations is that the ICC provided an umbrella organisation with facilities that met the religious needs of its subsidiary mosques and all Muslims. This encouraged leaders of mosque communities (*jamatbandi*) to become acquainted with one another, whereas in the Hindu population there was no such organisation. Furthermore, the fragility of the alliances between leaders of organisations is reflected in their poor acquaintance with one another. For instance, a high percentage of Muslims claimed some form of acquaintance with chairperson (75%) and vice-chairperson (64%) of the ICC. Well over half of the Muslims sampled (65%) did not know the other Muslim leaders. Many had not heard of the chairperson of the Pakistani Association, who received as much press coverage during 1972-76 as did the Sikh leader of the VHP. As the manager of the first Muslim bank to be established in Bolton, his picture appeared in the local newspaper where his bank and its services were advertised. Yet 74% of the sample had not heard of him. Only a small number of respondents (32%) had heard of the chairperson of Lena Street Mosque. He was the least well known of the Muslim leaders and yet became one of the best known to the white politicians and BCCR (Chapter Six). This bears out a point that the majority of leaders of Muslim organisations are known only to members of their organisations.

Likewise, Hindus were relatively unacquainted with their leaders. The majority (63%) of them knew or knew of the Sikh leader, which equates with his prominence as a leader of the VHP and the publicity that was associated with his position. Less than 50% of respondents were acquainted with his vice-chairperson and even fewer were acquainted with the other leaders of Hindu organisations. Only 24% of Hindus sampled could claim acquaintance with the chairperson of the Saibaba movement, and even fewer knew of the officers of the Mandhata Patel Association (24%), the Shree Kutch Swaminarayan (21%) and Shree Swaminarayan Mandir (18%). Knowledge of leaders across religious groups was even poorer. No leader was as widely known to both Hindus and Muslims as the Sikh leader of the VHP; 10% of Muslims knew of him as compared with less than 5% of Hindus who knew the chairperson of Lena Street Mosque, the Muslim leader who had received the greatest publicity. This also points to leaders having little contact with other leaders and other Gujaratis outside their organisations. Gujaratis knew the leaders of their organisations and a few had heard of other leaders; the leaders themselves were often not acquainted with other leaders. Thus alliances could only be fragile, but their awareness of the funds to which members had access through the BCCR, the semi-political and informal arena it provided and the opportunity to build alliances with other ethnic leaders and politicians encouraged competition. Leaders who represented their organisations on BCCR came to see themselves as an elite. As such they had an opportunity to become acquainted with each. They were asked how well they knew the chairpersons and secretaries of eight prominent Hindu, Muslim and Pakistani organisations. Eight organisations were selected because, firstly, they were independent of each other; secondly, the chairpersons and secretaries with one exception lived in Bolton. The vice-chairperson of the VHP who lived in Blackburn had his roots in Bolton. The findings suggest that generally Muslim leaders are better acquainted with one another than are Hindu leaders. For instance, most Hindu leaders (80%) had not heard of the chairperson of the Shree Kutch Swaminarayan Mandir and 92% had not heard of the chairperson of the Shree Swaminarayan Mandir. Since these leaders had so little knowledge of each other, there was little co-operation between them, even though their organisations shared similar interests, such as burial within 24 hours. Common interests brought the Muslim leaders together: they represented organisations which shared the same religious needs, and most of these shared a common identities as members of the ICC and as Muslims. The strong ties of close friendship, which linked them to their communities, enabled them to develop weak ties with those who did not belong to their organisations and communities. They could establish weak ties with leaders and members of other Gujarati and Pakistani organisations and with white politicians and other white people holding positions of influence. The strength of these weak ties lay in the ease and little commitment with which leaders could establish them and then break them. This added to the fragility of alliances.

To summarise, in this Chapter I argued that ethnic leadership was based upon a highly fragmented Gujarati population. Thus there is little possibility of the emergence of a single overall leader, or even a Muslim or Hindu leader. Therefore, the leaders that exist represent organisations: some are social, some religious, and some are a combination of social and religious. Competition to produce cultural symbols that reflect their social identities in a competitive world drove most to join the BCCR, where they had an opportunity to increase their access to scarce resources (funds) and to establish alliances, however fragile, with both other ethnic leaders and elected white politicians. This situation, with the added opportunity of participating in an informal political arena provided by the BCCR, encouraged the emergence and development of ethnic politics. The next Chapter looks at the debates that provided the substance of ethnic politics.

Notes

1. Ten years later the formation of MJCCs functioned just like buffer organisations but had the advantage of appearing to give minority representatives more direct representation.
2. Such issues as these encouraged the militancy of Asian and black leaders then and since then. The equal opportunities legislation has done little to resolve this difficulty. Though recognition of inequalities by members of ethnic communities has continued, the leaders who are emerging today are different from those of the 1970s and 1980s.

7 Quest for space: politics and ethnic politics

In the previous Chapter I argued that the distinction between participation in formal politics and ethnic politics is crucial to understanding the different purposes that each served. The suggestion that there are five (or three) possible forms of participation by black people in politics (Layton-Henry, 1984; Solomos, 1989) gives the impression that they all provide ways in which black people can relate to the political system. These five different ways are dissimilar in so far as they do not enable black people to participate in the same kind of politics. They can be separated into three forms of political activity. Firstly, ethnic politics is not strictly about participation in formal politics, but about competition between and within ethnic communities for scarce resources. Politicians may utilise ethnic links to collect votes, but then ethnic leadership is reduced to a device for vote catching. The idea that there is space for an ethnic political body of some kind in a party political system is unrealistic. Ideologically, it is possible to conceive of some kind of body that might assert a right to express ethnic interests at a political level (Parekh, 1991). Participation in the formal political system, through social class allegiances, voting, and participation in political parties, must by definition exclude ethnic political bodies, such as ethnic communities or organisations. Democracy in Britain is organised on the basis of political parties. This Chapter will explore the inter-relationship between formal and ethnic politics and will also focus on how ethnic politics developed to meet an ethnic need to capture the ungoverned space between and within ethnic communities and the white community.

The emergence of ethnic politics coincided not only with the period of freedom that CRCs had prior to the review in 1988, but also when ethnic communities became committed to establishing signs advertising their presence in Bolton. It was a period of growth for the ethnic consumer community. Ethnic communities imposed their culture upon the town by establishing mosques and temples. These organisations supported ethnic religion and cultures such that the wider social system – education, health, business, industry - had to accept and if not espouse, at least recognise. This shift towards consumerism in the 1970s was made possible by two factors, firstly, the lack of access to governed space other than through voting and secondly, competition for ungoverned space within and between both ethnic communities and the white community.

In the 1970s, governed space was controlled and dominated by white politicians, the established political parties and the local authority. The form that control took was over permission to change the existing use of space for the production of ethnic cultural signs. Ethnic organisations, as part of their growing awareness of the value of their floating votes, also recognised that they controlled the production of signs and symbols. The argument that control of this space enabled the state through local and national government to devalue the space in which ethnic communities lived is persuasive (Smith, 1989). Competition for ungoverned (devalued) space was not of great concern to those who controlled it, so long as what happened to it did not affect the value of the governed space. Ungoverned space was available for capture because it was not seen as economically valuable or politically important. Therefore, ethnic politics involved competition for resources and ungoverned space in which to develop cultural signs. These included the establishment of ethnic enterprises and community ventures, which formed the beginning of a process of cultural reproduction and consumerism, enabling Gujaratis to establish themselves as consumers and producers of their culture.

The main competitors for ungoverned space and the production of ethnic signs were the ethnic communities. Both formal politics and ethnic politics provide the dynamics which made possible competition for scarce resources, such as funds, land and property, but also for the mobilisation of ethnic support. In local and national elections, support for candidates and representation on political bodies was not the responsibility of the local CRC, but was the responsibility of other organisations, such as political parties and local authorities. However, local CRCs inadvertently supported ethnic competition for ungoverned space, because they enabled them to maintain links with the ethnic communities and organisations. What the CRC provided was a stage on which leaders could establish or break the fragile alliances to gain access to resources or support. All seemed to benefit by this relationship, until the CRE removed immigration and nationality cases from the remit of CRCs in their review in 1988. Through this decision they began to demolish the arena in which ethnic politics flourished. Although this change in role reduced ethnic politics, it did not totally remove it. For instance, as noted elsewhere, recently Oldham CRC was closed down, because ethnic politics had led to a take-over by one ethnic cohort.

This Chapter will focus attention on two forms of political activity: firstly, ethnic participation in formal politics, which is concerned with governed space; and secondly, activity within ethnic organisations, showing how leaders competed for cultural domination of ungoverned space.

Governed space: ethnic participation in local politics (1970-1979)

During the early 1970s the issues which concerned Gujaratis shifted from the problems of immigration, nationality and settlement to dependence on benefits, unemployment, housing and education. The locus of these issues stems from particular sources. Dependence on benefits was explained by vulnerability to unemployment, low wages, lack of qualifications and/or skills, a lack of knowledge of English and racial discrimination. Housing became an issue when South Asians, and particularly Ugandan Asians, found themselves needing housing at a time when those wanting it had to form queues and be identified on lists (Rex and Moore, 1971; Bristow, 1979; 1976; 1975; Smith, 1989). Racial discrimination impinged upon all of these aspects of the lives of South Asians. Smith (1989) argued that governments had devalued the areas and housing in which black people resided. Arguments about black people accepting these conditions on the grounds that they were an improvement over what they had left behind in the subcontinent (Dahya, 1974) served to conceal the political issues. Because the housing that these people lived in was devalued, they could not compete equally with other town or city dwellers for better housing and residence in better areas (Smith, 1989; Rex and Tomlinson, 1979). Participation in the formal political system became essential if South Asians were to persuade the politicians to provide better access to funds to improve these areas and the housing within them. I shall begin by looking at Gujaratis' participation in the formal political system and then look at how they used ethnic politics to resolve inter- and intra-community matters through competition for cultural space.

With no political link between the ethnic organisations and ethnic communities and the formal political machinery, in the 1970s rank and file Gujaratis found themselves unable to communicate their views to councillors and MPs unless they did so through their white elected representatives. From their point of view a political vacuum existed, since there were no elected Muslim or Hindu councillors who could represent their views in formal political arenas. From the point of view of the politicians there was no vacuum, since the electoral system that brought them to power gave them the right to act as decision-makers on behalf of the electorate. Moreover, at this time few people from ethnic communities held positions in national political arenas. Although later in the 1970s and 1980s more Asian and black people were elected as local councillors in Blackburn, Bradford and some of the London boroughs, they had relatively little influence as they were in the minority and had to support political party views. Initially, there were no MPs from these minority communities, but by the 1990s there were six. As Anwar (1994) notes, the total number of MPs has not increased and the number of ethnic councillors has dropped.

During this time in Bolton, with the exception of two councillors (an Asian and a West Indian who were committed to representing their political parties) the councillors and MPs were white. The Asian was first elected in 1967 as a Conservative councillor in Little Lever ward. Later he stood as an independent, and in the 1973 local elections he shifted his allegiance to the Liberal Party and lost. Since his success, no Asian has stood successfully in any election in Bolton. Since then, with the exception of the West Indian councillor, all councillors have been white to this day. These two men took the view that their responsibility was to represent their constituents and not their ethnic communities. The West Indian councillor, who lost and later regained his seat, has held it ever since and recently was elected mayor. Although he is committed to supporting his political party, he consistently argues for equal opportunities for minority communities. However, he has never supported an ethnic political argument.

By treating grassroots political activity as a form of factionalism (Rex and Moore, 1971:117) attention was shifted to black or ethnic participation in the formal party political structure. This had the effect of focusing attention on formal political participation and also on the lack of black people who held political office as councillors or MPs. Consequently, the political role of ethnic communities at the local level was overlooked, giving the impression that there was little, if any, role for them locally other than to provide social and psychological support for their members. Ben-Tovim *et al*, (1986) drew attention to the importance of ethnic communities in local politics by exploring the relationship between the CRC and the Labour Party in Liverpool. These authors recognised the key role the CRC played in providing ethnic communities with access to political participation through political parties. What these authors did not recognise is that ethnic communities were involved in two contexts: the first being formal political issues and the second being ethnic competition for ungoverned space. Anwar (1994) has consistently demonstrated that not only have South Asians been assiduous voters, but they have also made consistently little progress towards gaining access to political positions. Not surprisingly, Solomos and Back (1995) found racism was a barrier hindering the participation of black people in local political parties. The barriers lie within the political party system, which are controlled by white party members. Unlike the two ethnic councillors mentioned above who were committed to party politics, Gujarati leaders found themselves under increasing pressure to fill a political vacuum, which separated their growing communities from effective political participation. In theory, opportunities exist for these Gujaratis to participate as voters, as non-voters, and as political party members seeking nomination as candidates. In practice, elected councillors believed that to support these men as candidates would be detrimental to the interests of their political parties, because they would place personal ambition above the interests of their ethnic supporters and their parties. Thus Gujaratis along with the other ethnic minorities had little, if any, hope of electing a candidate who also had responsibilities in an ethnic organisation. The buffer to political participation was not the local CRC but the local political parties.

Two factors have assisted the political parties in exercising control over ethnic leaders. Firstly, the Gujaratis maintain that 'big men are not good'. Secondly, the political parties argued that any support for ethnic candidates would place them in a dilemma; they would have to choose between their commitment to ethnic organisations and communities and their commitment to their political party. The latter belief has persuaded white politicians that a South Asian candidate would place his personal ambitions over and above those of the party. Consequently, the ethnic candidates tended to share few social characteristics and qualifications in common with the main body of the South Asian population and were allocated unwinnable seats. For instance, at what appeared to be their first attempt at supporting a South Asian candidate, the Conservative Party selected a Kutchi Swaminarayan, who represented his temple on both the BCCR and VHP, to stand in Bradford Ward. This ward was a traditional Labour stronghold with a high percentage of ethnic minority voters. In 1973 at the local election for the new Metropolitan Borough, Labour won 77% of the votes; in the 1976 local election Labour was re-elected with 69% of the votes and in 1978 the Labour candidate received 86% of votes cast. The Asian candidate stood in the 1978 election and received 10% of the votes. Not even the substantial South Asian population in this ward supported him. A number of reasons were offered to explain his lack of support by Gujaratis; some objected on the grounds of his belief in the Swaminarayan religion, others claimed that he did not show the kind of behaviour expected of candidates looking for votes. A few years later the Conservative Party supported a Muslim woman candidate, a professional person. She received a similarly low number of votes to the Swaminarayan. Reasons included claims that she spoke English, was a Muslim, was a woman, and had not canvassed in a manner likely to attract votes. The West Indian, who has managed to hold on to his support over twenty years, argues that he is not an Afro-Caribbean, that he supports equal opportunities, opposes racism but supports his party's line. It took the Labour Party to the late 1980s and early 1990s to support another ethnic candidate. The man they selected was an Afro-Caribbean who was also the representative of his community and an outspoken critic of the local authority. He too was given an unwinnable ward, which was dominated by Conservative supporters. He polled only a few votes and was fortunate to hold on to his deposit. Thus the kinds of minority candidates who were putting themselves forward for consideration or were being selected for support were not prominent people, with the exception of an elected chair of the Afro-Caribbean community, and were often in the minority within the minority communities.

This situation encouraged the development of elitism amongst ethnic leaders, which became associated with the weaker links of friendship that ethnic leaders established with MPs and councillors. Access to councillors and their officers was regarded as a desirable asset, that leaders should have. Though access to elected politicians within the forum provided by the BCCR did not guarantee that leaders' views would be heard, it did provide opportunities for them to negotiate with politicians. An analysis of their views of the relationships with the two MPs is instructive. Fourteen (92%) of the fifteen Muslim leaders questioned had heard of Mrs A.Taylor MP, and all had heard of Mr D.Young MP. Nine considered them to be acquaintances or friends. Some 76% (19) of Hindu leaders had heard of Mrs Taylor MP, but only 44% (11) had heard of Mr Young MP. Eight Hindu leaders claimed to be acquainted with Mrs Taylor and three claimed to be acquainted with Mr Young. In 1976 the Muslims had more contact with these MPs than did Hindu leaders. An explanation for this is based upon the Muslims making a greater effort to attend the surgeries of these MPs. They always invited MPs to visit mosques and their involvement in the Lena Street Mosque event brought them into contact with the MPs (see below). Finally they believed that the Labour Party was more prepared to support them than were the Conservative Party. Muslim and Hindu opinions about Conservative and Labour Party policies may have been based upon misapprehensions, but, broadly speaking, they were similar. They supported the Labour Party, believing that it was sympathetic to their cause. Most respondents gave two reasons for supporting this Party. Firstly, they argued that the Conservatives had opposed India becoming independent in 1947. Secondly, many believed that the Labour Party was not opposed to immigration and was not responsible for the immigration laws (Layton-Henry, 1984:152-156; Rex and Tomlinson, 1979:87; Lawrence, 1974: 138- 140). This latter reason was the most commonly given one for their dislike of the Conservatives (Table 7.1). The politicians regarded their ties with ethnic leaders as a form of friendship; ethnic leaders looked to the politicians for political respect.

Table 7.1
Do you think of yourself as a supporter of which party?

Political party	Hindu	Muslim	Total	%
Labour	105	67	172	66.8
Conservative	26	21	47	18.2
Liberal	6	1	7	2.7
No party	6	6	12	4.6
Don't know	11	9	20	7.7
Total No.	154	104	258	100%

Both major political parties made concerted efforts to capture these ethnic votes. The difficulty they had was to find arguments to persuade Gujaratis to vote for them while not alienating their white supporters. Political parties depend upon the involvement of their supporters, paid and unpaid, for their success in local and national elections. The involvement of Muslims and Hindus in political parties in 1976 had not led to the election of a Gujarati MP, although during the 1970s the Conservative Party supported two Gujarati candidates in local elections. As the ethnic vote became increasingly important (Layton-Henry and Rich, 1986:104; Anwar, 1986: Chap.5; Layton-Henry, 1984:146; Anwar, 1980: 14-15; Anwar and Kohler, 1975: 10), the political parties not only sought to capture it, but some also supported Asian and black candidates in an effort to win ethnic votes. In the 1974 election the power of the ethnic minority vote was felt for the first time. In many towns the Asian vote was instrumental in swinging control away from the Conservative Party to the Labour Party (Anwar and Kohler, 1975). Bolton experienced a similar swing, which saw the Labour Party wrest control of the town from the Conservatives. It brought to the political scene Mrs A. Taylor MP and Mr D. Young MP, each of whom contested and won a seat in the two elections held during 1974, which they held until the constituency boundaries were redrawn in 1983. By 1976 both Hindus and Muslims supported the Labour Party, which accords with other findings. For instance, the high percentages of 'don't know' (31%) and 'do not vote' (29%) answers given by ethnic voters to a Conservative Party canvasser in a local election in Bradford ward in 1974 reflect insecurity and a commitment to the Labour Party. High percentages of both Muslims (81.7%) and Hindus (77.9%) sampled claimed to have voted in this election. This commitment to political participation is reflected in a recent survey of electors of Asian origin (BREC, 1990, *Bolton Metropolitan Borough: Survey of the 1990/91 Electoral Registers for Electors of Asian Origin*). The commitment of this sample to voting in elections was comparable with that of white electors. The number of respondents who did not vote was small - Muslims (12.5%) and Hindus (20.8%) - and even fewer could not vote. This bears out the conclusion that Gujaratis' commitment to vote was (and still is) strong.

However, political parties in Bolton remain reluctant to support Gujarati candidates in elections. When they do so, they put them into wards with established opposition majorities. Between 1975 and 1980 the Conservatives nominated two candidates, a Hindu man and a Muslim woman. The woman, a staunch member of the Conservative Party, participated in party activities. For instance, she and her family canvassed regularly for the Party in wards that had high numbers of Asian residents. Although she participated in BCCR activities, she was not directly linked to any Muslim organisation. Her work as a professional separated her from, and placed her in opposition to, the male-dominated local Muslim communities. For instance, she was more articulate than most of the men; attached little importance to caste community membership, arranged marriage, the customary role of women and *purdah*, dowry and cousin marriage; opposed Islamic attitudes to contraception and regarded herself as a much stricter and better Muslim than most local Muslims. Thus, she was unlikely to attract Muslim male and female voters who had none of her advantages and skills. She posed no threat to other Conservative councillors, since she was unlikely to win a seat in an entrenched Labour ward. Nevertheless, her nomination by the Conservative Party was interesting, unusual and innovative.

Until recently the Labour Party did not nominate any South Asian to stand in an election, although it has provided financial and political support for Gujarati organisations. The Conservative Party has offered little direct support to these organisations, but it has provided opportunities for Gujaratis to stand in local elections. Overall there is not only little support for Gujaratis within the local political parties, but together they act as effective buffers blocking career paths for Asians in local politics. Therefore, it is not surprising that the majority of Gujaratis considered that they were 'not strong supporters' of any party (Table 7.2 below). The data show that more Muslims than Hindus described themselves as 'strong supporters'. To some extent this can be explained by the commitment of Muslims to the Labour Party and the support they received from it, whereas the Hindus, possibly by coincidence, were not involved in events which could have been turned by either Party to political advantage.

Few Gujaratis sampled expressed a commitment to participation in political parties. No more than 10% stated that they were willing to be associated with a specific party and only 3.9% were willing to contribute to work in a party office. More Hindus than Muslims were involved in party offices, but more Muslims than Hindus identified with a particular party. No one sampled had agreed to wear a party rosette or attend party meetings. Some 8% of Hindus and 11% of Muslims had placed a party poster in the window of their homes during elections. Some 8%

of Muslims and 3% of Hindus had canvassed on behalf of a party and no more than 3% had worked in a party office. An explanation for this is that in the 1970s to become openly associated with a party may have attracted some form of racially motivated attack. Nevertheless, the Conservative Party relied on their supporters to use their personal influence to influence voting; the party supported candidates in local elections. The Labour Party depended for support on the goodwill that their councillors and MPs could win through resolving personal problems and organisational difficulties; they did not support any Asians as candidates in elections. The sample was unwilling to work in political party offices, on the streets or to advertise their party allegiances.

Table 7.2
Support for political parties

Are you a:	Hindu	%	Muslim	%	Total	%
Strong supporter	44	28.6	50	48.1	94	36.4
Not strong supporter	89	57.8	42	40.4	131	50.8
Don't know/No Answer	21	13.6	12	11.6	33	12.8
Totals	154	100	104	100.1	258	100

The Gujaratis attached importance to personal contact with MPs and councillors. This is reflected in their responses on what they would do if dissatisfied with a locally- taken political decision. Both Muslims and Hindus attend the surgeries of Mrs A.Taylor MP and Mr D.Young MP.[1] Most Muslims stated that, if they had a problem, they would contact MPs first (79.8%) and then local councillors (78.8%). If this form of action proved to be ineffective, then they were willing to consider some other form of action, such as hold protest meetings or marches (24%), campaign against a candidate (19%) or even refuse to obey the law (16%). If dissatisfied, they were willing to become politically active and believed that they could count on a reasonably wide degree of agreement and support across their community.[2] In comparison, Hindus were less committed to political action. Fewer Hindus than Muslims were prepared to contact their councillors (61.7%) and MPs (55.8%). Even fewer were ready to consider attending a protest meeting or march (16%), campaigning against a candidate (11%) or refusing to obey the law (14%). Thus, the impression these data give is that Gujaratis are law-abiding; unlike the panic with which black people were associated either in the 1960s (Hall *et al*, 1978) or in the recent debates surrounding the stop and search law, they are not inclined towards destabilising the state. Muslims had more contact with politicians than Hindus, various requests for planning permission associated with mosques or a place for use for worship and changes in procedures to enable them to meet the requirements of Islam, brought them often into conflict with the politicians and the local authority. Hindus have had less cause to seek support from local politicians regarding decisions taken by the local authority. In the 1970s, many still experienced feelings of insecurity since coming here as refugees from Uganda, and they were reluctant to select more positive forms of political action.

The knowledge councillors and MPs had of their Gujaratis was flawed and limited. The leaders and the led had commitments with which the politicians were unfamiliar. For instance, the Mandhata Patels, the largest Hindu caste, expressed a need for separate religious and community facilities from those of the VHP. Politicians interpreted this as factionalism. Some Muslims expressed the view that the town ought to provide them with a community centre. Councillors dismissed this as wishful thinking. Many of the sampled expressed a need to have their representatives in local government. The response to this was that they had elected their representatives: white councillors. When asked if the representation of their interests by local councillors was adequate, the majority stated that they were inadequately represented. Some 73% Hindus claimed that they were inadequately represented compared with 60% of Muslims. This can be explained in terms of the relatively low contact they had with the politicians. A small percentage (21% and 11%) of Muslims and Hindus thought that the councillors performed their jobs adequately and an almost similar percentage could offer no opinion on the performance of the councillors.

That the Gujaratis were aware of their political position is borne out by their response to the form of representation that they considered acceptable. When the sample were asked to comment on the form of representation they would like, they were uncertain. Between 42% and 54% of Hindus and Muslims respectively are unclear how they wish to be represented on local authority bodies, or were not aware of, or were uninterested in, their achieving some form of positive representation in local politics. However, a significant number of Hindus (33.8%) and Muslims (34.6%) believed that co-opted Gujarati representatives would provide a solution to representation on local committees. They were less certain about having Asians elected as councillors. Equal opportunity legislation in the 1980s set out to remedy this gap in representation (Ball and Solomos, 1990). The majority of the sample believed that they were inadequately represented at the national level. The majority (62%) of Gujaratis expressed the view that they were inadequately represented nationally by MPs (Table 7.3), but a minority (21.3%) took the opposite view. Of these a third of the Muslims interviewed, who seemed to have more contact with the councillors than did Hindus (14%), claimed that they were adequately represented.

Table 7.3
Adequacy of national political representation

Representation	Hindu		Muslim		Totals	
Adequate	22	14.3%	33	31.7%	55	21.3%
Inadequate	101	65.6%	60	57.7%	161	62.4%
Don't know	26	16.9%	9	8.7%	35	13.6%
No answer	5	3.2%	2	1.9%	7	2.7%
Totals	154	100%	104	100%	258	100%

Political space

The Gujaratis were victims of their own dilemma. On the one hand they stated that would not accept anyone who was not a Gujarati to represent them (Chapter Six). Technically, this was possible in the 1970s, although the political parties were not committed to making this option work. Local political party leaders resolved this difficulty by arguing that to co-opt Gujaratis would undoubtedly encourage factionalism. Representation in the 1980s and 1990s was expected and was supported by equal opportunities legislation, but this is not effective. For instance a person is usually selected rather than elected, and who they represent is in doubt with those are supposedly represented. Furthermore, it only exacerbated the problems of representation. It focused attention upon appointments and representation within the Local Authority, but neither the Local Authority nor political parties were prepared to provide the minorities with political representation, power or even an agreed process for the selection of representatives. On the other hand they could not (and still cannot) elect an ethnic candidate in an election, since they did (do) not dominate the voting in any ward. They also expressed dissatisfaction with the existing representation of their interests by elected MPs. Unable to achieve political representation by the accepted political process and prevented from selecting their own representatives for co-option, the Gujaratis were rendered politically ineffective. When asked for reasons why they thought that representation is inadequate, most of sample did not answer the question (76%). Those who gave a reason stated that there is no representation and linked this to discrimination. They amplified this answer by saying: 'No Asian Members of Parliament', 'Members of Parliament don't listen', 'They only come when they want votes', 'Different laws apply to us', 'Members of Parliament discriminate' and 'They are prejudiced and misguided'.

By the 1970s Gujaratis were defining the situation in social, economic and political terms, which laid down some of the social boundaries around ethnic communities. This required ethnic communities and organisations to become consumers and producers of cultural signs. This is as much a political development as an economic one. To produce cultural signs, ethnic organisations had to achieve control over ungoverned and devalued space. This was made easier by the low economic value that Local Authorities and politicians placed on space within the inner urban areas, and particularly those in which ethnic minorities resided. Interest in this space changed when the usage that it was to be given affected the lives of the local white community. To an extent it removed a major competitor from the competition between ethnic communities for control of the ungoverned space. This left ethnic communities and organisations to compete for it. This competition formed the basis of ethnic politics and the local CRC provided the forum in which it could take place. By doing this, the local CRC became, like other CRCs, a hostage to its own future.

Ungoverned space: ethnic politics and the CRC (1970-1979)

This section of the Chapter is concerned with the way in which ethnic leaders competed within the town for which would raise them from being consumers of the culture of others to the level of consumers and producers of their own cultural signs. The space in which this development took place was seen by the white community as having low social, economic and political value, that is, it was racialised. Competition for ungoverned space within it was left open to contest by the ethnic communities; but competition for governed space outside this area involved formal political participation. The contest for ungoverned space provided the dynamic for the development of ethnic politics. CRCs looking for ways to relate to ethnic communities allowed ethnic politics to develop, since it gave CRCs direct contact with the grassroots leadership and provided ethnic communities with both the opportunity and an arena in which to contest this ungoverned space. Furthermore, it enabled ethnic leaders to relate this competition to the existing political structure. It also gave politicians the opportunity to establish contact with ethnic leaders (CRE, 1997:4, paras 2.3-2.4). Thus ethnic politics could, for a period of time, become part of local, and to a lesser extent, national politics.

Ethnic politics, far from being a form of factionalism (Rex and Moore, 1971:117) enabled ethnic communities to relate their development as consumers and producers of culture to the local economic and political situation. 'It is at the local level that the newcomers, individually and collectively, have attempted to fashion new economic, social and political relationships that affect their lives directly' (Katznelson, 1973:152). Furthermore, concentrating on local events allows the analysis of racial and ethnic divisions both to be grounded and located within a political economy framework (Solomos *et al*, 1983:12-13). Therefore, ethnic politics was one of the most important forms of political participation. For too long the effects of racism in local level politics had been ignored or interpreted in terms of national level politics. Local authorities with the direct or indirect support of the State (Smith, 1989) have concealed ethnic politics, thus devaluing the contributions and demands of local ethnic leaders and ensuring that the able ones would not achieve political prominence, while keeping up the demand for Asian support on local issues. The content of ethnic politics embraced events which involved some form of demand for, dispute or control over ungoverned space either between Gujaratis or other ethnic communities or the white community. These events enabled ethnic leaders to develop a political dialogue between one another and the elected politicians that involved the construction and demolition of fragile alliances. It is not just what happened that was important, but how leaders, councillors, BCCR and the local authority debated the events. The debate is critical to the analysis, because they reflect changing perceptions from powerlessness to power. The level of ethnic politics became an indicator of the way that ethnic leaders were seen to be reacting to the control imposed upon them by the State. This reaction developed into protesting about their lack of, or unequal access to, public resources. The dialogue drew upon the language and symbolism of racism, open or closed, which was typical of the period between 1972 and 1976.

These events were typical of those experienced by Asian or black populations living in other British towns. By typical I mean that these events serve as a representative example of a particular type of response by a minority to decisions made and not made by local politicians. Typical is a relative term and has levels of applicability. To what degree so called 'typical' events are unique to this Gujarati population is difficult to say without adequate comparative data. However, the kinds of issues that provided the content of events were similar to those that have been described for ethnic communities in Manchester (Macdonald, 1989), Liverpool (Gifford *et al*, 1989; Ben-Tovim *et al*, 1986), and Nottingham (Katznelson, 1973). They also are similar to many reported over this period in the media, such as conflicts in mosques and over planning permission for mosques and temples, single sex schools and *halal* food in schools. The events became not only a protest against local decisions over unequal access to public resources and to positions in the formal political hierarchy, but also a process for negotiating social identities and allocating political responsibility.

Ethnic leaders used these occasions to debate the degree of politicians' public commitment to anti-racism. As the importance of Gujaratis' votes became recognised as important in local politics, leaders used their positions as officers of organisations to exert influence on politicians. Leaders sought to trade votes for influence. In this way politicians became aware of the potential of ethnic leaders to 'develop their own politics of resistance' (Hall, 15/7/85). National events made manifest racial issues with which most Asians and black people could sympathise and agree; for instance, those associated with immigration and nationality. Local events made manifest the imbalance in power relations. Debates about events were attempts by leaders to negotiate for more favourable forms of political participation. Negotiations brought together into one arena (provided by the CRC) ethnic identities, notions of space, and the construction and demolition of fragile alliances between leaders themselves and other CRC members. Therefore, an analytical framework needs to take account of the different spaces in which events occur, the social identities of all of these participants, and the social identities of the negotiators.

Events selected were chosen because they involved leaders, and to a greater or lesser extent, with other Asian, black and white participants. Some attracted the attention of the media but failed to attract the attention of leaders; others did not achieve media attention but found enthusiastic advocates amongst the leaders. Leaders championed events which they believed would give them opportunities to challenge the allocation of political control. They also enabled leaders to marshal support, real or fictitious, and to establish fragile alliances with other leaders and their supporters. In this sense, debated events became micro-movements within a much larger and more widespread antiracist movement across Britain. Events were selected for analysis were chosen on the basis of the following criteria. They:

1.   were public;
2.   provided opportunities for a public definition of the power relationship between black and white;
3.   provided leaders with opportunities to negotiate for new identities; and

4.   allowed for the allocation of political responsibility.

During the period of the research many events occurred; a few have been selected. Of those that have not been selected, leaders and white politicians did not debate some. These included rape, assault and drug cases involving Asians and white people. Apart from some leaders and politicians expressing feelings of condemnation, they attracted little attention.   Others were debated and also made the headlines in the local press and a few made the national press. Four events were selected which illustrate the range of negotiations of leaders in their attempts to challenge power relationships. The dynamic element is provided by the process of negotiation of labels that enabled leaders and white politicians to define the political space between them and their relative political status (Miles, 1982:60). This space is not neutral: governed space is racialised and politically controlled and carries a high political value; ungoverned space is devalued space and carries a low political as well as economic value. On the one hand, the characteristic which accompanied events that occurred in ungoverned space was the lack of political and police (where appropriate) concern. On the other hand, events which occurred in governed space were perceived by the local authority and police to affect the lives of those living in it, thus efforts to control these events were quickly put into place.

A model for the analysis of events might separate space from responsibility (Diagram 2 below). Earlier (Chapter One) I distinguished between governed and ungoverned space, the former being valued and contested in formal political arenas and the latter being devalued and contested only by ethnic communities. There is a relationship between the allocation of responsibility and the value attached to different spaces. Since ungoverned space is racially devalued (Smith, 1989) what occurs within it either attracts little attention from local authority and the state or it attracts panic responses from the police or politicians. Events in governed space are politically contested through the existing formal political channels. What occurs in ungoverned space may been seen as politically dangerous by the white politicians, while what occurs in governed space is seen by them as controlled and acceptable. The model set out below incorporates sets of social identities which reflect social proximity to or social distance between communities as perceived by Gujaratis, that is, the 'us' and the 'them' (Wallman, 1978: 207). These social identities are used as labels for communities, but their social boundaries can alter depending upon the perceptions of those in and outside them. They are mental constructs (Cohen, 1985).

The relationship between ungoverned and governed space is ascending and descending orders of social identities, the 'us' and 'them'. These changes in social identities are reflected in changes in the perceived sizes of group social boundaries. The allocation of responsibility at the local and national level of local and national government is reflected in the racialisation of this space. Ungoverned space in which ethnic communities could develop control as producers and consumers of ethnic culture was devalued and racialised space. As devalued space, neither local nor national government was actively concerned with allocating responsibility for settling social relationships between ethnic communities. Governed space, which was not racialised, was valued. This was space over which local and national government had control. The ethnic groups in this space are less clearly defined, and their social boundaries are much vaguer. Space and the allocation of responsibility provide a framework for analysing events in the local political context.

Diagram 2
Relationship between space and responsibility

Space	Responsibility	
	Waived	Allocated
Ungoverned	faction, caste, sect 'us'	Hindu, Muslim 'us'
Governed	Asian, Indian	foreigner, alien, immigrant, coloured 'them'

Ungoverned space with responsibility waived

The following three events reflect attempts by ethnic communities to take control of ungoverned space for the purpose of becoming the producers and consumers of ethnic culture. Local and national government waived their responsibility over activities that occurred within this racialised space.

Baruchi vs. Surti take-over of Peace Street Mosque (1969-76) In 1969 Deobandi Surtis attempted to seize control from the Deobandi Baruchis of all mosques in Bolton by taking control of Zakariah Mosque in Peace Street. As both the first mosque and the headquarters of the Islamic Cultural Centre (ICC), it had a special place in the local Islamic population. Although local mosques are controlled by a founding community, only Zakariah Mosque is controlled by the whole Islamic community. Control of the ICC gave the dominant faction control of this mosque and control of Bolton's Islamic community. Each faction sought to impose its will upon the management of Islamic affairs, since they held different views on how Muslims should pray, conduct themselves in everyday life, and respond to local politics. For instance, Baruchis held one view on these matters and Deobandi Surtis another.

As each faction gained control of the ICC, they would remove the *imam* of Zakariah Mosque and invite one of their choice to take office. A Surti committee appointed the first imam of Zakariah Mosque. A year later at the AGM open conflict between members of these factions culminated in assaults, broken windows and the take-over of the mosque committee by Baruchis. They replaced the *imam* with one of their choice. In 1976 the conflict broke out again between these factions over the appointment of an assistant *imam* to Mosque who was the nephew of a prominent local Surti. The Baruchis claimed that the Surti was unsuitable for the post because his relatives here were embroiled in an unsavoury affair involving a Surti man whom, it was alleged, had attempted to rape another Surti's wife. This, they argued, demonstrated the unsuitability of the candidate. It was further alleged that some Baruchis even wrote to the Home Office and the local CRC giving reasons as to why he should not be allowed into the country. Neither the Home Office nor the CRC responded to the letter. The latter stated that this was a mosque affair which only the Baruchis and Surtis could settle. The conflict at its height, it was claimed by one Surti, involved a stabbing by a Baruchi and the smashing of the mosque windows. The police were called to the incident, but found no injured person.

In a description of a similar dispute, Anwar observes that no satisfactory solution was found (1979:163-165). He also notes that outsiders like the CRC and police were involved, as they were in this incident. Both descriptions point to flaws in the conditions of employment of *imams* at that time (Chapter Six above; Anwar, 1979:164), which made the mosque committee that appointed them all-powerful. A difference between the dispute in Rochdale and in Bolton that is that the mosque leaders in Rochdale were educated men with the knowledge and the financial resources to go to court (Anwar, 1979:164). Those in Bolton were less educated and without the financial support to settle, and therefore did not consider going to court a realistic solution. Those in Bolton appealed to no person and no organisation for a final decision; rather, they endeavoured to manipulate influential outsiders into taking up specific positions and to use force to achieve their goal.

This conflict continued into the 1980s when a Baruchi chairperson of the ICC decided to charge Surtis £25 for funeral services while making them free to Baruchis. This led the Surtis to dissociate themselves from the ICC arguing that it did not have the authority to decide who could be buried in the cemetery. Since no agreement could be reached within the ICC, it was brought to the BCCR to resolve. In the debate, the ICC representative conceded that the ICC did not control burials in the cemetery and agreed to withdraw the charge for funeral services to Surti Muslims. Furthermore, the ICC representative acknowledged that the inability of Muslims to settle such disputes amongst themselves supported the argument that without any accepted structure for leadership in the Islamic community, using outsiders to settle disputes was a reasonable solution. Control of the ICC over the interpretation of Islamic culture Bolton rested with whichever faction was in control at the time.

In the late 1980s these two factions clashed again in the ICC over the election of officers to manage Makki Mosque. The police and CRC were invited by one faction to attend the election in order to ensure that the other did not use force or cheat. However, both organisations chose not to attend when they realised that they were being used. When the Baruchi ICC representative, who previously had tried to force Surtis to pay for funeral services, commented on this dispute in the CRC, he merely expressed his shame at the behaviour of his fellow Muslims, but gave no indication of how the matter would be resolved. The involvement of outsiders in such inter community disputes is a recognised tactic where there are no clear forms of social or political control (Frankenberg, 1957).

184

Outcasteing of a Hindu (1975-1976)   This event involved the public outcasteing of a Hindu family, and as such demonstrates the power of a caste committee to control its members, their social conduct, and even demand that they behave in a way that is good for the caste. This event can be separated into three stages. The first is the husband's decision to separate from his second wife and to marry another woman; secondly, the family and caste conflict that accompanied this decision, and thirdly, his decision not to go through with the third marriage. The result was that his caste association outcaste him and his family.

Briefly, this man sent his second wife back to Gujarat, divorcing her there and leaving her destitute. Having chosen another woman to be his wife, his sons discovered that she already had two sons. To ensure that her sons would not benefit from the family wealth they had achieved through marriage to their father, they forced their father to sign a change of deed. Thus they removed him from a position of authority. Now he was undecided as to whether or not to proceed with the marriage. On the one hand, if he did not marry her, his sons would return the deeds to him and regain his position of authority. On the other hand, if he did not marry her, his caste association would outcaste him and his family. To avoid being outcaste he sought the help of the Sikh chairperson of the VHP, the chairperson of the Islamic Culture Centre, a solicitor, and the director of the CRC. None chose to become involved. He decided to withdraw from the marriage. His caste association outcaste him and his family, making their decision public in a letter sent to caste members instructing them to avoid contact with him and his family. In the opinion of a Pakistani barrister, to whom the father was referred by the chairperson of the ICC, the letter was libellous. The father chose to take no further action.

The caste association was concerned about this man's treatment of his previous wives and was determined to protect their members. It is alleged that his second wife died as a result of his neglect. This man's daughter's wedding took place about the same time as the decision to outcaste him. Few people turned up for it. Once the bridegroom heard about the outcasteing he beat his wife. Nobody helped her. The outcasteing had implications for the man's younger children at a local primary school. All their cousins shunned them and none of their relatives could visit or speak to them. It also would have consequences for his children who in the future might want to marry. They could not marry within caste. It is an instance of an event occurring in ungoverned space within the Gujaratis' communities. Nobody wanted to get involved. The unwillingness of anyone to become involved in this and the previous event is an indication of the social difference between ungoverned and governed space (Lash and Urry, 1994). In the former instance religious culture and in the latter instance caste culture, practical measures such as support for the entry of members into the UK, the reduction of dowries, and the right of caste members to caste support, became strategies for strengthening ethnic culture.

Ungoverned space with responsibility allocated

Unlike the events described above, the next events originated in governed space. Through them ethnic culture intruded into governed space in a way that challenged the control of the politicians, employers and representatives of the state. Rather than challenging law and order, these events challenged cultural control. They included the demands by Muslim mill workers to celebrate the holidays associated with *Ramadan*, such as *Eid-ul-Fitr*, which were not recognised by employers. To this day, the employers have refused to recognise these holidays. When the Muslims, either Gujaratis or Pakistani or both, object to these conditions, they are accused of acting as a 'union within a union' (President of the United Textile Factory Workers Association (*BEN*, 26/4/74). Similarly, between 1974-75 Muslims requested the right to twenty-four hour burials; permission was being given to Muslims in neighbouring towns like Blackburn. Although this was a national issue (*Muslim Burials*, CRC, 1975:6), the impression was given that this was only of concern to Muslims. It was also of concern to Hindus who cremate the dead within 24 hours, but the reaction to Muslim demands ignored their interests. The two events selected illustrate the concern with control and particularly that mobilised in response to Muslim demands. This bears out Said's argument that those in the West fear Islam (1981). The first deals with the demand by a small Muslim sect for land and the second involved a schoolboy who grew a beard.

Lena Street Mosque Issue (1973-1976)   This event began as an apparently insignificant request for planning made by a group of Gujarati Berelewi Baruchis who had decided to separate from Tayabiah Mosque, then under Deobandi Baruchi and ICC control. Amongst their reasons for separating was that they found a particular prayer format to be unacceptable. They established their new mosque in a shop owned by a member of the sect. In 1973 Bolton Corporation's planning committee considered a proposal from the *Anjuman-E-Islamma* branch of the Muslim faith to use a house in Ulleswater Street for prayer, until they could find suitable land on which to build a mosque. Their application for planning permission was made, they claimed, in an effort to resolve growing conflict between the two sects who had to share the mosque. The committee refused their request for use of the house for prayer (*BEN*, 24/3/73) and this decision was upheld by the corporation (Council after 1974) (*BEN*, 5/4/73). The sect reapplied for permission to use the house in December 1973, and again planning permission was refused.

In some neighbouring towns such as Blackburn, Muslims were allowed to use houses as prayer centres, but Bolton resisted this trend. Embittered, their leader left town and another man took over the leadership. Now known as the *Anjumane-Ahle-Sunnat-W-Jumat* and numbering about 200, their next attempt to obtain planning permission to use a house for prayer was unsuccessful. This new leader, who owned an old 'co-op' store in the area, proposed that the sect should use it as a mosque. When he applied for permission for change of use of this property, the Planning Committee rejected his application suggesting that the sect find other premises (*BEN*, 13/8/74). In defiance of this decision, these Muslims continued to use the store, which became known as Lena Street Mosque. Bolton Council served notice on the sect to close it (*BCCR Minutes*, 23/8/74). Now local white residents began to protest about the cars, noise and broken bottles in the vicinity of the mosque. In December 1974 the Council served an enforcement notice on the sect to close the mosque. The sect had 56 days in which to find alternative premises. Apparently, the council should have served this notice on the leader in August 1974, but they were uncertain as to who owned the premises. Thus it was not served until December 1974. The sect said, 'We are prepared to move to another building, if the council will find us one' (*BEN*, 8/1/75). A Labour Party councillor made Granada TV aware of this dispute. They interviewed the mosque leader for the local evening news, thus publicising the plight of the sect (*BEN*, 23/1/75). The Conservative chairperson of the planning committee criticised Granada for showing this footage, claiming that the Council was not given an opportunity to put their case. What began as a micro-ethnic dispute had grown into a major political issue involving the local authority, the politicians, political parties, the sect, the residents and the media. Once the social boundaries of those who saw themselves as supporters of the sect widened to include all Muslims, local Labour Party councillors and Labour MPs, the sect leader could appeal against the closure. Thus he delayed the Council's decision by at least a year until a public inquiry had been held.

Trades Council rallied to the support of the sect giving as its reason a letter they claimed to have received from Muslims suggesting that the National Front was inciting opposition to the mosque amongst local white residents (*BEN*, 20/2/75). By now the dispute was three years old. The issues had become clear-cut: as one councillor put it: 'Can a minority of the immigrant community do just what they please?' 'Do planning regulations apply equally to members of all sections of the community?' (*BEN*, 6/3/75). Towards the middle of 1975, the housing committee was authorised to negotiate with the sect over the terms for the lease for a plot of land on which they could build a mosque. The sect accepted the offer, but it took a further five years before they had sufficient funds to begin building the mosque. During this time they continued to use the 'co-op' as a mosque.

This is an apt illustration of how the social boundaries between two sects in dispute, in which the wider Gujarati communities and the white community had little interest, could be extended to involve all local Muslim communities, the Hindu communities and local politicians. A little dispute between two sects became a major political dispute. Eventually, the local council was pressurised into making available land to one of the smallest sects in the Asian community at the time. This dispute also shows how ethnic politics impinges upon local politics and how to separate it from local politics is in itself a form of racism. A small powerless Muslim sect had defied the might of the council and had effectively placed legal and political constraints on it. The social process of extending social boundaries is central to the development of communities as producers and consumers of ethnic culture.

The second event illustrates how quickly local government was to take up a particular position, when confronted by an ethnic community that challenged the rules of the establishment.

Bearded schoolboy (1974-1975)   A Muslim student in the final year of his CSEs at a local school grew a beard allegedly as a sign of his intention to become an *imam*. The headmaster drew the pupil's attention to an unwritten rule prohibiting students from wearing beards. At his father's behest the young man left his beard untrimmed. The headmaster asked him to trim his beard to scissors depth. With the young man's permission, the headmaster demonstrated what he meant by this. The boy's father's adviser, a Baruchi Muslim, construed this act as assault and argued that the headmaster ought to be charged accordingly. The pupil was excluded and the headmaster asked the father to provide written evidence to support his argument. If he received such evidence, he said that he would waive his objections, allowing the young man to return to school wearing a beard. If evidence could not be provided, then the boy could return to school only after shaving it off. Conclusive written evidence could not be produced. The father did not allow his son to shave his beard. A confrontation situation developed between the boy, his father, his father's advisers, the headmaster and his advisers from the local authority education department and the BCCR.

The Baruchi adviser used this event to widen the social boundaries of those affected by inviting the local MP and a few Labour councillors to condemn the decision of the headmaster as being intolerant and discriminatory. He also sought the support of all Muslims arguing that the headmaster's decision was anti-Muslim. He proposed that the Muslims should hold a public demonstration outside the local education offices against the decision. Unable to provide conclusive written evidence in support of his argument, he received neither support from the politicians or the Muslim communities. The confrontation fizzled out. Some three or four months later, the boy's father was persuaded to send his son beardless to complete his schooling. For schools the issue remains. What should schools do when an ethnic or religious community challenges generally accepted rules? The headmaster argued that had he agreed to allow this pupil to wear a beard, under school rules he would have discriminated against white pupils who had accepted the rule not to wear beards. At a meeting of headmasters held in 1975, they established a principle that left headmasters to deal with each case on its own merits. This failed to satisfy the Muslim minority, who claimed that headmasters, BCCR and politicians favoured the Christian community. This event was debated on five occasions within the BCCR without any conclusion being reached. No councillor or MP intervened in this dispute. Many Muslims believed that the Baruchi wanted to achieve an influential position in the ICC, and this event gave him an opportunity to raise himself to a position of political prominence.

This event highlighted a number of critical issues. Firstly, this event was one of many forerunners of the blasphemy debate. English law does not recognise the limits of non-Christian religions. Individual headmasters will continue to make decisions on their merits. Secondly, the local CRC could (a) not contain such a dispute, (b) not act an intermediary, (c) not act as an effective political pressure group, and (d) did not act as a buffer. Thirdly, this issue showed how an ethnic event could escalate into a political one with possibly legal implications involving, potentially, the whole Islamic community. Fourthly, an almost identical event occurred in 1992. The decision taken by a different headmaster in the same school was the same. The Muslims were incensed and put pressure on their councillors, school managers and headmasters to change the decision. So far little has changed. This time young Muslims talked about withdrawing their votes at the next election, but this threat seems to have come to nothing.[3]

These events fall into governed space between communities with undefined social boundaries. Groups described by terms like Indian and Asian are virtually meaningless. During the period 1972 to 1976 two events occurred which required Gujaratis and Muslims in particular to define their positions within the wider society. Some white children broke some of the windows of Zakariah mosque while playing cricket in the grounds. A Muslim member of the mosque committee took one child to his parents demanding that they pay for the broken windows. The parents claimed that this Muslim had assaulted her son. The police, after seeing all parties, dropped the matter. The other event began as a complaint by Gujarati customers against shopkeepers who profiteered by raising the prices on rice and oil. The claim made was that prices had soared far beyond the rate of inflation by as much as 400%. Muslim customers wrote letters of complaint to the press (*BEN*, 7/1/74), and formed themselves into an Asian Consumers Watchdog Committee (*BEN*, 7/1/74; *Guardian*, 8/1/74). The shopkeepers responded by forming themselves into the Association of Asian Traders (*BEN*, 24/1/74). Asians took up the accusation of price raising by Asian shopkeepers all over Britain. Here it took the form of Muslim accusing Hindu. The CRC advised the members of the Asian Watchdog Committee to contact the Prices Commission in Manchester. Subsequently, the Asian Watchdog Committee wrote a letter to the Prices Commission; a copy appeared in the local press. The CRC sent a letter to the Consumer Protection Committee in Greater Manchester council and nominated a Gujarati to sit on the Consumer Protection Committee. However, the Committee received no letters of complaint. Without letters of complaint the Committee could do nothing and the issue faded away.

This began locally as an event involving Gujaratis complaining about Gujaratis and then grew into one in which Asian complained about Asian. The setting up of a separate body to bring local issues of concern to a national body failed because locally the Gujaratis, like other Asian minorities, did not wish an internal matter to be resolved by an external body.

Governed space with allocated responsibility

This final set of events occurred in political space that represented the greatest threat to the white community, and the decisions taken reflect the racialised nature of the power relationship between local and national government and the state and those who are perceived to pose a threat. Four events occurred which make explicit the threat that those labelled immigrants posed for governments and the state. Two will be discussed briefly and two in more detail.

In-Company Language Training Scheme (1974)   In 1974 a CRC meeting discussed a proposal from the textile industry to establish what became known as the In-Company Language Training scheme and to select two ethnic representatives to sit on the management panel. Employers stated that they did not want to involve religious organisations in the discussion. The scheme was intended to provide

English tuition for Asian workers in their own time. It assumed that most of them were unable to speak English. The leaders from the Gujarati, the Pakistani and Afro-Caribbean communities reacted strongly to the employers' assumptions that black people were powerless. In particular the leaders objected to the assumption that white employers knew what was best for their immigrant workers. The Sikh leader of the VHP wanted to know why the employers had not approached the ethnic communities. He pointed out that the employers would have to deal directly with ethnic workers. He suggested that the employers approached the CRC in order to (a) avoid approaching ethnic organisations, (b) to avoid union involvement of any kind, and (c) to make use of the CRC's buffer role. The Sikh and an Afro-Caribbean member believed that the unions might just support their black members in this debate, particularly the Asian workers' organisations.

Then the ethnic leaders questioned why the responsibility of selecting the two representatives had been passed on to the CRC. The Sikh said: 'Who are they? Who will select them? They will just be rubber stamps. They represent nothing'. Ethnic communities could not accept that two individuals could represent their interests. No two people selected in this way would be accepted as representing ethnic interests. Gujaratis could not accept one ethnic leader, let alone two individual representatives with no standing in the communities. The result of the debate was a decision to send the employers a list of addresses of ethnic organisations with a letter stating that it was their task to approach them and suggest some form of selection. Questions were raised about the colour of the other members. Then the debate moved on to question the scheme's use of workers' time for training. The view taken was that all training should be in the firm's time and at their expense. A point was made that English was being treated as a charity commodity. One Muslim leader observed that he had survived in his community without any training in English. Finally, the Sikh asked why women had not been included in the scheme and then he observed that the scheme, was created just to enable immigrants to be able to say 'yes please. Thank you sir'.

The allocation of responsibility in this debate shifted from the caring employer to the view that they were white racists, because they refused to take on the responsibility of selection themselves and refused to involve the ethnic communities. Implicit in the debate was the assumption that all those who were not fluent in English could be labelled as black, inferior and uneducated people, in need of help and who should be grateful for all the help, and the support of the white community, whatever the price. As it involved governed space and white cultural signs, the ethnic leaders could unite in their opposition to the employers and their scheme. It was also a plea by the ethnic leaders and their organisations to be seen by white employers to be reasonable. To this extent it was also a bid by ethnic leaders for the recognition of ethnic culture. A further point, which needs making, is that here a group of employers tried to use the CRC as a buffer organisation. Because the CRC provided an arena for the discussion of ethnic politics, rather than acting as a buffer, it responded by forcing the employers to recognise ethnic organisations and their responsibilities to their members. In other words, the local CRC took a far more active role in promoting antiracism than it is given credit for.

Vishwa Hindu Parishad trip to the Isle of Man (1975)   This proved to be another instance when blame was attributed to an ethnic community for an event that took place in governed space without any evidence to support it. The VHP accused the Isle of Man police of insensitive treatment because they represented an ethnic minority. During a visit to the island in 1975 this party of Hindus visited a church in which there was a valuable statuette. Sometime after they left the church the statuette was discovered to be missing. On their arrival at the ferry terminal, with the agreement of their representatives, men and women were 'searched' by the police on the quayside in full view of everybody. On the conclusion of the search, the police were asked for a letter stating that the statuette had not been found. On June 30 1975 a letter was received clearing them of the theft and thanking them for their co-operation. When the Sikh chairperson was informed of this experience, he took up the issue of the police search at a BCCR meeting. He complained that, although the police searched the Hindus, the white couriers and other European visitors were not searched. 'Therefore, this was a blatant instance of racial discrimination.' The CRC supported his argument and suggested that he write to the Chief Constable of the Isle of Man. This he did, adding that it was also an insult to Boltonians and sent copies of it to the CRC, MPs, councillors, Mayor and the Home Office. He regarded the search to be an insult to himself, to the women and to any self-respecting person. The BCCR sent letters in support of his complaint to the governor-general and Chief Constable of the Isle of Man.

This event was an instance of how responsibility was presumed initially to lie with members of an ethnic community, and the treatment they experienced from the police in governed space was indicative of racialised status. The apologies that were received later shifted responsibility back on to those who were responsible, in this instance the police. This event also illustrates how the local CRC supported ethnic organisations in responding to alleged racist behaviour. Again, far from being a buffer organisation, the CRC responded to a political situation. It provided the all-important arena in which these issues could be made political.

'Farnworth girl paid to marry immigrants' (1976)   This event focused the attention of ethnic leaders and white members of the BCCR on the local white community's perception of them as immigrants and the racism associated with it. Black people's experiences of immigration control, queuing and split families are well established in the literature. For the local white community, immigration was linked to racism and the solution was reduced to immigration control. At the time the local National Front party supported this solution publicly with letters to the Press and marches in neighbouring Blackburn. This event served to support such ideas about white Bolton and Britain being swamped by black people. An emotive headline appeared in the local press, which read: 'I was paid to wed immigrant - girl' (*BEN*, 7/4/76). The Press reported that a white girl in Farnworth was being paid to marry immigrants, so that they could establish their right to remain in Britain. This was followed by another story of a local Pakistani, who stated in court that he had paid £1,000 to obtain a passport to provide him with entry into Britain (*BEN*, 15/6/76). Although these reports were mentioned at CRC meetings, they were not discussed. The politicians and leaders made no

comment. Both events could have provided opportunities for leaders to protest against establishment racism, but they avoided all discussion of such events.

This event was noted not because of the predictable and well-rehearsed debates surrounding the racialisation of immigration, but because a letter appeared in the local press in which a Muslim was reported to have said immigration should be stopped (*BEN*, 28/5/76). The letter stated that he favoured a reduction in the numbers of immigrants coming into Britain, so that those already here might experience greater security. Furthermore, he suggested that this would clarify the position of those who were migrants and those who were British. 'If immigration were allowed to continue', he was reported to have said, 'racial clashes could result and resentment would arise between the employed and the unemployed. There were not enough jobs to go around and he was in agreement with some of the things the late Enoch Powell MP had said' (*BEN*, 28/5/76). The reaction of most leaders to this report was: 'the writer has a choice. He should keep quiet or pack his bags, leave and give other people a chance. People from East Africa holding British passports have nowhere to go except here. At least the people from India and Pakistan have a choice. We must allow Asians in, even if it means cutting down immigration from other countries'. He was cast in the role of a traitor to his people. Later, Muslim leaders reported that Muslims threatened him with assault if he ever repeated such statements.

This debate highlighted a different side of immigration. The public was sympathetic to the Press reporting the plight of the woman, as it supported the public's racialised view of black people. As such, both reinforced prevailing ideas about the racialisation of immigration, but it raised issues of citizenship. The Sikh leader of the VHP argued that Britain had a responsibility to Asians coming from East Africa and suggested that those coming from the subcontinent had a much greater choice of countries to which they could migrate. The author's arguments about identity and belonging are elaborated in more recent literature on immigration and nationality (Cohen, 1994; Castles and Miller, 1995). Immigration is still of central concern today to the Gujaratis and Pakistanis. A recent survey in Bolton has shown that the one service which is no longer provided by the CRC, but which these communities consider to be of major concern, is one that provides advice and support on immigration and nationality matters (Mulla, 1995).

Conclusion

Political participation in governed space was limited to voting. Local political parties selected few Gujaratis as candidates. When they were selected, they were given unwinnable wards. The political parties restricted Gujaratis' participation in formal politics, although they wanted the ethnic vote. Other forms of political participation are relatively meaningless, since they are so difficult to identify. The evidence for withdrawal or a refusal to vote is lacking. Many local young Muslims refer to it as a possibility. Locally, control over governed space is valued, and because it is valued, ethnic issues, whatever form they take, are relegated to other arenas. Thus the responsibility for political control remains firmly rooted in the white controlled political party.

Some events analysed in this Chapter illustrate changes in the allocation of responsibility in governed and ungoverned spaces between the white and Gujarati communities in Bolton. The analysis shows how the allocation of responsibility over events involving ethnic organisations in ungoverned space was waived by local and national government. Where the involvement of ethnic organisations took more politically acceptable forms, such as religious organisations, responsibility was avoided where possible. The allocation of responsibility over events involving less clearly defined groups, such as Asians, Indians, immigrants and foreigners, was attributed initially to members of ethnic factions. Only when this was resisted was responsibility allocated to others. In the 1970s this pattern of allocation of responsibility symbolised the control over the production and consumption of cultural signs in ungoverned and governed space in British towns and cities. The difficulty Gujaratis and other members of ethnic communities have in achieving support from the political parties is a measure of their lack of control over production and consumption of cultural signs in governed space. Their control over ungoverned space was treated as of little importance.

Ethnic politics and local CRCs gave ethnic organisations and their leaders opportunities to challenge the allocation of responsibility in governed space which disappeared with the changes in their role. 'The place of the REC as a forum for political leadership of local minority ethnic communities is, therefore, a far diminished one. Leadership is far more likely to reside with those who have sought and achieved mainstream elected office' (CRE, 1997: paras 2.3-2.4). In other words, ethnic communities lost their initiative to gain some control over ungoverned space when they lost the informal political arena in which they could develop ethnic politics. Two important political changes in attitudes towards ethnic minority communities demands for political participation occurred in the period between the 1980s and 1990s. The first change was the recognition of the importance of equal opportunities (Ball and Solomos, 1990) and the second led to the growing respectability of other cultures embodied in the concept of the diversity of culture. The principles that underpin them are important and necessary. Neither can provide equality, because they do not address the issue of ethnic identity. Whether or not ethnic identity is regarded as important today is open to question. While there is a need to recognise ethnic diversity, its incorporation into the formal political process is little more than an aim (Parekh, 1991). Although neither of these changes in attitudes to the ethnic minorities has increased their access to positions in the formal political hierarchy, they have increased people's awareness of the absence of ethnic culture signs. The events themselves have not changed as much as the political climate around them. The disastrous election of John Taylor in Gloucester exemplified this grassroots party control and the consequences of the absence of a potential MP who could have contributed to the changing face of Parliament.

In effect, control of governed space and the production of signs remains under the control of the white community, local and national governments and the state. The globalisation of industry and politics has changed the character of ungoverned space to a large extent, except in the sense of lawlessness. Local and national government initiatives have led to the redevelopment of much of the ungoverned space of the 1970s. The effect of this has been to localise and globalise ethnic organisations and ethnic social identities. This has depoliticised ethnic organisations, while giving ethnic businesses the opportunity to produce ethnic cultural signs for consumption. This is the subject of the final Chapter.

Notes

1. On the basis of her records between 1975-76 of persons who attended her surgeries for advice and support, Mrs A.Taylor MP estimated that a third were Asians (personal communication).
2. Muslims have shown in their opposition to Rushdie's *The Satanic Verses* that they are prepared to oppose the law if they do not agree with a decision.
3. This issue has surfaced again this year, but the way in which it has reappeared is slightly different to the occasion mentioned above. The arguments are unchanged. This time the petition from the mosques received the support of two Muslim governors of the school. The petition was circulated to more organisations and some MPs.

8 Conclusion

The recognised shift of migrants from being powerless outsiders to people with full rights to live in Britain is confirmed by their change in status to citizens. Originally seen as cheap and exploitable labour (Miles, 1982) with few responsibilities to the country in which they had found work, and more responsibilities to that from which they came, the transformation brought about by citizenship has had economic and political implications which have emerged with time. Three changes in status are important. Firstly, as people who came to save money (Anwar, 1979) and act as workers meeting the needs of capitalists (Miles and Phizacklea, 1984), these South Asian Gujaratis have become 'strollers and consumers in new crowded urban spaces' (Featherstone, 1996:72). Secondly, citizenship gives them a right to cultural participation (Amin, 1997; Urry, 1997) in their ethnic communities as well as in British society generally. Thirdly, they have become the 'good tourist' (Urry, 1997). Citizenship for these South Asians provides them with rights in the place where they live, but it adds rather than restricts the social identities they draw upon in their daily lives. They belong to a wider global society whose members move around seeking locations which might provide a socially acceptable place of residence, only to move on again when the impulse arises. The changes in British society from Fordism to post-Fordism have left South Asians detached in a social location that still fails to protect them from racism and racialisation. With no way of politically expressing their cultural diversity and no ethnic political representation, they are free of the social constraints that once bound citizens to their countries.

Post-Fordism is associated with the cultural process of aestheticisation of everyday life. This process has confirmed citizenship for ethnic minorities while also depriving them of the resources necessary to allow them to remain ethnically distinctive. The combination of deskilling of an ethnic community that was experiencing an empowering process of citizenship ensured that their contribution as consumers would remain difficult, if not tainted, with racism. Anwar's (1979) recognition of the lure of wealth that drew the Asian to a racialised Britain that was antagonistic towards black people, now encourages them to look to a new form of equality, that is, 'not hiding or apologising for one's origins, family or country, but requiring others to show respect for them' (Modood, 1996:115) for more mobile social identities. The lack of economic and social integration of most South Asian populations has made more apparent the importance of the need to develop 'a notion of public ethnicity, of redrawing our understanding of the private and the public' (Modood, 1996: 185). The efforts of Asian communities' to establish ethnic politics and its suppression by the state need to be seen in terms of the struggle by the former to achieve social, economic and political recognition as citizens and consumers.

The Conclusion is set out in three parts: the first provides a summary of the analysis present, the second part looks at the position of the Gujarati population in Bolton today, and the third part consist of some concluding ideas.

Ethnic politics: a summary

I began by arguing that the process of settlement and the work available to Gujaratis in Bolton, which were similar for South Asians living elsewhere, allowed for racism to become explicit. It also enabled these ethnic populations to form distinct communities around social and religious organisations. The pattern of settlement was partly influenced by the way in which the state racialised its various dimensions of control (Smith, 1989) and partly by more localised factors, such as the availability of housing, the kind of work available, and a general sharing of experiences of migration and racism.

The growth of the ethnic population provided the social basis for the emergence of community organisation. Initially, members provided through their own efforts the capital that was used to purchase, refurbish or alter buildings for social and religious use. Through these efforts, ethnic communities made an impact on the local and national political economies. Most immediately, these achievements not only enhanced Gujaratis' social and religious facilities, but more importantly, they changed the landscape. They did this by competition for governed and particularly ungoverned space. This process partly became a response to racism (Ballard, 1994) and partly both enhanced ethnic culture and partly set it apart within British culture.

By generally investing in social networks that drew their close friends from their own communities, the Gujaratis strengthened their own social position rather than weakening it by investing in weaker relationships with those in stronger positions (Lin, 1982; Blau, 1964). Thus ethnic communities within populations, such as those of the Gujaratis in Bolton, in becoming aware of their political position recognised the importance of their votes with their lack of effective means for political participation.

Competition for ungoverned space by ethnic communities which not only brought this space to the attention of those with control, like local authorities, but it also explains why much of the early political activity had to do with planning permission. The lack of 'operational' minarets on mosques is evidence of the degree of local political power that was brought to bear on ethnic communities and changes to the urban landscape. It was not only these changes that were important: more import was their symbolism; namely, they signified the existence of new consumers. Consumption brought ethnic communities into the political arenas not as seekers of benefits, but as architects of a changing landscape. Thus it is through ethnic politics that ethnic communities could fashion their social identities and to begin to conserve and rebuild their cultures.

Initially seeking support against racism and disadvantages that accompanied it, ethnic communities turned to the local CRCs, which had been developed to support them. At the same time local CRCs, as part of a wider race relations strategy, had an independence that allowed them to offer their clients, members of ethnic communities, political support. For CRCs the support they received from members of these communities was a measure of their ability to meet the needs of their clients. Immigration and nationality matters dominated the lives of these ethnic citizens and their families. This also provided local CRCs with opportunities to extend their role as the defenders of the rights of the racially disadvantaged. This was transformed into local confrontations between ethnic leaders expressing their views and demands for the debate of issues that characterised their demands for space. Meanwhile the politicians endeavoured to marginalise these issues partly to reduce their own political vulnerability to being seen as black supporters and partly to protect themselves against ethnic leaders who were believed to be acting for themselves. This one-sided relationship was tempered by the politicians' need for the ethnic vote and their belief that ethnic leaders could possibly influence this vote. The fragile alliances that were constructed between competing ethnic organisations were attempts by ethnic representatives and CRCs to forge political roles for the former and to encourage the recreation of ethnic culture. Politicians and the state saw the former as a threat to stability and the latter was initially regarded as evidence of assimilation rather than integration.

Networks of social relationships, which underpinned ethnic social organisations, provided structures for leadership and support. With hierarchies of social identities these social organisations were able to use the informal political arenas provided by CRCs to exploit the flexibility of unity and detachment. From being all Muslims at one moment, they could separate into as many different communities as their identities allowed. The flexibility to segment was to prove to be a major weakness in the structures of CRCs. While Bolton CRC, like other CRCs, viewed the development of informal political arenas as providing ethnic leaders with access to local politicians at a time when they had no significant voice (Ben-Tovim *et al*, 1986, 1992). Others saw it as giving ethnic minorities through another form of political contact, an advantage that they themselves did not have (Solomos, 1989). However, the lack of success of ethnic people within political parties (attributable to racism) confirmed for CRCs the need to facilitate such contact. Although members of ethnic communities have had varying success in being supported by their political parties for election as councillors and MPs, their success did not reflect either the size of the ethnic population or the ideologies sometimes expressed by the state to recognise ethnic diversity (Swann Report, 1988).

The CRCs' commitment to providing this access might be seen as a reaction to the buffer functions of other bodies involved in race relations at the time (Katznelson, 1973). Thus the rise and the fall of ethnic politics as a feature of local politics lasted only as long as local CRCs could facilitate such access in addition to the political participation provided by political parties. Possibly, arguments about such access advantaging ethnic communities compared to white communities, led to the demand by governments for greater accountability of the activities of CRCs. A series of reviews of CRCs by the CRE culminated in reports by Gay and Young (1988), and more recently by CRE (1997). The former report brought about major changes in the roles of CRCs and these brought to an end ethnic politics as well as removing immigration and nationality from CRCs' agendas. In effect this broke the link between ethnic communities and CRCs and required both to reconsider how they might form new relationships and on what basis. These changes brought to an end ethnic politics.

Three points need to be made about ethnic politics. The first point is that ethnic politics was not just about gaining better and more equitable political representation in local politics and political parties, but also about gaining access to urban space as consumers. What this analysis demonstrates is that the consumption by the ethnic communities was relatively limited. Besides Gujaratis creating ethnic villages in which they and other minority people could move safely and find familiar goods, the desire to establish community and religious centres has become a goal in itself. The symbolism attached to these structures changed the skyline and took up urban space that intruded politically and economically upon the white community's control over space. To this extent ethnic diversity has been made apparent and suggests that the interests it represents are in a part of the town which is socially, economically and politically devalued (Smith, 1989). While these physical structures symbolise the presence of ethnically different communities, they also symbolise their inferiority and separation.

The second point is that ethnic politics was about developing structures of support and leadership in a political environment in which they had no direct form of political participation or representation. The choice they had in theory was whether or not to establish alliances within the Gujarati population alone, with non-Gujarati minority communities or with the white community (Lin, 1982). The analysis of friendship showed that Gujaratis close friends were Gujaratis' from the same religious background as themselves. Their friendships with members of other minority communities were minimal, as were their friendships with members of the white community. Friendship became reflexive (Lash and Urry, 1994); it enabled Gujaratis to define different levels of social commitment to those with whom they interacted in daily life. Friends who were of lesser acquaintance were also the ones who were perceived to be the less trustworthy (Granovetter, 1977). The boundaries of the primary zones of Gujaratis' social networks symbolise socio-geographical boundaries that separate them from others. Thus both in a geographical and social sense Gujaratis claims upon physical and social space symbolise their position within Bolton society.

The third point has to do with the economic niche they occupied. Gujaratis came originally to supplement and/or complement local labour in failing industries. Gujaratis filled a niche in a textile industry which was competing both with imports from outside Britain, and with demands within Britain to modernise. Thus the skills these workers acquired, often through minimal training, were sufficient for the purposes of the mill owners to keep going, but were insufficient to make a major difference to their survival. Employment ensured that these workers were enskilled with skills that were not transferable to other industries. Exploitation extended to giving these workers skills that could not be used in other industries and other work, possibly with the exception of homeworking. With the eventual collapse of the textile industry, Gujaratis and some of the other minorities employed by this industry found themselves not only jobless but also unemployable. They had to compete with other jobless people among whom were white people, whose potential baseline skills and education gave them an advantage. The Gujaratis who were successful in business were a minority within a minority. They were also people who preferred to employ workers who were white rather than Gujaratis. Thus consumption by Gujaratis themselves did not use white controlled space or symbolism desired by white consumers: they continued to intrude into devalued space and thus gave it new value.

This set the racial scene for the 1990s. By the end of the 1970s and into the early 1980s Gujaratis were able to accumulate earnings, were still in employment, still had some ethnic political representation and were beginning to transform their surroundings as well as having them transformed by urban renewal programmes. The recessions changed the scene for the ethnic population in a number of significant ways. The process of modernisation of the racial equality structure also contributed to this change. Therefore, the issues that have become central to these minority communities today have less to do with integration and assimilation and more to do with the their resistance to racism.

It is the changes in the role and functions of the local CRC that I shall address next and then move on to consider a recent survey of mainly South Asians in three wards in Bolton.

CRC and ethnic communities in Bolton: into the 1990s

Gay and Young's (1988) review of the role and functions of local CRCs changed them. They defined their objectives as (a) to work towards the elimination of racial discrimination and (b) to promote equality of opportunity, and good relations, between persons of different racial groups (CRE, *A Good Practice Manual*, 1991:4). The functions of CRCs are policy development, public education, community development and casework, mainly concerned with complainant aid, that is, racial discrimination based upon the 1976 Race Relations Act. Casework connected with immigration and nationality and social, housing and personal issues and a range of other casework all became the responsibility of other voluntary organisations. With these changes, as well as with a new degree of accountability to the CRE, local RECs lost a membership, which had personal experience of immigration and nationality. This service has now been moved to organisations which specialised in such work, and people with problems relating to counselling and advice, health matters or social concerns had to approach those organisations that were funded to provide such a service. This was a way in which the government could encourage these voluntary organisations to take full responsibility for their clients, including those from ethnic minorities.

The number of local RECs nationally is now about 100 (CRE, 1995, Annual Report), which is only slightly down on the numbers in existence in the 1970s and slightly up on those in the 1980s. As a CRC is evidence of the presence of an ethnic minority population, CRCs in turn are evidence of the widespread activities of the CRE and of the involvement of members from ethnic communities in race related issues. With the removal of ethnic politics from REC agendas, the involvement in the new functions of RECs has brought into them new membership which, if Bolton's REC is taken as an example, will be much younger than it was ten years ago. The point at issue is, if these organisations were once a focal point for ethnic politics, then the change in their functions has had a considerable impact on such political activity by removing it. Now all of these ethnic communities will have to relate to the political structure through activities involving local political parties and elections. This will require the submergence of ethnic issues within wider social class debates and relegate ethnic political issues to the mosque or temple. Both at the local and national level, ethnic issues have to be taken up by mainstream political representatives and their political parties as political issues generally and possibly as a means to attract more ethnic members.

The effects of these changes on local RECs and their immediate membership (a) made them more accountable to the CRE, (b) removed the issues that were central to the lives of most of their members, namely immigration and nationality (for Bolton see Mulla, 1995), (c) separated RECs from their grassroots support, (d) brought about changes in membership, (e) brought new debates on to agendas, and (f) led to a change in the name of these organisations from CRC to REC. These changes removed ethnic politics from REC agendas, which also implied reducing the risk of ethnic sectional take-overs. These changes were calculated to make racism an issue for wider political concern. Solomos and Back's (1995) study of politics in Birmingham suggests that this process is likely to be hindered by continuing racism within local organisations and local political parties. During this period of development, RECs viewed the CRE with some suspicion seeing it as responsive to its paymasters, the government. The most recent review of the roles and functions of RECs by CRE in 1997 initially did little to dispel these feelings. The results of this review confirm the changes that resulted from the previous review, namely that RECs have to address racial discrimination in terms of policy development, public education, community development and casework (Gay and Young (1988) and become even more accountable to their paymasters and clients. While these changes are generally intended to bring RECs into the 1990s, they also reflect changes in the state's attitude to racism.

As the ethnic composition of the membership of RECs begins to include more younger people and more women, the danger of their being taken over by ethnic sections fades. This new membership, if anything, is likely to be even less tolerant of racism than its predecessors. These changes in the membership and changes in functions has removed the REC from being the focus for ethnic political activity. Thus ethnic politics waxed as CRCs searched for support in the 1970s and waned with the changes to its functions at the end of the 1980s and into the 1990s. Thus Solomos (1989) is right to regard ethnic politics of little concern after 1988, but the importance of ethnic politics now needs to be located in debates about pluralism, justice and a public culture. To some extent Parekh (1991) began to address these issues when he argued that diversity should be recognised politically. The days of black sections in political parties are over, and now ethnic voters have to participate on the same grounds as other voters. Ethnic issues are disappearing from the political agenda; they were becoming subsumed within the class-based issues and party political participation. That ethnic politics had ever existed is in itself remarkable in a country that has chosen not to enshrine ethnic representation in its political structure.

The opportunity to develop ethnic politics should be seen as a form of resistance to racism which gave the migrant, who had few rights and little wealth, the opportunity to participate in politics. With political parties controlling ethnic participation, citizenship is not a substitute for the lack of ethnic political participation.

Gujaratis in Bolton: the 1990s

Some 20 years on, the Gujarati population seems not to have changed in any major way with the exception of moving from a position of almost full employment to being one of groups experiencing the highest unemployment. Other changes are less obvious. In this section I shall look at housing, family size and employment and unemployment. I shall draw on the findings in the 1991 Census and the *Economic and Social Audit of the 3Ds area of Bolton (ESA3Ds)* (1996).[1]

Population

The size of the population has changed little since the 1970s; the Gujarati population has remained at about 13,000. In the 1970s the total ethnic minority population comprised about 6.7% of the total population, whereas today it is closer to 8.3% (Census, 1991). Gujaratis comprised 4.9% of the total population in 1976; today they comprise 5.2%. These differences may be accounted for by a fall in the size of the white population. Bolton has still the largest Indian community in Greater Manchester. The Indian community is still characterised by a younger age profile than the white community; 62.5% of whom are under 30 years of age compared with 40.7% of in the white community (Census, 1991). The *ESA3D* survey found that over a third of the ethnic residents sampled were born in Britain and only 9 held Indian citizenship. This can be taken as a measure of stability. Although the population is growing as more migrants from the Indian subcontinent come to join it, this growth is less driven by a search for work and more by the pressure to find appropriate marriage partners (Mulla, 1995).

Pattern of settlement

The pattern of settlement has changed only in terms of being extended in certain directions. Parts of the inner urban wards in which Gujaratis found housing in the 1970s have been demolished and replaced with green areas. The quality of housing and amenities in the areas in which they first settled and still live have improved with the injection of funds and improvement grants, but compared with those in the outer suburban areas the houses continue to be of lower value. In other words, the Gujaratis and other South Asian communities have consolidated themselves in Halliwell, Central, Burnden, Derby and Daubhill, the area in which they lived in 1976. There has been some expansion in the area of settlement, partly brought about by the redrawing of ward boundaries in the 1980s and partly by expansion. South Asian settlement encircles the town centre (Map 2). It is in some of these inner urban areas that the greatest overcrowding in housing is to be found and still some housing is marked by a lack of amenities. Although South Asian families are still some of the largest, the average number of children in these families is dropping (Census, 1991).

An explanation for the relative lack of movement of Asians into the suburbs can be explained by the low value of the housing, partly by the lack of demand for these houses and possibly by the suppression of housing values arising from the selling and exchanging of houses between Gujaratis. A further explanation for the lack of movement may be attributed to the improvement in local schools as a consequence of the implementation of the national curriculum, and the establishment of more mosques, temples and community centres together with a general modernising of these areas. Other factors that have contributed to the stability of this population are, firstly, in the 1980s, the availability of housing improvement grants and the building of new housing in the areas. Secondly, South Asians experienced financial hardships as a result the loss of jobs in a declining textile industry and declining manufacturing sector generally.

Housing was a key issue in the 1970s. The availability of poor quality housing, a lack of resources, and a political inability to compete for better resources symbolised the position of South Asians in Bolton. In Chapter Two (above) I show how homeownership prior to the survey rose from 32% to 64% at the time of the research. Saunders (1990) commented on this rise in Asian homeownership. By 1991 Indian homeowners had risen to 81.5% making them the second highest group of homeowners in the town (Census, 1991). The highest are Pakistanis of whom 82.6% are homeowners. Some 44% of the *ESA3D*s sample of Indians had lived in this area from 10 years to over 30 years. Arguably, a high proportion of homeownership points to the presence of a stable ethnic population.

Another factor that could have influenced homeownership is employment. In the 1970s Gujaratis found work easily, so easily that they could walk out of a job one day in the certain knowledge that they could find a similar job three to four months later. Until the 1980s South Asians could still find work in a declining textile industry and declining manufacturing industry. After this time, work in the manufacturing sector and declining textile industry became difficult to find. This resulted in the disappearance of jobs which had attracted this Asian workforce. Now the loss of opportunities for work has reduced their earning capacity. This may have added to the inability of South Asians increasing significantly their share of privately owned properties after the 1980s. These changes not only deprived South Asians of jobs and earnings, but they also deskilled them for work in the new textile industry that replaced the old one. With the exception of a few successful business and professional South Asians, who have been able to move into middle and upper class white areas, the majority of South Asians are still living in the same areas in which they first settled in the 1970s.

Unemployment and employment

In 1976 only 5% of the sample were unemployed and this included one or two retired people. Almost 50% of the sample worked in the textile industry and only 3.5% held professional jobs (Chapter Two). The majority of the sample held jobs which were of lower middle class or working class status, irrespective of individual qualifications. In 1991 of the 13,356 Indians living here only 4,901 (36.7%) were working and comprised 4% of the total workforce. Most of these Indians held full time jobs, but an increasing number are taking up part time work. Self-employment rose generally from 7.7% in 1981 to 10.7% in 1991; and Asians accounted for much of this growth. Some 16.8% are in some form of self-employment. The move towards self-employment was once attributed to Asians being able to escape from racialised situations (Smith, 1976). In a post-Fordist society which is based on flexibility and encourages the development niche industries and markets, South Asians express a preference for self-employment will find opportunities to establish their own businesses. Much of ethnic minority self-employment takes the form of corner shops, small clothing manufacturing and soft furnishing businesses. One of the most successful of these is a food and clothing materials business which recently made the headlines in their battle with Saab to keep their trade name 'Memsaab' on certain foodstuffs. These and a few Asian businesses, which retail electrical goods and clothing, stand out as larger developments from the small corner shop. The impact of South Asians on the town as major consumers of culture is limited to religious and social developments and niche markets.

Today the majority of Indians are employed in similar proportions in the same industrial sectors that they were employed in the 1970s. In the Borough the social class profile of South Asians shows that are in professional occupations than another other ethnic group with the exception of the Chinese. Unemployment has had a major impact on the South Asian communities. The unemployment rate for Indians was 24.2% compared with 9.4% for the white community and 30.7% for the Pakistani community (Census, 1991). This gives an average of 25.4% unemployment in the ethnic minority communities. The unemployment rates for Indians in Greater Manchester is lower (17.5%) than for those living in Bolton. This possibly can be explained by the heavy dependence of Indians in Bolton upon a collapsing textile industry. The rate of unemployment for South Asians under 25 is 30.5% compared with 17.3% for the white community. With the exception of the Chinese, the other ethnic communities share in this trend.

In terms of qualifications, although Asian communities place a high social value on educational aspirations (Penn *et al*, 1991), according to the Census they have the lowest number of people with a UK degree. Thus the overall profile of the Indian and Gujarati community in the borough suggests that the main changes lie in employment and unemployment and in the lack of change in housing. The paid work, which once provided South Asians with the resources to move to better

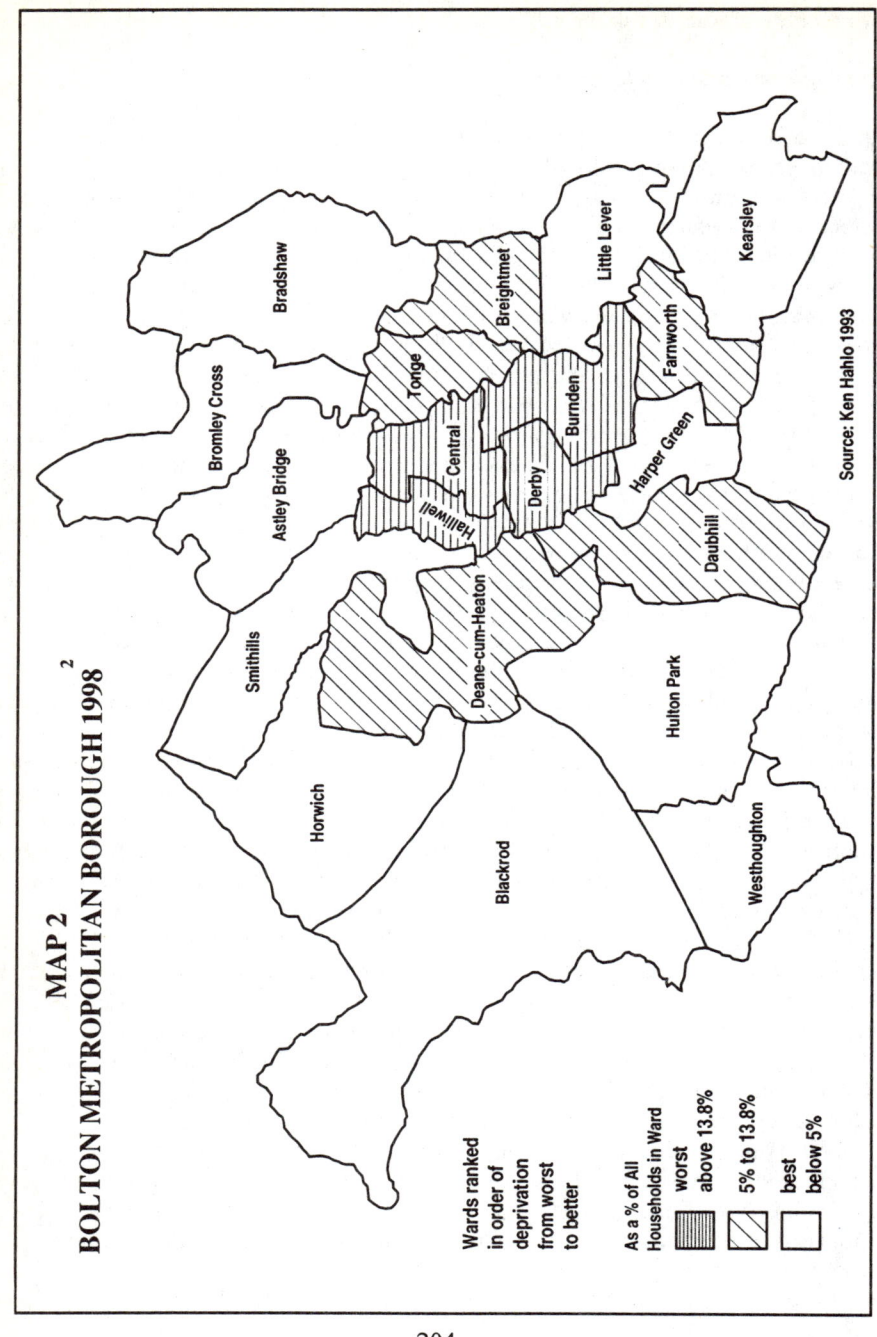

MAP 2
BOLTON METROPOLITAN BOROUGH 1998 [2]

Bradshaw

Breightmet

Little Lever

Kearsley

Bromley Cross

Tonge

Burnden

Farnworth

Astley Bridge

Central

Derby

Harper Green

Halliwell

Daubhill

Smithills

Deane-cum-Heaton

Hulton Park

Horwich

Blackrod

Westhoughton

Source: Ken Hahlo 1993

Wards ranked
in order of
deprivation
from worst
to better

As a % of All
Households in Ward

worst
above 13.8%

5% to 13.8%

best
below 5%

housing areas, was taken up by more qualified white workers. Consequently, the disadvantaged South Asian workers have remained disadvantaged by their colour and lack of appropriate skills.

More importantly, these South Asians came to work in a textile industry that was under threat internally from the then government, which required it to modernise and to clean up its production, and externally from cheaper imports from foreign producers who could bring their products to British markets. With white women leaving millwork, men having left it earlier, the South Asians provided neither simply replacement or supplementary labour to fill this labour vacuum (Chapters One and Two above). These new industrial textile plants manufacture materials to meet the needs of changing globalised markets. The skills once acquired by these South Asians are now of little use. For instance, a mill on Swan Lane, which once employed about 3000 workers, after modernisation employs 500. Thus the period in which the labour intensive mills declined and disappeared also marked the period of massive deskilling of a South Asian work force. The decline of the manufacturing sector and racism ensured that they would become unemployed and gradually and increasingly unemployable.

Penn (1994:74) notes that 1.4 million jobs were lost in the 1980s in the textile and clothing industry in Europe and about 200,000 jobs were lost in these sectors in Britain (1994:75). The trend in the growth of multiply unemployed in ethnic families has become a feature of Bolton's South Asian communities. The jobs in the textile and clothing sector have changed with new methods of production, demand for shorter runs and a need to meet global competition. This new textile industry demands higher qualifications from its employees. These qualifications do not match the training that the Asian migrants received when they first came to work in the old textile industry. Even after the decline in the textile industry, Asians are still twice as likely as white workers to be employed in the manufacturing sector (ESA3Ds, 1996). This suggests that the skill level of the South Asians have not changed much, that the skills they bring to the workplace have not changed, that they are having to accept lower pay for longer hours, and are experiencing increasingly longer periods of unemployment. The explanation for such a large rise in unemployment lies in the disappearance of the textile mills and the general decline in the textile and clothing sectors along with the development of new high tech textile and clothing industry with a demand for qualified staff (Penn, 1994: 82-85). In other words, the South Asians who first came to find work in the mills are being rapidly deskilled. Although some Asian workers earn higher wages than white workers sampled, overall more Asian workers earn less than the white workers do. Generally, Asian women earn less than Asian men. The findings of the ESA3Ds survey shows that male and female ethnic workers received less training, found fewer jobs, experienced more racial discrimination, were faced with language barriers and experienced longer periods of unemployment than did white men and women. An explanation for the lower pay and less secure employment of Asians needs to take into account racial discrimination, deskilling and the lack of qualifications (Jenkins, 1989; Penn, 1994, ESA3Ds, 1996:23).

The dependence of the South Asian population on the manufacturing sector has not changed, which leaves these workers vulnerable to deskiling and unemployment. However, Asians encourage their children to have high aspirations and to find work in more secure, prestigious and better paid sectors than their parents and their white peers (Penn *et al*, 1991). While the aspirations of South Asians may be higher than those of their white peers (Penn *et al*, 1991), the difficulties of coping with racial discrimination remain. It remains to be shown if the Asian children can achieve their aspirations. Although racial discrimination is regarded as a crime, and the number of racial discrimination cases taken up nationally and locally by the CRE is on the increase, the practice of discrimination has become both subtler and less invisible. More South Asian workers are unemployed or, if employed, were earning less on average than white workers.

Over the twenty years that have elapsed between the 1976, 1991 Census and 1996 survey, the vulnerability of the economic position of the South Asian population in Bolton has changed little. They were and still are a section of the population that is, vulnerable to poverty, deskilling and discrimination, but now they are citizens and not migrants. The effects of this lack of change in their overall location in Bolton is further influenced by their continued lack of access to political resources and to their location within consumer culture as consumers rather than producers. In this final section of the conclusion I shall briefly consider the demise of ethnic politics and the absence of legislators and interpreters in South Asian communities.

Consumerism and race

The quest of ethnic minority communities for social, economic and political space in which to develop and thereby to increase access to scarce resources after the 1970s became increasingly dependent upon their ability to achieve representation in the formal political arena. Continued residence and the acquisition of citizenship has given this one-time migrant community security, but this in itself has not added to their ability as a community to achieve better access to resources than that which they had twenty years ago. A number of factors have contributed to this continued state of being. These include the change in the role and functions of the REC (and therefore the CRE), the demise of ethnicity and ethnic politics, the role of religious and community organisations, migration, culture and political participation.

In conclusion I shall argue that to be a stroller and consumer the Asian has to contribute to the production of signs and images which identify his/her ethnic origins and set them alongside other consumable signs and images. The local, rather than the global, provided the site of change for Asians who had come to seek work and now find themselves in a post-modern world in which their place can be secured through the market place. Racism needs to be seen as part of a struggle to achieve equality within an urban location. Part of this struggle became one of attempting to achieve political recognition locally in a declining economic situation. This shift to a commitment to settle here was translated into a commitment to elevate social, religious and cultural needs over those of over those of local industrial demands (Geddes, 1994; Ballard, 1994). Rather than South Asians being 'prisoners of the Beveridge dream' because of rising unemployment (Williams, 1994:83), they have become citizens within a commodifying labour relationship that extends from a declining manufacturing sector to a rising service class (Lash and Urry, 1988) and new local markets that bring the global within reach of local consumers. Support for South Asian commitment to citizenship are a raft of pressures, these include the efforts of successive governments to control immigration through the 1981 Nationality Act, 1986 visa controls, 1987 Immigration (Carriers' Liability) Act, 1988 Immigration Act, 1990 British Nationality Act, 1993 Asylum and Immigration Appeals Act and 1996 Asylum and Immigration Act. British categories of citizenship are designed to separate those who have no rights from those with limited rights (certain categories of non-patrials) and those with full rights, citizens (R. Cohen, 1994; (Department of Immigration and Nationality, Annual Report, 1995). Although such legislation would appear to clarify the status of citizens, it has had at least two consequences. Firstly, South Asian migration has declined and is no longer politically of central importance to British industry; most pressure is coming from migrants leaving other third world countries (Department of Immigration and Nationality, 1995, Table 3.4). Secondly, Asian Britons, however, want to bring in partners to fulfil the conditions of arranged marriages for their children as well as bringing in their elderly parents, who are becoming increasingly dependent on them. For South Asians immigration and nationality remain issues of importance (Mulla, 1995). Control over immigration and nationality has been effectively translated from political control over labour to control over citizenship, (Castles and Miller, 1993). This form of control still meets the needs of the state and government, and in so doing controls the flow of new immigrants into its black communities.

The shift from migrant to consumer has invested in the ethnic consumer a gaze that gives them the same power and opportunity as any other consumer to consume and produce. However, in rust-belt towns, like Bolton, ethnic communities have become trapped in a deskilling process that has left them as vulnerable to racism and capitalism as migration did almost half a century ago. Migrants are consumables; their labour can be bought. The change from consumable to consumer involves a major shift in power, and in an age when consumerism predominates, the position of consumers is a reflection of their social class position.

Since their arrival, they acquired citizenship and some degree of wealth. Migration is still a national issue, but the mechanisms of immigration control have been extended to all migrants, irrespective of where they come from. Migration is not just a 'black' issue. This does not mean that South Asian migration has ceased. It has been reduced as a consequence of measures of control over the past 25 years, but it has not ceased. Immigration and nationality are major concerns in South Asian communities. Although changes in the social and economic positions of South Asian communities have occurred, their access to political power has changed little. The changes to the role and functions of CRCs (now RECs) have removed the informal political arena that once encouraged the development of ethnic politics. Now without ethnic politics, these citizens still have relatively little access to political positions through political parties. The shift in the importance of migration and access to citizenship have contributed to depoliticising ethnic organisations, and removing ethnic politics generally. The ethnic communities depend upon political parties for access to political positions. Their access to scarce resources is still also dependent upon white politicians and the construction of a shared public culture. To quote: 'even if some of the conditions are necessary to a participation in a shared public culture, such as the rights of citizenship, a public culture or a national identity cannot be equated with the formally legal or institutional. A sense of society, of effective as opposed to nominal membership in a shared public culture, over and above private and communal affiliations, may be dependent on different things with different people' (Modood, 1996:188).

Culture and consumerism

One aspect of ethnic culture was the formation in the 1960s and 1970s of ethnic communities and religious organisations. At one time Ballard R and C (1977) observed that the formation of such communities and organisations were major steps in the process of developing ethnic identities. Without a political arena in which their leaders can wield ethnic support in their interests as well as those of other political supporters, ethnic organisations, community and religious, are reduced to the level of other voluntary organisations. Their political activities are welded to those of these other voluntary organisations. The issue about ethnic political representation has been forgotten, and ethnic interests are now social class and political party interests. Of the five forms of political participation outlined by Layton-Henry (1984) social class participation remains along with other negative forms of participation. The removal of ethnic politics has become complete (Solomos, 1989), although Parekh (1991) has argued for its continued recognition in politics at a regional level. Religious organisations are still the most obvious sign of an ethnic presence in the town and the appearance of new religious buildings is evidence of further ethnic activity. Now this activity has become more focused on the ethnic community served by the organisation and it has become associated with the development of organisations to serve the needs of the elderly in the community. A number of religious communities, such as the VHP, Barbodan Society and Mosque communities support their own elderly or the Asian Elders Initiative which provides support for elderly people from all ethnic communities. The functions of ethnic organisations are changing and becoming community led.

The importance of religious and ethnic organisations lies not only in their change in roles, but also in that they continue to act as the flaneurs in the ethnic communities. They perform a public function when ethnicity can be put on display at festivals and on religious occasions Cohen (1991). Tourism is one aspect of the aestheticisation of a definable period of time which can be given monetary value (Urry, 1990). Three steps can be identified as marking the passage of South Asians to their position in British society today. Firstly, South Asian culture is gazed upon by the wider society. The notion of the diversity of culture still attracts social and political gazers. Like the tourist, the white gazers only consume their samosas and saris; they do not provide anything for the makers of the samosas and saris to consume. Secondly, South Asian organisations and entrepreneurs are entering the markets as major consumers of space and resources. The urban landscapes in some towns and cities have been changed by the building or conversion of old buildings in temples and mosques. They have added a new cultural dimension to the aestheticisation of urban landscapes. Thirdly, South Asians are achieving status as the providers of consumables, clothing, electrical goods (particularly computers) and ethnic foodstuffs. Ethnic goods and services are available to consumption and they form part of an expanding flexible post-Fordist market. Thus South Asians are part of the process of aestheticisation of daily life.

Other aspects of aestheticisation of everyday life include shopping, public displays, art, and culture. This process is expressed through three senses, namely, the emergence of artistic subcultures, the project of turning life into a work of art and the rapid flow of signs and images which saturate the fabric of everyday life (Featherstone, 1996:66-67). These changes are expressed not only through architecture and art, but also through signs and images which introduced into urban locations a dreamlike power to tempt the consumer. To quote Featherstone: 'Hence the consumer society becomes essentially cultural as social life becomes increasingly deregulated and social relationships become more variable and less structured by stable norms. The overproduction of signs and reproduction of images and simulations leads to a loss of stable meaning, and an aestheticisation of reality in which the masses become fascinated by the endless flow of bizarre juxtapositions which takes the viewer beyond stable sense' (1996:15). Race relations, along with other areas of social behaviour, has been deregulated and hollowed out, and social relationships have been destructured, creating opportunities for the social reconstruction of new signs with new meanings. This allows ethnic minority communities to construct signs and symbols based upon consumerism which can become understood in new and different ways by their own members as well as by others in society (Back, 1996; Hall, 1992). The exchange of meanings has to take place in some marketplace, and it has to take forms that open meanings to others. The producers and consumers need to benefit from the exchange: the former need to locate their signs where they have the greatest effect and the latter need to be able to view them and have access to them. Signs which are accessible and have a potentially high exchange rate are cultural items, like art, music, food, and clothes. Control or dominance of a cultural item allows an ethnic minority community to become recognised and gain opportunities to alter status.

Much of this conclusion, however, argues that the South Asians, and Gujaratis in particular, in Bolton are still disadvantaged economically and politically, irrespective of the existence of legislation supporting equal opportunities and racial equality. As consumers they continue to be disadvantaged, because their history in the locality has left them in a position of a consumer who can purchase only the less desirable signs and symbols that carry the more valued meaning in a consumerist culture. The formation of ethnic communities symbolised by newly acquired religious sites no longer marks a process of change in control of the inner urban areas. All that it stands for is an ethnicity located in an outdated ethnoscape (Appadurai, 1990), which now does little more than identify one Asian community from another community of citizens belonging to the same country. The history once attached to the moving landscape of the migrant has become compacted into a collection of memories which are losing their meaning in a globalised world. These old ethnicities are losing their meaning through what Urry (1990b: 20) refers to as a 'process of deterritorialisation', and new ethnicities are emerging which locate ethnic citizens within a local and a global context. The former involves greater sharing of common identities through citizenship; therefore what ethnic communities have also experienced is a process of reterritorialisation. This has enabled Gujaratis to redefine their ethnicities in relation to local and global environments. The former process has reduced their ethnicities to 'movements of opposition' (Appadurai, 1990: 296-300) which are part of local citizenship. They reflect common issues of locality and environment.

However, the process of reterritorialisation offers potential for association of new ethnicities with ethnicities that are and were part of other scapes, ethnoscapes, finanscapes, mediascapes, and ideoscapes. The Rushdie affair is an example of this process, that is, the potential of diverse communities with different citizenships sharing a common identity in response to a political situation. Urry (1990b) argues that it is the sharing of concerns associated with globalised environmental issues that generate identities to which citizens from different countries can commit or oppose themselves. There is no simple progression from local identities to globalised identities; local ethnicities have little meaning now in a global environment unless they can be linked to 'ideologies of states or movements of opposition' (see Urry, 1990b: 20; Appadurai, 1990: 296-300).

A consequence of this is that South Asians have to stroll and consume the sought-after products of white producers. Generally only the wealthy South Asians can buy the desirable signs of consumerism which identify them as modern consumers. The division between the wealthy and poor South Asians is growing, and is confirmed in Bolton through the movement of the former into good upper class housing areas, leaving the others in the inner urban areas. It raises a question in the local geo-political context that is, now being answered, namely 'who is the native?' (Spivak, 1985:134,147 quoted in Rattansi, 1994). The Gujarati is now a Briton, and as such shares local ethnicities with other non-Gujarati locals. This includes a reduction in the need for Gujaratis or South Asians or black people to be represented in a pluralistic nation state.

With the demise of ethnic politics, ethnicity has been reduced to an item that can be paraded in an arcade for the benefit of consumers and other strollers. It has become an item for display of cultural identities and differences without being commodified. The continual expansion of ethnic social and religious organisations, no longer having political meaning, they have been transformed into organisations with a social meaning not dissimilar to other kinds of voluntary social organisations. Only the mosque and temple intrude upon the local skyline. Ethnic producers copy others. The production of ethnic commodities in addition to ethnic foodstuffs, which are already commodified, would bring the ethnic into the marketplace. What is still missing locally are interpreters and legislators. Without interpreters who can re-attach ethnic identity to commodities and thus commodify ethnicity, ethnic communities shop along with others for globalised products that carry globalised values. The creation by ethnic communities of commodities with globalised values, in addition to food, would bring them closer to the process of aestheticisation of ethnic culture and thus closer to the construction of a shared public culture. This

210

would bring the ethnic minority, and the ethnic and exotic, into and alongside the traditional, modern, historical and postmodern in British society.

Notes

1. Though the *ESA3Ds* survey is the most recent research to be done in Bolton, the findings are often based on small samples. Why they often had high refusal rates is not always made clear.
2. This Map is constructed from the outline for the 1990 *District Trends* (Bolton Metro) with data drawn from *Deprivation in Bolton*, 1994. Bolton Metropolitan Borough.

Appendix I
Research methodology

This Appendix is organised in two parts; the first addresses issues of research methodology and the second sets out the sampling.

The aim of this Appendix is to clarify selected aspects of research methodology. Three issues will be addressed: firstly, the degree to which the approach influenced or was influenced by the researcher moving across cultures; secondly, the degree to which it impinged upon the understanding of the usage of the concept of culture; and thirdly, how the above issues were affected by or were modified by the collection and analysis of data. The first part deals with research methodology, and the second part deals with fieldwork matters and interviewing.

Research methodology

The first issue concerns whether or not a social anthropological or sociological approach predominates or to what extent the analysis can be described as ethnographic. The second issue concerns the concept of culture and how the cultures of ethnic minorities relate to British culture. The third issue focuses on the consequences of interpretation of data drawn from a cross-cultural situation. These three issues are intertwined and influence each other.

As this book focuses on an area that is situated at an interface between white British and Gujarati cultures within British society, it raises questions about research done across cultures. These include detailing the approach, and also issues raised when a researcher from one culture claims to record and analyse the views of those belonging to another culture. Whose views are being recorded? To what extent does the community studied subscribe to the stated views? Can a person belonging to one culture accurately record the views of members belonging to another culture? Some of these latter concerns will be discussed below.

The subject of this book focuses on how Gujaratis used ethnic politics to exploit a gap between the grassroots, the local political party and the formal political structures. The aim is not to provide a total description of Gujarati culture or of social life in Bolton. My interest is in political interaction between Gujaratis, white politicians, members of BCCR (later REC), the wider public and the Press. Thus, the research needs to take account of Gujaratis' socio-economic position, the religious organisations which provide them with structures of leadership and support, their perceptions of community, the social networks that structured these communities, their perceptions of political representation and their participation in local politics. In presenting an analysis of the observable social actions of Gujaratis and the meanings that these actions were intended to provide for certain audiences, I am making explicit what they made explicit. In doing this I am contributing to existing sociological debate about race and race relations. This is an exercise to provide an in-depth understanding of their social world.

Research that involves crossing ethnic and/or cultural boundaries raises questions about approaches. In this research an anthropological and sociological approach are combined. An assumption was once made that the difference between these disciplines lay in their approaches and subject matter. Today, however, both disciplines utilise a wide range of approaches and study a wide range of subject matter. In anthropological and sociological research, qualitative and quantitative techniques are combined (Bryman, 1988:147; Cicourel, 1981). There is no firm separation between the techniques used by one discipline and those employed by the other. Practitioners of both draw on a range of techniques of data collection and analysis appropriate to the subject studied (Ballard *et al*, 1994; Solomos and Back, 1994). A range of approaches and techniques was used to collect data, including both macro- and micro-approaches. Techniques of data collection included nonparticipant and participant observation, case studies and a questionnaire, which all provided data for network analysis. Recognising the dangers of employing a micro-approach which 'runs the risk of losing touch with social reality and imposing instead a fictional non-existing world constructed by the scientific observer' (Bryman quoting Schutz, 1988: 52), this study is situated within a macro-approach. Most of the research concentrated upon a microcosm of actions that occurred within the arena provided by Bolton Council for Community Relations and Bolton generally. The research also draws on the wider aspects of local social interaction and to an extent on national events to make sense of political activity.

Another aspect of the debate about approaches revolves around the issue of the extent to which research on another culture, and what is loosely termed anthropological content, forms ethnography. As Mair (1966:7) noted, any book that goes beyond description focusing on general theoretical issues, cannot be regarded as ethnography. Hammersley has taken a more critical view of ethnography concluding that it is not a useful category for thinking about social research methodology (1992:203). It forms part of a more complex approach to social research. In the process of carrying out this research, a view is provided of aspects of Gujarati social life. In doing this, as an informed outsider, I am providing a view of ethnic and local politics. Most politicians who are involved in local politics have greater or lesser experience of ethnic politics; thus they are to an extent familiar with ethnic politics. Their familiarity is based upon a selective process that is not intended to explain ethnic politics but to utilise it to promote or diminish support. From another point of view this study may be described as ethnographic, since it involves both ethnography and analysis, which is particularly appropriate to a study of racism. To quote Willis: 'The role of ethnography is to show the cultural viewpoint of the oppressed, their 'hidden' knowledges and resistances as well as the basis on which entrapping 'decisions' are taken in some sense of liberty, but which nevertheless help to produce 'structure'' (Willis, 1981:201-3, quoted in Clifford and Marcus, 1986: 179; see also Willis, 1979: 119-126, 171-179). Such an approach seeks to make explicit through ethnography the extent of institutional racism in local politics (Solomos and Back, 1994). In particular it raises an important issue about central values.

If politics is concerned with the definition and maintenance of central values, which are concerned with state security (Campbell, 1990), then the decisions of the state and through it governments reactions to the arrival of the West Indians in 1948 and the South Asians in the 1950s concern central values. Reactions to the racial unrest in the late 1970s and 1980s suggests that the State and governments still based their responses to black people on racialised notions of security (Gifford, 1989; Benyon and Solomos, 1987). Whether grounded in history (Fryer, 1984) or in more recent politicisation of immigration (Solomos, 1989; Layton-Henry, 1992), racialised reactions received either overt or covert support. As W. Brown (1992) argues the masculinisation of the state also allows for the racialisation of the state. However, for ethnic minorities to share in these values, two processes need to take place. Firstly, although central values can change, it cannot be easily achieved in a situation of fear (Hall *et al*, 1978). Secondly, racialised barriers may prevent central values from becoming shared with minority communities. Efforts by minorities to change central values to accommodate their local, national and global experiences and social values have been associated more often in the past with protest than with peaceful accommodation. Cohen's (1994) argument that the clarification of Britain's external boundaries has led to the generation of multiple social identities within Britain implies that the state has to recognise that members of minority communities are equal to other Britons. The complexity of this issue has been explored by Parekh (1991) when he argued that the social logic of pluralism implies some form of cultural and political equality (also Layton-Henry, 1984; Back, 1996:1-6). The tacit acceptance of the existence of cultural and political equality does not imply that the state recognises multiculturalism. CRE Annual reports continue to reflect the continuing existence and persistence of racism and racialised barriers in British society.

The second issue concerns the understanding of the concept of culture. The approach taken here is that Gujaratis are part of British society; many were citizens at the time of the research and now probably all are citizens. During the 1970s they perceived themselves as being inside rather than outside British society; but they believed that the government saw them as outside rather than inside British society. If living in a multicultural society implies the existence of diverse communities linked by a complex web of cultural similarities and differences, then the central values of the society should reflect the views of these communities (Parekh, 1991; Back, 1996: 1-6). While this does not preclude the possibility that there are other interpretations, it makes no attempt to recognise that members of minority communities and white people might dispute the centrality of these values (Modood, 1996). More importantly, the state's lack of commitment to antiracism raises questions about what can be shared in a plural society.

The debate about British society being a unitary society or a multicultural or plural society may explain the different approaches of governments and the state to minorities within the society. In the debate about whether or not Britain is a pluralistic or multicultural, Parekh (1991) has argued that the conditions of the former have not been met, and Rex (1987; 1986) has shown how the latter model is little more than an ideal type. This notion accepts the idea of British society being comprised of a number of cultures (multicultural) all of which are accorded equal freedom of expression within the private domain and a unitary set of institutions in the public domain (Rex, 1987:228). However, Rex observes that such a society as he describes is an ideal model and does not exist as yet. However, his model suggests that a multicultural society is one consisting of communities between which the cultural differences are a matter of degree and not kind.

Gujaratis distinguish between themselves and those who are not Gujaratis; they also distinguish between Gujarati Hindus and Muslims. There is an implicit assumption that people who are British can have different social identities and still be British (A.Cohen, 1982; 1985; 1986); while people who have both a different social identity and a culture with roots overseas may be socially perceived as not British, irrespective of their actual citizenship (R.Cohen, 1994). Cohen (1994) argues that people's perceptions of belonging are based upon the clarity of the definition of a British identity that either allows for their incorporation or separation from being British in a changing world. This is a highly subjective process. It is possible for members of these ethnic communities to recognise their social isolation from belonging to British society based upon their social and cultural differences. It is equally possible for members of these communities to accept their social identity as British by not giving sufficient importance to cultural differences. Arguably, it is within this framework that in a local context black and Asian Britons may perceive themselves to have disadvantaged access to scarce resources as an indication of their being socially and geographically isolated (Smith, 1989). The social identities which separate them from British culture may be explained in terms of their resistance to the destruction of their cultures. To this extent, ethnic resistance to the denigration of their cultures can be explained in terms of antiracism. The notion of 'between two cultures' is an approach which is based on the idea that maintenance of culture is regarded as a sign of social resistance to racism (Ballard, 1994) and cultural domination (Khan, 1982). Ethnic politics forms a key part of this resistance to cultural domination, because it is used to extend the participation of ethnic minorities in politics without losing their culture.

The argument behind this thesis is that Gujaratis living here may have separate social and ethnic identities and separate cultures, but they are British citizens much in the same way as are others (Cohen, 1982; 1985; 1986). In other words, living here does not require Gujaratis to give up social values and beliefs that they recognise as Gujarati and replace them with 'British' values. Similarly, white Britons do not need to accept Gujarati social values: they need to respect them as part of the broader concept of cultural diversity (Education for All, 1985), or justice (Modood, 1996). The social values that Gujaratis living here recognise as Gujarati are assumed to be accepted as Gujarati by people living in Gujarat. This implies that ethnic communities at home and abroad share similar social values and identities that are located in a South Asian diaspora (Shaw, 1988; Werbner, 1989: Watson, 1977). The argument implicit in this research is that ethnic politics is a new response that employs existing and new Gujarati social identities. Gujarati culture is a social construction that draws on some elements of British culture while separating itself from others (Ballard *et al*, 1994; Solomos and Back, 1994; Robinson, 1986; Ben-Tovim *et al*, 1986); in other words it has become a hybrid culture (Werbner and Modood, 1997).

A perception of Gujaratis political position vis-à-vis other communities is that they should have some political representation that makes them more equal to the white community, that is, it would set them apart by advantaging them. However, such a political initiative was not forthcoming for at least two reasons, firstly racism and secondly an unwillingness of the state to support an initiative which could undermine the existing democratic system. Over time changes in their status to citizens and the state's uncompromising view of ethnic politics contributed to the demise of ethnic politics. This has in effect left ethnic minorities to cope with racialised party politics (Solomos and Back, 1994; Saggar, 1990) and with the knowledge that they are regarded as no different from other voters. Although state claims to support multiculturalism, this support has been limited to acknowledging cultural diversity without removing ethnic minorities' disadvantaged access to scarce resources, without improving their political representation. An implication of this approach is that their perceived adherence to South Asian culture and to the location of their social identity in a South Asian diaspora is to be explained as a form of resistance to racism (Ballard, 1994). Thus the politicisation of multiculturalism is another form of racism.

It is accepted that to study other cultures, particularly those separated from British society by geographical distance, involves a major shift by the researcher from the familiar to the unfamiliar. Any attempt to plot the steps that link the familiar to the unfamiliar is an exercise in degree. As Sharrock and Anderson point out: 'Once different monolithic cultures have been decomposed into cultural differences, the problem of understanding and its near relation - the problem of meaning - becomes a great deal more tractable' (1982:131). The approach adopted here is no different from that adopted by others: in studying ethnic politics I am analysing a Gujarati view of a political process which both Gujaratis and white politicians could recognise. Therefore the approach taken here is that ethnic politics is about ethnic differences and not about the clash or meeting of two monolithic cultures.

The third issue considers how the above approach and interpretation of the concept of culture relates to the collection of data and the analysis of data. The combination of approaches is reflected in the range of methods of data collection and the range of techniques for data analysis.

Aspects of the approach employed share much with the symbolic interaction approach. An advantage of this approach is that it recognises the importance of the ordinary Gujaratis' interpretations of the everyday social and political world that underpinned their social actions and social meanings. It emphasises the political strategies and tactics which Gujaratis consider appropriate to ethnic politics, such as the importance of the role of social and religious organisations, labelling and social meanings embedded in Gujaratis' body of common sense racism. The concept of ethnicity draws attention to social boundaries (Cohen, 1985) based upon Gujarati perceptions of social identities in a political arena, the fragile alliances that link Gujarti leaders into competition for space.

To collection of data involved crossing cultural boundaries into Gujarati society, learning about aspects of Gujarati culture, and gaining some understanding of their view of local politics, ethnic politics and racism in politics. This raises a number of important issues about the relationship between British culture and that of ethnic groups like Gujaratis. The extremes of this debate suggest that, on the one hand, a researcher cannot cross culture boundaries, and, on the other hand, that total immersion is possible. This presupposes that a monolithic culture exists in which a researcher can avoid becoming or can choose to become immersed (Clifford and Marcus, 1986). Amongst the questions such a study raises is what kind of a view and whose view does a researcher provide - that of the researcher or that of the subjects researched? To some degree this study presents a version of an outsider's view of insiders' views (Sharrock and Anderson, 1982:121). Where the approach used here diverges from that used by others is that Gujaratis are treated as 'only interpretative actors', no attempt has been made 'excavating the meanings that they have for the actions they take' (Sharrock and Anderson, 1982:131).

Working across cultures

The approach used in this study of ethnic politics and racism in local politics involved the use of both micro- and macro-methods for the collection of data. Considerable amounts of data were collected by participant and nonparticipant observation. Additional data were collected by means of case studies and a survey. Therefore, this study combines qualitative and quantitative forms of analysis; in particular it brings together a qualitative analysis with a computer analysis of the data in general and with a highly formalised computer analysis of the data on social networks (see also Werbner, 1989; Mitchell, 1967).

In the 1970s, working across cultures presented established difficulties, such as the need to bridge the language gap through the use of an interpreter. Attempts to employ Gujarati students as interviewers to overcome some of these difficulties ended in frustration. These students claimed that as young men they could not interview older men, particularly of those of their fathers' generation and, if Hindu, they could not interview those belonging to other Hindu castes or Muslim men. The difficulties that I experienced trying to persuade these Gujarati students to do the interviewing suggested that being a Gujarati may have given a researcher some advantages, such as the language, but it could also be disadvantageous. A person might be seen to compromise Gujarati social values or undermine the ethnic identity of others as a Hindu interviewing Muslims or vice versa. Three Muslims, who interviewed some Muslim men for me, struggled even more than I did. When the VHP agreed to help with the interviewing of the Hindus, their interviewers had the support of their organisation help them overcome the difficulties associated with accessing information that many regarded as private.

When I interviewed, with or without an interpreter, I could move from a Hindu to a Muslim respondent without offence being taken. Although respondents might have been suspicious of my motives, only time could prove them right or wrong. Furthermore, they could choose to conceal information from me without causing offence, knowing or believing that I might never gain access to it. Had I been a Gujarati, I could have gained access to it. Since Gujarati interviewers were seen as members of their community, first and foremost, it was more difficult for them to separate their roles as members from those of interviewers. Possibly, a Gujarati who was an outsider might have had easier access to this information. In the circumstance, I would argue that not being a Gujarati was an advantage when working in these close Gujarati communities. For instance, there was an advantage in being able to show respondents, whom I did not know, that I was unaware of critical pieces of information.

Two different methods were used to collect data on social background, marriage patterns, religious beliefs, membership of religious organisations, caste associations and communities, friendship and social association, social class position and employment, political allegiances and opinions. These were participant observation and a questionnaire; in terms of the material collected they support and enrich one another. The collection and analysis of one set of data illustrates the combination of approaches well. For instance, observation allowed me to verify to an extent the complex and detailed data on patterns of social association, friendship and close friendship in particular, which I collected by means of the survey. On the one hand, the combination of methods of data collection and analysis gives these data a depth which sets them apart from the other data. On the other hand, the some of the data collected by observation and survey can be separated from the social network data, collected by the survey, by virtue of the complexity and precision of its analysis by computer. These data provided an important source of information about social identities, and on social perceptions of social distances between communities and ethnic groups. These data became the linchpin for the analysis of structures of leadership, because (a) they brought together diverse approaches and different methods of data collection with complex methods of data analysis, (b) they link the overall analysis, and (c) above other data they required a crossing of cultures and an exchange of trust.

This research takes as its analytical starting point 'the notion of a shared set of meanings and understandings', and 'what it seeks to demonstrate and not what it is predicated on' (Sharrock and Anderson, 1982:133). These authors argue that a researcher should concentrate upon 'those things which allow him to act'. 'The idea of the actor as an interpretative actor does not require the attribution of shared meanings' (Sharrock and Anderson, 1982:133), which need to emerge from the analysis. Therefore, no attempt is being made to understand the meanings the Gujaratis attach to social actions, but to treat them as interpretative actors. What is attempted is to explain their view of participation in a shared political process rather than to treat their interpretations as a form of causal attribution. This requires some knowledge of their social organisations and culture as well as some knowledge of the social constraints which form part of their social world, but I do not offer an interpretation or description of their culture or social meanings associated with it.

Social network analysis allowed me to meet these rigorous principles for the understanding and interpretation of the views of actors and analyst.

Data collection and questionnaire

The aim of this Appendix is to provide additional background information on the methods and difficulties experienced collecting data, and in particular to focus attention firstly on the selection of the sample, secondly, construction of the questionnaire, thirdly, piloting of the questionnaire, fourthly, recruitment of interviewers, and finally, on difficulties in interviewing. The research project was carried out in two overlapping stages: the first stage involved the use of nonparticipant observation (1971-76) and in the second a survey (1975-76). Time was spent with Gujaratis in their homes, temples and mosques, shops, businesses, in some of the schools their children attended, political meetings, electioneering, weddings, funerals and other social events. Data were collected on social, economic, religious and political relationships within and without the Gujarati communities, using the case study method to collect data on particular political events and on leaders.

Selection of the sample

Addresses of 400 people with Asian names were randomly selected from the electoral register with the intention of interviewing 200 Hindus and 200 Muslims distributed residentially across the town (giving a 5% sample). Selecting the sample was difficult, because not all Gujaratis were on the electoral register in 1973, not all those on the register with Asian names were Gujaratis, and some Gujarati names are similar to Pakistani names. A sample of 400, therefore, seemed to be reasonable. For reasons given below this sample could not be achieved.

A final sample of 258 adult men was selected from a sampling universe of an estimated 8,000 households, which is a 3.23% sample. The majority of these men were over the age of eighteen (2 were 16yrs and 5 were 17yrs, and one Muslim, who was older than eighteen, refused to give his age). The sample comprised 104 Muslims and 154 Hindus. The majority of Hindus were Gujaratis; four came from other parts of India: one was a Sikh, the chairperson of the VHP (1975-1977). All but two of the Muslims claimed not to be Gujaratis; one was a Gujaratis but preferred to be called a Turk or South African. This is a study of Gujaratis who comprised 95% of Bolton's ethnic population; no attempt was made to include other minorities. At the time no adequate population lists were available and crosschecking the lists of members of Gujarati organisations with the electoral register would have been a long and difficult task. Some organisations did not wish to make their lists of members available to me, and some individuals belonged to more than one organisation. Although I cannot for statistical reasons argue for randomness, this sample can at least be regarded as an aggregate. Statements can be made about the Bolton community which would bear generalisation.

This study of ethnic politics involved only men, since no women at that time held positions in social and religious organisations which might have brought them into prominence and into informal or formal political arenas. Therefore, little mention is made of women; this is a bias in the sample. In the 1970s, men held most of the key positions in ethnic organisations and women appeared to be disinterested or were prevented by men from becoming more involved. Although I came across the occasional woman teacher in a mosque, they had no discernible influence in mosque politics. Hindu women held positions within caste associations, sects and the VHP, but few were in prominent positions in Bolton. In Gujarati communities in Bolton there was, and still is, no evidence of the emergence of voluntary and self-help groups which in other parts of Britain have given women opportunities to play more public roles. Moreover, given the social values surrounding the role of women in Gujarati society, as a man I could not have gained access to the views of the women. By the time the interviewing began, I knew little about women's involvement in community affairs. Later, I learnt that Hindu women belonging to certain caste organisations had their own committees, elected their own chairpersons and joined the men's caste association committees when taking decisions on caste matters. Unfortunately, none of these women lived in Bolton, so they could not be interviewed, but this does not mean that they are not prominent in Asian communities elsewhere in Britain. Indeed, recent literature points to the roles played by Asian women in industrial disputes, in work, business, and self-help organisations and in local politics.

Construction of questionnaire

The questionnaire was based upon data collected by participant and nonparticipant observation, and has allowed much of the observed data to be presented in a more structured form. Not only does this mean that quantitative and qualitative data could be brought together, but also it meant that this made possible a formal analysis of data which, at first sight, might appear unstructured. For instance, a formal analysis of Gujarati social networks is to be found alongside an analysis of data based on nonparticipant observation, such as that on ethnic political events. The blending of qualitative and quantitative analysis occurs in many parts of the book (Chapters Three to Seven).

Taking one of these areas as an example, it is possible to show how each approach supported the other. For instance, Gujaratis' ideas about friendship, communities and common sense racism depended upon the collection of data that could be analysed by both formal and informal processes. Data on the qualitative aspects of friendship were formalised through the use of a survey, thus making it accessible to quantitative and formalised network analysis. Data on who has access to social information, where they meet, how frequently they meet and who is excluded from sharing 'public knowledge' was initially obtained using micro-techniques. Then it was formalised into questions that appeared on a questionnaire. Data on perceived social equivalence of knowledge and the deployment of this knowledge in the context of the political arena by leaders could not be formalised. Nor was it possible to formalise the collection of data on negotiations which took place in the BCCR. This was part of a co-operative process which led to the creation of an oral history that in turn gave depth and complexity to community life (Emmett, 1982:208).

The questions for the questionnaire were based on the knowledge gained in the first two years of research from semi-participant observation. To some extent the construction of the questionnaire became associated with the selection of interviewers. Individuals and organisations which I approached for help with interviewing, sought to have questions they did not approve of modified or deleted before agreeing to assist with the interviewing. The process of modification became linked to a process of approval. This process formed the pilot stage. The questionnaire was modified on at least four occasions before it was administered. Having discussed the schedule with an advisor in the SSRC Survey Unit, it was again modified. It was now estimated to take about an hour to administer. Trials proved that it could take between an hour to three hours to complete. It was destined to take even longer to complete with Gujaratis who spoke no English.

I approached some Muslim friends in Blackburn for help: one was a teacher, one a radio announcer, and one the secretary of the Indian Workers' Association. They objected to questions on nationality, length of residence in Britain, questions which too obviously distinguished between Hindus and Muslims, and questions which explored political involvement. They agreed that these questions might produce the kind of information I wanted, but believed that many of those interviewed would suspect that the answers could be used against them. Asians, they argued, felt insecure in Britain, since they did not have equal rights. 'If we ask for what are regarded as general rights, white people look at us as if we have demanded special rights. We are not asking for favourable treatment, just for fair and equal treatment.' One cited the case of an Asian drug smuggler which had appeared in a local newspaper: 'Not only was he sentenced to four years imprisonment but he was also to be deported. Had he been white, he would only have been sent to prison for a couple of years. When an Asian breaks a law like any other Briton might, he is dealt with more harshly than the transgression warrants.' It later became apparent that their fears were shared by other Muslims and Hindus Gujaratis.

In their opinion the questions should reflect general opinions and not those of particular Asian communities. Not long after these discussions, the police in the Northwest arrested some 200 Asians on the grounds that they were illegal immigrants. Such occurrences continued to support Asians' fears about their insecurity in Britain and served to make them wary of answering questions about their backgrounds and giving political opinions. Generally, they were unhappy about answering questions and many who completed the survey believed that there would be repercussions. There was no way in which I could alleviate their fears and suspicions.

It was noteworthy that some of the officers of the VHP criticised the same questions and for the same reasons as had these Muslims. However, the former criticised a number of other questions, including those which identified differences in caste and religion. Questions, which implied that members of different castes could or would not support members of other castes, had to be deleted. Evidence has shown that Hindus continue to attach great importance to caste differences.

One question that was singled out as problematic was that on the length of time a person had lived here. In the opinion of those Hindus and Muslims I consulted, respondents would not give such information. They argued that illegal immigrants, their relatives and friends would not wish to be identified. Any Gujarati could believe that by answering a question on length of residence in Britain, he was providing the police with relevant information about his status in this country, albeit through an alternative channel. No Gujarati organisation was prepared initially to accept responsibility for confidentiality on my behalf Therefore, however valuable the question was on length of residence, it had to be removed. The omission of this question detracted from the analysis of settlement patterns. Another question that posed problems related to information about the home village. Although most respondents answered it, many feared possible repercussions. They said that the Indian Government had the right to seize property owned by Indians who were British nationals resident in Britain. Some Gujaratis answering this question feared that by giving the names of their villages, their families in India might be made to suffer. The question was asked and was answered.

Questions on close friends raised fears. The majority of the respondents argued that to give this information was being too personal. Although they acknowledged that I did not ask for names, initials or addresses, they felt that all close friends could be traced. This could be taken as a measure of their insecurity as well as of their closeness as a community. They also felt uneasy about answering some of the questions on politics, such as 'Do you think that people like you have too much political power, too little or about the right amount?' Certain parts of other questions on political behaviour were criticised for similar reasons. All the questions were subjected to intensive scrutiny and as a result, many were modified and in a few instances, parts were deleted. To my knowledge these fears turned out to be groundless. This did not mean that I altered the questionnaire, but rather it pointed to the importance of making apparent the differences between Hindus and Muslims, between friends and acquaintances and information. The questions about villages remained in the questionnaire. However, ignoring their criticism of the questions on length of stay and nationality could have proved to be insensitive, and, given their fears, it was tactful to modify those questions. Their reactions to questions define to some degree their social construction of their ideology as migrants and black people in Britain.

Piloting of the questionnaire

Two Muslim friends came from Blackburn to help me pilot the questionnaire. We did one interview, which highlighted some of the major difficulties. I learnt how difficult it was to translate some of the questions into Gujaratis. I learnt that, even after shortening the questionnaire, it could still take three hours to complete. It took this length of time to complete even in the hands of an interviewer who understood the questions, spoke Gujarati and an interviewee who was not suspicious about how the information might be used. This interview proved to be instructive in other ways; the issues it raised were typical of the problems met throughout the survey. For instance, from the addresses I had drawn on my random sample, they selected the addresses of a brother-in-law and a brother-in-law's brother-in-law. They explained to me that they felt happier interviewing people who were related to them, came from the same village, from the wife's village, or villages of close friends. This meant that respondents could trust them with answers to personal questions. Moreover, the respondents could not ask the interviewers to leave the house if they did not wish to continue with the interview. The point was made that a Muslim interviewer would not voluntarily go into the house of any Muslim with whom he could not establish a social link. An argument suggests that interviewees may be more reticent answering questions put by those they know, because the answers go 'on record' in the community. Barley (1986) suggested that even when an interviewer knows a person, responses could be inhibited. The reason he gives is that the interviewee may be placed in the position of a gatekeeper, who has to decide whether or not to pass on this information to a friend who may or may not know it.

An implication of this was that I should have identified every family selected and then found interviewers who knew them. This was an impossible task, since I could never be certain that I could match an interviewer with a family selected in terms of similar religious beliefs and acquaintanceship. It also called for a depth of knowledge of the community which I did not possess. Thus it became apparent that a random survey would fail. Consequently, a solution was for me to interview as many Hindus and Muslims as possible. The other solution lay in trying to obtain support from Gujarati organisations to assist with interviewing. In the end I settled for both of these solutions, but it meant abandoning the idea of a random sample. Another solution might have been to bring in an Asian research firm from elsewhere, but this was ruled out on the grounds of expense.

Recruitment of interviewers

Recruiting interviewers is supposedly a simple task. The problem is to train them. In this instance recruitment of interviewers presented the biggest problem. Initially I found a group of 'O' and 'A' level Gujarati students at Bolton Technical College (now Bolton College), who said that they were willing to interview. When they saw the questionnaire they began expressing doubts. Initially, they said little, and a few indicated that they had never heard of some of the caste groups. Payment was discussed along the lines suggested to me by the Social Science Research Council Survey Unit. The students said that their lecturer would inform me of their decision. Some weeks later I received a message stating that the students were unwilling to help, but no reasons were given. Then I learned that some thought that I should be offering £2.00 per questionnaire rather than 50-60 pence. Later a few students informed me that they had refused because they were unwilling to ask people, whom they did not know and who were older than they were, or questions which were too personal. The question of the rate of pay was just a way of saying that they were not prepared to do the interviewing.

At this stage I was ready to give to the interviewers a randomly drawn sample.

However, the refusal of the students to do the interviewing ensured that I would have to do most of the interviewing myself and would not have the time, manpower or finance to carry it out. To an extent this resolved another issue. When I realised that I would have to do the bulk of the interviewing, I decided against translating the questions into Gujarati and/or Urdu. Apart from this, some of the questions proved to be particularly difficult to translate and had to be simplified.

After the refusal of the students to help, the search began for other interviewers. I approached some Muslim friends and the VHP for help and support, who scrutinised each question. This led to further modifications. I approached the VHP when I realised that I could not complete a survey of 200 Hindu heads of households without assistance and community support. Three influential members agreed to help. Two other influential men volunteered to help. One was a member of the Mandhata Patel Association and the other was a supervisor at a local mill, whose father was an influential Kanbi in the Kutch community. He had links with the three sections of the Hindu community, including through the VHP. These included the Leva Kanbis and Kadva Kanbis.

The ground rules laid down by the VHP were that no Hindu interviewer could interview a Muslim; no Hindu student could ask anyone but his father to answer personal questions about home village, caste and subcaste membership, religious affiliations and politics. No Hindu student is likely to know the answers to these questions, as his parents are unlikely to have told him. No Hindu student can ask Hindus who are both unrelated and also his seniors such questions. No Hindu would feel happy asking his close friends such questions. As the VHP supported the venture, at least I was assured of some questionnaires being returned.

Judging, however, from the range of questionnaires completed by Hindus, they drew on Hindus from a wide range of backgrounds, castes, sects and beliefs. Where the survey can be demonstrated to be non-random is in the selection of respondents in relation to the area in which they live. The majority of the Hindus who completed questionnaires live in areas surrounding the town centre. I attempted to remedy this by interviewing a few Hindus who lived in some of the other areas of the town: most of them were doctors or successful businessmen. As one friend observed, they would have refused to complete the questionnaire had the interviewer belonged to a lower caste or been less educated than them. A total of 130 schedules were returned to me by the VHP of which 108 were complete and the remainder were incomplete. One prominent member of the VHP claimed that he could interview 250 Hindus. When I took up his offer he did not manage to interview anyone. On another occasion I approached a prominent member of the Shree Kutch Swaminarayan Mandir organisation for help. However, he made it clear that he wanted nothing to do with the research. Members of his organisation did complete some of the questionnaires. The reason for his refusal, which came to light later, was that he opposed to VHP and its chairperson. Unlike the VHP, the Swaminarayans and Shree Kutch Swaminarayans are committed to maintaining differences of caste and sect.

In comparison with the VHP, the Muslim organisations large and small made no offer to help with the interviewing. If anything, they obstructed it. In a meeting with four influential Muslim members of the ICC I asked them for support. They represented the views of those most opposed to my research. Later at a meeting in one person's house I gave my reasons for conducting a survey, I took them through it and my reasons for wishing to interview Muslims. Four issues surfaced as the discussion progressed which were never resolved. After looking through the schedule, one man said 'When we left India, we left it behind us. Now we are British, we have British passports. There is no point in asking us about Baruchi and Surti and our differences. We live here.' These very differences, which I found divided the Muslim community, were those which these men argued were irrelevant to their lives in Bolton and Britain.

An issue arose from my stating that I should interview as many Muslims as possible if I intended my survey to be scientifically acceptable. The idea of my interviewing individuals was rejected. One Muslim said 'We can tell you all about Indians, you don't need to interview them'. Later on, when I attempted to interview him, he was reluctant to answer the questions and refused to name the streets in which his close friends lived. He also argued that his answers would become data and that this would be later used against him and the Muslim community. He wanted to know what I was giving to the Muslim community in return for the information I wanted. Although there was little that I could do for interviewees, occasionally I was able to refer them to those who could help them. A Muslim 'A' level student refused to complete a schedule for this very reason. He turned around an old adage: 'one man' poison is another man's profit'.

Related to this issue was another. Which Muslim organisation would act as guarantor for the survey if they agreed to help me? One man volunteered his friend. Though all four men were old friends, they selected the one man who came from a different district in Gujarat to the others and was a Surti; the other three were Baruchis. The person they picked argued that the matter should be put to the ICC; in fact it never was put to this organisation. Although all four agreed to being interviewed, none volunteered to be interviewed. It was weeks later through another Muslim friend that I was able to persuade three of these Muslims to agree to be interviewed. The fourth man refused totally. The ICC refused to co-operate, although I did later receive help from a few individual members. This placed the bulk of interviewing of Muslims on me.

Problems with interviewing

Gujaratis were reluctant to answer questions on their personal and political life, and to overcome this reluctance was not easy. With the VHP taking over some of the interviewing, these fears were to some extent diminished. Nevertheless, the questions left incomplete were the ones thought to be too personal, such as the one on close friends. The only way that I as an interviewer could allay peoples' fears was by referring them to someone whom they knew, and whom I had already interviewed. This was not always possible, since it depended upon my knowledge of the interviewee prior to interviewing them. An element of luck became associated with the exercise. If I could mention the name of a person the interviewee respected, then the interviewee might agree, if not, he was likely to refuse. I also had to find an interpreter to enable me to interview the Muslims. This is where the previous two years of getting to know the Gujaratis helped. I knew a number of them, and this gave some of them confidence to answer the questions and me the knowledge of who might prove to be of the greatest help with a particular interviewee.

Of the 104 Muslims interviewed, Muslim friends interviewed 16. One prominent member of the ICC interviewed 5 men and then refused to do more, arguing that he could not ask his friends to complete some of the personal questions. He too reiterated the problems which the two Blackburn friends had mentioned to me: no Muslim will or can ask friends or strangers to answer personal questions.

My interpreter, who was once a member of the BCCR, knew a large number of Gujaratis, both Muslim and Hindu. It was easy for me to interview persons whom he knew.

I interviewed the remaining 83 interviewees with support of my interpreter. He accompanied me to about 70 houses. He also took me to Hindu families who were opposed to the VHP, so I did in practice cross the divide. As an interpreter, he was able to communicate with respondents; he knew exactly when and how to joke with them and how to phrase the questions in Gujarati. Furthermore, he was also well known to Muslims as a prominent member of the Muslim community. Secondly, he devoted time to helping Muslims and Hindus with their personal and immigration problems. Consequently, with his support I was able to obtain answers to all of my questions; in fact, I could even have asked those questions which I had to delete.

Generally, my experience showed that the few Muslim interviewers who helped me with the interviewing of Muslims experienced far more difficulty persuading Muslims to answer these questions than I did. Being a Gujarati and carrying out research in his/her own community is not necessarily an advantage. Sometimes being quite different and easily distinguishable is more of an advantage. At least then people can hide their views without being placed in compromising positions. The complexities of working across cultural boundaries have altered little. Recent research into families in a Gujarati Hindu community in Leicester shows that many of the difficulties that I experienced in the 1970s are still present in Gujaratis communities in the late 1990s (Goodwin et al, 1997).

Appendix II
Analysis of primary zones of social networks

Many ways of analysing social networks and the primary zones in them exist; the method of analysis used here reduces the links between close friends in a social network or zone to an optimum spanning tree (OST) (Deo, 1974). Some have drawn attention to the application of algorithms to network analysis (Mitchell, 1979). Since the relationships between the anchor point and his close friends in this research is by definition of the same value, that is, they are all his close friends, it can be ignored in the calculation. It is the social relationships between close friends that are of interest. OST analysis reduces the total number of links to a minimum set which link each individual only once to another individual.

In graph theory an OST is defined as the minimum set of optimum links. In this instance the tree defines a pattern of friendships that connect four or more people identified as close friends by a respondent. Weightings are attached to different intensities of friendship. A primary zone consists of the total number of links between close friends as described by a respondent. They can vary in intensity from kin to close friend, ordinary friend, acquaintance, stranger and hostile. Using Kruskal's algorithm to identifying optimum spanning trees, a computer plotted the optimum spanning trees for every respondent anchoring zones of close friends with four or more close friends. Zones of less than four persons are too small to have more than one OST. Zones containing ten close friends have matrices consisting of ninety possible links. An OST analysis provides one of a number of possible sets of optimum links between the set of close friends. Where close friends are connected by different intensities of friendships, the possible number of OSTs increases. Where all close friends are close friends of each other, the optimum spanning tree is the same irrespective from which point it started. The result is that different trees have different total scores and patterns.

One of the products of this form of analysis is a score which is calculated from the total value of each branch that makes up the final tree (Table A4 (i) and (ii)). Another feature of this form of analysis is that clusters of close friends within a social network can be easily identified. Below are examples of OST analyses.

Optimum spanning tree analysis: respondent No.6

Five close friends   (5) 4 2 5 5 5 5 5 5 5 5
This is the matrix   4 2 5 5
as it appears as   0 5 5 5
completed in the   0 0 5 5
schedule.   0 0 0 5

     2 1 3
Weightings are in   4 1 2
near columns;   5 1 5
the middle and   5 2 3
far columns identify   5 2 4
to which relation-   5 2 5
ship the weightings   5 3 4
are attached and   5 3 5
these are ranked by   5 4 5
weight.   2 1 3 1 1
     2
The optimum spanning   4 1 2 1 1
is constructed in   6
terms of the lowest   5 1 4 1 1
weighted relation-   11
ship.   5 1 5 1 1
Total weight of OST =   16

Weightings of relationships between close friends

Kin = 1, Close friend = 2, Ordinary friend = 3, Acquaintance = 4,
Stranger = 5, and close friends = a,b,c,d and e.

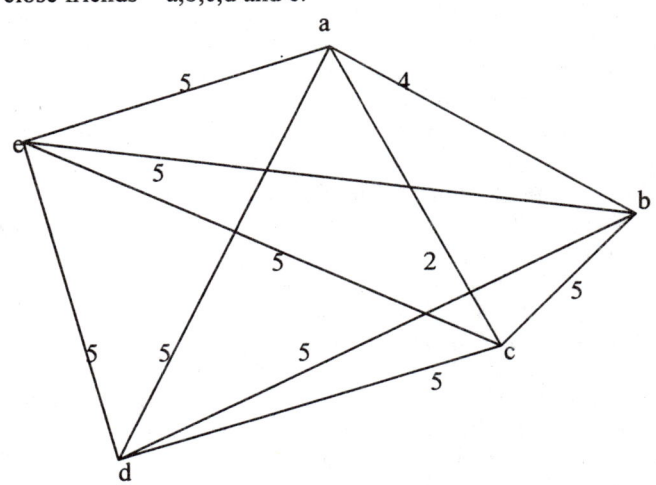

Optimum spanning tree analysis: No.29

Six close friends: (6) 3 5 2 5 5 2 5 1 2 4 5 3 2 4 2

```
3 5 5 5 5
0 2 5 1 3
0 0 2 2 2
0 0 0 4 4
0 0 0 0 2
 1 2 5
 2 2 3
 2 3 4
 2 3 5
 2 3 6
 2 5 6
 3 1 2
 3 2 6
 4 4 5
 4 4 6
 5 1 3
 5 1 4
 5 1 5
 5 1 6
 5 2 4 4
 1 2 5 2 2
 1
 2 2 3 2 2
 3
 2 3 4 2 2
 5
 2 3 6 2 2
 7
 3 1 2 1 1
 10
```

Weightings of relationships between close friends

Kin = 1, Close friend = 2, Ordinary friend = 3, Acquaintance = 4,
Stranger = 5, and close friends = a,b,c,d and e.

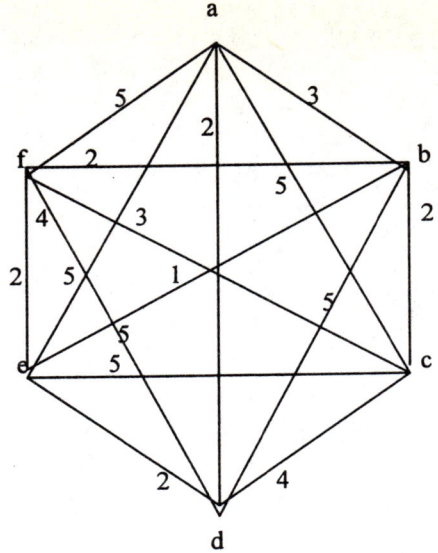

Bibliography

Allen, S. 1982. 'Perhaps a seventh person?' In C. Husband (ed). *'Race' in Britain: continuity and change*. London: Hutchinson.

Allen, S., Bentley, S.and Bornat, J. 1977. *Work, Race and Immigration*. Bradford: University of Bradford.

Allen, S. and Wolkowitz, C. 1987. *Homeworking: Myths and Realities*. Basingstoke: Macmillan.

Amin, A (ed). 1997. *Post-Fordism: a reader*. Oxford: Blackwell.

Anwar, M. 1979. *The Myth of Return*. London: Heinemann.

Anwar, M. 1980. *Votes and Policies: Ethnic Minorities and the General Election, 1979*. Commission for Racial Equality. London: Elliot House.

Anwar, M. 1984. *Ethnic Minorities and the 1983 General Election*. Commission for Racial Equality. London: Elliot House.

Anwar, M. 1986. *Race and Politics*. London: Tavistock Publications.

Anwar, M. 1991. 'Ethnic minorities' representation: voting and electoral politics in Britain, and the role of leaders'. In P. Werbner and M. Anwar (eds), *Black and Ethnic Leaderships*. London: Routledge.

Anwar, M. 1994. *Race and Elections: the participation of ethnic minorities in politics*. Monographs in Ethnic Relations No 9. Centre for Ethnic Relations. Warwick: University of Warwick.

Anwar, M. 1996. 'What Impact has the Race Relations Legislation made on British Race Relations?' Paper presented at the conference *'From Legislation to Integration?' Twenty Years of the Race Relations Act 1976'*. Warwick: University of Warwick.

Anwar, M. and Kohler, D. 1975. *Participation of Ethnic minorities in the General Election, October 1974*. Community Relations Commission. London: Elliot House.

Appadurai, A. 1990. 'Disjuncture and difference in the global cultural economy', *Theory, Culture and Society*, 7, pages 294- 310.

Asian Social Development Agency Ltd. 1996. *An Economic (and linked Social) Audit of the 3Ds Area of Bolton (Derby, Daubhill and Deane)*. Bolton: Bolton Metropolitan Council.

Back, L. 1996. *New Ethnicities and Urban Culture: racisms and multiculture in young lives*. London: UCL Press.

Bakshi, P., Goodwin, M., Painter, J. and Southern, A. 1995. 'Gender, Race and Class in the Local Welfare State: moving beyond regulation theory in analysing the transition from Fordism', *Environment and Planning*, Vol.27, pages 1539-1554.

Ball, W. and Solomos, J.(eds) 1990. *Race and Local Politics*. Basingstoke: Macmillan.

Ballard, R. 1994. *Desh Pardesh*. London: Hurst & Co.

Ballard, R. and Ballard, C. 1977. 'The Sikhs: The Development of South Asian Settlements in Britain.' In J.L.Watson (ed). *Between Two Cultures*. Oxford: Basil Blackwell.

Ballard, R.and Kalra,V. S. 1994. *The Ethnic Dimensions of the 1991 Census: a preliminary report*. Dept. of Religious and Theology. Manchester: University of Manchester.

Banks, M. 1991. 'Competing to give, competing to get: Gujurati Jains in Britain'. In P. Werbner and M. Anwar (eds), *Black and Ethnic Leaderships*. London: Routledge.

Banton, M.P. 1972. *Racial Minorities*. London: Fontana.

Barley, N. 1983. *The Innocent Anthropologist*, Harmondsworth: Penguin Books.

Barnes, J. 1971. 'Networks and Political Processes'. In J.C.Mitchell (ed) *Social Networks in Urban Situations*. Manchester. University Press: Manchester University Press.

Barot, R. 1972/3. 'A Swaminarayan Sect as a Community'. *New Community*, Vol.2, No.1, pages 34-37.

Barot, R. 1980. *The Social Organisation of a Swaminarayan Sect in Britain*. Ph.D.Thesis. University of London: SOAS, unpubl.

Barth, F. (ed). 1970. *Ethnic Groups and Boundaries*. London: George Allen & Unwin.

Bauman, Z. 1995. *Legislators and Interpreters*. Oxford: Polity Press.

Bauman, Z. 1988. *Freedom*. Milton Keynes: Open Unversity Press.

Becker, H.S.1963. *Outsiders*. New York: The Free Press.

Beetham, D. 1970. *Transport and Turbans*. Institute of Race Relations. London: Oxford University Press.

Bendix, R. 1966. *Max Weber: an intellectual portrait*. London: Methuen.

Bentley, S. 1972/73. 'Intergroup Relations in Local Politics: Pakistanis and Bangladeshis'. *New Community*, Vol.II, No.1, pages 44-48.

Ben-Tovim, G., Gabriel, J., Law, I. and Stredder, K. 1986. *The Local Politics of Race*. London: Macmillan.

Ben-Tovim, G., Gabriel. J., Law, I., Stredder, K. 1992. 'A political analysis of local struggles for racial equality'. In P. Braham, A.Rattansi and R. Skellington (eds). *Racism and Antiracism*. London. The Open University: Sage Publications.

Benyon, J. and Solomos, J. (eds) 1987. *The Roots of Unrest*. Oxford: Pergamon Press.

Bhabha, H. K. 1994. *The Location of Culture*. London: Routledge.

Blackburn, R. and Mann, M. 1981. 'The Dual Labour Market Model'. In P. Braham, E. Rhodes and M. Pearn (eds). *Discrimination and Disadvantage in Employment: the experience of black workers*. London: Harper and Row Publishers.

Blau, P.M. 1967. *Exchange and Power in Social Life*. London: John Wiley & Son.

Bohning, W.R. 1981. 'The Self-feeding Process of Economic Migration from Low-wage to Post-Industrial Countries with a Liberal Capitalist Structure.' In P. Braham, E. Rhodes and M.Pearns (eds). 1981. *Discrimination and Disadvantage in Employment: The Experience of Black Workers*, London: Harper & Row.

Boissevain, J. 1968. 'The Place of Non-Groups in the Social Sciences', *Man*, Vol.3, pages 542-556.

Boissevain, J. 1974. *Friends of Friends*. Oxford: Basil Blackwell.

Bolton Council for Community Relations. 1977. *Area Profile*: Bolton.

Bolton Metropolitan Borough. 1984. *District Trends*: Bolton.

Bolton Metropolitan Borough. 1987. *District Trends*: Bolton.

Bolton Metropolitan Borough. 1990. *District Trends*: Bolton.

Bolton Planning Department. June 1976. *Bolton Metropolitan Borough Plan*. unpublished.

Bolton Racial Equality Council. 1990. *Bolton Metropolitan Borough Survey of the 1990/91 Electoral Registers for Electors of Asian Origin*.

Bott, E. 1971. *Family and Social Network*. London: Tavistock.

Brah, A. (1982). 'The South Asians. Minority Experience', Educational Studies: a 3rd level course. *Ethnic Minorities and Community Relations*. Part 1, E354, Block 3, Units 8-9. Milton Keynes: The Open University Press.

Brah, A. 1992. 'Difference, Diversity and Differentiation'. In J. Donald and A. Rattansi (eds). *Race, Culture and Difference*. The Open University. London: Sage Publications.

Brah, A. 1992. 'Women of South Asian origin in Britain: Issues and Concerns'. In P. Braham, A. Rattansi and R. Skellington (eds). *Racism and Antiracism*. The Open University. London: Sage Publications.

Braham, A. Rattansi and R. Skellington (eds). 1992. *Racism and Antiracism*. The Open University. London: Sage Publications.

Braham, P. and Rhodes, E. 1985. *Employment,Education and Community*. Milton Keynes: Open University Press.

Braham, P., Rhodes, E. and Pearn, M. (eds). 1981. *Discrimination and Disadvantage in Employment: The Experience of Black Workers*. London: Harper & Row.

Brewer, J.D. 1984. 'Competing understandings of common sense understanding: a brief comment on 'common sense racism'. *British. J. of Sociology*, Vol.35, pages 66-74.

Bristow, M. 1975. 'Uganda Asians in Britain, Canada and India: Some Characteristics and Resources.' *New Community*, Vol.IV, No.2, pages 155-166.

Bristow, M. 1976. 'Britain's Response to the Uganda Asian Crisis: Government Myths v. Political and Resettlement Realities', *New Community*, Vol.V, No.3, pages 265-279.

Bristow, M. 1979. 'Ugandan Asians, Racial Disadvantage and Housing Markets in Manchester and Birmingham', *New Community* Vol.VII, No.2, pages 203-216.

Brooks, D. and Singh, K. 1978/79. 'Ethnic Commitment versus Structural Reality', *New Community*, Vol.VII, No.1, pages 19-30.

Brown, C. 1984. *Black and White Britain: The Third PSI Survey*. London: Heinemann.

Brown, C. 1992. 'Same Difference: The persistence of racial disadvantage in the British employment market'. In P. Braham, A.Rattansi and R. Skellington (eds). *Racism and Antiracism*. The Open University. London: Sage Publications.

Brown, W. 1992. 'Finding the man in the state', *Feminist Studies*. 18, No 1, Spring, pages 7-34.

Bryman, A. 1988. *Quantity and Quality in Social Research*. London: Unwin Hyman.

Burrows, R. and Loader, B. (eds). 1994. *Towards a Post-Fordist Welfare State*. London: Routledge.

Campbell, D. 1992. *Writing Security: United States foreign policy and the politics of identity*. Manchester: Manchester University Press.

Castles, S. and Kosack, G. 1973. *Immigrant Workers and Class Structure in Western Europe*. London: Oxford University Press.

Castles, S. and Miller, M. J. 1993. *The Age of Migration: International Population Movements in the Modern World*. London: Macmillan Press.

Castles, S., Booth, H. and Wallace, T. 1984. *Here for Good*. London: Pluto Press.

Central Statistics Office. 1977. *Regional Statistics*. No.13. London: HMSO.

Centre for Contemporary Cultural Studies. 1983. *The Empire Strikes Back*. University of Birmingham: Hutchinson.

Chaudhuri, N.C. 1979. *Hinduism*. London: Chatto and Windus.

Christopher, J. B. 1972. *The Islamic Tradition*. London: Harpers Row Publishers.

Cicourel, A.V. 1981. 'Notes on the integration of micro- and macro-levels of analysis'. In K.Knorr-Cetina and A.V.Cicourel (eds). *Advances in Social Theory and Methodology: Toward an Integration of Micro- and Macro-Sociologies*. Boston: Routledge and Kegan Paul.

Clarke, C., Vertovic, S. (eds). 1990. *South Asians Overseas*. Cambridge: Cambridge University Press.

Clifford, J. 1988. *The Predicament of Culture*. London: Harvard University Press.

Clifford, J. and Marcus, G.E. (eds) 1986. *Writing Culture: The Poetics and Politics of Ethnography*. Berkeley, University of California Press.

Cohen, A. 1991. 'Drama and politics in the development of a London Carnival'. In P.Werbner and M.Anwar, Black and Etnic Leaderships in Britain. London. Routledge.

Cohen, A.P. (ed) 1982. *Belonging: Identity and social organisation in British rural cultures*. Manchester: Manchester University Press.

Cohen, A. P. 1985. *The Symbolic Construction of Community*. Tavistock Publishers: London and Ellis Harwood Ltd.

Cohen, A.P. (ed) 1986. *Symbolising Boundaries: Identity and diversity in British cultures*. Manchester: Manchester University Press.

Cohen, R. 1994. *Frontiers of Identity*. London: Longman.

Cohen, B.G. and Jenner, P.J. 1981. 'The Employment of Immigrants: A Case Study within the Wool Industry.' In P. Braham, E. Rhodes and M.Pearn (eds) *Discrimination and Disadvantage in Employment: The Experience of Black Workers*. London: Harper & Row.

Coleman, J., Katz, E. and Menzel, H. 1977. 'The Diffusion of an Innovation among Physicians.' In S.Leinhardt (ed) *Social Networks: A Developing Paradigm*. London: Academic Press.

Community Relations Commission. 1975. *Muslim Burials*. London: Elliott House.

Commission for Racial Equality. 1978. *The Nature and Structure of Local Work for Racial Equality*. London: Elliot House.

Commission for Racial Equality. 1984. *Hackney Housing Investigated* London: Elliot House.

Commission for Racial Equality. 1989. *A New Partnership for Racial Equality*. Community Relations Group of MSF and National Association of Community Relations Councils.

Commission for Racial Equality. 1991. *Annual Report*. London: Elliot House.

Commission for Racial Equality. 1995. *Annual Report*. London: Elliot House.

Commission for Racial Equality. 1997. *A Fundamental Review of the Public Service Role of Racial Equality Councils. A Summary Report*. KPMG. London: Elliot House.

Dahya, B. 1974. 'The Nature of Pakistani Ethnicity in Industrial Cities in Britain'. In A.Cohen (ed) *Urban Ethnicity*. A.S.A. Monograph. 12. London: Tavistock.

Dalton, M. and Daghlain, S. 1989. *Race and Housing in Glasgow: The Role of Housing Associations*. Commission for Racial Equality. London: Elliot House.

Daniel, E., Daniel, L., Hahlo, K. G., Smith, G., Wood, S. 1996. *Business Security Survey: a survey of business security and crime in the Bolton 3Ds Area*. Bolton Institute.

Davies, M. 1990. *City of Quartz*. London: Verso.

Deo, N. 1974. *Graph Theory with Applications to Engineering Science*. New York: Englewood Cliffs. Prentice-Hall.

Department of Education and Science 1985. *Education for all: Report of the Committee of Enquiry into the Education of Children from Ethnic Minority Groups* (The Swann Report). Cmnd 9453. London: HMSO.

Desai, R. 1963. *Indian Immigrants in Britain*. London: Institute of Race Relations. Oxford University Press.

Dorson, R.M. 1959. *American Folklore*. Chicago: University of Chicago Press.

Drucker-Brown, S. 1984. *Participant Observation in Sociology and Social Anthropology*. SSRC. Ref.G00250004.

Dumont, L. 1972. *Homo Hierarchicus*. London: Paladin.

Dwyer, R. 1992. 'Caste, Religion and Sect in Gujarat: Followers of Vallabhacharya and Swaminarayan.' In R. Ballard. *Desh Pardesh*. London: Hurst & Co.

Eade, J. 1989. *The Politics of Community: The Bangladeshi Community in East London*. Aldershot: Gower.

Eade, J. 1991. 'The political construction of class and community: Bangladeshi political leadership in Tower Hamlets, East London'. In P. Werbner and M. Anwar (eds). *Black and Ethnic Leaderships*. London: Routledge.

Emmett, I. 1982. 'Place, community and bilingualism in Blaenau Ffestiniog'. In A.P. Cohen (ed). *Belonging: Identity and social organisation in British rural cultures*. Manchester: Manchester University Press.

Erbe, W. 1977. 'Gregariousness, Group Membership, and the Flow of Information'. In S. Leinhardt (ed). *Social Networks: A Developing Paradigm*. New York: Academic Press.

Evans-Pritchard, E.E. 1967. *Nuer Religion*. Oxford: Clarendon Press.

Featherstone, M. 1996. *Consumer, Culture and Postmodernism*. London: Sage Publications.

Ferguson, K. E. 1984. *The Feminist Case against Bureaucracy*. Philadelphia: Temple University Press.

Firth, R. 1973. *Symbols: Public and Private*. London: Allen & Unwin.

FitzGerald, M. 1987. *Black People and Party Politics in Britain*. Runnymede Research Report. The Runnymede Trust.

Fortes, M. 1970. *Kinship and the social order: the legacy of Lewis Henry Morgan*. London: Routledge & Kegan Paul.

Frankenberg, R.J. 1957. *Village on the Border*. London: Cohen & West.

Fryer, P. 1984. *Staying Power: The History of Black People in Britain*. London: Pluto Press.

Gay, P. and Young, K. 1988. *Community Relations Councils: Roles and Objectives*. Commission for Racial Equality London: Elliot House.

Geddes, M. 1994. 'Public Services and Local Economic Regeneration in a Post-Fordism economy.' In R. Burrows and B. Loader (eds). *Towards a Post-Fordist Welfare State?* London: Routledge.

Gerrard, N. 1981. 'The Tuberculosis Environment'. *Geographical Magazine*, 53, July, pages 641-644.

Gifford, Lord, Brown, W. and Bundy, R. 1989. *Loosen the Shackles*. Guildford: Karia Press.

Gilroy, B. 1994. *Black Teacher*. London: Bogle-L'Ouverture Press.

Gilroy, P. 1987. *There Ain't No Black in the Union Jack*. London: Hutchinson.

Gilroy, P. 1993. *Small Acts: Thoughts on the Politics of Black Cultures*. London: Serpents Tail.

Gilsenan, M. 1979. *Recognizing Islam: An Anthropologist's Introduction*. London: Croom Helm.

Gluckman, M. 1971. 'Preface'. In E. Bott. *Family and Social Network*. London: Tavistock Publications.

Goffman, E. 1970. *Stigma: Notes on the Management of Spoiled Identity*. England: Penguin Books.

Golden, S. 1995. *A Survey of developments in the Bolton and Bury textile and clothing industry and their impact on the training and skill level of the workforce*. Unpubl M.Phil. Thesis. Bolton Institute of Higher Education.

Goldthorpe, J.H, Llewellyn, C. and Payne, C. 1980. *Social Mobility and Class Structure in Modern Britain*. Oxford: Clarendon Press.

Goldthorpe, J.H. 1981/82. 'Social Standing, Class and Status'. *Survey Method Newsletter*, ESRC, pages 8-11.

Goode, W.J., and Hatt, P.K. 1952. *Methods in Social Research*. London: McGraw-Hill.

Goodwin, R., Adatia, K., Sinhal, H., Cramer, D. and Ellis, P. 1997. *Social Support and marital well-being in an Asian Community*. York: Joseph Rowntree Foundation.

Goulbourne, H. 1991. 'The Offence of the West Indian: political leadership and the communal option'. In P. Werbner and M. Anwar (eds). *Black and Ethnic Leaderships*. London: Routledge.

Granovetter, M. 1977. 'The Strength of Weak Ties'. In S. Leinhardt (ed). *Social Networks: a developing paradigm*. London: Academic Press.

Grillo, R. D. 1985. *Ideolgies and Institutions in urban France: the representation of immigrants*. Cambridge: Cambridge University Press.

Hahlo, K.G. 1980. 'Profile of a Gujarati Community in Bolton'. *New Community*, Vol.8, No.3, pages 295-307.

Hahlo, K.G. 1993. *Gujaratis in Bolton: the Leaders and the Led*. Unpublished Ph.D Thesis. The Open University.

Hahlo, K. G. 1994/95. 'Gujaratis in Bolton: The Leaders and the Led'. *Association of Open University Graduates Journal*. The Open University, pages 17-21.

Hahlo, K.G. 1996. 'Community, Culture and Identity among Some South Asians In Britain.' In S. Stern-Gillet, T. Stawek, T. Rachwat and R. Whitehouse (eds*). Culture and Identity: Selected Aspects and Approaches*. Wydawnictwo Univesitytetu Slaskiego, Katowice.

Hall, S. 1981. 'Racism and Reaction'. In *Five Views of Multi-Racial Britain*. Commission for Racial Equality. London: Elliot House.

Hall, S. 1985. *The Gulf between Labour and blacks*. Guardian. 15th July.

Hall, S. 1988. 'Brave New World'. *Marxism Today*. October, pages 24-29.

Hall, S. 1990. 'Cultural identity and Diaspora'. In J. Rutherford (ed) *Identity*. London: Lawrence and Wishart,

Hall, S. 1992. 'New Ethnicities'. In J. Donald and A. Rattansi (eds). *'Race', Culture and Difference*. London: Sage.

Hall, S. and Jacques, M. (eds). 1989. *New Times*, London: Lawrence Wishart.

Hall, S., Critcher, C., Jefferson, T., Clarke, S. and Roberts, B. 1978. *Policing the Crisis: Mugging, the State, and Law and Order*. London: The Macmillan Press.

Hammersley, M. 1992. *What's wrong with ETHNOGRAPHY?* London: Routledge.

Hamnett, C. 1989. 'Consumption and class in contemporary Britain'. In C.Hamnett, L. McDowell and P. Sarre (eds). *The Changing Social Structure*. London: Sage Publications.

Hann, C. 1987. *Living in Terror: A Report on racial violence and harassment in housing*. Commission for Racial Equality. London: Elliot House.

Hann, C. 1988. *Homelessness and Discrimination: Report of a formal investigation into the London Borough of Tower Hamlets*. Commission for Racial Equality. London: Elliot House.

Hardy, P. 1972. *The Muslims of British India*. London: Cambridge University Press.

Hart, J.W. 1970/71. 'The Sociometry of Poverty'. *British J. of Social Psychiatry*, No.4, pages 83-87.

Hay, C. 1994. *Moving and Shaking to the Rhythm of Local Economic Development: Towards a Local Schumpeterian Workfare State?* Lancaster Working Papers in Political Economy. Political Economy of Local Goverance Series. Working Paper 49. Lancaster: Lancaster University.

Hebdige, D. 1991. *Subculture: the meaning of style*. London: Routledge.

Heineman, B.W. 1972. *The Politics of the Powerless*. Institute of Race Relations. London: Oxford University Press.

Hill, A. F. and Jordan, E. C. (eds). 1995. *Race, Gender and Power in America: The Legacy of The Hill Thomas Hearings*. Oxford: Oxford University Press.

Hill, M.J. and Issacharoff, R.M. 1971. *Community Action and Race Relations*. Institute of Race Relations. London: Oxford University Press.

Hill, V. 1977. *Some Aspects of the Social Geography of Bolton*. Thesis presented to Jesus College. Unpubl. Univ of Oxford.

Howe, D. 1988. *From Bobby to Babylon: Blacks and the British Police*. London: Race Today Publications.

Immigration and Nationality Department (IND), 1995. *Annual Report.* London: Home Office.

Jeffers, S. 1991. 'Black Sections in the Labour Party: the end of the ethnicity and godfather politics?' In P. Werbner and M. Anwar (eds), *Black and Ethnic Leaderships.* London: Routledge.

Jenkins, R. 1992. 'Black Workers in the Labour Market: The Price of Recession'. In P. Braham, A. Rattansi and R.Skellington (eds). *Racism and Antiracism.* London: Sage Publications.

Jessop, B.1990. *State Theory.* Cambridge: Polity Press.

Jessop, B. 1992a. 'From Social Democracy to Thatcherism'. In N. Abercrombie and A. Ward (ed). *Social change in Contemporary Britain.* Cambridge: Polity Press.

Jessop, B. 1992b. *From the Keynsian Welfare State to the Schumpeterian Workfare State.* Lancaster Group Working Paper No 45. Lancaster: University of Lancaster.

Jessop, B. 1993. 'Towards a Schumpeterian Workfare State? Preliminary remarks on Post-Fordist Political Economy', *Studies in Political Economy* .40, Spring, pages 7-39.

Jessop, B. 1994. 'The Transition to Post-Fordism and the Schumpeterian Workfare State.' In R. Burrow and B. Loader (eds). *Towards a Post-Fordist Welfare State.* London: Routledge.

Jessop, B. 1997. 'Post-Fordism and the State'. In A. Amin (ed), *Post-Fordism: a reader.* Oxford: Blackwell.

Jessop, B., Bennett, K., Bromley, S., and Ling, T. 1988. *Thatcherism.* Cambridge: Polity Press.

John, DeWitt. 1969. *Indian Workers' Association in Britain.* Institute of Race Relations. London: Oxford University Press.

Joint Working Party on Structure Plans in Greater Manchester Employment Sub Group. (1972). *An Analysis of Industrial Change 1959-1971.* Bolton Metropolitan District.

Jordan, W. D. 1971. *White over Black.* Maryland: Penguin Books.

Josephides, S. 1991. 'Organisational splits and political ideology in the Indian Workers Assocations'. In P. Werbner and M. Anwar, (eds). *Black and Ethnic Leaderships.* London: Routledge.

Kalka, I. 1991. 'Striking a bargain: political racialism in a middle-class London borough.' In P. Werbner and M. Anwar (eds), *Black and Ethnic Leaderships.* London: Routledge.

Kapferer, B. 1973. 'Social Network and Conjugal Role in Urban Zambia: towards a reformulation of the Bott hypothesis'. In J.Boissevain and J.C Mitchell (eds) *Network Analysis: Studies in Human Interaction.* The Hague: Mouton.

Karn, V., Keneny, J., and Williams, P. 1985. *Home Ownership in the Inner City.* Aldershot: Gower.

Katznelson, I. 1973. *Black Men, White Cities.* Institute of Race Relations. London: Oxford University Press.

Khan, V. S. 1982. 'The role of the culture of dominance in structuring the experience of ethnic minorities.' In C. Husband (ed). *'Race' in Britain: Continuity and Change.* London: Hutchinson & Co Publishers.

Knoke, D. and Kuklinski, J. H. 'Network analysis: basic concepts'. In G.Thompson, J. Frances, R. Levacic, J. Mitchell. (eds) 1993. *Markets, Hierarchies and Networks..* London: Sage Publications.

Knott, K. 1992. 'Gujarati Mochis in Leeds: From Leather Stockings to Surgical Boots and Beyond.' In R. Ballard (ed). *Desh Pardesh.* London: Hurst & Co.

Knowles, C. and Mercer, S. 1992. 'Feminism and Antiracism: an Exploration of the Political Possibilities'. In J. Donald and A. Rattansi (eds). *Race, Culture and Difference.* The Open University. London: Sage Publications.

Kosmin, B. 1979. 'Exclusion and Opportunity: Traditions of work amongst British Jews.' In S.Wallman (ed) *Ethnicity at Work*. London: Macmillan.

La Gaipa, J.J. 1977. 'Testing a Multidimensional Approach to Friendship.' In S.Duck (ed) *Theory and Practice in Interpersonal Attraction*. London: Academic Press.

Lash, S. and Urry, J.1988. *The End of Organized Capitalism*. Oxford. Polity Press.

Lash, S. and Urry, J. 1994. *Economics of Signs and Space*. London: Sage Publications.

Laumann, E.O. 1973. *Bonds of Pluralism: The Form and Substance of Urban Social Networks*. New York: John Wiley & Son.

Laumann, E.O. 1979. 'Network Analysis in Large Social Systems: Some Theoretical and Methodological Problems.' In P.W.Holland and S.Leinhardt (eds). *Perspective on Social Network Research*. New York: Academic Press.

Laumann, E.O. and Pappi, F.U. 1976. *Networks of Collective Action: A perspective on community influence systems*. London: Academic Press.

Lawrence, D. 1974. *Black Migrants: White Natives*. London: Cambridge University Press.

Lawrence, E. 1983. 'Just plain common sense: the "roots" of racism.' In Centre for Contemporary Cultural Studies. *The Empire Strikes Back*. Hutchinson: University of Birmingham.

Layton-Henry, Z. 1984. *The Politics of Race in Britain*. London: George Allen & Unwin.

Layton-Henry, Z. 1992. *The Politics of Immigration*. Oxford: Blackwell.

Layton-Henry, Z. and Rich, P. 1986. *Race, Government and Politics in Britain*. Basingstoke: Macmillan.

Le Lohe,M. 1983. 'Voter Discrimination against Asian and black candidates in the 1983 General Election.' *New Community*, Vol.11, No. 1/2, pages 101-108.

Lee, R. 1995. 'Look after the pounds and the people will look after themselves: social reproduction, regulation and social exclusions in Western Europe', *Environment and Planning*. October. Vol 27. pages 1577-1594.

Leinhardt, S. (ed). 1977. *Social Networks: A Developing Paradigm*. New York: Academic Press.

Lemert, E.M. 1972. *Human Deviance, Social Problems and Social Control*. New York: Engelwood Cliffs, Prentice-Hall.

Lin, N. 1982. 'Social Resources and Instrumental Action.' In P.V.Marsden and N. Lin (eds) *Social Structure and Network Analysis*. Beverley Hills: Sage Publications.

Longworth, J. H. 1997. *The Cotton Mills of Bolton* Bolton: Bolton Museum and Art Gallery.

Lyon, M.H. 1972/73. 'Ethnicity and Gujarati Indians in Britain.' *New Community*, Vol.2, No.1, pages 1-11.

Lyotard, J. F. 1988. *The postmodern condition: a report on knowledge*. Manchester: Manchester University Press.

MacDonald, I. 1989. *Murder in the Playground*. London: Longsight Press.

MacDonald, J.S. and MacDonald, B.K. 1964. 'Migration, Ethnic Neighbourhood Formation and Social Networks'. *Milbank Memorial Fund Quarterly*, 42, 1, pages 82-97.

Mama, A. 1992. 'Black Women and the British State, Race Class and Gender'. In P. Braham, A. Rattansi and R.Skellington (eds). *Racism and Antiracism*. London: Sage Publications.

Mandelbaum, D.G. 1972. *Society in India*. Vols. 1 & 2. Berkeley: University of California Press.

Marcus, G.E. 1986. 'Contemporary Problems of Ethnography'. In J.Clifford and G.E.Marcus (eds). *Writing Culture: The Poetics and Politics of Ethnography*. Berkeley: University of California Press.

Mayer, A.C. 1966. 'The Significance of Quasi-Groups in the Study of Complex Societies.' In M.Banton (ed) *The Social Anthropology of Complex Societies*. A.S.A. Monographs No.4. London: Tavistock Publications.

238

Mayer, A.C. 1973. *Caste and Kinship in Central India*. Berkeley: University of California Press.

Mayer, P. 1962. *Townsmen or Tribesmen?* Cape Town: Oxford University Press.

McKinlay, J.B. 1973. 'Social Networks, Lay Consultation and Help Seeking Behaviour.' *Social Forces*, Vol.51, pages 275-292.

McLennan, G. 1995. *Pluralism*. Open Univeristy Press, Buckingham.

Miles, R. 1982. *Racism and Migrant Labour*. London: Routledge & Kegan Paul.

Miles, R. 1989. *'Racism'*. London: Routledge.

Miles, R. 1993. *Racism after 'Race Relations'*. London: Routledge.

Miles, R. and Phizacklea, A. 1984. *White Man's Country: Racism in British Politics*. London: Pluto Press.

Milner, D. 1975. *Children and Race*. England: Penguin Books.

Misra, S. 1964. *Muslim Communities in Gujarat*. New York: Asia Publishing House.

Mitchell, J.C. 1967. 'On Quantification in Social Anthropology'. In A.L.Epstein (ed) *The Craft of Social Anthropology*. London: Tavistock Publications.

Mitchell, J.C. 1971. 'The Concept and Use of Social Networks.' In J.C.Mitchell (ed) *Social Networks in Urban Situations*. Manchester: Manchester University Press.

Mitchell, J.C. 1974. 'Perceptions of Ethnicity and Ethnic Behaviour: an empirical exploration'. In A.Cohen (ed) *Urban Ethnicity*. A.S.A. Monographs No.12. London: Tavistock Publications.

Modood, T. 1988. "Black', racial equality and Asian identity'. *New Community*, Vol.XIV, No.3, pages 397-404.

Modood, T. 1992. *Not easy being British: Colour, Culture and Citizenship*. Runnymede Trust and Trentham Books: Stoke on Trent.

Modood, T. 1996. "Race' in Britain and the politics of Difference.' In D.Archard (ed) Philosophy and Pluralism. Cambridge University Press, Cambridge.

Moore, R. 1975. *Racism and black resistance in Britain*. London: Pluto Press.

Morris, H.S. 1968. *The Indians in Uganda*. London: Weidenfeld and Nicholson.

Mulla, A. 1995. *Placement Report: Applied Community Studies*. Unpubl. Manchester Metropolitan University.

Nancy, J-L. 1991. *The Inoperative Community*. Minneapolis: University of Minnesota Press.

Nesbitt, E. 1992. 'Valmikis in Coventry: The Revival and Reconstruction of a Community'. In R. Ballard (ed). *Desh Pardesh*. London: Hurst & Co.

Nicholas, R.W. 1965. 'Factions: a Comparative Analysis.' In M.Banton (ed) *Political Systems and the Distribution of Power*. A.S.A. Monograph 2. London: Tavistock Publications.

Niemeijer, R. 1973. 'Some Applications of the Notion of Density.' In J.Boissevain and J.C.Mitchell (eds) *Network Analysis: Studies in Human Interaction*. The Hague: Mouton.

Ogden, R.H. 1966. *Industry and Employment in Bolton*. General Report. Bolton. Borough Planning Office.

Owen, D. 1994. 'Spatial Variations in Ethnic Group Populations in Great Britain'. *Population Trends*. No 78.Winter. OPCS. London: HMSO.

Paine, R. 1969. 'In search of Friendship: an exploratory analysis in 'middle-class' culture'. *Man*, Vol 4, pages 505-524.

Parekh, B. 1991. 'Britain and the Social Logic of Pluralism', *Temps Modernes*, July. Vol 46. No 570. pages 83-110.

Parekh, B. 1994. 'Some reflections on the Hindu diaspora', *New Community*, Vol 20. No 4. July. pages 603-620.

Peach, C. 1978/79. 'British Unemployment Cycles and West Indian Immigration - 1955-1974.' *New Community*, Vol.VII, No.1, pages 40-43.

Pearson, M. 1986. 'The Politics of Ethnic Minority Health Studies'. In T. Rathwell and D. Phillips (eds), *Health, Race and Ethnicity*. London: Croom Helm.

Penn, R. 1994. *Bolton Bury TEC Local Labour Market Assessment*. Bolton Bury TEC.

Penn, R., Scattergood, H. 1991. *Career Aspirations of Fifth Formers in Rochdale*: University of Lancaster.

Phillips, D. 1981. 'The social and spatial segregation of Asians in Leicester.' In P.Jackson and S.J.Smith (eds) *Social Interaction and Ethnic Segregation*. Institute of British Geographers. Special Publication. No.12. London: Academic Press.

Philpott, S. B. 'The Montserratians: Migration Dependency and the maintenance of Island ties in England.' In J. H. Watson (ed). *Between Two Cultures: migrants and minorities in Britain*. Oxford: Basil Blackwell.

Phizacklea, A. 1990. *Unpacking the Fashion Industry*. London: Routledge.

Phizacklea, A. and Miles, R. 1992. 'The British Union Movement and Racism'. In P. Braham, A. Rattansi and R.Skellington (eds). *Racism and Antiracism*. London: Sage Publications.

Piore, M.J. and Sabel, E .F. 1984. *The Second Industrial Divide*. New York: Barri Books.

Pocock, D. (1972). *Kanbi and Patidar*. Oxford: Clarendon Press.

Pocock, D. (1973). *Mind, Body and Wealth*. Oxford: Basil Blackwell.

Power, J. with Hardman, A. 1976. *Western Europe's Migrant Worker*. Report No 28. Minority Rights Group.

Rattansi, A. 1994. Western racism, ethnicities and identities in a 'postmodern' frame'. In A. Rattansi and S. Westwood (eds). *Racism, Modernity and Identity on the Western front*. Cambridge: Polity Press.

Rattansi, A. and Westwood, S. (eds). 1994. *Racism, Modernity and Identity*. Cambridge: Polity Press.

Rex, J. 1986. *Race and Ethnicity*. Milton Keynes: Open University Press.

Rex, J. 1987. 'The Concept of a Multi-Cultural Society'. *New Community*. Vol.XIV, No.1/2, pages 218-229.

Rex, J. and Moore, R. 1971. *Race, Community and Conflict*. Institute of Race Relations. London: Oxford University Press.

Rex, J. and Tomlinson, S. 1979. *Colonial Immigrants in a British City*. London: Routledge & Kegan Paul.

Robinson, V. (1979). 'Choice and Constraint in Asian Housing in Blackburn'. *New Community*, Vol.7, No.2, pages 390-396.

Robinson, V. (1980). 'Correlates of Asian Migration to Britain: 1959-74'. *New Community*, Vol 8, Nos.1 and 2, pages 115-122.

Robinson, V. 1986. *Transients, Settlers and Refugees: Asian in Britain*. Oxford: Clarendon Press.

Rushdie, S. (1988). *The Satanic Verses*. London: Viking.

Rushing, A.W. 1978. 'Status, Resources, Societal Reactions, and Mental Hospital Admission'. *American Sociological Review*, Vol.43, No.4, pages 521-533.

Sacks, H. 1985. 'Notes on Methodology'. In A.J.Maxwell and J.Heritage (eds). *Structure of Social Action*. Cambridge: Cambridge University Press.

Sagger, S. 1992. *Race and Politics in Britain*. London: Harvester Wheatsheaf.

Said, E. E. 1981. *Covering Islam*. London: Routledge and Kegan Paul.

Sassen, S. 1990. *The Mobility of Labor and Capital: A study in International Investment and Labor Flow*. Cambridge: Cambridge University Press.

Saunders, P. 1990. *A Nation of Home Owners*. London: Unwin Hyman.

Saunders, P. 1989. 'Beyond housing class: the sociological significance of private property rights in means of consumption'. In L.McDowell, P.Sarre and C.Hamnett. *Divided Nation*. London: Hodder & Stoughton.

Saxelby, C.H. (ed) (1971). *Bolton Survey.* S.R.Publishers.

Scarman, The Rt.Hon. The Lord. (1981). *The British Disorders, 10-12 April 1981.* London: HMSO.

Schutz, A. 1964. *Collected Papers II: Studies in Social Theory.* The Hague: Martinus Nijhoff.

Schutz, A. 1976. 'The Stranger.' In G.Bowker and J.Carrier. (eds) *Race and Ethnic Relations.* London: Hutchinson.

Scott, D. 1972/73. 'West Pakistanis in Huddersfield: Aspects of Race Relations in Local Politics'. *New Community,* Vol.2, No.1, pages 38-43.

Sharrock, W.W. and Anderson, R.J. 1982. 'On the Demise of the Native: Some Observations on and a Proposal for Ethnography'. *Human Studies,* Vol. 5, pages 119-135.

Shaw, A.1988. *A Pakistani Community in Britain.* Oxford: Basil Blackwell.

Sherrington, P.C. (n.d.). *Asian Immigrants in England with Particular Reference to Bolton.* Thesis unpubl.

Sivanandan, A. 1990. *Communities of Resistance.* London: Verso.

Small, S. 1994. *'Racialised Barriers'.* London: Routledge.

Smith, D. J. 1976. *The Facts of Racial Disadvantage.* London: PEP.

Smith, S.J. 1984. 'Negotiating ethnicity in an uncertain environment'. *Ethnic and Racial Studies,* Vol.7, No.3, pages 360-373.

Smith, S.J. 1989. *The Politics of 'Race' and Residence.* Cambridge: Polity Press.

Solomos, J. 1989. *Race and Racism in contemporary Britain.* Basingstoke: Macmillan.

Solomos, J. 1991. *Black Youth, Racism and the State.* Cambridge: Cambridge University Press.

Solomos, J. 1992.'The Politics of Immigration since 1945'. In P. Braham, A. Rattansi and R. Skellington (eds), *Racism and Antiracism.* The Open University. London: Sage Publications.

Solomos, J. and Back, L. 1995. *Race, Politics and Social Change.* London: Routledge.

Solomos, J., Findlay, B., Jones, S. and Gilroy, P. (1983). 'The organic crisis of British capitalism and race: the experience of the seventies'. In *The Empire Strikes Back.* Centre for Contemporary Cultural Studies. University of Birmingham. London: Hutchinson.

Tambs-Lyche, H. 1980. *London Patidars: A case study in urban ethnicity.* London: Routledge & Kegan Paul.

Taylor, H. 1976. *The Half-Way Generation.* London: NFER Publishers.

Thompson, G., Frances, J., Levacic, R., Mitchell, J. (eds). 1993. *Markets,Hierarchies and Networks.* London: Sage Publications.

Townsend, P. 1979. *Poverty in the UK.* Harmondsworth: Penguin Books.

Townson, J. and Moorhouse, T. 1979. *Asians in Blackburn – 1978 Survey.* Blackburn: Blackburn Council for Community Relations.

Troyna, B. 1992. 'Can you see the join? : An Historical Analysis of Multicultural and Antiracist Education Policies'. In D. Gill, B. Mayor and M. Blair (eds). *Racism and Education: Structures and Strategies.*The Open University. London: Sage Publications.

Troyna, B. and Hatcher, R. 1992. *Racism in children's lives.* London: Routledge.

Turner, V.W. 1962. 'Three Symbols of Passage in Ndembu Circumcision Ritual: an Interpretation'. In M.Gluckman (ed) *Essays on the Ritual of Social Relations.* Manchester: Manchester University Press.

Urry, J. 1990a. *The Tourist Gaze.* London: Sage Publications.

Urry, J. 1990b. *Globalistion, Localisation and the Nation-state.* Lancaster Regionalism Group, Working Paper 40. University of Lancaster.

Urry, J. 1997. 'Globalisation and Citizenship'. Paper presented at a conference on *Citizenship for the 21st Century.* University of Central Lancashire.

Verma, G. K. (ed) 1989. *Education of All*. Lewes: Farmer Press.

Wallman, S. (1978). 'The Boundaries of 'Race' Processes of Ethnicity in England'. *MAN*, Vol.13, No.2, pages 200-217.

Wallman, S. (1979). 'Introduction: The Scope for Ethnicity'. In S.Wallman (ed) *Ethnicity at Work*. London: Macmillan.

Walvin, J. 1984. *Passage to Britain*. Hammondsworth: Penguin Books.

Ward, R.H. 1973. 'What Future for the Uganda Asians?' *New Community*, Vol.II, No.4, pages 372-378.

Warde, A. 1994. 'Consumers, Consumption and Post-Fordism'. In R. Burrows and B. Loader (eds). *Towards a Post-Fordist Welfare State?* London: Routledge.

Warrier, S. 1992. 'Gujarat Prajapatis in London: Family Roles and Sociability Networks'. In R. Ballard. *Desh Pardesh*. London: Hurst & Co.

Watson, J.L. (ed). 1977. *Between Two Cultures*. Oxford: Basil Blackwell.

Weber, M. 1978. *Economy and Society*, Vols. 1 and 2. Translated by R. Gunther and C. Wittich. Berkeley & London: University of California Press.

Werbner, P. 1979. 'Avoiding the Ghetto: Pakistani Migrants and Settlement Shifts in Manchester'. *New Community,* Vol.7, No.3, pages 376-389.

Werbner, P. 1989. *The Migration Process*. Oxford: Berg.

Werbner, P. 1996a. 'Allegories of Sacred Imperfection', *Current Anthropology*. Vol 37. Supplement. February. pages 55-86.

Werbner, P. 1996b. 'Fun Spaces: on identity and social empowerment among British Pakistanis', *Theory, Culture and Society*. Vol 13. November. pages 53-80.

Werbner, P. and Anwar, M. (eds). 1991. *Black and Ethnic Leaderships*. London: Routledge.

Werbner,P. and Modood,T.1997. *Debating Cultural Hybridity*. London & Jersey. Zed Books.

West, C. 1994. *Race Matters*. New York: Vintage Books.

Whitehead, M. 1987. *The Health Divide: Inequalities in Health in the 1980s*. London: Health Education Council.

Williams, F. 1994. 'Social Relations, Welfare and the Post-Fordism debate'. In R. Burrows and B. Loader (eds). *Towards a Post-Fordist Welfare State*? London: Routledge.

Williams, R.B. 1984. *A New Face of Hinduism*. Cambridge: Cambridge University Press.

Willis, P.E. 1979. *Learning to labour*. Farnborough: Saxon House.

Wrench, J. 1992. 'New vocationalism, old racism and the careers service'. In P. Braham, A. Rattansi and R. Skellington (eds). *Racism and Antiracism*. London: Sage Publications.

Wrench, J. and Solomos, J. (eds). 1993. *Racism and Migration in Western Europe*. Oxford: Berg.

Wright, P.L. 1968. *The Coloured Worker in British Industry*. Institute of Race Relations. Oxford: Oxford University Press.

Yancey, W.L., Erickson,E.P. and Juliani, R.N. 1976. 'Emergent Ethnicity. A Review and Reformulation.' *American Sociological Review,* Vol.41, No.3, pages 391-403.

Ziya-ul-Hasan, F. 1963. *The Deobandi School and the Demand for Pakistan*. New York: Asia Publishing House.

Past-into-Present Series

IRELAND

Padraig Lane

B T BATSFORD LTD London

First published 1974

© Padraig Lane 1974

ISBN 0 7134 2845 7

Computer composed in England by
Eyre & Spottiswoode Ltd at Grosvenor Press, Portsmouth
Printed by The Anchor Press, Tiptree, Essex
for the Publishers
B T Batsford Ltd, 4 Fitzhardinge Street, London W1H 0AH

Acknowledgments

The author and Publishers wish to thank the following for permission to reproduce copyright illustrations: the Commissioners of Public Works in Ireland for fig 4; the Mansell Collection for fig 6; the Ulster Museum for figs 8, 9, 13, 30, 35, 56, 57; the Trustees of the British Museum for fig 24; the National Library of Ireland for figs 33, 34, 36, 39, 40, 44, 45, 47, 48, 49, 53; the Irish Sugar Company for fig 66. The other illustrations appearing in this book are the property of the Publishers.

Contents

The Illustrations

Introduction: the Political Background

Romans, Celts and Danes

Agricola, the Roman governor of Britain from about AD 77 to 84, devised a plan to conquer the Irish Celts, or *Scotii* as the Romans called them. Maybe he was remembering how the Celts from Gaul had sacked Rome in 350 BC. The Irish kings had always been a thorn in the side of the Romans in France and Britain — they were constantly sending parties of armed raiding ships searching for plunder and slaves. In the end, however, the Roman legions were never sent to Ireland. Perhaps it was too far away for them. Soon after, the family of Niall of the Nine Hostages was able to force the kings of the other six provinces in Ireland to recognize the rulers at Tara as the most powerful in the island, and they began collecting tributes or taxes of cattle and hostages as a sign of their power.

By the time the Danes or Norsemen began raiding Ireland, the power of Tara was under challenge. It was the ruler of Munster, Brian Boru, who was given command of the army which defeated the Norsemen at Clontarf near Dublin, in the year 1014. The Norsemen were never able to rule the country but they had meddled in its politics by supporting the rulers of Leinster against Tara, and these in turn had fought alongside the Danes at Clontarf.

1 Lough Erne was a political frontier between the kings of Tara, Connaught and Ulster.

2 The Irish Kings (*left*) were forced to make peace with Henry II since their rough-and-ready soldiers were no match for the Norman barons.

The Normans

There was great rivalry among the rulers of Munster, Leinster, Connaught and Ulster for the high-kingship of Ireland in the years between 1014 and 1169, and this eventually brought the Normans into Ireland. Once again, the rulers of Leinster, this time the king of South Leinster, Dermot MacMurrough, encouraged the foreigners. Dermot fled from Wexford to the camp of Henry II in France, seeking out soldiers to help him recover his kingdom — he had been on the losing side of the struggle for the high-kingship, which Rory O'Connor of Connaught had won. Dermot thought that once he had made himself high-king of Ireland he would be able to get rid of the Norman knights. Henry II, however, had different ideas. He had often thought of conquering Ireland, and this was his opportunity. He sent the Earl of Pembroke, known as Strongbow, across to Ireland, apparently to help Dermot MacMurrough.

Having captured the cities of Waterford and Wexford, Strongbow reached Dublin. The Irish, under the command of the high-king Rory O'Connor surrounded the city, but they were caught by surprise when the Normans swept suddenly out. The Normans had better weapons, wore chain-mail suits and visors, and used their cavalry with skill. They easily defeated the rough-and-ready Irish and, in 1175, the Irish were forced to recognize Henry II as overlord, in feudal fashion. Rory O'Connor was appointed to act as his deputy. Strongbow, however, was recognized by marriage as the ruler of South Leinster; Hugh De Lacy was made ruler of North Leinster; then, after the defeat of the Irish in Ulster by John De Courcy in 1177, most of Munster was granted to the Norman knights Fitzstephen, De Cogan and De Braose. This made Henry's agreement with the Irish high-king almost worthless, since Norman knights now controlled most of the country O'Connor was supposed to be ruling. In 1250, indeed, Connaught was captured by the Norman knight De Burgo.

The kings of England later claimed personal rights of ownership to the lands in Ireland granted to Norman knights. The Irish Parliament called in 1297 was a sign that the English kings, through the agency of the Norman barons, had gained control over more than three-quarters of the island. The Irish chieftains remained on sufferance in small corners of their former territories. The English king kept personal control over the cities of Dublin, Wexford, Waterford, Cork and Limerick, as well as an area around Dublin that stretched down along the coast to Arklow, as a measure of security. This latter area was the centre of English domination over Ireland, and was known as the Pale.

3 (*Opposite*) the Irish chieftains were gradually driven into the wilder parts of the country. From their strongholds in the woods, they raided the English Pale for cattle.

How the Irish fought back

In 1261, at Callann in Co Kerry, and again in 1270, at Athankip near Carrick-on-Shannon, the Normans were beaten in battle by the McCarthys of Munster and the O'Connors of Connaught. The Irish had discovered that the mail-coated, axe-carrying Danish-Scots fighters (called gallowglasses) were magnificent mercenary soldiers, and a match for any Norman knight.

The link between Ireland and Scotland was strengthened for a brief period in 1315, when Robert Bruce and his brother Edward joined forces with the Irish in an attempt to gain control of the island. They planned to make Edward Bruce king of Ireland, while Robert became king of Scotland. The Bruces failed, but the Irish continued to win back their lands from the English. King Richard II made two attempts in 1394 and 1399 to check the Irish, but merely lost his own throne in England. The Hundred Years' War and the Wars of the Roses again prevented the English kings from conquering the island once and for all. Indeed, it seemed that the great Norman families in Ireland, the Desmonds, Fitzgeralds, Butlers and Burkes, were becoming more Irish in their ways, and steadily usurping the control of the English monarchs.

The Tudors

However, after Henry VII had gained control in England, he realized the danger of a conspiracy between the great families in Ireland and his English and foreign enemies. In 1494, he sent Edward Poynings over to Ireland to prevent the great families from becoming too Irish in their ways. He also forbade Ireland's Parliament to pass laws without the king's permission. Later still, his son Henry VIII took away the political control of the greatest of these families, the Fitzgeralds of Kildare. He forced the Irish chieftains to surrender their lands in token fashion, and had himself declared King of Ireland. He had thus confirmed the claims of Henry II to power over the island.

4 The gallowglasses were mail-coated mercenary soldiers who helped the Irish chieftains fight back against the Norman invaders.

5 Art MacMorrogh, the Gaelic King of Leinster, like the other Irish kings and chieftains, used the security of the forests to launch surprise attacks on the English armies sent to defeat him.

The Irish, however, rebelled time and time again against the increasing restriction of their freedom. The Tudors in their turn believed that the King of Spain would use Ireland as a base from which to attack England. So the Desmond rebellion in Munster and Hugh O'Neill's Nine Years' War in Ulster were defeated. The Battle of Kinsale in 1603 marked the end of the power of the native Irish.

The Stuarts, Cromwell and King William

As soon as the native Irish were defeated, the Normans who lived in the Pale, and who had remained more English in their ways, became restless — they felt that their Catholic religion was prompting English officials to remove their power and lands too. In 1642, they joined with the native Irish who were rebelling in Ulster in one last desperate effort to get their lands back from English settlers. A Parliament or Confederation was set up at Kilkenny in token loyalty to Charles I, against an English Parliament that was anti-monarchy, anti-Catholic and anti-Ireland. However, after Cromwell had gained control in England in 1649, he brought an army over to Ireland that defeated royalists and rebel Irish alike in bloodthirsty fashion.

When the Stuarts were restored in 1660, the Catholics in Ireland were not given back their lands. This meant that when James II was driven off his English throne in 1689, because of his catholicism, he found support in Ireland.

9

In 1690-91, the Jacobites (supporters of King James) and the Williamites (supporters of King William) fought for overall control in Ireland. At Derry, the Boyne, Aughrim and Limerick, the armies of King James were defeated.

Irish politics from 1691 to 1801

Until 1778, the Irish Protestant landowners, who represented the interests of English settlers in Ireland, lived on an island that was largely ruled by England. Then the example of the American War of Independence and the manner in which Irish industries had been neglected for the benefit of English businessmen, prompted a demand for Free Trade and a Free Irish Parliament. When this was set up in 1782, it soon became known as Grattan's Parliament, because of Henry Grattan's leadership in the struggle for freedom.

The Parliament, however, did not give citizens' rights in full to everyone, and this combined with the example of the French Revolution and the cruelty of the landlords to tenants brought about the establishment of a secret society called the United Irishmen and, in 1798, led to rebellion. In 1801, the English Prime Minister, William Pitt, frightened by the support given to the rebellion by the French, passed the Act of Union, which abolished the separate Irish Parliament, and brought the whole island under the control of Westminster. From 1801 to 1921, Ireland was part of Great Britain, under the name of the United Kingdom.

The Act of Union

The Act of Union was not accepted by the Irish people. In 1803, Robert Emmet led a rebellion in Dublin; in 1848, the Young Ireland leaders copied the example of the revolutions in Paris and other European cities; and, in 1867, the Fenians started a serious rebellion. Other leaders of the people tried more peaceful means to win freedom for Ireland again. Daniel O'Connell, Butt and Parnell attempted in turn to get enough support in the Parliament at Westminster to end the Act of Union. Finally, in 1914, the Irish were promised that Home Rule, or Irish freedom, would be given to them as soon as the First World War was over. By that time, however, the Protestants in Ulster were vociferously objecting to the end of the Act of Union, while in the rest of Ireland a secret movement was preparing to fight for a better form of freedom than a Home Rule government that still gave powers to England. During Easter Week, 1916, a rebellion broke out in Dublin in support of an Irish Republic, led by the heads of the secret movement, the Irish Republican Brotherhood, and supported by James Connolly and the Citizen Army who wanted a Socialist Republic.

The effort of the insurgents failed in military terms in Easter Week, 1916, but it inspired a war fought from 1919 to 1921, which ended with the formation of a Free State in Southern Ireland. The Ulster Protestants, or Unionists, had their wishes catered for by being granted a separate state of Northern Ireland within the United Kingdom. It contained six of the Ulster counties, excluding Donegal, Cavan and Monaghan. Stormont was the centre for the Ulster Parliament.

6 Edward Carson was a brilliant barrister, born in Dublin in 1854. He led the campaign in Ulster from 1910 to protect the interests of those who wished to keep the link with Britain, and served with the British government during the First World War.

1921 to the present

A Civil War broke out in Southern Ireland between those who accepted the new freedom and those who believed it was not enough. This ended in 1923. In 1932, Ireland's Free State, like Canada, Australia, South Africa and New Zealand, was given full rights to make its own treaties and arrange its own affairs. In 1936, the abdication of Edward VIII in England provided an opportunity to remove all royal connection with the Free State, which ceased to be a British Dominion. In 1949, the Irish Free State declared itself a Republic.

In January 1973, Southern Ireland (and Northern Ireland by virtue of being deemed part of Britain) entered the EEC and thereby became part of the greater political unit governed by the Treaties of Rome and Paris. Brussels, not Dublin, London, or Belfast, is now the political centre for the island of Ireland. Perhaps, after all, Agricola had the last laugh.

1. Farmers and Townsmen, to 1300

Settlements

About 5,500 years ago, Stone Age farmers came to live on the north coast of Co Mayo. They provided for themselves the simple needs of their small community. They lived in small clusters of huts, timber posts covered with sods and thatched with rushes. By 200 BC, when the Celts arrived, Bronze Age metalworkers had introduced the idea of living on artificial islands in the lakes. These islands, called crannogs, were surrounded by a wooden stockade, and approached by a zig-zag causeway, or path of stepping stones, under the surface of the water.

The Celtic warriors, with their chariots and iron swords, felt secure within their ring forts. These ring forts consisted of earthen mounds topped by wooden palisades. The fort entrances were guarded by dogs, such as threatened the legendary hero Cuchullain as a boy, and the farmers and craftsmen lived on the green areas between the mounds. Separate huts were used as separate rooms. The mud-caked wattle houses of the nobles were only distinguished from those of ordinary people by their decorations — the use of ornamented wood, and the silver and gold inside. They also had a roughly-paved floor with a central, kerbed hearth.

After Ireland became Christian in AD 431, monks developed the art of overlapping stones without mortar so that the walls met finally in a ridged roof.

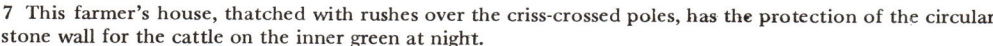

7 This farmer's house, thatched with rushes over the criss-crossed poles, has the protection of the circular stone wall for the cattle on the inner green at night.

8 The overlapping stones of this chapel come together without mortar in a ridged roof.

From 837, the Vikings, in their settlement at Dublin, chose to use timber rather than stone when building. They surrounded their earthen rampart up from the River Liffey with a wooden stockade, interweaving ash, elm and hazel rods horizontally through upright rows of round posts. Houses of squared timber, mortised together and sheeted with boards for protection against the weather, were also found in the Viking settlement. The first cathedral in Dublin after the Vikings became Christians was the timber cathedral of Holy Trinity. The very height formed by the earthen rampart of the Vikings gave the High Street in Dublin its name. Other streets got their titles from the tradesmen who lived there, like Shoemaker Street, and Fishamble Street the fish market.

The Viking settlements at Dublin, Wexford, Cork and Limerick were the first towns in Ireland. Before these towns emerged, the craftsmen and farmers, who lived within or around the boundaries of monasteries and ring forts, were isolated in the country. The Vikings now built timber streets, and used stone culverts for drainage and refuse.

The Normans brought the development of towns a stage further. As they conquered the island from 1169 onwards, they created towns of the contemporary English type around their stone castles. They surrounded these towns with walls of mortared stone. A tax, called murage, provided money for building the walls.

Trade

The early Stone Age farming people in Ireland had sent stone axes and tools from Co Antrim to their kinsfolk in England. The Bronze Age metalworkers had traded their gold and bronze jewellery as far away as the Mediterranean and Baltic for bright blue glass from the East and amber from Scandinavia. Later, however, the aonach or market, held annually at the Celtic high-kings'

13

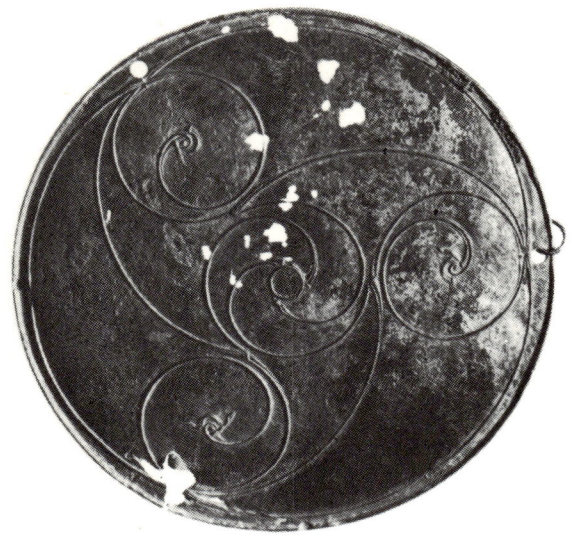

9 The metalworkers used intricate designs with which to decorate their work. These designs were based on mathematical knowledge, and very often derived from worship of the sun.

stronghold at Tara, was as much a social occasion as an exchange of goods. The ring forts and monasteries had farmers and craftsmen to provide their own needs. Barter was conducted in cattle, or with a measure of silver called a shekel.

The Vikings revived the trade in Baltic amber when they settled at Dublin, Wexford, Waterford, Cork and Limerick. By 1300, they had also established a flourishing trade in wine with Bordeaux. Winetavern Street in Dublin was the centre of Norman Dublin's wine trade. When Prince John was granting a charter of civil liberties to Dublin in 1192, he protected the trade of the wine merchants by ordering that no foreign merchant could have a tavern nor sell wine in the city. The foreign merchants could only sell wine from a ship. Wine had, however, been imported into Ireland from AD 600 in exchange for skins, wolf-dogs and hawks.

Money

The Vikings' ability as merchants is suggested by their use of folding scales for weighing. The first coins used in Ireland were those of the Viking King Sitric, who minted silver pennies in Dublin in 995. Later these reached other Viking towns like Limerick. However, they were out of circulation by the time the Normans came in 1169. From 1189, Norman coins were circulating in Ireland, although it was not until 1202 that King John established a special Irish coinage minted in Dublin. Carrickfergus, Trim, Limerick and Waterford all had legal or illegal mints at some time or another. As the Normans became involved in wars with France, the coins in Ireland became debased. In 1299, Edward I forbade the use of worthless coins like 'pollards' and 'crokards'.

14

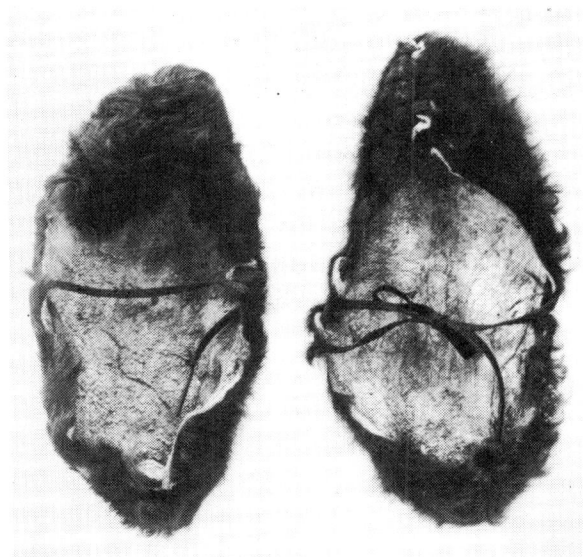

10 The skins of animals, sewn and bound by simple needles, served as footwear. Such shoes were still worn by islanders off the coast of Ireland at the beginning of the twentieth century.

Guilds

Apart from wine, the Vikings also traded in silk. Prince John's charter in 1192 also protected the merchants who traded in corn, hides and wool. Before 1169, most trading contact between Vikings and Normans went through Bristol. The Normans added new ports such as Drogheda and New Ross to the existing Viking ports. They also established regular fairs and markets in the villages that grew up around their castles. By 1300, there were 38 market towns and ports around Cork.

Dublin and New Ross, as elsewhere, had merchant guilds. Even a small village like Innistioge, on the Nore river in Co Kilkenny, was allowed by the prior of the abbey in 1220 to have 'a merchants' guild and other guilds'. Fullers, saddlers, vintners, cordwainers, heliers or tilers, millers and masons were only a fraction of the craftsmen and merchants who formed these guilds.

The making of clothes

There were many different crafts involved in the clothing business alone. Fullers, glovers, weavers, skinners, embroiderers and tailors are only some of them. The wives of the first farmers in Ireland used bone needles and spindles of stone and bone to gather skins together and to spin wool for clothing. By the Iron Age, from 200 BC, iron needles were in use alongside the earlier tools. To judge from the number of such needles and spindles dug up by archaeologists at the Celtic ring fort settlement at Knowth in Co Meath, there must have been garment-makers in great numbers and of great skill.

Certainly the requirements of the Celtic nobility were no less exacting than those of fashionable people today. The noblemen and ladies wore a rectangular woollen cloak, either dark or else brightly dyed, which was embroidered with

15

stitching at the hem, and fastened on the shoulder or breast with a gold brooch. Next to the skin they wore a tunic and hood of unbleached linen. This undyed tunic was ornamented at the hem, reached down to the knees, and was gathered in at the waist by a girdle. Working men wore baggy trousers and a short coat, while the the women wore a plain woollen tunic.

The Vikings in Dublin also used leather and silk. In 1970, archaeologists began to excavate old Dublin. Among the ruins, they discovered finely-woven hair nets. The Vikings had also developed weaving to the point of beating the weft threads into the warp with wooden sword-like tools. When Prince John granted his charter to Dublin in 1192, cloth was being sold by the same measure as wool, in ells. Cloths called russets and habersets already demonstrated the demand for variety in the merchants' wares.

Metalworkers

The development of metalworking had also taken place. The 'Beaker Folk' who had come to Ireland by 2000 BC, brought with them the art of fashioning molten tin, copper and gold into bronze and gold weapons, tools, cauldrons and, above all, gold ornaments. They used moulds and crucibles, twisted and sheet gold to make collars, torques and gorgets and necklaces called lunulae which were shaped like the moon. They also made cloak fasteners and bracelets of gold. Their skill was later used by the Christian monks to create the beautiful crosses and chalices, bindings for books and containers for relics which were required by the Church.

The use of iron after 200 BC made possible the manufacture of iron sickles and iron harnesses for agriculture. A smith was an honoured member of his community, and even King Conor MacNessa did not consider it beneath his dignity to dine with one.

There were also enamellers and stone-carvers who made ornamented High Crosses. The carpenter with his adze and auger made wooden shears, vats for ale, solid wheels for carts, ploughshares, mills and refectory tables for the monasteries. A legendary seer advised the men of Ulster not to burn such useful timber as yew and ash, which was used for vats and cartwheels.

When the archaeologists discovered the remains of the old Viking city of Dublin, they found that many craftsmen from different crafts used to work near each other. Leather-workers made clothing; cobblers used deerskin or cattle-hides for footwear and re-used the uppers of worn shoes to make new, smaller ones for children; comb-makers used the antlers of deer. Similarly, iron-workers and nailers made knife blades, iron locks and keys, spindles and nails. Alongside them worked wood-turners, using lathes for wooden bowls and rectangular, single-piece platters; coopers turning out staves for barrels; and carpenters and shipwrights manufacturing fine Viking ships.

Food and farming

The presence of towns and trade encouraged better farming. The first farmers on the coast of Co Mayo, 5,500 years ago, built drainage-proof stone walls around 16-acre (6.5-hectare) oval fields. Then they either made ridges and furrows with a crude spade of stone or bone or, lacking a mould-board on their ploughs with which to turn the sod, they cross-ploughed the earth until it was broken enough for sowing with wild grain. Later, from the Iron Age of 200 BC, iron sickles and harnesses for ploughs and harrows, as well as wooden ploughshares, permitted domesticated grain to be grown on a much larger scale. After AD 700, water-driven mills replaced the hand-turned querns or grinders for extracting meal from the grain, which was threshed with flails. Cormac, son of Conn of the Hundred Battles, is supposed to have brought the first mills and millers over from Scotland.

Of course, even from earliest times, cattle, sheep, pigs, wild boar, deer, fish and fowl were eaten. The legend of Bricriu's pigs, which could be eaten but came alive again, shows the value people placed on pork as a food. In Celtic Ireland, the king and wise men always got the prime steak at dinner. The allowance for each day was strictly regulated. Two cows, two salted pigs and two freshly-killed pigs were on the menu for dinner, to be shared among 100 men. They washed the food down with mead brewed from honey.

The sort of food eaten in Dublin after its foundation can be judged from the numerous skulls of cattle dug up by archaeologists. Pork, grain, wild nuts and berries, besides imported figs, were also eaten. Under the Normans, almonds became a favourite dish.

While the Christian monks had fenced in fields with stone walls, it was the Normans who introduced to Ireland the idea of the three-field system of crop rotation. The infields belonged directly to the lord of the manor. The land beyond this was given out to firmari or farmers, gavillers, betaghs or cottiers. These were either free or unfree tenants, who paid for the land in money, kind or labour.

Cows at that time cost between 25p and 67p each; sheep 3p to 5p; pigs 7½p to 10p; lambs 2p, and ordinary horses anything between 67p and £2. Oxen were very important because they were used for ploughing — the tails of the beasts were yoked to the plough. A team of four draft oxen might cost from £1.25 to £1.55.

11 The rough combination of iron and timber made ploughs and harrows that could effectively till the earth.

12 Wool and wheat were two valuable products of the Norman farms in Ireland during the Middle Ages.

Wool was a major commodity in those days. Among other things, it provided revenue for the king. Between 1280 and 1282, one king obtained £2,966 from the sale of Irish wool. Wool sold at about 1p per pound.

Wheat was also important for supplying food for the English armies in France. In 1255, 2,000 crannocks of wheat were ordered to be sent from Ireland to Gascony. Oats and rye were also sown. One of the duties of a betagh or villein was to provide workmen for the sowing, weeding and harvesting of the landowner's grain. On one estate in 1333, for instance, the betagh was obliged to find, for each three acres (just over a hectare) under tillage, three men in autumn for one day's work at wheat and two men at oats. Each man hired was paid less than ½p a day. Men were also wanted to turn the hay, and to cart the hay and grain to the mill. The landowner himself must have supplied the equipment for the farming — at 8p, a scythe was much too expensive for an ordinary labourer to buy. Finally the lord rewarded the labourers who helped at the harvest by giving nearly 4p towards the expenses of the hocmet or harvest feast.

The native Irish preferred to move their cattle around like nomads. They used to raid the lands held by the Normans, and steal cattle to add to their herds. In summer, the cattle were taken up onto the mountains, as in Switzerland, where huts were built and butter made. This was known as booleying.

How government regulated life

In Celtic Ireland, from about 200 BC onwards, lawyers or brehons laid down the rights and social position of everyone in the community. Men were divided into three classes — free, unfree, and slaves. A man's social position was judged by the number of cattle he held from the chieftain. Craftsmen were considered free men because of their skills. Anyone who unjustly killed or injured another was not imprisoned but had to pay compensation instead. Each freeman had a guarantor or bailsman who acted on his behalf at such times. The unfree had no such rights as citizens, while slaves were regarded as even lower than the unfree workers and labourers.

The Normans brought to Ireland their feudal system of government, with vassals, who held land from the lord in return for rendering him service, and serfs or unfree tenants below them. The Norman administrative system, with its jury, sheriff, burgesses, reeve, coroner and Parliament, entirely replaced that built up under the Irish kings. By order of Parliament, in 1297, the Lord of the Woods was made responsible for making roads 'flat, wide and cleared of briars and trees' so that criminals who fled to the bogs and woods might be swiftly pursued. Horses, including the small type known as the hobby horse, had to be made available for these manhunts. Ireland had never known such a security system.

In towns and cities the mayor and burgesses dispensed justice in their own court, the Hundred, which was held fortnightly. Charters of liberties granted to cities and towns assured freemen that they could be tried, for 'murdrum and other crimes', only by their fellows and only in the Hundred. Debtors, too, would be called to account there. The part of Dublin known today as the Liberties was once governed by such a charter.

Education, language and religion

The laws known to the brehons or judges, like the verses sung by the bards or poets, were not written but passed down from generation to generation, by word of mouth. Ogham, the first writing used in Ireland, was a series of regular strokes cut on pillars of rock, and the edges of wooden staves, quite unsuitable for long inscriptions. The Roman alphabet was first introduced to Ireland by St Patrick and his fellow missionaries in the fourth century AD.

The first settlers in Ireland, pagan sun worshippers, did, however, leave religious symbols on their tombs. The pre-Christian Irish believed that their gods, of whom Aengus was the most powerful, lived on the River Boyne. The most splendid of their tombs are to be found at Knowth, Dowth and Newgrange, all near the River Boyne. The Druids, priests of the pagan Celts, presided over great feasts held to celebrate the coming of spring, summer, the harvest and winter. Later, these feasts were given a Christian meaning.

In Celtic Ireland, certain families provided the teachers for both the noblemen's sons and for poor students. These teachers were given land by the chieftain, and each teacher then fed, clothed and taught his own students. These schools were an early type of boarding school. The students lived in huts grouped around the hut of the teacher, although other students lived with families or friends nearby. The poor students often had to serve the sons of nobles in return for their tuition, and were not allowed to wear the same clothes as the wealthier boys. The sons of noblemen were taught literature, horsemanship, chess, swimming and the use of weapons, while girls were taught sewing and embroidery. At the higher schools, the student had to spend 12 years learning the different kinds of verse, grammar, history, astronomy and law.

Not all of a boy's education came from his teacher. At that time, children were often sent away from home to be reared by a foster parent, usually another nobleman but perhaps of lesser rank. Under his foster father, the young boy learned the arts of war, statesmanship and cunning. Old legends often tell how the sons of kings were taught by magicians; the legendary hero, Cuchullain, received his training in the lands of the enchantress Sorcha. Fionn, another legendary hero, was said to have become a great athlete by being beaten up and down a steep hill by his tutor.

Christianity

It was St Patrick, originally a slave, who first brought Christianity to Ireland. He realized that if the pagan high-king who ruled at Tara could be persuaded to favour him, the Druids would not be allowed to stop him preaching. So he lit a great fire on the Hill of Slane, near Tara, as a celebration of Christ's teaching. This angered the Druids who were holding their own ceremony. St Patrick, as he had hoped, was brought before the high-king to be punished. But, using the three-leaved shamrock, he taught his captors the Christian faith. Although the high-king himself did not become a Christian, he allowed St Patrick to teach the faith freely. As a sign of Christ's greater power, St Patrick knocked down the statue of Crom, the old pagan god. The statue, like Stonehenge, was a worshipping place for the Druids.

After St Patrick, monks set up monasteries all over Ireland and often went to remote places to pray. Glendalough, established by St Kevin, was very lonely, as was Ciaran's retreat at Clonmacnoise. Other monks travelled to Scotland and Europe to spread Christianity during the Dark Ages, after the collapse of the Roman Empire. Columbcille (or St Columba) founded a famous monastery on the island of Iona, off the coast of Scotland.

The scholars at the monasteries began to attract students, and monastic schools grew up. In these schools, however, the stress was on more Christian subjects rather than the arts of war. The Christian monks not only brought writing into the schools but also Latin and foreign languages to be used alongside the native language, Irish.

It was in the medieval monasteries that some of the most splendid books ever produced by hand were created. These were largely copies of Latin manuscripts relating to the Old and New Testaments of the Bible, and were

13 The regular series of strokes on stone, seen at the bottom of this standing pillar, was the first form of writing, known as ogham. Christian crosses on the upper half show a new use for the pillar by the monks who later came to Ireland.

14 The monks spent long days and nights with quills and dyes illustrating with intricate designs the vellum on which they copied rare books.

painstakingly illustrated. The Book of Kells and the Book of Durrow, both in Trinity College, Dublin, are two of the most famous of these volumes.

Vikings and Normans

The pagan Viking raiders were attracted to Ireland by the wealth of the monasteries there. After the Battle of Clontarf in 1014, the Vikings living in Irish towns became Christian too.

The Christian Church in Ireland, however, followed a rather independent line, and not the ideas of St Bernard of Clairvaux, which were favoured by the popes of the time. So, in 1155, to make the Irish conform, Pope Adrian IV apparently encouraged Henry II of England to bring Ireland under his control. It was to help in this process that the Benedictine monastery at Holy Cross was established in 1135, and the Cistercian monastery of Mellifont in 1142. Later still, the Dominicans, the Franciscans and the Augustinians came to the island primarily as Norman orders, laying emphasis on pilgrimages to the Holy Land and on joining crusades. Many of the Normans from Ireland did go on crusade, and the mummified bodies of crusaders lie in the vaults of St Michin's Church in Dublin. The Knights Hospitallers, the order founded during the crusades, also came to Ireland.

Like the earlier Irish monks, the Norman religious orders created schools, but they laid stress on Norman-English culture rather than on the native Irish learning. Furthermore, the Norman idea of a young man's education was that of a training for knighthood and chivalry.

21

2. Life under the Norman Lords, 1300-1600

Order in the towns

Just as today local councils, the police and government provide for roads, cleanliness and health, public order and consumer protection, so a medieval town's ruler ensured that conditions were suitable both for business to prosper and for citizens to live. Equally, just as taxes and rates now provide the money for public services, so the liberties granted to medieval towns in their charters permitted the ruler to levy duties on goods brought into the town for sale. In 1549, for instance, duties of ½p per pound of ginger, and 1p per pound of saffron, and 1½p per pound of silk were levied on goods coming into Galway. The tax called murage provided funds for building and repairing the town walls. Other taxes included pavage, for paving streets, and pontage, for building and maintaining bridges. Roads and rights of way had to be kept free from

15 The building of town walls was necessary for defence. The murage tax levied on goods paid the costs of building the walls.

obstacles, and no-one was allowed to let his hedge hinder 'the common way'.

Public health was vitally important during the Middle Ages, when an open main drain ran down the street and people washed their clothes and the entrails of cattle in the public fountains. Houseowners in Kilkenny were ordered to clean the pavement outside their doors twice a week, and anyone who made a dung heap on the public street was liable to a fine of 5p. Pigs were forbidden to be fed 'upon the market place'.

When sickness came, which it did frequently, hospitals were available. In Galway, servant girls were sent round each Sunday collecting money for a hospital for the poor. The lease of a shop in Kilkenny in 1564 included the Corporation's right to occupy the house 'in case of plague, infection or illness being in the town'. Another merchant obtained a lease on condition that the best room was reserved for 'such as shall be infected of the disease commonly called the leprosy'. Since the plague of 1348-49, people had been terrified of disease. In 1566, however, Thomas Smyth, the apothecary and physician in Dublin, had to go out of business, because 'the greater part of this country folk are wonted to use the ministry of their leeches and such like, and neglecting the apothecary's science'. English settlers distrusted the practices of the leech or folk-doctor, who gathered his medicines on the hillside by moonlight, so

16 Carlow town with its ancient castle, bridge and weir.

seeming to hint of witchcraft. 'Rhubarb, sarsaparilla and aloes' were common cures, together with almonds.

All vagabonds were a nuisance. 'Idle bench-whistlers and luskish faitors', or corner boys, were banned from the streets. Gamblers who lured the workpeople into idleness were forbidden to play with 'cards, dice', and other 'unlawful games for money', on penalty of a £1 fine. Any citizen who began a street row, or drew a sword, dagger or knife, was liable to a fine of £5.

Besides providing for roads and sanitation, the ruler of the town had to ensure that the merchants built solid houses. They were ordered to construct stone houses 'with oaken timbers and slates'. Houses with thatch, always a fire risk, were forbidden within four metres of the town walls.

Citizens were also obliged to keep the gutters clean and keep the ditch or fosse that surrounded the town in good repair. Pollution of rivers was as much a concern as it is today. Lime-treated hides as well as flax were not allowed to be discharged into the River Corrib in Galway in case the salmon were destroyed. Mill streams also had to be kept clean.

Control of prices and wages

Today, public health officials inspect shops to make sure conditions are hygienic, whilst governments now regulate the correct measure and quality of goods to be sold. The prices of some goods are also laid down by the government.

In Irish towns and cities from 1300 to 1600 there were similar bye-laws to protect the interests of honest merchants and their customers. This was of particular concern wherever the native Irish settled in an outlying part of the town. In many places, of which Kilkenny is one, these areas still retain the name Irishtown. The principal merchants of the High Street usually disliked the shopkeepers of the Irish sector, who often charged less for their goods. There

24

were many regulations concerning the sale of goods. Meat had to be served clean by the butchers who were expected to wear spotless aprons. Nor were any horns to be near where the meat was exposed for sale. Similarly, badly-baked bread was prohibited, and loaves of varying weight were to be sold at different prices. Candle-makers were not to sell candles that were good neither for 'light nor sight', and butter could not be sold for more than ½p a pound. The trader who sold above this price was in danger of being fined 5p and imprisoned. Sellers of all foods were forbidden to 'take of the people very unreasonable gains' — in other words to sell beyond the market price. By 1600, however, the brewers in Dublin were reported to be selling beer at twice the amount charged in London, although they bought the malt at half the price the London brewers paid for it.

In 1513, a Galway bye-law prohibited the importing of honey into the city 'except it be good and merchantable'. It was noticed in 1585 that the town's glovers and skinners were not tanning their leather properly, and the weavers were not allowed to weave either linen cloth or single friezes that measured less than two and three-quarter metres wide.

If merchants were limited in what they could charge or manufacture, workmen were limited in what they could ask as wages. In 1300, and again under the Statute of Labourers in 1349, the wages of agricultural labourers were regulated in an effort to prevent Irish farm-workers from taking advantage of the scarcity of labour, or from leaving the manors of the Norman landowners altogether. It is clear, however, that the workmen in towns were equally restricted in what they could charge. In 1526, no carpenter or mason could accept more than 1p a day for his hire. Wages had very obviously not risen since 1333, because in Tipperary a man's wage for harvesting wheat and oats was still less than 1p a day. Nevertheless, in 1585, it was said that 'all artificers, craftsmen and common labourers, do take more than they should for their hire'.

Goods and markets

The market-place for cattle was called a shambles, and was separate from the market for other merchandise. Merchants sold their goods under the shelter of timbered penthouses or stone arcades that butted out from their houses, and used the cellars as store rooms. Rothe House in Kilkenny has been restored as an example of a typical merchant's house. In 1579, a widow was charged 15p rent for the 'lease of shop room under the new court house for 40 years'. Churches, like Christ Church in Dublin, were very often the centre around which the market was held. Wine was stored in the church vaults. In 1577, Queen Elizabeth I permitted only members of the Merchants' Guild to sell in the precincts of Christ Church, the area where the Vikings had bought and sold. Traders who were not members of a guild were expected to do business in the 'common hall'.

One of the functions of the Merchants' Guild of Dublin was the bulk buying of such goods as salt, iron, wine, coal, pitch and resin. From 1300 onwards, the goods on sale in most Irish cities included the skins of various livestock and wild animals, fish, sandals, coloured and white glass, timber, ironware, worsteds, canvas, ropes, silk, hemp, olive oil for making ointments, and lamp oil. The measure of quantity varied for different goods — a last of leather was 200 hides, a mease of herrings was about 670 fish, salt, coal and lime came in crannocks of 8 bushels, wine came by the tun or pipe, and cloth by the ell. By 1549, the quantity of ginger, cloves and spices imported showed how the demand for such luxuries had risen.

The king often chose special ports for the sole import or export of certain goods. In 1326, Drogheda was selected as one of these staple ports where all 'manner of merchandise was to be concentrated'. Similarly, Cork had a staple on the sale of wool, sheepskins and leather.

Cloth

The range of cloth available was considerable. In 1576, Dutch clothiers settled at Swords in Co Dublin, much to the annoyance of the Merchants' Guild and Tailors' Guild of Dublin. The silks, velvets, hollands, cambric and diapers produced by the Dutch affected the trade of the city merchants. Dublin's linen was said to be as good as any found in London, and its leather goods were comparable with those of Southwark. Waterford had established itself for its 'choice rugs', and Drogheda had given its name to a linen-and-wool mixture called drugget, which was used for the shirts and doublets of the Tudor armies. John Rothe, the merchant in Kilkenny, had a tucking mill for cloth finishing and so, probably, did other important merchants.

Wine, Spaniards and piracy

Ships coming into the ports controlled by Norman lords had to pay certain bonuses. The Earl of Ormond was one of the greatest of these lords, and in Limerick, for instance, every ship 'laden above 17½ butts or pipes' of wine had to grant his officers in the port one tun as 'prize' wine. The ship's captain had to leave the barrels of wine in the same position as they were when they were loaded, and not rearrange them so as to prevent the earl's officials from getting at the best wine. Blocking the gangway with barrels of poor-quality wine had apparently been a common trick. Much of the wine was bartered for fish.

Bretons and Spaniards traded along the Irish coast from Waterford to Carrickfergus. The Spanish Archway in Galway is a legacy from the days when Spanish traders plied along the west coast of Ireland. Besides wine, there was trading in iron, salt and gunpowder. English monarchs disliked this Irish trade with foreign countries and would have preferred ports like Bristol to be the centre for Irish trade. But piracy made it difficult for ships to trade along the east coast except between Waterford and Carrickfergus.

Banks and money

In Waterford, during the reign of Edward IV, there was 'want of small coins for change'. The fact that much of the merchandise coming to Ireland on the west coast was paid for with fish, hides or wool suggests that coins were not very important. Little English money reached Ireland from 1350 until 1460, when silver came into the country with the revival of trade. Spanish and French coins could also be found. Henry VIII's coins, known as groats, were the first in Ireland to have the Irish symbol of the harp on them. The groats, worth about 1½p each, were used alongside silver shillings in Elizabeth's reign. The Irish shilling, during Elizabeth's time, was called a harper because of the harp on it. The bad coins used for paying the soldiers were not popular with the merchants: 'No man cared to lay it up, and all things were bought at excessive rates'. Such was inflation that the Irish shilling was soon worth only 3½p, as against its original value of 5p. Rents for shops and houses were specified as being '14s (70p) Irish' or '10s (50p) English'.

Italian money-lenders and bankers traded in the principal towns of Ireland from 1300 onwards. The Riccardi of Lucca and the Frescobaldi of Florence had agents in many towns. King Edward II got a loan for the Scottish wars in 1322 from William Utlagh, a wealthy banker and money-lender in Kilkenny. Yet money-lenders were not altogether popular. In 1580, loaned money was being repaid at the rate of 'a peck of wheat or a good hide for the mark [or 66p]', a rate considered 'greedy, detestable and inordinate gains of living off interests'.

18 Suitors appearing before the Court of Exchequer. Note the chequered cloth used for calculation.

Strangely enough, even in the fourteenth century, the Court of Exchequer or Treasury in Ireland still used primitive means of counting. Counters were laid in rows on a chequered cloth on the table, and tallies and countertallies, square hazel rods notched in a particular way, were used as receipts.

Travel
Since much of the country was covered by woods and the Irish chieftains controlled great areas outside the Pale (the counties around Dublin) and the towns, travel was difficult and dangerous. Most of the roads were only muddy tracks, and bridges were wooden and very inadequate. However, in 1319, a bridge of stone was built across the River Liffey at Kilcullen. But when Sir John Perrot was conquering Munster in Elizabeth's reign, over two hundred years later, his soldiers still had to struggle through marshes, woods and rivers.

Life in the countryside
Gradually, from about 1450, the Norman landowners began to replace the old fortified castles with tower-houses. A winding staircase inside the walls led from the ground floor to the third storey. The second storey was often a hidden room reached through a trap-door in the upper banqueting hall. The floor of the banqueting hall was either flagged or wooden.

19 The banqueting hall was the most important room in a Norman tower-house.

The houses of the native Irish were much cruder. They lived in beehive-like huts covered by reeds, without windows or chimneys, and slept on the rush-covered floors in their clothes.

The rents charged by the Norman landowners show that their supply of food was varied. In addition to money, a tenant might have to pay in pigs, sheep, hens, 'twelve couple of rabbits' every week, and a dish of butter. The landowners also had orchards for growing leeks, herbs and apples.

The native Irish, however, lived on whey, blood drawn from the cattle, and roasted meat. In times of war, food was probably scarce, and it was said that wolves scoured the countryside of Munster after the wars during Queen Elizabeth's reign.

Clothes

Lord Clanrickarde's tailor's bill in 1578 tells us a great deal about the clothes then worn by Irish gentlemen. Doublets of satin, hose of velvet and yellow socks show a taste for quality and colour among men of fashion. Cloaks were of rich 'fine pipe', and ruffs and silk garters were essential for a fashionable outfit. Ordinary people wore more humble clothes. Clerks' gowns, jackets and jerkins were worn in the towns, together with full-sleeved smocks.

The native Irish continued to set their own fashions. The women were particularly fond of bright colours and many ornaments. On their heads they wore folded linen kerchers, the styles varying with the different provinces. The men wore a linen shirt or tunic and a leather or frieze cloak. They wore frieze caps with two lappets that buttoned under the chin. Outside the Irish areas, however, they were expected to wear clothes in the English style. Their cloaks were to be of 'country cloth', and contain no more than five ells of material. Saffron-coloured material was forbidden.

Entertainment

If life was harsh there were some compensations. By 1600, virginals were used to make music in the houses of the rich merchants, the guilds regularly organised pageants, and many Norman landowners had become attracted by the music of the Irish harpers.

The harp may have originated from the Egyptian cithara. It had one row of thirty strings in a frame of oak and red sallow, and was played with the help of specially sharpened fingernails. The earliest Irish harp in existence today dates from at least 1300 and is in Trinity College, Dublin. The harpers, however, were regarded by the government as a danger to the truly English way of life. Consequently, rhymers and bards, or poets, were banned from the castles of the Normans, and also from the towns.

Plays were performed inside Dublin Castle as early as 1528, just as they were performed at the court of the English king. The Lord Deputy was 'invited to a new play every day at Christmas', and the sum of 21 shillings and 2 groats

20 The gowns of a townswoman (*top*) and her daughter were of the best quality cloth.

(£1.08) was spent in providing wax tapers as props. The native Irish, however, preferred the more athletic entertainment of hurling a leather ball. And even the English enjoyed the outdoor pursuits of archery and hunting with falcons.

Schools, language and religion

When Henry VIII closed down the monasteries in the 1530s, it meant that the schools, hospitals, inns for poor travellers and refuges for the old and poor run by the monks also had to close. Even travel was affected since the monasteries had looked after the roads and bridges in their area. Because the Catholic religion was now banned, services were held in secret by the monks who had been turned out of the monasteries. Any wealthy person who did not attend the services of the State Church was fined £20.

In the monastery schools, 'young men and children, both gentlemen's children and others, both of man-kind and woman-kind' had been 'brought up in virtue, learning, and in the English tongue and behaviour'. Ever since the Parliament held at Kilkenny in 1366, the government had ordered that 'every Englishman shall use the English language and be named by an English name', leaving the Irish language as a forbidden subject. In 1537, at the same time as he closed the monastic schools, Henry VIII ordered that children should only be sent to schools where they could learn the 'English tongue, language, order, and condition'. After the monastery schools closed, private schools had to be started for the sons and daughters of merchants.

21 An Irish harper entertaining the guests at a chieftain's otherwise crude feast.

3. The Growth of Towns, 1600-1725

Life in the towns

The town councils employed several workmen whose functions have since gone out of use. The beadle's job was 'to turn strong beggars out of the town, and keep the pigs out of the streets'. He was also required 'to keep the channels of the streets of said town free from filth and dirt, and give notice to the scavenger to carry the same away'. Poor and needy men born in the town were allowed to beg, but had to have leaden tokens fastened to their caps to distinguish them from strange beggars. The beadle's pay for the year amounted to £12, while the scavenger got £16.

The town-crier's job was to walk the town every night in summer at 11 pm, 1 am and 3 am, and in winter at 10 pm, midnight, 2 am and 4 am, giving 'notice of the wind and weather and the time of the night'. The gate-keeper or watchman was to close the gates during winter from 8 pm to 5 am the following morning, but to allow the wicket gates to remain open until 9 pm. The ringer of the bells was to get 22½p a year.

A system of public lighting with lanterns was installed in Dublin in 1697. Cork had none until the eighteenth century. Town clocks were erected, usually at the expense of one of the wealthier citizens, on castle or church walls.

The borough councils continued to be concerned about hygiene. It was

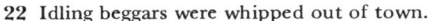

22 Idling beggars were whipped out of town.

31

ruled, for instance, that 'if any butcher leave the garbage of his cattle in the streets or suffer the blood to run in the gutters' he was to be fined 50p. The sale of blown, or bad, meat was forbidden. Instead 'wholesome, sweet and well-ordered shamble meat' was to be sold. Garbage was not to be thrown into the rivers and brewers were ordered not to brew with 'gutter water' in case the beer became infected and gave the town a bad image, as well as making its inhabitants sick.

Public services

In 1656, a public postal service was established to replace the military postal service, and by 1670 post houses were established in the principal towns. For about 4p or 5p letters could be sent to the remotest parts of the country. There was a fine for opening letters, which seems to have been a common occurrence. Travellers on the mail coaches were charged 1½p per mile per horse, payable at every livery station.

The first newspaper in Dublin was printed in 1685. It consisted of a single sheet of folio size paper, printed on both sides. It was in the form of a letter; each number began with the word 'Sir' and resembled the editorial in a modern newspaper. As the newspaper developed, it started 'containing an impartial account of the most material news foreign and domestic'. Advertisements were soon placed in the newspaper by merchants who wanted to make their goods known to customers.

Restaurants

In 1637, the first proper theatre was started in Werburgh Street, Dublin. About this time too, coffee houses and taverns began to appear and provided centres for both eating, drinking and conversation. But Fynes Morrisson, an Englishman who visited Ireland in 1617, did not consider the eating houses very good. He grumbled at the charge of 5p for an 'ordinary' meal.

23 The coffee house was a centre for writers and for conversation.

24 A man enjoying the pleasure of a clay pipe full of tobacco at a country tavern.

The ale was considered good, however, and the whiskey *aquavitae* strong enough to kill or cure a person. In Dublin, where there were only 4,000 families, there were at one time 1,180 alehouses and 91 public brew-houses. In 1633, Christ Church, Dublin, was reported to have had all its cellars turned into 'alehouses and tobacco shops'. In Kilkenny in 1671, licensers, collectors and receivers were appointed under the terms of an act to grant licences for the sale of beer and ale.

Business life

Tobacco seems to have been widely used by this time. Sir Walter Raleigh had introduced it at Youghal, when, so it is said, his housekeeper threw water on him, thinking he was on fire. Certainly, in Kinsale in 1663, the local merchants were concerned about strange traders who 'utter and retail tobacco' in the markets and at their own houses. The stench of tobacco shops frequently drew unflattering comments. By 1655 tobacco, 'taken in short pipes seldom burned', in other words clay pipes, was a great pleasure for most people. A 70-lb (28-kilo) roll cost £3.50.

Tobacco merchants were not the only ones to meet with disapproval. The

25 The merchant's well-stocked shelves brought profits to his ledger.

local merchants of any town still restricted business to suit themselves. Nothing was allowed to be sold in the market until a bell had been rung for the start of business. 'No husters retailing fruit, oysters, turnips, potatoes, basket-butter' were allowed to buy 'before tea in the forenoon on market days, and in the market-place, and on other days for the space of two hours'. This was to prevent 'forestallers' from meeting the country folk before the town merchants, and buying their produce cheaply in order to sell it dearly later. All goods that arrived at the town gates after they were closed were inspected — since the customs house was closed for the evening, such late goods were likely to be smugglers' goods. Finally, bakers were restricted to having one shop, the manchet shop or home. In these regulations lie the origins of the bye-laws which govern street traders, black-market merchandise and the public open markets of great cities today.

Guilds continued to exist. When Cromwell came to rule Ireland under the Protectorate, many members of the older guilds were refused permission, because of their religion, to continue in business or even to live in the towns. During this time, and later under the Restoration, many new guilds came into existence, and old ones were granted new charters. In Cork, for example, the Goldsmiths', Bakers' and Carpenters' guilds were established in 1656, the Coopers' in 1657, and the Wholesalers' and Retailers' in 1691. The Goldsmiths' Guild also emerged in Dublin at this time, although it had had a charter since Tudor times. It included saddlers, bridle-makers, pewterers, plumbers, braziers, glaziers and upholsterers, although it was for their silverwork during Georgian times that the guildsmen later became famous. An Assay Office would determine the quality of the workmanship, and mark approved pieces with the seals of the Assay Office, the maker and the year.

34

Trade

In 1609, the English government confiscated the lands of the Irish chieftains O'Neill and O'Donnell who were suspected of a conspiracy against King James I. To ensure Ulster's future loyalty to the English monarchs, it was decided to introduce English and Scottish settlers, and create new towns as fortified centres. The monarchy owed a considerable amount of money to the wealthy merchant corporations of London. Since these merchants could be expected to be capable of managing the confiscated estates in a business-like manner, large grants of land in Ulster were made to groups of London merchants, the skinners, goldsmiths, fishmongers, salters and drapers. With the help of other planters, as these settlers were called, they built up such towns as Londonderry, Armagh, Draperstown, Coleraine, Enniskillen, Salterstown, Belfast and Newry. These towns were given the right to return members to Parliament.

It was not until the 1680s, however, that Belfast began to develop into the fourth most important port in the country, and a busy market town. Indeed, in 1669, the most important ports, according to the amount of customs revenue collected, were:

Port	%	Port	%
Dublin	40	New Ross ⎫	
Cork	10	Wexford ⎪	
		Dundalk ⎬	1
Waterford ⎫	7	Baltimore ⎪	
Galway ⎭		Sligo ⎭	
Limerick ⎫		Killybegs ⎫	
Kinsale ⎬	5	Dungarvan ⎪	
Youghal ⎭		Donaghadee ⎬	not rated for custom
		Strangford ⎪	
Drogheda ⎫		Coleraine ⎪	
Londonderry ⎬	3	Dingle ⎭	
Carrickfergus ⎭			

The following ship's cargo list is typical of the goods brought from **Bristol** to Irish ports at the beginning of the seventeenth century:

II c of hoppes
di panni (2 rolls) Spanish silke
VI yards levant taffeta
a grosse of penny knyves
II dozen of bokes
VI feltes

Kinsale, in the middle of the century, recorded the arrival into harbour of the 'Virginia trade of 60 sail'.

The merchants of the Irish ports grew wealthy selling butter, salted beef, barrel staves, fish, wool and hides. In Cork, for instance, ten thousand bullocks were slaughtered in 1688, causing the Earl of Orrery to call it the 'ox-slaying' city. Much of the wealth was derived from supplying the fleet which went to the West Indies, and much trade went to France and Spain. However, most of Drogheda's trade in 1683 was with the English ports of Liverpool, Dover, Minehead and Workington, to which it sent wool, linen, yarn, corn, candles, soap, timber, beef, whiskey, and horses. It sent beef, butter, cheese, biscuits and herrings to Cadiz and the Canaries, and beef, malt and tanned hides to Rotterdam. Gradually, Belfast began to trade with the West Indies for sugar, and with America for flax seed and yarn. In 1698, Louis Crommelin brought linen-weaving to Lisburn. The French Huguenots, refugees from Louis XIV, had already begun silk-weaving in Dublin.

Customs houses were built in every port of consequence. In Dublin during the reign of James I, Wellington Quay was set aside for 'erecting cranes and

26 The quay at the Customs House was the only legal place to set goods ashore or to take them on board. Otherwise the king would lose the revenue from customs' duties.

wharves'. Later, Custom House Quay was chosen in 1662 as the only place for landing and handling trade. Similarly, weight houses and ballast offices were built in the ports, and tolls and fees charged for all goods entering and leaving the harbours. An alnager was appointed in each port to weigh cloth to ensure that it was the proper size and quality, and the butter merchants stamped their barrels according to quality.

Money

The Exchanges which were established from 1601 onwards by Queen Elizabeth to regulate the value of money, settled that £1 in English silver was equivalent to £1.50 in Irish. But things did not always run smoothly. War, of course, had a bad effect on the value of money. In Kilkenny in 1652, clipped, devalued coins from England, Spain, the Netherlands, France and other countries were in circulation. Gold coins were minted during the rule of the Confederate government in Kilkenny (1642-48), but both during Cromwell's wars (1649-52), and the Williamite war (1689-91), inferior coinage called gun money and siege money was produced to pay the troops. There was an outcry from the merchants of Dublin in 1722, when the English government granted William Wood, a Wolverhampton ironmaster, the patent to mint small copper coinage for Ireland. Jonathan Swift said 'Wood's halfpence' would ruin the businessmen; he wrote public letters condemning them under the pen name 'Drapier'.

The merchants in Irish towns had themselves been accustomed to minting their own small coinage when required. In Kinsale, in 1652, 1653 and 1654, one hundred pounds' worth, sixty pounds' worth and ten pounds' worth of copper farthings were minted. The value was shown on one side and the year and place of minting on the other. Later, in Dublin and Cork, the merchants issued their own coinage, and also notes and tokens. The butter merchants in Cork followed suit, and even an apothecary in Castle Street, Dublin, issued his own tokens.

There were, of course, plenty of bankers and money-lenders. Benjamin Burton, a banker in Dublin, was considered so reliable and prosperous that the phrase 'as safe as Ben Burton' was used to indicate a wise action. Similarly, Hoare's Bank in Cork was founded by a reputable firm of wine merchants. However, not all bankers were as honest. 'The banks are stairs whereby they climb into a knowledge of the merchant's fullness or want' was a common saying. Jonathan Swift wished for a law 'to hang up half a dozen bankers every year' because, like the banker Damer in Dublin, they were supposed to be charging too much interest and ruining the businessmen and ordinary people.

Houses

The English settlers in Ulster during the Plantation, as this period of deliberate colonisation was termed, were expected to build solid stone houses with a bawn or fortifiable grounds. The houses of their workers were usually like the timber-framed workhouses of contemporary English towns. One village of fifteen houses included two built of stone and lime, but this was unusual. The new town of Belfast was being built in brick at this time, and the house of the merchant John Rothe, in Kilkenny, was made of stone, with oaken ceilings. It had two cobbled courtyards with a private well in one of them.

Sir William Petty, who came to Ireland as a doctor with Cromwell's army, did a survey of the country. He found that, out of 200,000 homes, there were 160,000 mud hovels without a proper hearth or chimney. There were 24,000 homes with one chimney and 16,000 with more than one. There were 164 houses in Dublin with more than 10 chimneys, while the Earl of Meath's house had 27. A tax called the Hearth Tax was imposed which kept down the number of chimneys allowed for each house.

Travel

Many of the roads were still no more than rough tracks. It could take four days to travel from Cork to Limerick, a distance of about fifty miles. In 1612, an Act was passed which ordered the constables and churchwardens of each parish to gather together all the parishioners at Easter to appoint surveyors of the highways. These surveyors called on the landowners to supply free horses and vehicles for six days' labour each year. The labourers were to give six days' labour free. In 1634 this Act was replaced by another which allowed the Grand Jury in the county to levy a rate, the county cess, for roads and bridges. The compulsory labour continued.

The land

Three times during the period from 1600 to 1725, land in Ireland was confiscated and given to planters. In 1587, 480,000 acres (192,000 hectares) in Munster had been confiscated and divided among planters, including Walter Raleigh and the poet Edmund Spenser, on condition that they brought over English farmers, cattle and equipment. They got the land at a rent of a ½p an acre. In Ulster in 1609, 4 million acres (1.6 million hectares) were confiscated and divided among English and Scottish gentlemen and officials. These planters were called 'undertakers' because they undertook to bring tenants over to farm the land, and 'servitors' because they had served King James. Cromwell created a new plantation in the 1650s with about 6.5 million acres (2.6 million hectares) of good land. Finally, after King William defeated King James in Ireland in 1691, 1 million acres (0.4 million hectares) were distributed to William's followers. The ordinary Irish working men and peasants were kept on these planted estates to do the work.

Looking after cattle was the principal employment on the land. When Petty completed his survey for Cromwell, he found that there were 150,000 people looking after cattle, and 100,000 people tilling the land. Most of the open land was being fenced in, although cattle, which formed such an important export, still needed open grazing.

It was only natural that the food of the people should have been 'milk, sweet and sour, thick and thin' and 'bread in cakes . . . potatoes from August till May; mussels, cockles and oysters near the sea; eggs and butter, made very rancid by keeping in bogs. As for flesh they seldom eat it.'

27 Good roads were a blessing to the traveller, and brought benefits to the merchants.

Household goods

In 1685, an Irish nobleman listed his important possessions as five feather beds, bolsters, rugs and blankets costing £8, a cabinet at £2, and a great looking-glass valued at £2. The four-poster, or standing bed, had been used since 1600. There was also a pallet placed on a truckle-bed or 'flock' bed for the servant who slept in the master's room. Sheets were made from calico, canvas and holland. In the room was a 'linnercy cupboard'.

A gentleman's list of goods in 1633 included:

In the Kitchen. Pewter. 1 dozen and half of old pewter dishes, great and small, 6 saucers, 3 old chamber pots and two candlesticks . . . 1 old brass pot, 2 kettles, 3 skillets, and one ladle and skimmer. Iron. 2 iron pots, 2 spits, 2 small pair of andirons, 2 pair of pothooks, 1 pair of tongs, 1 gridiron, one old frying pan. 2 olde chests and a chair.

Another gentleman in Bandon, Co Cork, had in his kitchen a number of items like: 'Half a dozen of joined stools . . . Half a dozen of plain green cushions . . . A dozen of silver spoons . . . a small silver salt . . . A silver beer bowl'. Other items in the house included: '1 dozen of old diaper napkins, two towels, and 1 table-cloth of the same, 13s 4d. 10 old cotton napkins, 2 table-cloths, and rug, iiili. A table, with a coarse say carpet thereon, 5s'.

The poor

At the Charter or Bluecoat schools, poor boys were taught a trade. By 1705, Dublin already had a workhouse, which was the first building for the poor to

39

28 An oaken four-poster bed (circa 1600), carved for a gentleman's home.

be paid for by compulsory taxation. Taxes were placed on items such as sedan chairs and hackney coaches. Part of the workhouse was set aside for a Foundling Hospital. The unwanted infants were placed in a basket on the door, the bell was rung and the door revolved inwards.

In Cork, however, Skiddy's Almshouse for the poor of the city had been built much earlier, in 1620, and the custom of giving bread to the deserving poor of the city is still carried on today. In 1628, in Galway, the merchants of the town considered that charitable donations to the needy would be 'a hundred-fold rewarded, both in this and the other world'. They ordered, therefore, that poor widows should be given £10 from the city revenue, in memory of the 'widow who put her two small coins into the church collection in Christ's Jerusalem. The church provided the coffins for the dead paupers.

Education, language and religion

Since the rejection of the Catholic faith by Henry VIII, Catholic schools were not permitted in Ireland. In 1615, the king's officials came to Galway and discovered 'a public schoolmaster named Lynch, placed there by the citizens'. It was obvious that the parents had started to pay for a school of their own, and 'great numbers of scholars' were coming to the school from the province of Connaught and from the merchants' and landowners' families in Leinster and Munster. The schoolmaster must have been a good teacher because the king's officials said 'his scholars profited under him'. He taught them 'verses and orations', in other words poetry and other literature, as well as public speaking. But despite his good work he was forbidden to teach, and to make sure that he obeyed he was put on bail of £400. As a result parents had to send their children abroad to school, which was expensive. The will of a Galway merchant stated that his 'son, Patrick, who is to become a scholar', was to be paid '£20 sterling when he is ready and determined to go beyond seas to study' and £10 for every year of his studies.

Diocesan schools were set up to cater for the Protestant children. In 1611, the Corporation of Limerick paid the rent for the school, and the shops and clergy paid the master's salary. Almshouses were started, and many of them had schools for the poor as well. One wealthy merchant set aside £12 a year for a schoolmaster 'for instructing twenty boys in reading, writing and arithmetic'. £10 a year kept the school supplied with books and paper. Boys at these schools were later apprenticed to different trades, and a certain sum was set aside to pay for their fees as apprentices.

Many of the charitable schools for poor Protestant children were called Bluecoat schools because the boys were obliged to wear a 'uniform dress of blue and yellow'. In 1721, £20 was allotted for one of these schools, where 'twenty boys are taught to read, write, keep accounts, and to sing in the cathedral'. Again, a sum of £4 was put aside for the apprenticeship fee of each boy. Other charitable schools were known as Charter schools or Free schools. The boys from them were set to work on the school farms or looms. The children were 'ill-fed, ill-clad, and ill-taught; sickly, pale, miserable objects'. Those who complained were beaten.

29 This was the home of a Catholic merchant, once Lord Mayor of Galway, who was expelled for being a Catholic. Such a merchant would have been wealthy enough to send his children abroad for education.

Even after the defeat of the native Irish chieftains at Kinsale in 1603, Irish poets were still patronised by certain chieftains like the McCarthys of Munster. Many of the old families of Norman stock, such as the Butlers of Kilcash, Co Tipperary, also gave patronage to the scholars of Gaelic literature. The finest work of Irish scholars was, however, the collection of Irish manuscripts by four Franciscan friars from Donegal which led to the writing of the *Annals of the Four Masters*. In the English language, the greatest contemporary work was *The Faerie Queen*, written by Edmund Spenser at his plantation home at Kilcoleman Castle, Fermoy, Co Cork.

The Penal Laws, as they were called, were a series of restrictions on both the religion and education of Irish Catholics after the defeat of King James in 1691. But throughout Europe at this time, politics interfered in religious matters, and the Scottish Presbyterians who had settled in Ulster in 1609 were not allowed to worship in peace either. Many of the Presbyterian ministers travelled with their congregations to America, to find religious freedom there.

Indeed, because so many of the bishops and deans of the State Church cared more for wealth than for their duties, many of the Protestants in Ireland also suffered from lack of spiritual care. There were not enough clergymen available because the curates were paid so badly that none of them could stay very long in any one parish. Jonathan Swift complained bitterly about this neglect of the congregations.

If Presbyterians emigrated to America, French Protestants, or Huguenots fled to Ireland from France to escape the persecution of Louis XIV, as did the Palatines, German Protestants, in the eighteenth century. The Quaker Society of Friends had already been formed in Ireland in 1655.

4. Prosperity and Poverty, 1725-1815

The poor

The living conditions of people in the countryside and towns did not change much, although trade brought the country prosperity, and the landowners became very wealthy and lived in style. The food of the poor was still 'potatoes, milk and herrings, with oaten bread in summer'. Arthur Young, the English traveller, said that the poor 'have an absolute bellyfull of potatoes, and the children eat them as plentifully as they like'. They preferred oaten bread to wheaten bread. The poor also tried to forget their sorrows by drinking cheap whiskey which made them weak and liable to fever. Fever hospitals were finally set up in Dublin at the beginning of the nineteenth century, and the squalid houses and alleys cleaned up to help prevent epidemics.

Some 35,000 vagrants wandered the countryside. After the harvest had been gathered, the labourers drifted into the cities to beg. In 1743, there was a proposal to reduce the number of beggars in Kilkenny by licensing the blind and decrepit, and setting others to do spinning in the workhouse. In 1766, it was proposed that a poorhouse should be established in every county. These poorhouses were divided into one house for the old, one house for the sick, and a punishment or correction house for wandering beggars. The paupers had to wear a badge on their clothes. The beggars were punished with hard labour; the

30 Whiskey was readily available for all in the numerous taverns of Belfast.

letter 'V' was marked on their arm with gunpowder for a first offence, with a '2' added for a second offence.

Many of the beggars ended up in Dublin's Newgate prison. Footpads, or thieves, were taken straight from the dock to the gallows. The prisons were overcrowded and filthy — the clergyman who had to ask for his quarter's salary for visiting the sick and condemned in Newgate probably deserved his money.

The shortage of food caused many riots. In Cork, in 1728, the bad harvest caused a desperate mob to break open the cellars belonging to the mayor. Later the butchers who started selling the entrails of cattle abroad caused a riot among the poor of the city, who depended on this offal for food. In Kilkenny, in June 1768, there were oatmeal riots.

More trouble came when workmen were put out of work by bad trade. In Dublin in 1734, the weavers in the Coombe Street area attacked the shops of the woollen drapers who were importing English cloth. The weavers also objected to the introduction, in 1780, of gig mills and swivel looms that further threatened their jobs. In 1785, the Rector of St Paul's Church, Dublin, complained about a combination among the journeymen sawyers to extort unreasonable wages from their masters. Four employees were attacked for not joining in this early form of trade union. Asking for higher wages was considered 'injurious to the infant manufactures' of Ireland. It was scarcely surprising, then, that two journeymen coopers who downed tools in Cork in 1772 were whipped along the main street.

Conditions for some workmen were fairly good, however. Labourers in the Cork slaughterhouses earned about 5½p a day, and as much bread, beef and beer as they could eat or drink. Their fringe benefits included 7 lbs (3 kilos) of offal a week for their families. Masons' and carpenters' labourers got about 4½p a day, carpenters 12½p, sawyers 7½p and porters over 1p.

The servants of the landowners were, in their own way, better off. A coachman got £6 a year in 1700, as well as his uniform or livery, a hat, shoes, and stockings. By 1750, he was getting £10.50 as well as 35p expenses when his master was in Dublin. The gardener got £13.65 a year and the cook £10. The housemaid received £3 and the pantry boy £2. Ordinary men servants got between £3 and £4. Disobedient servants however, were whipped and caned.

The lives of the wealthy

The Georgian period in Ireland was an age of splendour for the landowners. They had beautiful country mansions and town houses. Their balls, their carriages, their meals and their retinues of servants were very expensive, but were supported by the high rents paid by the tenants on their estates. The value of the landowners' rents varied from £1,000 on the small estates to £20,000 a year on the Duke of Leinster's lands. Over £1¼ million was sent to England each year to the landowners who preferred living there. These absentee landlords were not very popular — they extracted wealth from the country without spending any of it on improving the farms or supporting the merchants.

Like most of the other landowners, however, the absentee landlords leased their estates to middlemen, and it was these men who were responsible for the burden of rents on the tenants. The middlemen would sub-let small parts of the leased estate at enormous profits, often, indeed, charging the same rent for a portion of the estate as they themselves paid for the whole. The discontented tenants formed secret societies called Whiteboys and Levellers to attack the houses, crops and cattle of those landowners who increased their rents or enclosed the common land for cattle. Cattle meant less ground on which the peasants could grow their potatoes, and less employment in sowing and reaping. The Whiteboys were so called because they used to wear white shirts or sheets as masks for identification at night. Levellers, on the other hand, gained their name by knocking down fences. Similar societies called the Hearts of Oak and the Hearts of Steel existed in Ulster. Most societies had a leader who signed himself fictitiously as 'Captain Right' or some such gallant name.

The actions of the secret societies usually had little effect on the wealthy landowners, except when they called on the government to supply troops in order to teach the midnight marauders a lesson. The wealthy landowners spent their days gambling, duelling, travelling abroad on grand tours of Europe, attending the Irish Parliament, visiting the theatres in Dublin, where the composer, Handel, conducted *The Messiah,* or resting at the fashionable spa of Mallow. Their interest in both gambling and horse-racing gave rise to the steeplechase, so-called because of a chase across open country and ditches to the steeple of Doneraile, Co Cork.

But most of their time was spent creating magnificent stately homes and gardens. Lord Orrery, at the beginning of the eighteenth century, spoke of the fine banqueting houses he had at Caledon. But the greatest buildings came after 1750, when mansions like Carton and Castletown in Co Kildare, Castlecoole in Co Fermanagh, Westport House in Mayo, Adare Manor in Limerick, and Lissadell in Co Sligo, began to appear.

31 The wealthy landowners spared no expense when building their stately homes in the countryside.

32 Portraits and lavish furnishings added to the elegance of a country mansion's drawing-room.

Squalor and splendour

The cabins of the peasants were 'scarcely distinguishable from a dunghill'. They were made from 'mud kneaded with straw'. The cattle and the people lived together inside these poor cabins. The sum total of their furniture consisted of 'a pot, a stool, a few wooden vessels, and a broken bottle'. In the town tenements, one could find 'from 10 to 16 persons, of all ages and sexes, in a room not 15 feet square, stretched on a wad of filthy straw, swarming with vermin, and without any covering, save the wretched rags that constituted their wearing apparel'. For this one room, a rent of between 5p and 10p a week was charged for each person.

In sharp contrast to this squalor, there was the luxury of the mansions belonging to the rich. The mansion of the Marquess of Downshire at Hillsborough, Co Down, was described in 1780 as having a frontage of specially imported Bath stone, with Ionic columns supporting the pediment. It had three storeys and a basement.

Robert Adam was the fashionable designer of furniture and fireplaces at this time. Mahogany began to replace oak as the most sought-after timber, and walnut was also popular. Plaster mouldings were used to decorate ceilings instead of timber, and plaster on the walls permitted the use of rich heavy wallpapers.

Narrow, wrought iron fireplaces began to replace the old open hearths. This meant that the numerous fires needed to heat such large buildings no longer required such cumbersome chimney-stacks. As well as native Kilkenny, Cork and Connemara marbles, white marble was imported from Italy. The marble was used for the sweeping staircases that rose from the great entrance halls, and also, in Regency furniture, to cover rosewood tables.

The library was an important room in a stately mansion. But the most important was the drawing room, which was the centre-piece in every house. Drawing rooms were lavishly furnished with damask, velvet and silk drapes, gilded couches and portraits — they were the scene of elegant conversation and social entertainment.

Silverware and Delft earthenware were very important items in a rich household. Irish silversmiths provided the table of a landowner with the following items — a pear-shaped teapot on four legs, an oval tray, spoons, tongs, a tea cannister, a sugar bowl with a lid, a jug with a lid, and candlesticks. Decorative country scenes were engraved on the silver. Blue, sepia, purple or white Irish pottery with a Chinese flower design made up the range of Delft in the mansion. Cut-glass decanters and claret jugs moulded in Belfast, Dublin, Cork, Newry or Waterford added to the splendour of the tables of the wealthy.

33 The stage coach provided reliable and fairly comfortable travel to and from the busy towns.

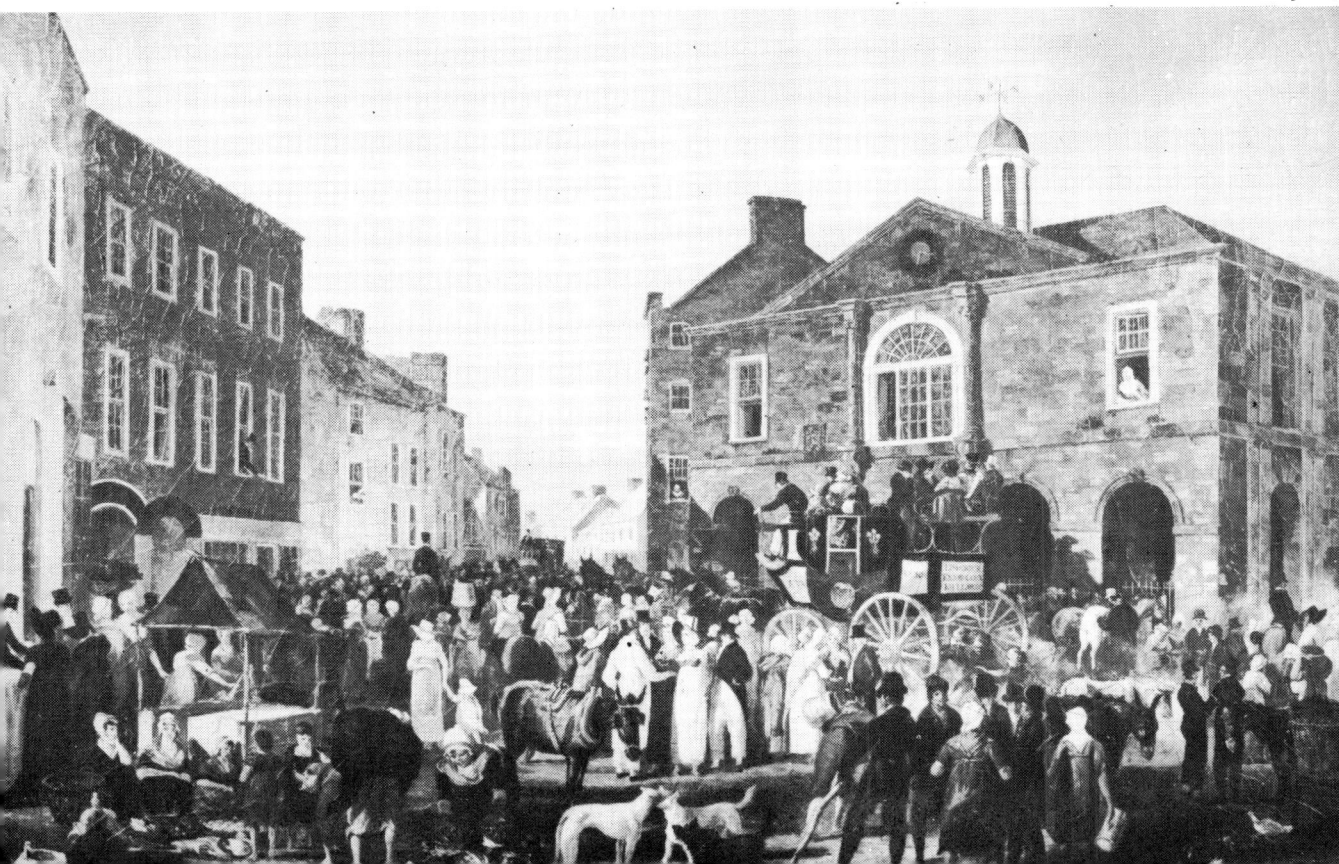

34 The country inn also provided the traveller with some comforts.

Transport

As early as 1730, stage-coaches were already running from Dublin to all the principal towns and cities of Ireland. They carried five passengers, four inside and one outside, and were an improvement on previous transport. In 1711, the Archbishop of Tuam considered that 'two or three days are required to rest on the road' to Dublin.

In 1729, turnpikes were established. Gates were placed across the roads at certain points, and tolls were charged on every vehicle passing through. The money was supposed to be used to improve the roads. But, on account of 'several hollow ways and of the many and heavy carriages frequently passing through the same', the roads in many parts were 'impassable for waggons, carts, cars, and carriages, and very dangerous for travellers'. The tolls charged give an idea of the type of traffic on the roads:

For every coach, chariot, berlin, chaise, chair or calash drawn by six or more horses, 5½p

For every coach, chariot, berlin, chaise, or calash, drawn by less than six but more than two horses, 2½p

For every coach, chariot, berlin, chaise or calash drawn by two horses or mules, 1½p

For every wagon, wain, car, cart or carriage or burthen or other carriage with four wheels drawn by four or more beasts, 5½p

For every horse, mule or ass, laden or unladen and not drawing, ½p

In 1760, Grand Juries were asked to make presentments or charges on the districts they thought required roads. Since it was mainly landlords who sat on the Grand Juries, many of the roads were arranged to suit the convenience of these landowners. The result was that the roads often took the longest rather than the shortest route. The importance of having good roads for the mail coaches led to improvements after 1784.

The vehicles in the towns included sedan chairs — a box-like carriage on poles carried by two men, one in front and one behind. These could be hired by people who did not own their own. 5p for the first hour, about 3½p for each hour after that, and 2½p for waiting were the charges for these first taxis. A calash was a two-wheeled carriage drawn by one or more horses, and driven by so-called Noddy Boys. The driving of carts and carriages was even then a danger to pedestrians.

The first canal in Ireland went from Lough Neagh, in Portadown, to Newry. It was used to bring coal down to the boats in Dublin. The Grand and Royal Canals running from Dublin to the Shannon brought grain to the city. But it was a slow form of travel. The instructions given to a merchant's servant who was to travel from Athy, Co Kildare, along the Grand Canal to Dublin, were most precise. He was 'to be met at Sallins by Larry who is to have 1 shilling (5p) for the Turnpike which he will have to pay at Athy, coming out, and at Kilcullen Bridge'. He was 'to give the horses a stone of oats at Dadd's in Naas,

35 The sedan chair allowed the ladies of Dublin to travel through the streets in gracious dignity.

and to put them up in Dublin at the Wheatsheaf in Thomas Street, near James's Gate' and was expected to need 'about 19 or 20 pence (7½ or 8p) for oats'.

The improvement of towns

Although Dublin was the principal city in Ireland, and most roads led to it, Belfast and Cork were also becoming increasingly important. But what were conditions like for the town and city dwellers?

In 1761, a Pipe Water Company was given powers to provide reservoirs and conduits. In 1743, nearly twenty years earlier, a merchant in Kilkenny was contracting for the supply of 'water-pipes' for the city of Waterford and again, in 1761, with an engineer in Cork for the supply of 'marble pipes'.

However, it was in the city streets that the greatest improvements came — the Wide Street Commissioners of the period were the forerunners of today's town planners. The streets were so narrow that two carriages could not pass, and so filthy that carriages were often knocked over by heaps of dirt. The great streets of modern Dublin were planned during this period, particularly during the time of the Free Irish Parliament from 1780 to 1800. Grafton Street, Dame Street, Westmoreland Street and Sackville Street were created as gracious thoroughfares. Other towns and cities copied Dublin's example, and a Mall, or gracious street, was built in Cork, Sligo, Westport and Lismore. Even the smallest towns and villages were often ordered around a central green called a 'Diamond'.

Besides widening and paving the streets, and building great stone bridges across the River Liffey, attention was also paid to creating great squares of Georgian houses. Fitzwilliam Square, Merrion Square, Mountjoy Square and others, resembled the similar squares in London. Pleasure gardens were provided, like Stephen's Green and the Rotunda Gardens, for teas and musical performances. College Green, in front of the Irish Parliament, and Trinity

36 The wide streets of Georgian Dublin were intended both to add distinction to the city and to avoid the danger and disease that lurked in the narrow streets of the older districts.

37 Inside the Irish parliament, 1790 — Crowds gather in the public gallery to hear the fine speeches.

College were the focal point for all Dublin. The city was also provided with splendid public buildings. Gandon, the architect and builder, designed the new Customs House, the Four Courts, and the House of Parliament in College Green.

In 1729, an attempt was made to provide public lighting in all towns by placing lanterns at intervals of 22 yards (20 metres) in the more public streets, and 33 yards (30 metres) in the narrow, darker streets. Later, mayors were permitted to charge the sum of 5p on each household in a parish for this service. By 1815, Dublin had six thousand lights hung on ornamental iron lamp-posts. But by then the old oil lanterns were out of date, and due to be replaced by gas lanterns, with which Cork and Dublin were both provided in 1819.

Hospitals

Hospitals were gradually being built for the sick, although they were stuffy, overcrowded, and lacked the medical knowledge of today. Dean Swift gave a large sum of money for the care of lunatics, and a special hospital was set up to look after mothers and infants. The Meath Hospital was provided by the Earl of Meath to care for the health of weavers. In 1765, county infirmaries were established throughout the country. As a result of the 1741 famine, there had been widespread starvation and disease; the danger of an epidemic was too real for the whole community to neglect the establishment of hospitals. The cesspools and refuse sewers outside each door, and the slaughter of cattle in the narrow city streets were other reasons why hospitals were so essential. Even today, however, the apathy of public officials permits the health hazard of sewerage effluent in rivers, lakes and the sea.

Selling

Merchants continued to use their own coins, tokens and notes. Many private bankers set up their own banks and printed so much paper money without proper security that they went bankrupt and ruined many businessmen. At other times, there was a scarcity of money, 'owing to the banks stopping payment'. Shopkeepers weighed coins to make sure they were not forgeries. The sheriff in Cork found a potter and his wife making counterfeit money in a garret. Frequently there was a shortage of small change. One customer in a shop had to wait for his change while the shopkeeper searched the neighbourhood for it in vain. In 1782, however, the Irish Parliament decided to regulate the currency by starting the Bank of Ireland. This was in the interests of businessmen and landowners. It prevented fraud by bankers, by making them liable for full payment of their notes.

Shopkeepers advertised their goods then just as they do now. A dyer advertised that he 'hath lately brought from London a new printing roll for stamping cambrics, calaminoes, German serges, serge-denims'. To add to his service, he told prospective customers that he 'likewise dyes and scours new and old silks of all sorts, both which he will perform at a reasonable rate'. A hatter claimed that he made 'ruffed hats of the newest fashions for Ladies and Gentlemen', and had 'supplied himself with a choice parcel of beaver for that use'. He was prepared to sell at 'the lowest profit'. A glover in Cork stated that there was 'just arrived from Dublin a choice parcel of the following goods — viz. cotton and linen checks, with all sort of the newest fashion stripes. Likewise buckrams, glaz'd linens, with a choice parcel of Irish handkerchiefs with some new fashion Scotch handkerchiefs' and with 'all sorts of linen drapery too tedious to insert'. The apothecary or chemist, on the other hand, advertised 'Essence of Peppermint — a most excellent remedy for the colic, gripes, hard drinking or sea sickness. Price 4s 10d half, the large, 2s 8d half, the

small bottle, with directions'. The hardware merchants had a 'new deal yard where may be had choice of timber, deals, scantling and slats of all sizes'.

Besides the shopkeepers, there were also street hawkers. The Dublin street song about Molly Malone, who 'wheeled her wheelbarrow, through streets broad and narrow, crying cockles and mussels, alive, alive o', represents the street cry of the fish-hawkers.

They shouted: 'Fresh Herrings, large Dublin Bay Herrings alive here — Here's a large fresh cod alive, here's large soles or plaices, alive, or fine Boyne salmon.'

The turf-seller called out: 'Buy the dry turf; buy turf, buy the dry turf — Here's the dry bog-a-wood — Here's the chips to light the fire; maids.'

The butter-seller cried his wares: 'Fresh butter, fresh butter, here — Here's the new milk hot from the cow, maids, come for your milk — Here's fine rich cream'.

Every year the guilds of Dublin put on what would be now considered a trade display. Each guild travelled on a carriage drawn by horses and showing the work they did. The weavers wore wigs of different colours and threw ribbons to the crowd; the hosiers had a loom weaving stockings; the millers and bakers had men dressed up in wheatsheaves; the butchers wore hides with long horns, and brandished knives; while the smiths had a working forge, and the shoemakers carried a golden slipper on a cushion. The Weavers' Hall and the Tailors' Hall were the centres for these guilds.

Weavers

Producing cloth was an important industry in Ireland. It was particularly important in Ulster, especially around Belfast. The weavers worked in their own homes and brought the cloth to linen-markets, such as the one at Lisburn. The cambrics were sold first. Then, when the clock struck eleven, the drapers jumped onto a stone stand and the weavers flocked about them with their

53

pieces. There was tough bargaining for the last penny or halfpenny extra. The drapers' clerks stood by them and wrote their masters' names on the pieces of cloth bought, together with the price. The clerks handed the pieces back to the sellers, and waited for the weavers to bring the cloth to the drapers' shops. Another hour was spent there measuring the cloth and paying for it — but always by cash. The bleaching of the cloth was very important. The bleacher also took out 'all stains, mildews, what kind soever'.

Trade

The Port News in every newspaper was watched with interest to see the comings and goings of ships and the cargoes they carried. A typical item was: 'Wind W. Arrived. *John and Mary*. Seville, fruit and wine for Dublin. Sailed. *Syren* of St Maloes, Bordeaux, beef. *Speedwell* of Punthally, Roley, Cheshire, tallow and tanned hides.'

Trade was so important that the carved figures representing the river gods on the Customs House were an advertisement for the industries of the various areas of Ireland. The carving of the Suir stood for the centre of the woollen industry; the Bann stood for the linen and distilling industry at Coleraine; and the Lagan stood for Belfast's linen industry. The Blackwater was there as a symbol of the apple-growing along that river. The figures of Neptune, Wealth, Mercury and Industry on the Customs House stood for the general importance of both trade and travel to the country.

Education, language and religion

The Penal Laws imposed as restrictions on Catholics and Presbyterians alike after 1691 were closely connected with the desire of a minority of State Church landowners to preserve their political, social and economic supremacy. But, as interest in religion declined with the influence of Voltaire, Diderot and Rousseau in France, so the Penal Laws were relaxed. In 1795, when Maynooth College was established by the government for the education of Catholic clergymen, most of the restrictions had gone, although the independent spirit of the Ulster Presbyterians resented the lack of proper parliamentary representation brought about by the Penal Laws. Most of them had obtained a good education in Edinburgh, and were aware of injustice. Furthermore, they had a strong religious fervour that contrasted with the indifference that John Wesley found elsewhere among Protestants in Ireland. The Catholics meanwhile had been obliged to attend religious services secretly wherever they could arrange them.

In 1704, Catholic schools were forbidden. While many parents smuggled their children to the continent for education, other secret schools were established. They were known as hedge schools, because the students were often taught under the shelter of a hedge by a wandering schoolmaster, who taught for a few weeks and then travelled on to another place. There are records of a hedge school in 1777 which had better shelter, but even this one had a hole in the roof for a chimney. The fees were 2p per week, and a halfpenny (¼p) for dancing. The door of the school was taken off its hinges

39 The Catholics were forced to hold their religious services in the open, by the sea in this instance. The rough-and-ready wooden chapel on wheels was able to be moved away in secret.

and laid on the clay floor for the dancing lessons. The hedge schoolmaster taught reading, writing and book-keeping. Near the coast, schoolmasters also taught navigation. Many of the schoolmasters were in fact poets, and could read Latin and Greek. One such tattered poet went into a bookshop in Cork and was handling a copy of Virgil. The bookseller, thinking he was ignorant, mockingly said he would give him the book if he could read it. This the beggar did, and kept the book. Needless to say, these schoolmaster poets taught and wrote in the language of the peasants — Irish.

Although the Presbyterians got an education in law, science and business in Edinburgh, like the Catholics they could neither become students nor get scholarships at Trinity College, Dublin. Many great writers in the English language had connections with Trinity College. Edmund Burke who wrote *Reflections on the French Revolution* and Oliver Goldsmith, author of *The Deserted Village* and *The Vicar of Wakefield*, were but two of them. Earlier, Jonathan Swift had written *Gulliver's Travels*, and the renowned English playwrights of the eighteenth century, Richard Brinsley Sheridan, George Farquhar and William Congreve, all had well-established Irish connections.

5. The Famine Years, 1815-1850

Farming

In 1800, Ireland had a population of about 5 million. By 1821, it had grown to 6.5 million, and by 1841 there were 8 million people. Although there were 14 million acres (5.6 million hectares) of land suitable for farming, 75 per cent of the people in fact lived on tiny farms of less than 5 acres (2 hectares). These little farms were usually on the poorest ground, since the large farmers controlled the best of the land. So, for most of the people, life was no more than a hard struggle to exist. If bad weather caused the crops, chiefly potatoes, to fail, the result was a disastrous famine, which of course affected the poor most severely. The famine came in 1845; by 1850, the population had fallen by over two million.

The land was owned by landlords who charged the people enormous rents for the privilege of living on the farms. These entries from one landlord's account book for 1833 show how they made their money:

Date	Money received	£	s	d
Jan 10	Recd from Tenants	375	13	6
Feb 6	Recd do do	89	9	7½
	Recd cow's fat & hide	1	16	0
	Recd for grazing	5	12	0
Feb 12	Recd for Butter sold	4	19	4
March 4	Recd from Redmond's tenants	282	13	5½
May 3	Recd from interest debentures	43	15	0
June 17	Recd for wool sold	16	18	11
July 31	Recd for wool sold 1832	8	3	1
Sept 18	Recd for wheat sold	4	8	6
Oct 23	Recd from Redmond's tenants	302	16	11
Dec 16	Recd for Interest stock 3½ per cent	43	15	0

Together with other rents and sales, the total income for the year was £2,613 14s 0½d (£2,613.70½); the bulk of this came from the tenants' rents.

Many of the landlords did not live in Ireland, and instead allowed agents and middlemen to manage their estates. These absentee landlords seldom cared how the people existed as long as they received their rents. The middlemen often charged very high rents, known as rack-rents. Tenants who could not pay were cruelly evicted, or had their cows, corn and household furniture taken by the sheriff. This confiscation was referred to as a distraint, and the bailiffs who knocked down the houses and the drivers who drove away the cattle were hated by the people.

40 The bogs supplied fuel as well as potato-ground for the Irish crofters

The high price of corn during the Napoleonic Wars (1792-1815) encouraged farmers to till more and more ground. Labourers were encouraged to grow a crop of potatoes on the rough land to prepare it for the corn crop. The farmer also had the advantage of being able to use these labourers to work his farm without payment, since the wages he should have paid were charged as rent for the potato ground. These labourers who squatted on the farmer's land and used the rough boggy ground, or conacre, for eleven months of the year were known as cottiers. Other labourers called spalpeens wandered through the countryside from spring to the end of the harvest trying to earn money to rent a patch of conacre. Many of the spalpeens or migratory labourers went to Scotland, Wales and England for work.

Much of the farmland was divided up in the rundale system, so that each peasant farmer had a strip of corn under cultivation in one place, alongside the corn strips of other peasants, and a strip of grazing land or potato ground some distance away. If anyone sowed his crop too late, or neglected the weeds on his own strip, it affected all the neighbouring crops. The cattle had to be kept away booleying, or at summer pasture, as long as the crops were in the ground.

The potatoes were the most important crop. First the grass, heather or furze on top of the sod was burned, to act as a fertiliser. Then lazy beds or drills were made for the seed potatoes. The lazy bed was simply a layer of dung spread on the flat earth with the seed potatoes put in it, and the earth shovelled over it from furrows on each side.

57

The lives of the peasants

The poor people depended entirely for their food on the lumper, a large potato. It grew plentifully and was very nutritious. The potatoes were eaten four times a day, roasted, boiled, made into potato cakes and boxty bread, or flavoured with salt or herrings if these were available. Their drink was always milk. During the summer months when the old potatoes were finished and the new potatoes not yet ready, the people ate cabbage or even sorrel and cresses. Shell-fish and dillisk, and edible seaweed, provided extra food for people who lived along the sea coast. Meat was rarely eaten, and when it was they were very careful not to tell the landlord's agent, in case he raised the rent. One boy, when asked by the agent, said he ate a piece of goose a long time ago, so suggesting the scarcity of meat in his home. The traditional pig kept by most families and fattened on the surplus potatoes was used to pay the rent and debts. In remote areas, any surplus grain that could not be taken to market because of the lack of roads, was made into illegal whiskey or poteen.

Some people lived in scattered collections of houses, often only one-roomed cabins made from mud and thatched with straw in which three generations of

41 A one-roomed cabin was often the only shelter for an entire family.

42 The thatched Irish cabins were usually very narrow. It was believed to be unlucky to build them wide.

the family, a pig and maybe even the cow all slept together at night. The cabins were always longer than they were wide because of a superstitious belief that to build them wider would reduce the size of the family.

Many people, however, lived in even worse circumstances. They sheltered in ditches or under turf-banks with rough roofs of furze over their heads. The houses of the weavers in Northern Ireland were rather better than elsewhere in the country because they earned money from spinning and weaving as well as from farming. But the homes of the weavers were also their workshops, which was a disadvantage.

Poverty, the workhouse and the famine
Work was scarce in Ireland, and even when it could be found wages were often only 2½p a day. This, and the fact that the potatoes often either withered away in the ground or were insufficient to feed the population, caused terrible poverty in the countryside. Families of labourers travelled the roads starving, or dependent on the charity of people who were not much better off than themselves. When landlords and large farmers realised that sheep and cattle earned them more money than either peasant labour or rents, they drove the peasants off their estates, so increasing the number of beggars on the road.

Eventually, in 1839, the government decided to establish a Poor Law system like the one operating in England, under the mistaken apprehension that beggars were beggars because they chose to be idle, and that harsh conditions in the workhouses would discourage such idleness. The money for keeping the poor in the workhouses was to be raised by the Poor Rate, a local tax on land. But the government also failed to realise that this would eventually beggar the

59

43 The spinning wheel could be worked outside the home in good weather to supplement the family income.

landlords as well, because there were no industries in Ireland, as there were in England, to drain off the surplus poor labourers.

The whole of Ireland was divided into 130 Poor Law Unions, each with a workhouse similar to the one in which Oliver Twist had to ask for more porridge. The people disliked the workhouse because it was a symbol of shame and disgrace. However, when the potato crop was blighted in 1845, and the potatoes rotted in the ground because of the hot, damp weather, the hunger of the people drove them to seek shelter in the workhouses.

Families going into the workhouses were broken up. Fathers and sons were put in the men's quarters, and mothers and daughters in the women's quarters. Many families never saw each other alive again — the overcrowded conditions caused disease and death among those already weakened by hunger. Corpses were carried out on carts day after day, to be thrown into mass pauper graves and covered with lime. Others were collected from along the roadsides, under bridges and from in their cabins. Dogs ate the bodies of those whom nobody had buried. Because of the danger of fever, corpses were often left in the cabins which were then knocked down on them as a sort of tomb.

At last, with more and more people wandering the countryside searching for nettles to eat or draining the blood from cattle, some grain was sent to the country by Sir Robert Peel, the British Prime Minister. This was Indian meal, a hard-shelled grain grown in America. At first, it could neither be milled nor cooked properly in Ireland. Furthermore, because it was thought that handing it out free to the starving people would be interfering with ordinary business life, the Indian meal had to be sold to the people through the shops. The money to buy this meal from the shopkeepers had to be earned by building roads, piers, and other public works. But both Sir Robert Peel and Lord John Russell, a later British Prime Minister, forgot that starving people cannot work, and that there were few shops in western Ireland. Eventually the government had to hand out the Indian meal directly to the people. By that late stage, however, thousands had died, despite the efforts of charitable people like the Society of Friends to provide soup-kitchens for the hungry.

Emigration

The government, as well as many landlords, often argued that the surplus population of Ireland would have to be sent to Canada, the United States or Australia. There had, indeed, been emigration before the famine. In the 1830s, shipowners, anxious to have some kind of cargo in their timber-carrying ships on the return journey to America, lowered fares to a price which farmers and even labourers could afford if they sold their belongings. Many of the shipowners and captains, however, were unscrupulous, and carried too many passengers in too little space, and with insufficient food or water.

During the worst years of the famine, some landlords took advantage of the situation to clear their estates of paupers, on the pretext of doing so for the well-being of the tenants. Ships that were scarcely seaworthy were packed with passengers who were to be taken no farther than Quebec, Montreal or New York. Many of the ships sank at sea, but even on those that reached America many had died during the voyage, or arrived in a strange land without money and stricken with fever. One landlord was shot by the boyfriend of a girl sent to her death on one such coffin ship.

Traditional entertainments

Despite the hard life led by most people, they still had a great capacity for enjoying themselves. The girls with their red flannel petticoats and the boys with their knee-breeches and swallow-tailed coats danced at the patterns on feast days, and a piper was always sure of a welcome when he visited a village.

44 The piper was made welcome by the village lads in their swallow-tailed coats and knee-breeches.

45 A hurling match played between rival parishes. The glory of a parish was judged by its victory on the playing field.

St Stephen's Day was always an occasion for merriment, when 'wren boys' or 'straw boys' carried the body of a wren around in a holly bush, and groups of mummers acted out stories and songs. Weddings and funeral wakes were both occasions for entertainment. Indeed the wake, with its food, clay pipes, song and dance, was a pagan form of sending the dead soul on its journey to eternity.

Faction fights between rival groups or gangs from different parishes often broke out on fair days, with shillelaghs, or blackthorn sticks, used as weapons. Many of these factions were also secret societies, and gloried in colourful titles like the Shanavests and Caravats, because of the coloured waistcoats or neckerchiefs that they wore.

In Belfast cock-fights were popular with the poor. The weaving girls entertained themselves by visiting each other's homes, and singing and talking to each other while working at the spindle. Such a visit was called a keating.

Education, language and religion

The religious discrimination of the Penal Laws, which had been relaxed by 1793, was finally ended in 1829. This was due to the efforts of Daniel O'Connell, the political leader of the Irish Catholics, who persuaded the government of the United Kingdom, and particularly the highly respected Duke of Wellington, that it would be wise to grant Catholic Emancipation, or religious freedom.

In most country areas, even after 1800, the hedge schools or pay schools were still the only schools. In Tyrone, the famous novelist William Carleton went to a hedge school where rich and poor, Protestant, Catholic, Presbyterian and Methodist boys and girls 'were all congregated under the same roof, to the amount of from 100 to a 150, or 200'. Edmund Burke also went to one of these schools.

However, the very poor boys and girls in the cities often had no education. Edmund Ignatius Rice started a school at Mount Sion in Waterford for boys, and in Cork Nano Nagle formed a school for girls. These schools became known as the Christian Brothers' School, and the Presentation Convent School, because the men and women who taught in them devoted their lives, as religious brothers and nuns, to the cause of educating the poor.

Eventually the government decided that it was their responsibility to provide schools all over the country. These schools became known as National Schools. Although most of the children spoke only Irish, the teachers would only allow English to be spoken. Any child who used an Irish word was punished with a slap for each word spoken during the week. A rod, or tally stick, was tied around the neck of each child, and each slap due was shown by a notch in the rod. This was one reason why use of the Irish language declined. Another reason was that large numbers of Irish-speaking people emigrated, both during and after the famine. Business deals and court proceedings were all conducted in English, which led Daniel O'Connell to advise the permanent use of English. For a long time, the English used was of very poor quality, because most conversations were partly in English and partly in Irish, and many of the English words were misunderstood or badly pronounced.

There were also a few secondary schools. At Ballitore, Co Kildare, the Quakers had a famous school. The Duke of Wellington himself had gone to school briefly in Portarlington, Co Leix. The following advertisement in a newspaper gives an idea of what these schools taught.

Mr Cumming's Classical and Mathematical School
Business was resumed Monday 23rd.
In this Establishment, the most particular attention is paid to every branch of an English Education and the Youngest Pupils are accustomed to English Composition suitable to their capacities.

A 'Boarding and Day School for Young Ladies' stated that: 'The course of instruction comprises English in all its branches, Music, Drawing and French, Writing and Arithmetic. Plain and fancy work.'

While William Carleton emerged as a novelist from the pay school in Co Tyrone, the novelist, Maria Edgeworth, was fortunate enough to have her inventive father, Richard Lovell Edgeworth, to educate her in their home at Edgeworthstown, Co Longford. From there, she was able to observe closely the society of poor and wealthy in Ireland, observations on which she based her novel *Castle Rackrent*. Walter Scott admired her novels and visited Ireland in order to see her. James Sheridan LeFanu of Chapelizod, Dublin, was a novelist particularly noted for his ghost stories.

6. The Great Emigration, 1850-1914

Leaving for America

After the famine, Irish men and women continued to go to the United States. Between 1853 and 1898, 3,204,613 emigrants left Ireland. One member of a family in America would send home the money or the ticket for the next oldest to come over. Going to America was considered almost as a death, and an American wake was held to mourn the person leaving. This was a night of singing and dancing before the emigrant was accompanied for part of the journey to the port by weeping relatives and friends, whom he would never see again. It was also an opportunity for the shipping companies to earn a profit. They had agents in the Irish towns to sell passenger tickets. The following advertisement shows much eagerness to get custom:

Notice to Emigrants

Persons intending to Emigrate to any part of the United States or Canada can make the necessary arrangements for so doing, by applying either personally or by letter to the Undersigned.

First-class Steamers and Sailing Ships to select from. An early application is desirable

Nicholas H. Devine,
Emigration Agent.

Tubbercurry, Co Sligo.
February, 1867.

Another advertisement stated that: 'The magnificent Sailing Packet Ship, *Victory,* 2,000 tons, will sail for New York from Liverpool, on the 8th of April. Passage Rates from Liverpool, £3.10s [£3.50].'

The ships of the Inman, Cunard and Anchor Lines sailed from Queenstown or Cobh twice a week, and from Derry every Thursday. The menu for steerage passengers (the poorest), stipulated that: 'The supply of provisions consisting of tea, coffee, fresh bread and butter, beef, pork, soup, potatoes, etc, etc, cooked and served out at eight, one, and six o'clock, is without stint, so long as no waste is observable.'

Many of the passengers brought their own food for the journey, which consisted of oaten cakes. At the ports, the passengers had to be careful not to be misled by 'runners' into staying at inns where they would be charged far too much or have their money stolen. Many of the emigrants were paupers from the workhouses. These workhouse paupers were supposed to be given money to

46 These emigrants might never be seen again by their relatives in Ireland.

support themselves on arrival, and women were to be supplied with the following outfit:

1 dress	1 pair of boots
1 jacket	1 hat or bonnet
2 woollen petticoats	2 towels
2 sets of underclothing	1 brush and comb
2 pairs of stockings	Sewing and knitting materials
2 handkerchiefs	1 rug or coverlet
1 shawl	1 bag or box

In fact this was luxury, and often an entire family of five would be sent across the sea with £5 from the workhouse's Board of Guardians.

Farming after the famine
The great numbers who emigrated changed the way of life for those who remained at home. The dollars that were sent back home meant that the rent could be paid or an extra cow bought. The very small farms were joined

47 Many Irishmen made their livelihood as drovers, driving pigs and cattle to the fairs.

together in 15 to 25-acre (6 to 10-hectare) farms that could be managed by the labour of a family. The only remaining son of the house inherited the farm, and the dowry of the girl he married could be used either to increase the number of cows on the farm, or to provide a dowry for his sister when she married. It was always hoped that farms gained by marriage would at some time be added to the home farm. Many of the cows used for milk and butter on these farms were, in fact, hired out from large dairymen.

Even after the famine, the people still had to pay rack-rents to the landlords. Many of these landlords were speculators who bought estates cheaply from bankrupt gentry, in the hope of getting a good return on their investment. They either cleared the tenants off altogether and substituted cattle and sheep, or increased the rents. At an auction of their own farm, people were forced to bid a rent higher than they could possibly pay from the profits of farming. The 'gale days', the days in November and May when the rent was due, were worrying times for the tenants, especially when there was a 'hanging gale'. A 'hanging gale' was an arrangement with the landlord which allowed the tenant to fall into arrears with the rent. This however, was of very doubtful value to the tenant — it brought him deeper into debt, leaving him more at the mercy of the landlord and so increasing the likelihood of eviction. In Ulster, however, there was a custom whereby a tenant could not be evicted if he paid a fair rent; the custom also allowed him to sell the interest or good will on his farm. This meant that any improvements he made would not provide an excuse for raising his rent, nor could they be confiscated without compensation from the landlord.

When bad harvests and competition from American corn and cattle hit the farmers' profits during the Agricultural Depression between 1876 and 1890, Irish farmers tried to get rent reductions from their landlords, but were refused. In order to protect themselves from eviction, they organised the Land League, in the manner of a trade union, under the leadership of Charles Stewart Parnell and Michael Davitt. In 1881, Gladstone passed an Act of Parliament guaranteeing them the rights of the Ulster Custom — the right to security of tenure on payment of a fair rent, and the right to sell their interest in the farm when leaving it. Land Courts were set up to regulate the amount of rent that should be charged according to prevailing agricultural prices. Later still, the landlords

48 Police protection for a landlord's bailiff, who is evicting a tenant for not paying his rent, and removing the furniture from the house.

were encouraged to sell the farms to the tenants. Arthur Balfour, George Balfour and George Wyndham passed Land Purchase Acts after Lord Ashbourne had set a precedent in 1886 by providing advances to the landlords for their land. These advances were to be repaid in annual instalments, or annuities, by the tenants who purchased the land.

In 1858, reaping and threshing machines began to be used in earnest by farmers, replacing the scythe and sickle to gather the harvest. These machines helped to save the cost of paying labourers, whose pay had risen from 3p a day at the time of the famine to 7½p a day during the harvest in 1858.

Many farmers, of course, preferred to keep servant boys for farm work rather than hire expensive casual labour at peak periods. At hiring fairs, servants hired themselves out to the farmers for a period of eight months, from March to November. A fee of £6 and their keep was the usual bargain, and the servant could be prosecuted if he broke his contract. Dairymaids were also hired; every year the dairymaids of Kerry went in search of work in the rich dairy lands of Limerick.

By 1878, the plough had largely replaced the spade for farm work, but lack of knowledge about the threshing machines was still causing accidents to the workmen. By the 1890s, farm workers were worried that machinery was replacing them altogether, and when the Co-operative Creameries began to supply machinery at lower cost to the farmers, they objected. The creameries were set up by Sir Horace Plunkett after 1896. Their aim was to improve farming, and to ensure that foreign groups did not gain control of marketing, and therefore of the price, of butter, milk and other farm produce. The quality of farming was also improved by the establishment of a Department of Agriculture and Technical Instruction in 1898. The Royal Dublin Society had previously been encouraging the improvement of breeds of cattle, sheep, pigs and farmhorses. The Spring Show and the Horse Show held every year at the RDS grounds in Ballsbridge, Dublin, originated from these exhibitions. Other agricultural shows developed at Cork, Balmoral in Belfast, and in country towns.

Food

After the famine, people were afraid that the potato crop might fail again. The increased use of porridge, or stirabout, mixed with milk, was an indication of a change in eating habits. People also began to eat more meat. American bacon was the cheapest meat on the market and it was often bought just to give to the servants. Tea soon became a favourite with the people. In fact, farmers' wives began to complain that the labourers would refuse to take their meals unless tea was served with the food. The tea, brewed for a long time, was very strong. It was also said to weaken the workmen's muscles.

Baker's bread used only to be available in the towns. By the 1880s, however, it was being taken into the countryside in delivery vans. Most food though was still bought in the general stores set up in the villages by the 'gombeen man'. He was a dealer who bought the eggs, poultry, milk, butter, vegetables and other produce from the country people at low prices, but charged them high prices for the tea, sugar, candles, tobacco and other items they bought in his shop. He

49 Servant girls bringing milk in churns to the Co-operative Creameries, which protected the price of milk for the farmers of Ireland.

charged particularly high prices to those who bought on credit while they waited for money they had earned picking potatoes or cutting corn as migratory labourers in Scotland, or else waiting for the spring fairs when they could sell their calves, lambs and yearling cattle. Shopkeepers often recovered credit given to customers by grazing cattle on their land. Christmas was a great occasion for regular customers because they could be sure of getting a Christmas box from the shopkeeper.

Houses

As money came in from America, so the houses of the people improved. Many still remained thatched with straw, but some were now roofed with slates. The houses were whitewashed with lime to keep them clean and healthy. The dung heaps that used to be kept outside the door and bred disease also began to disappear, especially as a result of the cholera danger in the 1860s. Finally, in

69

50 The shopkeepers had a busy time on Christmas morning handing out the Christmas boxes.

1883 with the Labourers Housing Act, and in 1888 with the Congested Districts Board, money was provided for knocking down unsanitary houses and replacing them with properly designed council cottages. Congested Districts were so named because they were areas where too many people lived on land too poor to support them. Improved housing including slated roofs, began to appear as contact between towns and countryside increased. Furthermore, the emigration to America of so many of the very poorest people meant that there were fewer poor-standard houses of mud left, without windows or chimneys.

51 The fishing village of Claddagh in Galway, with its houses thatched and whitewashed with lime.

52 The hunt was a popular pastime for the gentry.

Entertainment

The houses of the country landowners were the centres of fashionable society. Recitals, in which the music and songs of Thomas Moore were prominent, were held there. The diaries of Constance and Eva Gore-Booth of Lissadell, Co.Sligo, show that the ladies painted and conversed politely about literature.

Both gentlemen and ladies were extremely fond of hunting. The Galway Blazers and the Scarteen Black and Tans were famous hunts, and hunting scenes are vividly recalled in the writings of Edith Somerville and Violet Martin of Ross. Horse-racing, particularly steeplechasing at Punchestown, Fairyhouse, or Galway itself, was fashionable, although Irish horses also won the great English Derby at Epsom in Surrey.

The Royal Irish Automobile Club was founded by car enthusiasts in the 1880s, when cars were still the prerogative of the wealthier classes.

The ordinary people enjoyed horse-racing, too, as suggested by John Millington Synge's play, *The Playboy of the Western World.* As bicycles became popular, cycling for pleasure was accepted. Trains, trams and bicycles made visits to sea resorts quite easy.

The Gaelic games of hurling and football were organised in the 1880s. In earlier times all the young men of each parish competed with each other in driving a leather-covered ball across the fields, as vividly described in Canon Sheehan's novel *Glenanaer.* Now, in the 1880s, goalposts were set down in a field and teams were confined to less than twenty men. The hurley was a bit like a hockey stick, except that it had a broad base with which to hit or lift the ball. Gaelic football was quite different from soccer — the players were allowed

71

to handle and kick the ball from the hand. The ball could not be carried the length of the field, however, as in modern rugger. But both the oval-shaped ball and the carrying of it originated in 'gad', the older form of Gaelic football which was introduced to England from Tipperary by William Webb Ellis.

Throwing the hammer as an athletic exercise was another popular sport, and for many years Irishmen were Olympic champions in hammer-throwing, shot-putting and jumping. The hammer-throwing contest in the novel, *Knocknagow,* by Charles Kickham, was drawn from Irish life at the time.

Education, language and religion
It was from the lives of the people, as seen by the gentry in their big houses, that the world famous Anglo-Irish literary revival sprang in the late 1890s. From the conversations of Lady Augusta Gregory of Coole Park, Edward Martyn of Tullyra Castle, Co Galway, and William Butler Yeats of Sligo came the idea of founding the Abbey Theatre in Dublin. In this theatre the plays of Yeats and Lady Gregory were first performed, along with those of J M Synge, Sean O'Casey, and T C Murray. George Moore of Moore Hall, Co Mayo, was a celebrated novelist of his day, as was James Joyce later, after the publication of *Ulysses* and *Finnegan's Wake.* George Bernard Shaw, too, was born in Dublin.

The Irish language was revived by Dr Douglas Hyde, who was later the first President of the Irish Free State. It became a curriculum subject in national, secondary and university education. In fact, Patrick Pearse, the young head-master of St Enda's school, who later led the Easter Week rebellion in Dublin in 1916, realised that the existing educational system destroyed learning, by paying teachers for results gained in useless memorised knowledge. This led him to call it 'the Murder Machine'. Instead, he taught his pupils to love the Irish language and Ireland's history.

Much of the educational problem derived from the difficulty Irish Catholics had in getting any education at all. Many who would not otherwise have bothered, wanted to learn to read and write so they could write letters home when they emigrated. After the famine, the Catholic Church was able to establish a number of secondary schools, and even began a university under the guidance of Cardinal Newman, with Gerard Manley Hopkins, the poet, as teacher. The National University, established in 1908, gave Catholics an opportunity for higher education, alongside the opportunities for Protestants at Trinity College, and Queen's University, Belfast.

From the time of the famine onwards, there had been a remarkable spirit of fervour in the religious faith of Catholics, Protestants and Presbyterians alike, which contrasted sharply with the growing hostility to religion arising out of new scientific discoveries and Marxism. This religious fervour was also apparent among the Nonconformist churches of Great Britain, and led Gladstone to sever the link between the Church of Ireland and the political state in 1868. This was known as disestablishment.

7. Town Life, 1850-1914

Transport

In 1841, the Sligo Mail Coach took 15 hours 15 minutes to reach Dublin, and charged £1.50 for the journey. By 1866, the Midland Great Western Railway was offering an excursion train leaving Sligo at 10 am and reaching Dublin by 5.40 pm, a journey of only 7 hours 40 minutes at a fare of 37½p. The freight charge for goods was only about 1p a mile. Such a change of pace and cost not only meant a greater movement of people, but also introduced new goods at cheaper prices to the country towns.

Of course, not everyone had been able to afford to travel in the stage coaches, or even on the ½p a mile Bianconi cars introduced in 1815 by an Italian peddlar. These long, open cars seated twelve or so passengers back to back against a central ridge, with their feet resting on a foot rail. The Irish jaunting car which carried tourists at Killarney was rather similar, though more highly sprung. But most people still travelled on foot, and continued to walk up to 50 or more miles (80 kilometeres) as they journeyed to the emigration ports.

By 1898, bicycles were on sale in most towns at £10.50. At the end of the First World War in 1918, motorcars were selling at £105. The increasing number of two-horse and four-horse trams in towns during the last twenty years of the nineteenth century allowed people to live in the suburbs and yet

53 The railway from Dublin to Kingstown (Dunlaoghaire) was the first such passenger service in Ireland.

54 The Bianconi cars provided a cheaper and wider network of road transport.

still work in the centre. A penny fare brought passengers in from Dalkey to Dublin, a journey which today would cost 10p. The Dublin to Kingstown (Dunlaoghaire) Railway, laid in the 1840s by Jonathan Pim, was another link between the suburbs and the city centre.

Money

Just as important to business as cheaper transport of goods was the ready availability of a stable form of money. As late as the 1820s, private banks in Munster went bankrupt and ruined businessmen, farmers and poor people who had entrusted their savings to the banks. Joint Stock Companies were then allowed to form the Northern, Provincial, National and Hibernian Banks. The increased number of shareholders gave more security to the banknotes, but even in the 1850s the Tipperary Bank, headed by John Sadlier, went bankrupt because of the misuse of its funds. The importance of the banks is shown by the fact that when disaster struck the farmers in 1878 they were unable to get any credit from the banks, largely because in the years following the Land Act of 1870, when their greater security of tenure made the farmers worthy of credit, they had borrowed heavily for personal spending.

Many people preferred to put their savings in the post office, and the government judged the prosperity of the country from the total in post office savings accounts. The Limited Liability Act of 1862 encouraged business by securing businessmen against complete bankruptcy. It was also recognised by Parliament that Ireland had in the past been taxed too highly, which had prevented business from growing.

74

Because most of the people who worked on the land or as labourers in the towns scarcely had any money to spend, Irish businessmen could not risk competing with the factories of Great Britain for a small market. A labourer with only 60p to spend was unlikely to make any manufacturer wealthy — for that, he needed a market in Britain. Of course, the very fact that the labourer had only 60p to spend made the cheaper clothes, shoes and other household requirements more attractive to him. The railway brought these cheaper English goods within his reach.

Belfast and Londonderry

The population of Belfast grew from 37,277 in 1821 to 75,308 in 1841. By the First World War, the population was 400,000. The reason for this rapid growth was the increasing number of labourers needed in the Harland and Wolff shipyards and the linen mills. Because of the depth of Belfast Lough, and its proximity to the coal and iron areas of Scotland and Lancashire and the great ports of Glasgow and Liverpool, Belfast was able to switch to the steam-powered method of spinning linen in the 1820s. Belfast was also a great shipbuilding area, and specialised in great iron ships with turbine engines. The *Titanic* was the most famous, if also the most unfortunate, of its ships. Belfast had always had trading links with America, and its tobacco industry developed rapidly. Ropemaking industries and other allied services grew up to serve the needs of the shipbuilders.

Londonderry was not quite as busy as Belfast, but it also had shipbuilding industries, tobacco factories and, particularly, shirt manufacturers. Small towns near Belfast, like Lisburn, Lurgan, Portadown and Dungannon, Built up their importance as centres for linen mills.

Industry and trade

Until the time of the famine, most of the bigger country towns had breweries, tanneries, ironworks, flour mills and woollen mills. Mountmellick, Co Leix, for instance, although now only a market town, has ruins of old factories to show why the industries built up there by Quaker businessmen led to it being called the Manchester of Ireland. After the famine, and particularly after the introduction of the railways and of fast steamers from Britain, the industries in the smaller Irish towns began to disappear. In Wexford, Dublin and Drogheda, farm machinery was still being made, particularly ploughs, and in cities like Cork and Waterford butter and bacon exports created work. In Drogheda, the firm of Grendon, which after the famine had built railway locomotives and girders for bridges had, by the 1880s, gone out of business. Sadly, this was typical of most industries. Dublin alone had the large Jacob's biscuit factory, Guinness's brewery and the Jameson and Power distilleries. Their slowness, or inability, to adopt new milling machinery affected flour and grain mills throughout the country.

Country towns, however, were still hives of activity. In the 1850s, 'monster houses' began to appear. They were a form of shop which dealt in several lines of merchandise within the one building — women's wear, men's wear, linen

55 Guinness's brewery grew to be the largest of the many breweries in Irish towns and cities. Irish grain to support these breweries was in plentiful supply until the middle of the nineteenth century.

drapery, woollen drapery, hosiery, haberdashery and hats, all items that had previously been sold in separate shops.

The type of clothes that people wore changed as well. In 1823, the men in the towns wore a 'buff vest, a swallow-tailed coat with bright buttons, a frilled shirt with ruffled cuffs, and a large gold seal hanging from the fob'. Even in the countryside, the men wore 'blue coats, corduroy breeches, and blue stockings' in 1845, and the women wore 'a blue petticoat with a printed dress turned back and pinned behind, coarse shoes, and blue or black stockings (when they have shoes), a blue cloak, with a hood to put over the head, in case of rain'. The fashionable ladies of the town wore coal-scuttle bonnets, sombre dress and 'sandal shoes with ankle ties'. By 1913, men wore lounge suits, while women were dressed as anywhere else in Britain.

Even the appearance of the shops had changed. In 1823, shops had 'low fronts and small windows of little panes that were cleaned perhaps once a month and protected . . . with strong iron railings on the outside', but by 1875 shops had a 'whole storey of plate glass reaching almost to the ground'. By

1869, city stores in Dublin were prepared to deliver parcels on the same day by rail, as far out as to Bray.

But even one small village, in 1897, had 90 skilled tradesmen, including 30 coopers, tinsmiths, tailors, weavers, saddlers, stone masons, blacksmiths, and 10 bakeries. There were 14 public houses compared with only 5 today. The village had fairs every 4 years and a weekly pig, butter and fowl market, to add to its activity. The fair day, with its long rows of carts and peddlars, was a very important occasion in Irish towns.

Life in the towns

Living conditions in both the cities and towns were very bad. In Belfast, the factory workers lived in small, brick, back-to-back houses, with narrow lanes running between the rows of houses. Under the 1878 Improvement Act, new artisans' dwellings were built, but the older ones still remained.

In Dublin the slum tenements were even worse. Twenty-seven out of every 1,000 children under five years old died. Tuberculosis killed many of the workers. Even in country towns there were slum tenements. People drank water from sewage-filled rivers. From 1850 onwards, the Artisans' Dwellings Acts tried to improve workers' houses by condemning unsanitary, unsafe and overcrowded dwellings. In 1864, there was compulsory inoculation against cholera, but scarlet fever, another dangerous disease, often broke out as a result of the presence of dung heaps and contaminated food. Imported rag clothing

56 These drab houses for Belfast's factory and shipyard workers were a feature of the Industrial Revolution.

peddled by dealers was always a danger. The poverty of the people who, in 1913, often lived on less than 75p a week for a family of seven, left them undernourished and prone to disease. Their diet usually consisted of bread and butter and American bacon at 2p a pound. Their poverty also left them at the mercy of slum landlords and pawnbrokers.

Trade unions

Until trade unions were recognised in 1868, the Combination Laws in both Britain and Ireland prevented workers from protecting their living and working conditions. But, despite the Combination Laws, workers frequently did combine to try and improve matters. In Cork in 1831, opposition to the use of imported carpenters in the building of the North Infirmary led gangs of wandering workmen to waylay the unpopular strangers and give them severe beatings. In Cork and Limerick in 1870, there was a general strike at mills, potteries, timber-yards and docks, sparked off by the opposition of the tailors to the use of sewing machines. In Dublin, the carpenters and coach-builders were violent. Railway workers or navvies were striking as early as 1858 on the Midland Railway from Tullamore to Athlone.

The success of the Dockers' Strike in London in 1889 introduced into Ireland the Gasworkers' and General Labourers' Union, the Dockers' Union and the Amalgamated Firemen's and Railwaymen's Union. But it was not until James Larkin formed the Irish Transport and General Workers' Union in 1910, as one giant union for all general labourers, that most workers in Ireland were prepared to stand up to the employers. James Connolly and Larkin had already attempted to organise the shipyard workers and the mill girls in Belfast against sweated labour at low wages.

In 1913, the great Lock-Out occurred in Dublin. The owner of the trams organised the other employers of carters and dockers to break the power of Larkin's trade union. After weeks of starvation, the striking workmen had to go back to their work at the employers' rate of wages. The strike had been as much against the shocking living conditions of their families as it had been for higher wages.

57 The Soviet Russian leader, Litvinov, helped Larkin to lecture to the workers of the Belfast shipyards, on their way home from work in the evenings.

78

8. Changes in the Twentieth Century

Money

When Southern Ireland gained its freedom in 1922, it decided to have its own special form of currency. The figures of the various river gods on the Customs House, signs of the prosperity of eighteenth-century Ireland, were printed on the notes. On the coins, the hen and her brood of chickens, the pig, the horse, the salmon, the snipe, the hare and the bull were stamped as symbols of thrift, industry and care, or the goods for which Ireland was famous, particularly agricultural produce. English notes and coins continued to be used side by side with the new Irish coinage. The Northern Bank in Belfast kept its special notes.

Today, of course, Ireland has a decimal currency. But it still has the harp imprinted on one side, like the famous harpers of Tudor times, with designs from old Celtic manuscripts on the other face. Credit cards, travellers' cheques and hire-purchase facilities are the twentieth-century means of exchange and payment, although they are not altogether unlike the bills of exchange used in the seventeenth century. The modern Bank of Ireland marks a connection with the prosperous eighteenth century, for it is housed in the building where the meetings of Grattan's Parliament were held.

Power for industry

The age of steam power was not yet over, but electricity had now to be provided on a large scale. Until 1927, private generators were used. In 1927, however, the waters of Ireland's biggest river, the Shannon, were harnessed to supply electricity. Water was not the only source of power used for driving the turbines. Over the whole country, there were large areas of bogland and peat. Local people had always cut the turf for fuel, just as coal had been mined. In twentieth-century Ireland, this has been harvested on a large scale by hand, or

58 This hydro-electric generating station on the River Lee, near Cork, is a perfect example of how natural resources can be harnessed for the country's improvement.

59 Instead of forming coal or oil the vegetation of prehistoric Ireland decayed and hardened into peat. The harvesting of peat by such modern machinery has been copied in many countries.

more especially in recent years by giant mechanical turf cutters. Machinery was used to make milled or powdered turf, for briquettes, in Co Offaly — the first instance of its use outside Soviet Russia. The turf was then burned in generating stations, such as Portarlington, to drive the turbines. Anthracite was used at Arigna, Co Leitrim, where coal-mining had gone on since the eighteenth century, because it was so cheap. Today, oil or gas is used as well. There is no atomic power available as yet, but there is said to be natural gas off Kinsale, Co Cork, as in the North Sea. It is certain that the Bronze and Iron Age metalworkers at their charcoal furnaces would no more have dreamed of such power stations than those who cut down the woods for ironworking, or who used water to turn mill wheels.

Transport
By the end of the First World War, motor cars, buses and lorries were widespread. Like the arrival of train services after the famine, motorised transport brought changes in the delivery of goods throughout the country. Even before the war, engineers had realised that steamrollers were required to make roads that would be able to stand up to the new volume of traffic.

In 1932, the railway service in Southern Ireland was brought under the control of the State as Great Southern Railways, and in Northern Ireland, there was the Great Northern Railways. Besides this, many narrow-gauge railways operated on the smaller routes, such as the famous West Clare Railway, or the Ballinamore, Co Leitrim, line. But still the pony and trap was the most common form of individual transport in country areas, while tram tracks in cobbled streets showed the continued use of trams, particularly in Dublin.

The creation of the Aer Lingus national airline was, however, an acknowledgment that the twentieth century had arrived, with a form of world transport to stand alongside the traditional vehicles. Alcock and Brown significantly had landed at Clifden, Co Galway, on their trans-Atlantic flight, and Shannon Airport was established, before the age of modern long-distance jets, as a necessary servicing stop from Europe to America.

Farming
The arrival of the tractor was of course the most important change to take place in farming. It was advertised as 'capable of doing the work of six horses either in mowing, reaping, hauling or threshings. The same advertisement was selling 'Mowing machines, binders, hayrakes and swath turners', along with 'Combination threshing sets'. But the old steam threshing machines, and even hand threshing, continued to be used for years until the modern combine harvester arrived.

Spraying potatoes with copper sulphate from a cylinder on the farmer's back was the first advance into the twentieth-century use of chemicals in farming. Today, the use of nitrates and phosphates is an accepted feature of Irish farming and, at Arklow in Co Wicklow, the Irish government has sponsored a modern plant for their production. The use of silage in cattle feeding has been made possible by the use of these fertilisers on grass land.

60 Dublin Airport today handles the arrival of Jumbo jets.

Shopping

Older people look back on the past and regret that the good old days of cheaper prices are gone. Rises in wages and the cost of manufacture and transport have forced prices upward. In comparing the prices in 1900 and 1930 the following changes would be most noticeable:

	1900	*1930*
Men's readymade suits	8s 6d (42½p)	20s 0 (£1)
Men's trousers	2s 11d (14½p)	4s 6d (22½p)
Men's overcoats	9s 6d (47½p)	16s 6d (82½p)
Blankets	2s 11d (14½p)	8s 6d (42½p)

Most country people certainly got their local tailor to make their clothes cheaply.

After the Civil War in Ireland (1922-23) and the Second World War (1939-45) which involved Northern Ireland, employment was scarce, so that people in both country and urban areas had very little surplus spending money. As in the rest of Britain, the textile mills and the shipyards in Belfast were going through a bad period, and the workers there suffered even more than elsewhere.

The period from 1929 to 1950 was one of general economic depression, caused by the Wall Street crash, the Second World War, and, in Southern Ireland, the Economic War with Britain. This Economic War arose out of an argument over the continued responsibility for paying back in land annuities the money lent for the buying of the landlords' estates, and also over the extra taxation that had been imposed on Ireland by the United Kingdom after 1800. This meant that Irish cattle and farm produce could not be marketed in Britain, while British coal and industrial products were unable to find a market in Ireland. Calves were slaughtered and the meat given to the poor. The farmers lost a great deal of money. Rationing of food was introduced during the Second World War and wages were controlled. However, the war did bring prosperity to Northern Ireland, because of the employment wanted by munitions factories, shipyard and aircraft production, and clothing for the armed forces.

In such circumstances of restricted money and opportunity for spending it, it is not surprising that shopping practices did not greatly change. In country areas, the combined grocery, hardware and public house establishment continued to exist. In the cities, great stores like Roche's, McBirney's, Arnott's, Switzer's and Clery's either improved on the business they had done in the nineteenth century, or else emerged under new ownership. Eason's, the retail newsagents that had figured in the 1913 Lock-Out, still continued in their specialised sphere, as did family firms such as Bewley's in tea and coffee. It was not until the 1960s that American-style supermarkets and self-service stores began to compete with the specialist stores, as the Monster Houses had done in the 1850s.

Housing and health

Because there was very little surplus spending money available to either governments in Ireland from the beginning of the First World War to the end of the Second World War, the improvement of housing was a slow process. In Northern Ireland nissen huts were often used as houses; and in Southern Ireland, thatched cabins in the countryside, and slums in the cities, continued to exist. Some of the worst slum areas were cleared, but it was not until the Coalition Government in Southern Ireland had the use of Marshall Aid, and the Northern Government had the benefits of the welfare state, that the housing shortage could be tackled by building the great housing estates of Creggan, Bogside, Ballybeen (Dundonald), Andersonstown, Ballyfermot, Crumlin, Ballymun and Ballyphehane, around the cities of Derry, Belfast, Dublin and Cork.

The National Health Insurance scheme, introduced in Lloyd George's budget

61 Thatched cottages like these, once a feature of the Irish countryside, are getting rarer every year.

of 1911, brought some benefit to the poor of Ireland, although the degrading old Poor Law system of relief, imposed by the Medical Charities Act of 1856, continued to be used. Unemployment benefits did come to the aid of the poor, however, although farm workers were neglected until the 1930s. The Old Age Pensions Act of 1905 had been even more important because it gave dignity and independence to the old who would formerly have gone to the workhouse to die as paupers. T C Murray's play, *Spring,* movingly shows what an old man feels when he is no longer an unwanted person. The Southern Irish government got rid of the indignity of the old workhouse system by accepting that it is a government's duty to look after citizens who have worked for their country in their prime. The Northern Ireland government also adopted the social welfare programmes of Britain.

However, it was not until after the Second World War that a campaign to end tuberculosis was launched in both Northern and Southern Ireland, with the aid of modern drugs and special hospital services. The Irish Hospitals' Sweepstake had been an ingenious way of obtaining money for building hospitals and paying for their upkeep and services to the sick. Football pools also help to finance them today.

Entertainment

Winding up the gramophone for an evening's entertainment would have been the first thought of our grandfathers, and perhaps even our fathers. The records of John McCormack and Caruso, or the dance bands of the twenties and

62 A display of posters for Irish plays outside the Abbey Theatre in Dublin.

63 Playing bowls on a country road in Cork — a unique form of sport.

thirties would have been the life and soul of a gay evening. The arrival of the cinema would have been an even greater form of entertainment. A daily newspaper in 1929 advertised for Cork: 'Richard Barthelmess in *Weary River*. A First National Vitaphone Production.'

The Abbey and Gate Theatres in Dublin were producing exciting productions of the plays of Sean O'Casey, Paul Vincent Carroll, Lennox Robinson and George Shields, while Micheal Mac Liammoir and Hilton Edwards directed and acted in modern world drama, or Denis Johnston's *The Old Lady Says No*.

In country towns, the arrival of a travelling stage show or 'fit up', or of a circus, was a seven days' wonder for young and old alike. Crossroads dancing in the summer was common until quite recently in country areas. Parish halls were erected for bazaars and dances, long before the age of the showbands and the building of dancehalls or discotheques in every third town.

For more athletic exercise, bowling an iron ball along the roads, hurling, golf and football were the favourite sports. Coursing hares with greyhounds, or playing pitch-and-toss or skittles at the cross roads were equally popular. In Belfast and Derry, pigeon-racing was much fancied, while cock-fights were held along the border counties.

85

9. Ireland: Common Market Country

Tourism

A modern visitor to Ireland would arrive by Aer Lingus, British Airways, or Cambrian jet at Shannon, Cork, Dublin or Belfast airports, or by car-ferry at Larne, Dublin, Dunlaoghaire, Rosslare or Cork. He would not be as weary as Jonathan Swift was after his journeys by sea to Dublin. At any rate, the stranger in Ireland today could rest in an ultra-modern hotel, a farmhouse guesthouse, a converted castle or landlord's mansion. He would certainly be better provided for than they were in one of the inns of 1600 because tourism is now an important source of income. He might prefer, of course, to have arrived in Ireland between 1750 and 1850 and stayed at a stage-coach inn or a canal hotel, but he could still visit one, as for instance at Robertstown, Co Kildare. He could even see how the ordinary people lived and worked at the folk villages and museums of Cultra outside Belfast; or Glencolumbcille in Donegal, Bunratty near Shannon Airport; Muckross House, Killarney and Kerry's folk theatre, Siamsa; Stradbally, Co Leix; and Rothe House, Kilkenny and Castleruddery, Co Wicklow. The visitor could then compare the past with the present.

Industries

Ireland today has industries all over the country, unlike the period from 1815 to 1918, when only Belfast and the surrounding area contained any heavy industries. The visitor would discover that the Belfast region still has its industries, but that now synthetic fibres have replaced linen in the textile industry. Giant companies like Michelin, Du Pont, Courtaulds and ICI are signs of the present age in industry.

Most factories in Ireland today are situated on industrial estates. These are sites specially provided by the government for groups of factories. An Industrial Development Authority and an Industrial Credit Corporation try to attract foreign industries to come to Ireland by providing them with these sites and by giving them grants and loans. The big cities beside ports and airports — Belfast, Drogheda, Dublin, Waterford, Cork, Limerick, Shannon and Galway — are the centres for these industrial estates. British, American, German, Dutch, French and Japanese industries are there to give employment to the workers of the cities. Cork, for instance, has the Verolme Dockyard, Pfizer Chemicals, Ford Motors, a steel mill and an oil refinery. So a port which from the time of the Danes onwards was dealing almost exclusively in food is today a city of heavy industry. Bantry Bay, which has a song about its fishing boats, is today a place where Gulf Oil tankers unload crude oil.

Ever since the Bronze Age in Ireland, it was thought that there was scarcely any mineral wealth in the island. But today silver, iron, lead, zinc and copper

86

64 Irish goods are exhibited at trade fairs all around the world.

are mined in great quantities from the richest mines of Europe at Tynagh, Co Galway, Gortdrum, Co Tipperary, Avoca, Co Wicklow and Navan, Co Meath. The miners work in better conditions than those who dug out the copper in the mines at Allihies, Co Cork, from 1811 to 1850, as Daphne Du Maurier described in her novel, *Hungry Hill*. But if the factories of the past produced smoke, the danger from industries of the present is pollution of the rivers and seas, and toxic chemicals in the air.

Today, manufacturers have to travel abroad to sell their goods. That is why exhibitions of goods made in Ireland are displayed in London, New York and Paris shops, and why the country has stands at World Fairs, like the great trade

65 The Irish country fair is still a lively business and social occasion.

fairs of the Middle Ages. Irish fashion, particularly in tweed, is a familiar item at such trade fairs.

Farmers and fishermen

Although markets are still held in country towns, they are fast disappearing. Instead of bringing their cattle to the market, the farmers now drive them to the central marts, where they are auctioned. The farmer, however shrewd, no longer has to strike his own bargain with the wily cattle dealers. In this way the farmer is assured of getting a more consistent and fairer price for his stock.

The farmer's life has changed in other ways in recent years. Combine harvesters save the wasted time and money of older days. Milking parlours, too, save the immense amount of time spent milking by hand, and ensure that the

66 The sugar beet is washed down with power hoses before being pulped at this sugar factory in Carlow.

farmer will obtain pasteurised milk acceptable to the creameries. The visitor to Ireland's countryside would notice that the creamery tankers now travel around collecting the milk, whereas before the farmers themselves brought the cans to the creamery in carts, or in the boot of a car. Veterinary surgeons help to eradicate TB and brucellosis from the valuable herds.

The government helps the farmer to market his crops and produce. The Milk Marketing Board, the Sugar Company, Erin Foods, the Grain Board and Livestock Board either buy the milk, sugar beet, potatoes and vegetables, wheat and cattle produced by Irish farmers, or else help to sell them abroad by advertising campaigns in Britain, America and Europe.

Fishermen are also helped by the government. In the past, fishermen were satisfied to fish in small boats near the coast, but today large trawlers are needed. Young fishermen are trained as skippers and given loans with which to buy their boats. The money earned for the country by fishing is an important part of the country's wealth. Killybegs, Co Donegal, Carna, Co Galway and Castletownbere, Co Cork have large fishing fleets and fish processing plants.

All the support given by the State to industry, farming and fishing represents the greater involvement of all governments today in the economy of their countries, which was formerly left to free enterprise by individuals. It is a form of nationalisation, and another facet of the welfare state.

Urbanisation

As in every Western country today, more people in Ireland are living in towns and cities, than in the countryside. This is an unfortunate feature of twentieth-century life. Apart from creating a need for more sprawling suburbs and high-rise flats, living in built-up suburbs lessens the individual's identity as a person, compared with his position in the smaller community of a village in the

89

67 The children in the new city of Craigavon enjoy a more pleasant playground than the bleak back streets of the old Belfast.

country. It also means that the countryside becomes deserted, and loses the life and customs of the past. Small communities lose their post office, school, police station, shops and village hall. Very often, because traffic requires bigger and better roads, villages are by-passed, and long-distance passenger and freight trains no longer stop at small stations. But as old towns die, new towns are born, and so the new city of Craigavon was built in Northern Ireland and Shannon grew up for the workers who served the industrial estate and airport.

Education, language and literature

Along the west coast of Ireland, in Donegal, Mayo, Connemara, Dingle in Kerry, and parts of Cork, Waterford and Meath, Irish is the most usual language spoken. But since Irish is taught in all the schools of Southern Ireland, and very often by choice in Northern Ireland, most of the people in Ireland speak two languages. English is, however, more generally used. Irish schools are not very different from those of any other country. After primary or junior school,

90

students attend a secondary school, technical school, comprehensive school or community school for three years until they obtain the intermediate Certificate or Group Certificate, which are equivalent to the CSE. Later they attend for two further years before obtaining the Leaving Certificate or Matriculation, and enter university or technical college.

Students in Ireland today are familiar with the writings of such Irish writers as Brendan Behan, Samuel Beckett, Thomas Kinsella, Seamus Heaney, Mary Lavin, Frank O'Connor and Sean O'Faolain, as well as being familiar with the music of Sean O'Riada. Radio Telefis Eireann, the Irish equivalent of the BBC, has all the advantages of satellite link-up and Eurovision to make the affairs and culture of the modern world familiar to all viewers. The world is made a smaller community both by television and newspapers, and by the greater frequency of travel abroad.

Conclusion
The Stone Age farmers who lived on the coast of Co Mayo, 5,500 years ago, would find Ireland today as interesting as the modern visitor stepping off the car-ferry or jet. The Stone Age farmers would be particularly and pleasantly surprised to find that the people of Ireland are now journeying back to Europe to find a better way of life. So, since 1 January 1973, a simple community of the past has become a part of the complex EEC of the present.

Further Information

Books

J C Beckett and R E Glasscock, *Belfast: Origins and Growth of an Industrial City* (BBC Publications, 1967).

M E Collins, *Conquest and Colonisation* (Gill and Macmillan, 1969).

M Craig, *Dublin 1660-1860, A Social and Architectural History* (Allen Figgis, 1969).

W H Crawford, *Domestic Industry in Ireland* (Gill and Macmillan, 1972).

L M Cullen, *Merchants, Ships and Trade, 1660-1830* (Gill and Macmillan, 1971).

L M Cullen, *Life in Ireland* (Batsford, 1968).

L M Cullen, *Six Generations* (Mercier Press, 1970).

K Danaher, *Irish Country People* (Mercier Press, 1966).

K Danaher, *In Ireland Long Ago* (Mercier Press, 1970).

K Danaher, *The Year in Ireland* (Gill and Macmillan, 1972).

E Gillespie, ed., *The Liberties of Dublin* (E T O'Brien, 1973).

D Guinness and W Ryan, *Irish Houses and Castles* (Thames and Hudson, 1971).

J Hawthorne, ed., *Two Centuries of Irish History* (BBC Publications, 1966).

G MacGearailt, *Celts and Normans* (Gill and Macmillan, 1969).

E McLysaght, *Irish Life in the Seventeenth Century* (Irish University Press, 1971).

T W Moody and J C Beckett, *Ulster since 1900,* parts 1 & 2 (BBC Publications, 1957).

T W Moody and F Y Martin, ed., *The Course of Irish History* (Mercier, 1967).

D O Muirithe, *A Seat Behind the Coachman* (Gill and Macmillan, 1972).

K B Nowlan, ed., *Travel and Sport in Ireland* (Gill and Macmillan, 1973).

M and C C O'Brien, *A Concise History of Ireland* (Thames & Hudson, 1972).

V S Prichett and E Hoffer, *Dublin — a Portrait* (Bodley Head, 1967).

A Ross, *Everyday Life of the Pagan Celts* (Batsford, 1970).

Educational Facsimiles

Issued by the Public Record Office, Northern Ireland:
The 1798 Rebellion; Irish Elections; The United Irishmen; The Act of Union; Eighteenth-century Emigration; Penal Laws; The Famine, 1845-1852
In the Jackdaw series published by Jonathan Cape:
Fenianism; Dublin, 1916

Pictorial

H Clark, *Ireland in Colour* (Batsford, 1970).

M Gorham, *Ireland from Old Photographs* (Batsford, 1971), and *Dublin from Old Photographs* (Batsford, 1972).

V McCutchem, *History of Railways in Pictures: Ireland,* Vols 1 & 2 (David and Charles, 1969, 1970).

Audio-Visual
The National Film Institute of Ireland's catalogue of 16mm Educational Films, and its catalogue of Film Strips, are splendid guides to the available audio-visual material relating to Ireland. Supplements to the National Film Institute's 1970 catalogue are issued annually. For material on record or cassette, the catalogues of Outlet Recording Co Ltd, Belfast, and of the Mercier Press Records are particularly useful. They have issued *Songs of the Irish Rising of 1798* and P Mac Aonghusa's *James Connolly*, as well as M Tierney's *Modern Ireland*. Veniss, Audio-Visual Aids Catalogues, Part 2, and Video Cassettes Catalogues (obtainable from 33 Queen Anne Street, London W1) are also of value.

Magazines
R Ffolliot, 'Men's Clothes in Ireland, 1660-1850', 'Women's Dress in Ireland, 1680-1880' in *The Irish Ancestor* No. 2, 1971, and 'Cottages and Farmhouses' in No. 1, 1972.
In *Ireland of the Welcomes* issued by the Irish Tourist Board: A J Went 'The Coinage of Ireland' in Vol 17, No. 4, Nov-Dec 1963; 'Eighteenth-century Dublin Street Cries' in Vol 13, No. 4, Nov-Dec 1964; M Bianconi 'King of the Irish Road' Vol 17, No. 4, Nov-Dec 1968.
The Arts in Ireland, Trinity Publications, Dublin.
Ireland, Journal of the Department of Foreign Affairs.

Table of Dates

AD	
c 80	The Roman governor Agricola plans to conquer Ireland, but never does.
431	Christianity is brought to Ireland by St Patrick.
1014	Battle of Clontarf, and the defeat of the invading Norsemen.
1175	The Irish are forced to recognise Henry II as overlord.
1192	Charter of civil liberties granted to Dublin by King John.
1530	Monasteries closed down by Henry VIII.
1603	Battle of Kinsale marks the end of the power of the native Irish.
1609	Land in Ulster is confiscated and divided up among English and Scottish settlers.
1690-91	Struggle in Ireland between the Jacobites (supporters of King James) and Williamites (supporters of King William) ends in victory for Protestant King William.
1691	Penal laws imposed to restrict Irish Catholics.
1782	Free Irish Parliament set up, under the direction of Henry Grattan.
1801	Free Irish Parliament abolished by William Pitt. Ireland becomes part of Great Britain.
1839	Poor Law system established in Ireland with workhouses for the destitute.
1845	The famine in Ireland; thousands die of starvation and disease when the potato crop fails.
1867	Fight for Irish freedom led by the Fenians.
1910	James Larkin founds the Irish Transport and General Workers' Union.
1913	The great Lock-Out in Dublin. Striking workers are forced to capitulate.
1914-18	The First World War.
1916	The Easter Week Rising fails.
1921	Formation of a Free State in Southern Ireland.
1939-45	The Second World War.
1949	Irish Free State declared a Republic.
1973	Both Northern and Southern Ireland enter the EEC.

Index